Declaratio

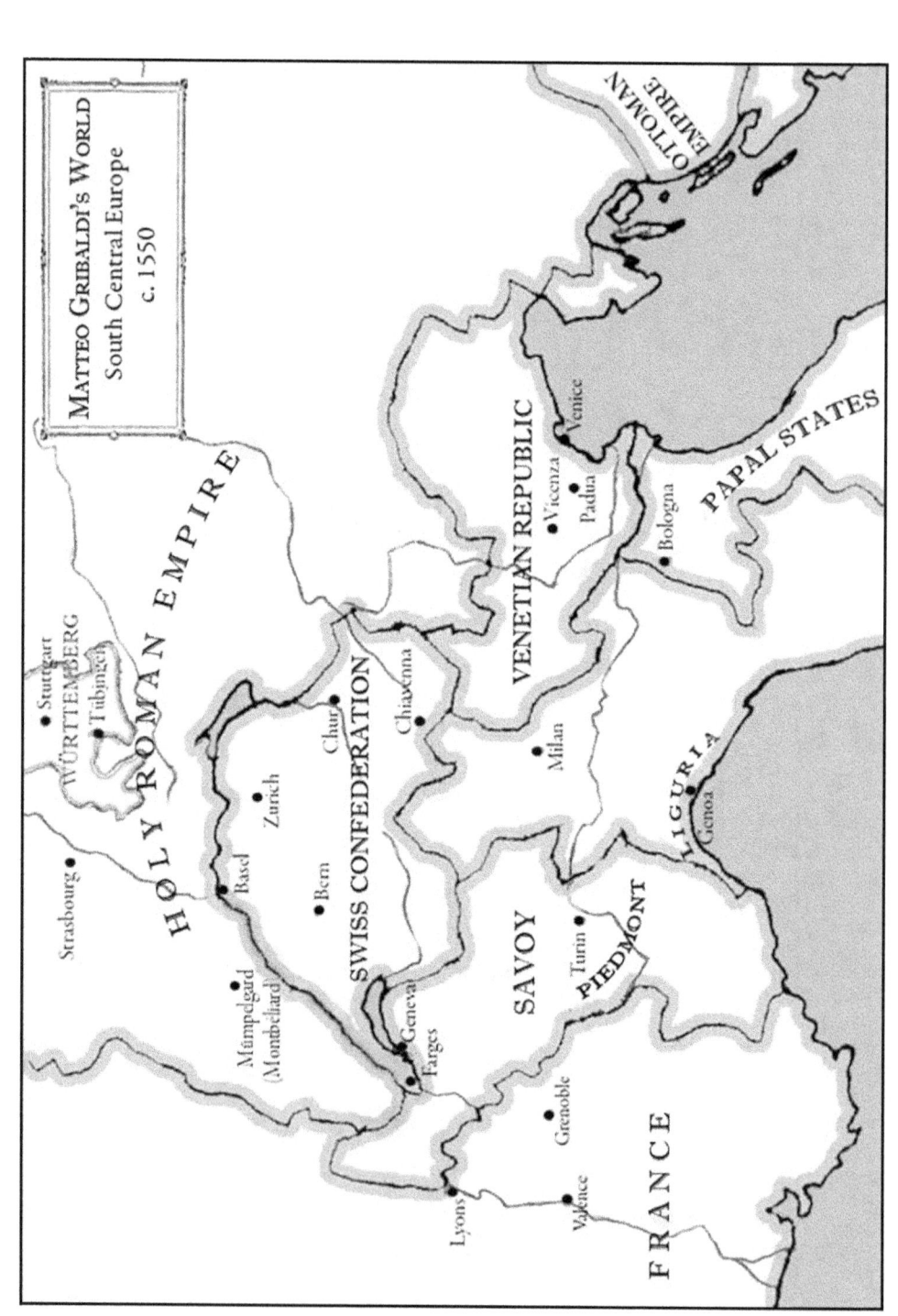

Declaratio

MICHAEL SERVETUS'S
REVELATION OF JESUS CHRIST
THE SON OF GOD

AND OTHER ANTITRINITARIAN WORKS BY

Matteo Gribaldi

translated by
Peter Zerner
with Peter Hughes and Lynn Gordon Hughes

edited by
Peter Hughes and Peter Zerner

Blackstone Editions
Providence, Rhode Island & Toronto, Ontario, Canada
www.BlackstoneEditions.com

© 2010 by Blackstone Editions
All rights reserved. Published 2010
Reprinted 2016
Printed in the United States of America

ISBN: 978-0-9816402-1-1

Contents

Foreword *by Sergio Baches Opi*	vii
Acknowledgments	ix
Key to Annotations and Abbreviations	xi
Introduction	xv
Notes on Sources, Transcription, and Translation	lx

DECLARATIONIS JESU CHRISTI FILII DEI
A REVELATION OF JESUS CHRIST, THE SON OF GOD   1
    Preface   2
    Book 1   8
    Book 2   20
    Book 3   42
    Book 4   80
    Book 5   110

APOLOGIA PRO MICHÆLE SERVETO
A DEFENSE OF MICHAEL SERVETUS   169

THESES DE FILIO DEI ET TRINITATE
THESES ABOUT THE SON OF GOD AND THE TRINITY   201

DE VERA DEI ET FILII EIUS COGNITIONE SERMO
A DISCOURSE ON THE TRUE KNOWLEDGE OF GOD AND HIS SON   213

LETTER TO THE ITALIAN CONGREGATION IN GENEVA   229

RELIGIONIS CHRISTIANÆ προγυμνάσματα
PRELIMINARY EXERCISES ON THE CHRISTIAN RELIGION   237

Chronology	251
Notes	263

Illustrations

Matteo Gribaldi's World: South Central Europe, c. 1550   *frontispiece*

Geneva in 1550   xiv
    From Sebastian Münster, *Cosmographia* (1550)

The Death of Servetus   xxi
    Detail from a portrait of Servetus by Christoffel Van Sichem (1607)

Declarationis Jesu Christi Filii Dei: a page from the manuscript   xxiv

View of Padua   xxxiv
    From the Nuremberg Chronicle (1493)

View of Tübingen   xxxix
    From the album of Prince Johann Wilhelm von Sachsen-Altenburg (c. 1616). Württembergisches Landesmuseum, Stuttgart, Inv. Nr. 1936/179

Map of Bern   xliv
    By Hans Rudolf Manuel (1549)

Handwriting samples from the *Declaratio* manuscript   lxii

Foreword

by Sergio Baches Opi
Director, Michael Servetus Institute

Michael Servetus (Villanueva de Sijena, 1511 - Geneva, 1553) has always been considered a *rara avis* as a scholar and theologian — an isolated soul who did not have any followers in his time and whose light was put out suddenly by John Calvin at the stake in Geneva. However, we now know that his death had enough influence in his time to cause a turning point in the debate in favor of freedom of conscience in Europe. Michael Servetus, along with Sebastian Castellio and a few other humanists of the XVI century, should be considered one of the fathers of freedom of speech and conscience. Their firm attitude and lifetime example set in motion the historical movement that, centuries later, would result in the recognition of these freedoms as fundamental human rights in modern constitutions and international treaties. Yet, despite their obvious importance, these names may be unknown to those who are not familiar with the history of the Reformation or the history of freedom of speech and conscience.

We at the Michael Servetus Institute have always been aware of the need to spread Servetus's legacy among the non-specialized public. We have also recognized the hindrances to doing so, given the historical distance and the fact that most of the works of Servetus and his contemporaries were written in Latin. For this reason we support efforts to translate and analyze his writings and other documents that illuminate aspects of his life and times.

During his relatively short life, Servetus wrote and published two important theological works, *De Trinitatis Erroribus* (On the Errors of the Trinity) and *Christianismi Restitutio* (The Restoration of Christianity). However, there is one work that has been attributed to Servetus by several prestigious scholars, but whose authorship has always troubled me: this is *Declarationis Jesu Christi filii Dei* (A Revelation of Jesus Christ, the Son of God). It is clear that this manuscript is linked to Servetus's theological thought and to his published writings, but it was not published during his lifetime, and seems to be written in a different style.

With this translation and study of *Declarationis Jesu Christi filii Dei*, Peter Hughes and Peter Zerner have made an important contribution to Servetus studies. This is the first English translation of *Declaratio* ever made. The introductory study examines the question of the authorship of *Declaratio* and concludes that the author was not Servetus but rather Matteo Gribaldi, a well-known Italian antitrinitarian.

Why, if this work is not by Servetus, is it important for an understanding of his work and legacy? As the introduction points out, the reattribution of *Declaratio* is not a loss, but a gain for the Aragonese theologian. It clearly proves that Servetus's legacy survived him and influenced other theologians and scholars, especially in Poland.

The Michael Servetus Institute warmly welcomes this work of scholarship and thanks the translators for their dedication and effort to complete this book. We are also indebted to Peter Hughes for sharing with us his research and conclusions on the authorship of *Declaratio* at an academic session organized by our Institute, held on November 1, 2008. In addition to his memorable lecture, Dr. Hughes and his family had the chance to visit the birth house of Michael Servetus, a place which has become a pilgrimage destination for Unitarians and Unitarian Universalists from all over the world and for all those who want to trace the origins of freedom of conscience.

For all the above reasons, our Institute is deeply proud of having the chance to co-publish this work with Blackstone Editions and hopes that this marks the beginning of a fruitful collaboration in publishing other books in the future.

The Michael Servetus Institute is a non-profit public historical institute located in the birth house of Michael Servetus, Villanueva de Sijena, Huesca, Aragón (Spain).
www.servetus.es

Acknowledgments

Independent scholars are among the most dependent people in the world. We could never accomplish our goals without great and timely assistance from both friends and strangers.

First of all, we would like thank the Michael Servetus Institute, which is supporting the publication of this volume. The Director of the Institute, Sergio Baches Opi, has consulted with us all during the project, connecting us with resources, and making suggestions that greatly helped us in our research.

Marian Hillar, the author of *Michael Servetus: Intellectual Giant, Humanist, and Martyr* (2002) and editor of the first English translation of Servetus's *Christianismi Restitutio*, who helped prepare the first transcription of *Declaratio*, generously provided us with photocopies of the *Declaratio* manuscript. We received copies of three other manuscripts from the Basel University Library, thanks to the kind assistance of Dominik Hunger of the manuscript department.

A number of other libraries deserve special mention and thanks: the Robarts Library, the Thomas Fisher Library, the Kelly Library, the Regis College Rare Book Library, and not least, the library of the Centre for Reformation and Renaissance Studies, all at the University of Toronto; the Rockefeller Library at Brown University; the Andover-Harvard Theological Library; and the Z. Smith Reynolds Library at Wake Forest University.

Ángel Alcalá, who has been in charge of the complete edition of Servetus's works in Spanish, has been an inspiration in our work. Carol Zerner, in addition to providing moral support, has also been consulted on many points of Latin translation and has done some translation from Spanish. Nancy Winter and Sergio Carletto helped us with translation from Italian.

Kathleen Parker provided proofreading, editing, and thoughtful comments on this project.

Peter Hughes would particularly like to thank the Michael Servetus Institute for the opportunity to present some of our discoveries about the authorship of *Declaratio* at the Institute's annual seminar in November 2008. The Institute hosted Peter and Lynn Hughes, and Lynn's mother, Marcelyn Gordon, on their visit to Villanueva de Sijena. Montserrat Foguet Gómez, a counselor of the Institute and Guide to the Michael Servetus Birth House, showed us around the museum and let us inspect the Institute library. Laura Tisaire and Jordi Serrano, assigned by the Institute to translate the lecture, were attentive, helpful, and friendly, and accompanied us throughout our stay. Mayor Alfonso Salillas and all of the people of Villanueva were very gracious and hospitable. It was an honor to be invited there and to be given a role in the moving annual civic candlelight commemoration of their native son, Michael Servetus.

Key to Annotations and Abbreviations

We have used a variety of annotations and typographical conventions to guide the reader through *Declaratio* and the other writings in this book, and to point out relationships between these and other texts.

Annotations in the Latin text

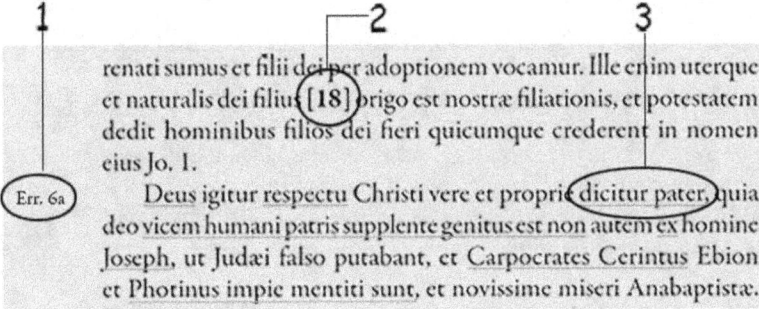

1. Cross-reference to page number in *De Trinitatis Erroribus* (marginal note).
2. Page number in manuscript or printed source. See Note on Pagination (page xiii).
3. Language copied or adapted from *De Trinitatis Erroribus* (underlined).
4. Text crossed out in the manuscript (strikethrough).
5. Footnote pointing out variant readings, copyists' errors, or other issues concerning the manuscript or printed source text.

Annotations in the English text

Note the inferential word *quapropter* [because of this] or *idcirco* [therefore], and you will grasp the meaning of the inference whereby the child is called the Son of God. Undoubtedly, this was because he was born from God and a virgin. The same understanding of the sonship of the man Jesus Christ is set forth in the book of Daniel, which calls him *a stone cut by no human hand*.[b] And likewise, Matthew explains that a virgin was made *pregnant by the Holy Spirit*, and that *what was conceived in her came from the Holy Spirit*. He would be the Savior, *Emmanuel, which means God with us*.[c] Note, therefore, that the power that was begotten and conceived in the Virgin's womb, which was the Son of God and is called God, was the man Jesus Christ.

Also note carefully what [the angel] says in Luke: "The son whom *you will conceive and bear will be called the Son* of God and *he will be great* in the sight of God; *and God will give him the throne of his father David*."[d] Thus Irenaeus[4] says in [*Against Heresies*], book 3, chapter 18:[5] "The angel, announcing the good news to Mary, says that he who is *the Son of the Most-High* is also the *son of David*."[e] He is the son of David, however, through his mother. But, since sonship is principally defined with reference to the father, David does not presume to call him his son, but rather his Lord. Thus, in the spirit of prophecy, he says about Christ, "*The Lord said to my Lord, sit at my right hand*."[f] Can the second person or hypostasis, whom [theologians] call the Son, *be made great* and receive from God *the throne of his father David*?[g] Would God say to it, *sit at my right hand*? In truth, however, all these things are said about the real Son, the man Jesus Christ.

A bit further on [Ignatius says]:

> For he who was born of a woman is the Son of God, and he who was crucified is also God of all creation, the Word, and [he who] made everything at the command of the Father. This the Apostle also corroborates, saying, *One God, the Father, from whom all things are, and one Lord, Jesus Christ, through whom all things are*.[e] And again, *One God and one mediator between God and men, the man Christ Jesus*,[e] {*who is the image of the invisible God* and} *the firstborn of all creation*,[e] *for in him were created all things in heaven and earth, visible and invisible. And he is before all things and in him all things hold together*.[f] And since he is not God over all things, but [God's] Son, he [proclaims] that he is ascending to him, saying, "*I am ascending to my Father and to your Father, to my God, and to your God*."[g]

1. Footnote giving source of quotation or reference (superscript letter).
2. Endnote containing discussion of the passage (superscript number).
3. Words in languages other than English (italics, followed by translation in square brackets).
4. Text added by translator to improve clarity (square brackets).

5. Quotation from a source other than the Bible (quotation marks). May contain footnotes, endnotes, Bible quotations, etc.
6. Quotation from the Bible (italics).
6a. Quotation marks are used for Bible quotations only when required by the sense of the sentence.
7. Long quotation (block quote). May contain footnotes, endnotes, Bible quotations, etc.
8. Text interpolated into a quotation (brackets).

Abbreviations

The following abbreviations are used for sources cited in footnotes, endnotes, and marginal notes.

Adv. Hær.   Irenaeus, *Adversus Hæreses*
Calv. Op.   *Ioannis Calvini Opera quæ supersunt omnia* (Corpus reformatorum)
Erroribus or *Err.*   Servetus, *De Trinitatis Erroribus*
PG   *Patrologia Græca* (ed. J.-P. Migne)
PL   *Patrologia Latina* (ed. J.-P. Migne)
Restitutio or *Rest.*   Servetus, *Christianismi Restitutio*

Note on Punctuations of Titles

As far as we know, none of the works included in this volume was printed during Gribaldi's lifetime. A number of them, however, were intended for distribution and were likely passed around in manuscript form, perhaps in multiple copies. We have chosen to treat these as published works and have therefore italicized the titles of *Declaratio*, *Apologia*, and *De vera Dei*. The quotation marks around "Theses" and "Religionis Christianæ" indicate that they were not published in any sense of the word.

Note on Pagination

Page numbers used in citations of *Declaratio*, *Apologia*, "Theses," and "Religionis Christianæ," as well as Servetus's *De Trinitatis Erroribus* and *Christianismi Restitutio*, refer to the page numbers on the manuscript. In the case of *Apologia* and "Theses," these are page numbers within the archival collection rather than those of the original manuscript (e.g. *Apologia* begins on page 18a). Depending on the conventions that were used when the page numbers were assigned, some of the manuscripts use "a" and "b" for recto and verso, while in others the pages are numbered as in a modern book. Because there is no extant manuscript of *De vera Dei*, the page numbers for that document are those of the transcription in Stanislas Lubieniecki, *Historia Reformationis Polonicæ* (Freistadt, 1685).

Geneva in 1550

Introduction

The Story of Michael Servetus

On the afternoon of Sunday, August 13, 1553, Michael Servetus, a Spanish fugitive fleeing France to escape the Inquisition, attended services at La Madeleine, one of three parish churches in Geneva, Switzerland.[1] His name was a byword for antitrinitarian heresy. He had only recently entered the city and was not planning on staying long, for he realized that he might be in as much danger from the Protestants in Geneva as from the Roman Catholics in France. At his lodgings at *La Rose d'Or*, close to the River Rhône and to Lake Leman, he had made arrangements with his hosts to be taken by boat across the lake in order to continue his journey through Switzerland to Italy. He later testified that "while in the city he hid as best he could in order to be able to proceed on his journey without being recognized."[2] But, as it was Sunday, and Geneva was the bastion of the Reformed Church of John Calvin, he felt obliged to go to church. Those who did not attend Sunday religious services might be reported and, if they could not satisfactorily account for themselves, were liable to punishment by the Genevan Consistory.[3] Since Servetus had no desire to call attention to himself, he bundled himself up, walked six blocks, and, staying as much as possible in the shadows, listened to the sermon.[4]

For over a decade Servetus had been practicing medicine in Vienne, a hundred miles away in France, just south of Lyons. Living under the pseudonym "Michel de Villeneuve," he had been a protégé of the liberal archbishop, Pierre Palmier, had lived in the archbishop's palace, and had been a respected citizen in the town. He had concealed his true identity because in 1531, when he was about twenty years old, he had written a notorious book, *De Trinitatis Erroribus* (On the Errors of the Trinity), which made him unwelcome among the Protestants of Switzerland and Germany and set both the Spanish and French Inquisitions on his trail.[5]

Servetus was born about 1511 in Villanueva de Sijena, a small town in Aragon in northeastern Spain.[6] He worked for several years under the tutelage of the Franciscan theologian, Juan de Quintana, who was a member of the Parliament (Cortes) of Aragon and later served as confessor to the Holy Roman Emperor, Charles V (Charles I of Spain). In 1527 Servetus probably accompanied Quintana to the historic Valladolid Assembly convened by the Spanish Inquisition in an attempt to pass judgment on the works of Erasmus. Having studied law during 1528 and 1529 in Toulouse, the headquarters of the Inquisition in France, Servetus must have been well aware of the frightening machinery employed by the Catholic Church to suppress heresy.[7] He later wrote that during the early 1530s he was terrified, for "I was hunted, high and low, by those who wished to kill me." As a result, "I concealed myself for many years among strangers, in great anguish of mind."[8]

Although Servetus could hardly be described as a representative Protestant, and although his ideas were rejected by all of the leading reformers, his book did much to confirm the suspicions of Catholics that Protestantism was falling away from Christianity as they understood it. Consequently, *De Trinitatis Erroribus* was a great embarrassment to Protestant apologists. The Basel reformer, Oecolampadius, with whom Servetus had lived in 1530, worried that others would consider the Swiss churches "responsible for such great blasphemy."[9] Martin Luther's Catholic opponent, Girolamo Aleandro, wrote, "Wherever the Spaniard may be, these Lutheran or Zwinglian heretics of Germany — if they are such true Christians, evangelicals, and defenders of the faith, as they pride themselves on being — ought to have punished him."[10]

The title, "On the Errors of the Trinity," might suggest that Servetus had composed an antitrinitarian work. It is so only in the sense that it is a grand assault on the established system of church dogma, for the doctrine of the Trinity was the principal rubric under which theologians had long been accustomed to discuss the nature of God and Christ. Unlike Unitarians, Servetus did not deny the existence of the Trinity entirely, nor did he dismiss its usefulness as a theological construct. Rather, he redefined the Trinity, along with all the scholastic terminology associated with it — person, hypostasis, oneness or unity, substance, nature, etc. — and reexamined the biblical words used to describe and define God.[11]

According to the orthodoxy accepted by both Roman Catholics and Protestants, the Godhead is a single substance, essence, nature, and being, composed of three coequal and coeternal hypostases or persons: the Father (the first person), the Son (the second person), and the Holy Spirit (the third person). The first person is an unbegotten pure spirit. The second person, Christ, or the Word (*Logos*) of God, begotten by the first person before time existed, has two natures, one fully divine and the other fully human. God created everything in the universe by means of the Word. Since Christ was the Word before his incarnation as the man Jesus, he is understood to have existed from the beginning. Likewise, as the Word, a spirit permeating the universe, he continued to exist side by side with the human Christ who lived and moved in a specific place and time. These two natures of the second person are considered distinct, but at the same time indivisible. Properties or qualities that belong to one of the natures of Christ are applied or transferred to the other by *communicatio idiomatum* (sharing of properties). By an application of this doctrine, it is permissible to say that God suffered on the cross, but this suffering is held to apply only to the second person, Christ, and not to the first, the Father, who is incapable of suffering. The third person, the Holy Spirit, is the agent of God who inspires and conveys grace to human beings. The Holy Spirit is said to "proceed" from the other two persons of the Trinity (or from the Father alone, according to the Eastern Orthodox Church).

By contrast, according to Servetus's *De Trinitatis Erroribus*, the Son of God — although he was God himself — was a man and, as such, did not have an existence in time prior to the incarnation. He only came into being when the Word was made flesh. In this transformation, the Word, as such, ceased to exist. Furthermore, in Servetus's view, the Word never had a separate existence, but, as the divine utterance, was just the way in which God operated in this world prior to the coming of Christ. Christ, the Son, on the other hand, was a real, living human creature — although, at the same time, he was inseparable from the being of God the Father. He had a single nature, different from that of God, which was a mixture of human and divine substance. He was, nevertheless, the image of the substance of God, the way that God could become known to humankind.[12]

Unlike orthodox Trinitarians, Servetus believed that there were no real internal distinctions within God. He thought the idea of three persons in the Godhead a useful one, but only as a way to label and describe the activity of God in the world. In this sense his theology can be thought of as modalist, like the Sabellian heresy of early Christianity, in which a unitary God is portrayed as putting on different masks (*personae*) in order to interact with human beings. But because of the concreteness of his picture of Christ, and his claim that Christ was different from God in nature or essence, Servetus's theology also resembles Arianism, a quite different ancient heresy in which Christ is seen as separate from and subordinate to God. Servetus vigorously rejected the identification of his theology as Arian, however, and claimed that Christ was not a lesser deity, as Arius had made him out to be, but was equal to God in power and one with God in unity and harmony of will. And since Christ has a single nature, there is no need for the doctrine of *communicatio idiomatum*. God the Father shared his divinity fully with Christ, but did not himself take on human qualities. God himself did not take on flesh, and he did not suffer.[13]

Unlike orthodox theologians, Servetus did not portray Christ as a sacrificial lamb, a victim to appease the wrath of God, but rather as the point of direct contact between God and humanity. He was the face of God, as much as human beings could understand it, and the source of the only true human knowledge of the nature of God. Servetus did not mention original sin — the doctrine of the inherent sinfulness of every human being descended from Adam and Eve after their fall from grace — for the doctrine was not important to him. He was less interested in human salvation than in divinization. Through knowledge of God, acquired through knowledge and faith in the Son and/or inspired by the Holy Spirit (an activity of God which proceeds from the Son), human beings could become adopted children of God, and discover themselves to be filled with God.[14]

Responding to the immediate, intensely adverse reaction to *Erroribus*, Servetus tried in his next work, *Dialogorum de Trinitate* (Dialogues on the Trinity, 1532), to argue his case more moderately and to cast his doctrines in a form and language more closely resembling established teaching, but this failed as well. Over the next two decades he continued his studies. He developed his expertise in Greek and Hebrew and became more skillful at scripture interpretation; rechecked his citations and quotations of ancient and medieval theologians; read more of the works of the church fathers and medieval scholastics as they became available in printed editions; discovered Jewish, Islamic, and Hermetic writings; and explored the ideas of Renaissance thinkers. He did all of this with a view to finishing his grand treatise, *Christianismi Restitutio* (The Restoration of Christianity), which incorporated revised and expanded versions of *Erroribus* and *Dialogorum*.

He hoped that this would prove to be the most complete, convincing, and best documented exposition of his thought.

Some of these new studies were performed in the course of, or initiated by, his various professional duties — as editor, physician, and lecturer. As Michel de Villeneuve, Servetus first began to work as an editor, eventually preparing editions of Ptolemy's *Geography* (1535, 1541) and of Sante Pagnini's translation of the Bible (1541-45). Inspired by one of his contacts in publishing, the medical writer Symphorien Champier, he studied medicine at the University of Paris. Servetus made good use of this study: it enabled him to trace the path of the pulmonary (or "lesser") circulation and to describe the aeration of the blood in the lungs. He recorded this discovery more than half a century before William Harvey's more complete description of the circulation of the blood throughout the body. Servetus published his findings, not in a medical treatise, but in his great theological work, *Christianismi Restitutio*, to illustrate how the souls of human beings breathe in the spirit of God and how the divine spark is communicated throughout the body.[15] Unfortunately, as the book was almost entirely suppressed, medical science long remained unaware of Servetus's contribution.[16]

Servetus cared much more about religion than he did about medicine. He would rather have been recognized as a theological revolutionary than a scientific pioneer. All the while he was living in France and practicing medicine as Michel de Villeneuve, he spent much of his free time researching, writing, and polishing *Christianismi Restitutio*. He was anxious to use this new work to convert Calvin, whom he had first met in Paris in the early 1530s, to his views. In 1546 he sent Calvin a draft manuscript of the new work. Calvin reported to his friend and colleague, Guillaume Farel, that he had received "a lengthy volume of [Servetus's] ravings" and wrote, "He proposes to come here, if that is agreeable to me. But I am unwilling to make any promises. For should he come, if I have anything to say about it, I will not allow him to get away alive."[17]

There are several sources of Calvin's extreme animus towards Servetus. One may be in the history of their personal relationship, perhaps a catalogue of wrongs committed or endured or a conflict of personalities during their student days in Paris. We do not know exactly when or how often they met in their youth. We do have a report of a meeting that did not take place. Around 1534 Servetus missed an appointment to debate with Calvin in the Rue St. Antoine. Calvin, who did show up, and who at that time was himself being sought by the French authorities, resented having been put in unnecessary danger.[18] Later, around 1546, after Calvin had sent him a copy of *Institutes of the Christian Religion*, Servetus returned Calvin's work with the margins so full of critical comments that Calvin compared him to someone who had gulped down a maddening potion [*hippomanes*]. "He filled it so completely with his insolent abuse, that not a page remained undefiled by his vomit."[19]

Calvin also had good reason to fear anything that would associate him with Servetus. In 1537, when Calvin was establishing himself as the leader of the church in Geneva, both his own and Farel's orthodoxy on the Trinity had been challenged by a minister in nearby Vaud, Pierre Caroli, on the grounds that they had avoided the terms "person" and "Trinity" in their writings. A minister in Basel, Oswald Myconius, wrote, "If [the Genevan ministers] attempt to reintroduce Arianism, as I hear they have begun to do, or rather the wicked error of the Spaniard Servetus, learned men will have something to say about it."[20] Although the charges of unorthodoxy against Calvin and Farel were officially dismissed by the Lausanne Synod in May 1537, the Swiss churches remained suspicious of Calvin's relegation of the Trinity to speculative, and not practical theology. These doubts contributed to the crisis that led to his exile from Geneva during 1538-41.[21] Calvin thus learned of the danger that any hint of antitrinitarianism, or rumor of association with Servetus, posed to his reputation and position. When Servetus turned up in Geneva in 1553, Calvin felt the eyes of the world upon him, scanning him for any doctrinal laxity. Accordingly, he was convinced that he had little choice but to be very severe.

Servetus might have remained undisturbed in Vienne had he not arranged for the printing of *Christianismi Restitutio* in late 1552. News of this reached Calvin, who, through an intermediary, on February 26, 1553, alerted the Inquisition to the presence of Servetus in Vienne. He later supplied evidence that was used by the prosecution in the trial. However, on April 7, before these legal proceedings were concluded, Servetus escaped from prison. He remained at large in France for four months, seeking to find a way to escape to the Venetian Republic, where he hoped that he might be unknown and safe. The route that he ultimately chose, unfortunately, led through Geneva, a city under the spiritual leadership of the man who had become his arch-nemesis.

On that August Sunday in Geneva, Servetus knew better than to go to the Cathedral of St. Pierre, where Calvin would be preaching. But even at La Madeleine, it was of no avail to have pulled his cap down and drawn his cloak partway over his face.[22] He was spotted and recognized by several people who had known him in France. The report was carried to Calvin, who informed the magistrates, and later that day Servetus was arrested at *La Rose d'Or*. He was imprisoned along with Calvin's secretary, Nicholas La Fontaine, who, as the official accuser, was liable for punishment if the charges proved false. After the Genevan Council examined the documents provided by Calvin through his secretary, and interviewed Servetus several times, La Fontaine was freed from jeopardy for having made the accusation.[23]

Servetus remained in prison, in uncomfortable and degrading conditions.[24] He was removed from his cell only to appear before the authorities on trial for capital crimes — including denial of the Trinity — until, on October 27, 1553, he was led outside the walls of Geneva and, with his book, *Christianismi Restitutio*, bound to his leg, burned at the stake. Guillaume Farel, who accompanied Servetus to the stake, later commented, "I could not get him to admit his errors openly and acknowledge that Christ was *the eternal Son of God*."[25] Instead, faithful until the end to his belief that the Word only became the Son when it took on flesh, Servetus is reported to have cried out from the flames, "Jesus, *Son of the eternal God*, have mercy on me!"[26]

The Death of Servetus

Nearly the whole print run of one thousand copies of *Christianismi Restitutio* was destroyed by the Protestant and Catholic authorities. Because only three printed copies survived, Servetus's last work, presenting the final version of his theology, was unknown to almost all of his contemporaries.[27] Those who would follow in Servetus's footsteps had to be content with his early works, *De Trinitatis Erroribus* and *Dialogorum de Trinitate*; or with others' descriptions of his ideas, including the hostile treatment by Calvin in *Defensio orthodoxæ fidei de sacra Trinitate contra prodigiosos errores Michælis Serveti Hispani* (A Defense of the Orthodox Faith in the Holy Trinity against the Monstrous Errors of the Spaniard Michael Servetus) and in the 1559 edition of *Institutes of the Christian Religion*; or with a manuscript, passed from hand to hand —*Declarationis Jesu Christi filii Dei* (A Revelation of Jesus Christ, the Son of God) — which purported to be the work of Servetus.

The Mysteries of Declaratio

Did Servetus write Declaratio? *Declarationis Jesu Christi filii Dei*, which includes a preface by "Alphonsus Lyncurius Tarraconensis"— the same pseudonymous author who had composed the better-known *Apologia pro Michæle Serveto* (A Defense of Michael Servetus, 1554) — first surfaced in 1559, when it was discovered among the possessions of Michael Zaleski (or Salecki), a Polish student who had been murdered in Tübingen, in southwestern Germany. This obviously heretical book was quickly confiscated by the authorities, and thus preserved for posterity, since it became part of the record of an investigation into the orthodoxy of the foreign student community in Tübingen.

When we first began to translate *Declaratio*, we took it for granted that it had been written by Michael Servetus. In Stanislas Kot's landmark 1953 article, "L'Influence de Servet sur le mouvement antitrinitarien en Pologne et en Transylvanie," in which he announced the discovery of this manuscript, which he had located in the Stuttgart State Archives, he proclaimed *Declaratio* to be a genuine work of Servetus. "To be convinced, it is enough to read a few pages," he wrote. "Not only does the point of departure prove it, as it is as similar to the first book, *De Trinitatis Erroribus*, as it is to [the last one,] *Christianismi Restitutio*; not only do many passages which are the same as those in *Erroribus* confirm it; but, above all, it shows the same train of thought [as Servetus] and the same style of writing as in his printed works: sometimes displays of scholarship, or powerful scripture argument;

at other times, passionate outbursts in which the author personally addresses the reader."[28]

Declaratio was also accepted as a genuine work of Servetus by Roland Bainton, the author of *Hunted Heretic* (1953), a biography that remains a standard work on Servetus. Ángel Alcalá, in the epilogue to his 1973 Spanish translation of *Hunted Heretic*, wrote, "The topics [in *Declaratio*] are the same [as in Servetus's published works] and there are no significant theological differences."[29] In 2004, Alcalá included *Declaratio* in his bilingual Latin/Spanish edition of Servetus's complete works. In the introduction to this volume he declared, "No one has raised any doubts that Servetus was the author."[30]

With scholars such as Kot, Bainton, and Alcalá having vouched for *Declaratio*'s Servetan authorship, we launched into our translation, the first of *Declaratio* into English. In the beginning our principal concern was to determine when *Declaratio* was written. We sought to find internal evidence to settle the question of whether the book was a very early work — an initial draft of *De Trinitatis Erroribus*, as Alcalá and Bainton proposed — or a work intermediate between *De Trinitatis Erroribus* and *Christianismi Restitutio*, as had been suggested by Kot.[31] The more we studied *Declaratio*, however, the more dissatisfied we became with both of these hypotheses.

As we investigated the relationship between the parallel passages in *De Trinitatis Erroribus* and *Declaratio*, it became clear to us that *Declaratio* had to be a revision of *Erroribus* and not the other way around. Thus the Alcalá-Bainton theory could not be sustained. However, this did not necessarily mean that Kot was correct. For, although we recognized that *Declaratio* is, in part, a revision of material taken mainly from book 1 of *Erroribus*, it does not contain, even in embryonic form, any of the highly developed Neoplatonist or anabaptist ideas found in *Christianismi Restitutio*. Nor does it mention any of the many passages and books cited or quoted by Servetus in *Restitutio* that were not already found in *Erroribus*, such as the Robert of Ketton translation of the Quran, Hermetic literature, and numerous additional references to the works of St. Augustine.

At this point we were compelled to consider a third hypothesis: that *Declaratio* was not written by Servetus at all. For it appeared to us to have been written by someone entirely ignorant of the progress of Servetus's thinking after 1531, who had theological ideas of his own to promote and was intent on taking the theology of *Erroribus* in a new, non-Servetan

Declarationis Jesu Christi Filii Dei
a page from the manuscript

direction. Furthermore, in a few places it was obvious that the person who had appropriated and adapted portions of *Erroribus* for his own use had misread the original text, so that the borrowed and edited passages in *Declaratio* became somewhat garbled.[32] Thus, midway through our translation, we stopped referring to the author as Servetus and adopted the rather more awkward "author of *Declaratio*." The question was no longer "When did Servetus write *Declaratio*?" but "Who wrote it, and when?"

We thereupon began to gather evidence of differences in theology, vocabulary, style, opinion, and the selection of authoritative source texts (the Bible, church fathers, etc.) between *Declaratio* and the known works of Servetus. In this way we were able to put together a quite detailed case to prove that Servetus could not possibly have written *Declaratio* (except, of course, for those passages copied directly from *Erroribus*).

For example, some key words used repeatedly in *Declaratio* — *passibilis, visibilis, crucifixus, unigenitus, mysterium, peccatum, redemptio,* and *sanguis*[33] — are seldom or never used by Servetus, which indicates that the author of *Declaratio* was concerned with theological problems, such as suffering, crucifixion, sin, sacrifice, and atonement, that were not of such great interest to Servetus. Among the numerous phrases often used in *Declaratio*, but not found in the corresponding sections of Servetus's books, are *ipsa veritas* (truth itself), *tota/universa scriptura* (all of scriptures), *religionis fundamentum* (basis of religion), *vera pietas* (true piety), *vita æterna* (eternal life), *evangelica veritas* (Gospel truth), *redemptio humani generis* (redemption of humanity). Also unlike Servetus, the author of *Declaratio* frequently heaped up words of similar meaning in pairs and triplets, narrowing down his meaning after the fashion of a lawyer. Among these are *persona vel hypostasis* (person or hypostasis), *dominus et deus* (Lord and God), *pietas et religio* (piety and religion), *proprium et unigenitum* (own and only-begotten), *gratia et veritas* (grace and truth), *verbum seu logos* (Word or Logos), and *blasphemia et impietas* (blasphemy and impiety).

Both Servetus and the author of *Declaratio* mentioned or discussed Islam, but there is a marked difference in the writers' attitudes. Although Servetus valued Islam less than Christianity and hoped to convert Muslims, Islam and the Quran are taken seriously in *Erroribus* and *Restitutio*, and are used to critique Christianity.[34] The author of *Declaratio*, expressing a more common sixteenth-century Christian outlook — especially in view of the power of the expanding Ottoman Empire — was dismissive of the Quran and referred to Islam as "the Mohammedan sect, so impious, false, and abominable, lurking about and gaining strength throughout the world."[35]

Unlike Servetus, whose direct quotations are almost invariably short and to the point, the author of *Declaratio* sometimes copied long passages from other authors. At one point in *Declaratio* there are six consecutive pages almost entirely filled with material taken from Irenaeus.[36] This kind of unprocessed textual appropriation is not found in the genuine works of Servetus, but can be found in several other places in *Declaratio*.[37]

Servetus cited passages from an impressive array of church fathers.[38] If we except passages copied or adapted from *Erroribus*, the only church fathers quoted in *Declaratio* are pseudo-Ignatius and Irenaeus. Further, the citations from each of these writers in *Declaratio* are all from a single work or a part of a work: seven from pseudo-Ignatius's *Letter to the Tarsians* and dozens from a few chapters of book 3 of Irenaeus's *Against Heresies*. Servetus, in his many citations and mentions of *Against Heresies*, almost never referred to this book and much preferred to cite book 1. Clearly, in Irenaeus, the two authors found different things to admire and emphasize.

In *Erroribus* Servetus drew liberally on book 1 of *Against Heresies* in order to ridicule Trinitarianism by comparing it to second-century Valentinian gnostic theology with its arcane terminology: "If we are permitted to hold this philosophy, how can we condemn the likes of [the gnostics] Marcus and Colorbasus, who, from the parables and from the letters and numbers in the words of sacred scripture, philosophize Triads, Tetrads, and Ogdoads, and also theorize the Demiurge, Bythos, Pleroma, and finally the various Aeons?"[39] Whereas Servetus claimed that the orthodox were no better than gnostics, the author of *Declaratio* took the position that most contemporary Christians actually were gnostics: "They conjure up a Word which remains invisible and incorporeal, and distinguish it from the visible Jesus, tearing Christ asunder. This was the heresy of Valentinus, against whom Saint Irenaeus wrote five books."[40] In book 3 of Irenaeus's *Against Heresies*, he found arguments, based upon scripture, with which to combat what he perceived as gnosticism dressed up as Christian orthodoxy.

Servetus and the author of *Declaratio* differ as well in their use of the available Latin translations of the Bible. In quoting from the New Testament, the author of *Declaratio* favored Erasmus's translation over the Vulgate more often than Servetus did. Even more telling are the quotations from the Old Testament. The Latin of the Pagnini Bible, which Servetus edited between 1541 and 1545, can be found in some of Servetus's Old Testament quotations in *Restitutio*. The Pagnini translation, however, was not used at all in the Old Testament quotations in *Declaratio*. In every passage that we checked, when the Pagnini Latin wording varies from the Vulgate, *Declaratio* always has the Vulgate version.[41] It seems unlikely that, if Servetus had written *Declaratio* toward the end of his life, he would have totally disregarded a version of the Bible which he had come to value and respect and to which he had devoted years of effort.

Dating *Declaratio*. Having established that *Declaratio* was not by Servetus, we thought that we might get a better idea of who actually wrote it, by first finding out when it was written. Our first clue was a striking and interesting word: "*neoterici.*" What did the author of *Declaratio* mean by *neoterici*? The word means people whose views or styles are up-to-date, fashionable, new wave, newer than new.[42] Our author distinguished *neoterici* from *moderni*, a word which he used to refer to writers going back to the time of William of Ockham. *Neoterici*, by contrast, must mean the newest of the new, current Reformation writers, most likely those who were still actively writing and publishing. Translating *neoterici theologi* as "contemporary theologians," the passage reads, "One of our contemporary theologians says that 'not even all the devils that there are could tear [his interpretation of] the passage away from him.'"[43] The passage under discussion here is Philippians, chapter 2. Therefore we needed to look for the source of this quotation in the exegetical works of theologians like Philip Melanchthon, Martin Bucer, Heinrich Bullinger, or John Calvin. We found it in the first place we looked, Calvin's commentary on Philippians. The commentary, it turns out, was not published until 1548.

This was just the first of several pieces of internal evidence that led us to date *Declaratio* later and later. For example, there are several references to "wretched anabaptists" who believed that Christ was begotten by Joseph.[44] Since about 1546, the Venetian Republic had been the base of a group of antitrinitarian anabaptists. They held secret meetings in and around the city of Vicenza and assembled at a forty-day convention in Venice in the autumn of 1550. Among the theological points agreed upon by the convention was one specifying that Jesus Christ was not God and that he was the normally-conceived child of Joseph and Mary.[45] This pushes the date for the composition of *Declaratio* past late 1550.

Furthermore, there is evidence within *Declaratio* that its author knew the ultimate fate of Servetus. He wrote, "If the visible Christ were again to proclaim himself the Son of God, [our theologians] would crucify him once more, or, according to today's custom, set him on fire and reduce him to ashes."[46]

Finally, there is a passage in *Declaratio* that appears to be a response to Calvin's commentary on Luke 1:35 in *In Harmoniam ex Mattheo, Marco et Luca* (A Harmony of Matthew, Mark, and Luke), issued in August 1555.[47] This publication date pushes the *terminus a quo* for the completion of *Declaratio* into late 1555. Allowing a period of time for the author to obtain a copy of Calvin's commentary and to finish writing *Declaratio*, and, at the other end, an interval for the manuscript to be passed from hand to hand amongst the Polish students before it was discovered by the authorities in 1559, we now estimate that the most likely date for the completion of the pseudonymous work is some time in 1557.

Identifying the author. At this point, although internal evidence gave us a rough idea of when *Declaratio* was written, we still had no precise evidence as to authorship. Therefore we began to line up our suspects. We even hoped that the author might have cleverly embedded his name in the text — perhaps in a code, cipher, anagram, or acrostic. The most likely place to look for such a clue was in the name of the purported author of the preface to *Declaratio*: Alphonsus Lyncurius Tarraconensis. Since 1559 this peculiar name has been identified as a pseudonym.[48] The same pseudonymous author also wrote the eloquent and better-known *Apologia*, a work highly critical of Servetus's arrest, trial, and execution which was issued only a few months after the event. There is a modest scholarly literature which debates the true identity of Lyncurius.[49] Various people have been proposed as the author of both *Apologia* and the preface to *Declaratio*. Those considered most often are three Italian exiles: the Basel professor of eloquence, Celio Secondo Curione; a peripatetic Bible scholar, Lelio Sozzini (Laelius Socinus); and a celebrated legal scholar, Matteo Gribaldi. It seemed to us that whoever was using the name Lyncurius for *Apologia* should also be our prime suspect for the authorship of the mysterious pseudo-Servetan *Declaratio*.

This imaginary Alphonsus was given the persona of a Spaniard, like Servetus. Tarraconensis is the ancient Roman name for northeastern Spain, the part that contains the Kingdom of Aragon, where Servetus was born and raised.[50] This seems a natural enough way of expressing solidarity with Servetus.[51] Alfonso had long been a common name for kings of both Aragon and Castile. Thus this first name might be a reference to Alfonso V, "the Magnanimous" (1396-1458), king of Aragon, Naples, and Sicily, and the patron and protector of Lorenzo Valla (1406-1457), a great Renaissance humanist much admired by the author of *Declaratio*.[52] Another notable Alfonso is Alfonso X of Castile, known as Alfonso the Wise (1221-1284).

The first and third names of the pseudonym, while rich with possible meaning, do not get us anywhere in identifying the mysterious author behind *Apologia*. Frustratingly, the name "Lyncurius" may be analyzed, using a complex series of allusions and multilingual plays on words, to suggest any or all of the three principal candidates: Gribaldi, Curione, or Sozzini. To begin with, under the supervision of Alfonso the Wise, a popular book on the magical properties of stones was translated into Castilian from the original Arabic. One of the stones described was the *lapis lyncurius*, amber, which got its name from its importation by the Greeks from Liguria, the region around Genoa, not far from where both Gribaldi and Curione were born. In Latin amber is also known as *succinum*. This word looks and sounds quite similar to the Latinized form of Sozzini, Socinus (though as etymology it is suspect).[53] Lyncurius, of course, also suggests Lyn-curio, and Curio is the Latin name of Curione.

The "Lync" part of the name could have been a classical reference to Lynceus, the lynx-eyed Argonaut who had the power of seeing through solid objects.[54] And solid objects might be a metaphor for the obscurity surrounding many theological ideas. In *The Praise of Folly*, Erasmus made fun of theologians who employed arcane terminology to describe their supposed knowledge about God: "There is an unlimited supply of such idle quibbles, and of others even more subtle. They concern instants, notions, relations, formalities, quiddities, and eccieties, which no one could make out unless they had eyes like Lynceus to enable them to see, through the deepest shadows, things that are not there."[55] Thus, although we cannot be certain precisely who suggested or designed the pseudonym, the name appears to make certain claims about the author: our Alphonsus was not only wise, but possessed a penetrating intellect.

Kot believed that Lyncurius was Celio Curione. He was seconded by David Pingree, who made an English translation of *Apologia* that was published in 1965. Delio Cantimori, a specialist on the subject of Lelio Sozzini, thought, as might be expected, that it was Sozzini. Uwe Plath contended that it was Matteo Gribaldi.[56] George Huntston Williams thought that all existing theories about the identity of Lyncurius "more or less cancel each other out." He identified Gribaldi as the author of *Apologia* because "his known views, style, career, profession, and itinerary comport well with the presence of a 'Lyncurius' manuscript in both Basel and Tübingen."[57]

We were not much convinced by the attempts of some scholars to establish the authorship of *Apologia* based on comparisons of style. For example, Pingree compared a "pedestrian" passage from one of Gribaldi's legal textbooks with a "magniloquent oration" by Curione in order to prove that Gribaldi was incapable of writing the brilliant rhetorical Latin of *Apologia*. All this proved to us was that Gribaldi — who was, it must be remembered, a lecturer celebrated for eloquence — wrote in a prosaic manner when it was appropriate for him to do so. In fact, Williams made an assertion to the opposite effect: "The impassioned style is much closer to the known works of Gribaldi than to those of the more placid and dry Socinus or the humanistically mannered Curio."[58]

Not having access to the manuscripts of all of the letters and treatises referred to by scholars in the debate about the identity of Lyncurius, we were not in a position to evaluate the many arguments that appeal to the evidence of handwriting and orthography. In any case there is no scholarly agreement about whose hand was responsible for each text.[59] What is more, since the extant *Declaratio* is a copy of a vanished original, written in four different unidentified hands, any appeal to handwriting and spelling is futile.

Despite the arguments of Kot and Pingree, we found it easiest to eliminate Celio Secondo Curione. Curione, as will be seen, did in fact edit some of Gribaldi's works, and it looks as though he had some kind of advisory hand in *Apologia* and possibly *Declaratio*. However, his own religious writings indicate that his theological concerns were quite different from those of "Alphonsus Lyncurius." In general, rather than challenging the doctrine of the Trinity, he avoided it.[60] The purpose of Curione's most celebrated theological writing, *De amplitudine beati regni Dei* (On the full extent of the blessed kingdom of God, 1554), was to argue that the majority of people, including the Jews and those who had never heard of Christ, would be saved.[61] This was the only radical religious idea for which he was prepared to risk the wrath of the Protestant authorities.

For a time, we thought that the mysterious author of *Declaratio* might turn out to be Lelio Sozzini. He used a form of the word *neoterici*, applied to Calvin and Calvin's contemporaries, in *Brevis explicatio in primum Joannis caput* (A brief explanation of the first chapter of the Gospel of John).[62] Moreover, a passage about Boethius in Lorenzo Valla's *De Elegan-*

tiis Latinæ Linguæ (On the elegance of the Latin language), which is discussed in *Declaratio*, is also mentioned in a work attributed to Sozzini, "Theses de Filio Dei et Trinitate" (Theses about the Son of God and the Trinity). However, the same passage is also cited in "Religionis Christianæ προγυμνάσματα" (Preliminary Exercises on the Christian Religion), a known work of Gribaldi.[63]

Looking again at "Theses," we were struck by how close its theology was to that of *Declaratio*. At the same time it was inconsistent with Sozzini's views as expressed in *Brevis Explicatio*. For instance, "Theses" lists several ways in which the Word might be related to the Son of God. In all of these the Word has existed from the beginning of time. But the basic thesis of *Brevis Explicatio* is that the Word did not exist until the beginning of the ministry of Christ.[64] Moreover, the explanation of the origin of Christ in *Brevis Explicatio* seems to be one that the author of *Declaratio* would associate with gnostics and "wretched anabaptists." Cantimori ignored the discrepancies between the "Theses" and *Brevis Explicatio*, commenting casually, "[Theses] helps considerably to fill out our picture of Lelio Sozzini."[65] On the contrary, we thought that "Theses," considered as a work of Sozzini, made our picture of his theology somewhat muddled and confusing. We began to suspect that Cantimori must have been mistaken in accepting "Theses" as Socinian.

Antonio Rotondò did not include "Theses" in *Lelio Sozzini Opere* (1986). We consulted his *"nota critica"* in order to learn his reasons for excluding this little work. He cited an article by Uwe Plath, which argued, on the basis of textual comparisons between "Theses" and "Religionis Christianæ προγυμνάσματα," that the former work was actually by Gribaldi.[66] In his discussion of *Apologia*, Rotondò called our attention to an even more valuable study, Carlos Gilly's *Spanien und der Basler Buchdruck bis 1600* (1985). Gilly makes systematic comparisons between another piece of pseudo-Servetan literature, *De vera Dei et filii eius cognitione sermo* (A Discourse on the True Knowledge of God and His Son), and the works of Gribaldi, which indicate that Gribaldi was the author of *De vera Dei*. He also analyzed the theology of *Declaratio* itself, showing how different it is from the works of Servetus and how much the ideas in the mysterious manuscript work reflect the ideas of Gribaldi.[67]

We gathered as many of the known and suspected works of Gribaldi as we could — *Declaratio, Apologia,* "Theses," *De vera Dei,* "Religionis Christianæ προγυμνάσματα," and a letter from Gribaldi to the Italian

Church in Geneva — together with descriptions of Gribaldi's theology in the correspondence of his contemporaries[68] and made our own analysis. We concluded that the theological sections of *Apologia* were written by the same person who composed *Declaratio*. The theology of the letter to the Italian Church is the same as that expressed in "Theses" and *Declaratio*. *De vera Dei*, clearly the work of the author of *Declaratio*, shares important themes and concerns with "Religionis Christianæ προγυμνάσματα." The memoir by Francesco Scudieri of his discussion with Gribaldi in Padua encapsulates the arguments and doctrine of *Declaratio*.[69] When we looked at all these documents together, along with with what is known about their provenance, the interconnections proved so many and so marked that they impressed upon us a unified picture of the thinking of a particular individual, who could be unequivocally identified as Gribaldi.

When we began the translation of *Declaratio*, we thought of it as part of a larger project, a new translation of Servetus's works. Then, after we became convinced that Servetus could not have written it, we thought of publishing it as the work of an unidentified pseudo-Servetus. Finally, our confidence in the identification of the author of *Declaratio* as Matteo Gribaldi became so great that it did not make sense to publish it under any other name. Since the other works of Gribaldi that form a key element in this decipherment are today hard to find, and since some of them have not previously been translated into English, we decided to translate them all and include them in our volume. This book, therefore, is not simply a translation of *Declaratio*; it has become as well the collected antitrinitarian works of Matteo Gribaldi.

The Story of Matteo Gribaldi

Matteo Gribaldi was born shortly after the beginning of the sixteenth century in Chieri, a town near Turin in Piedmont. He built his reputation during the 1530s and 1540s as a teacher of Roman Law at various universities in France: Toulouse, 1535-37; Cahors, 1537-40; Valence, 1540-43; and Grenoble, 1543-45. In the early or mid-1530s he married Georgine Carraxe, the heiress of Farges, an estate a dozen miles west of Geneva. Farges, like Gribaldi's native Piedmont, was part of the Duchy of Savoy. In 1536 the Protestant Swiss city of Bern conquered the area around Farges (the District of Gex) and controlled it for several decades to protect the newly-Protestant city of Geneva from attack by the Roman Catholic Duke of Savoy. Since

Georgine was illegitimate, her claim to Farges was hotly contested, but a Bernese court upheld the Gribaldis' right to the estate.

During his annual summer residences at Farges, Gribaldi visited Geneva frequently. On the evidence of a letter written to him by Calvin's close associate, the missionary evangelist Pierre Viret, by the beginning of 1542 Gribaldi already held Protestant views. "You have joined [the law] so closely to celestial philosophy," wrote Viret, "that neither impedes the other. Rather you have commanded [the law] to be the handmaid [of theology], in such a way that we can see that you practice law like a theologian."[70] However appealing his lectures may have been to Protestant listeners like Viret, during the remaining years that he lectured in France Gribaldi was, at least outwardly, a conforming Roman Catholic. He could not have been otherwise, for to have been identified as a Protestant, or even to have failed to attend mass, would have cost him his position and might have endangered his life.

Gribaldi did not display overtly Protestant, much less radical, leanings until after 1548, when he began to teach at the University of Padua. Padua was in the territory of Venice, whose government had, until 1547, been successful in keeping the Roman Inquisition from harassing its international community of merchants. The students and faculty of the university, many of them Swiss, German, or Polish Protestants, enjoyed some immunity from Roman Catholic religious supervision even after this time.[71]

The Inquisition began to take an interest in Gribaldi after he published a piece of Protestant propaganda in the form of a personal testimony about the deathbed agony of conscience experienced by a Protestant lawyer, Francesco Spiera, who, in 1548, had been forced by the Inquisition to publicly recant his beliefs.[72] Gribaldi wrote that Spiera "anticipated nothing better for himself in the end than the terrible verdict of a just God." The dying man felt that "although the mercy of God might eventually overcome all the sins of the world, nothing could benefit him, because he would be eternally condemned, and never written up in the book of life. Christ suffered and prayed only for the elect, not for him."[73] During this harrowing episode Gribaldi became the close friend of another of Spiera's comforters, the bishop Pierpaolo Vergerio, who had become a Lutheran. In 1549 Vergerio, about to be convicted of heresy, fled to Switzerland to escape arrest. Gribaldi wrote a letter recommending him to Calvin.[74] The ex-bishop soon strove to become a leader in various communities of Italian Protestants in exile.

Padua

Gribaldi's connections with Vergerio and with other prominent Protestants, including Boniface Amerbach, the heir of Erasmus's estate and Professor of Roman Law at the University of Basel, enabled him to be accepted as an orthodox Protestant for a number of years. He did not begin to develop definite radical views until around 1550, when he first received a copy of *De Trinitatis Erroribus* from the Italian expatriate publisher Pietro Perna. According to Perna, after reading it Gribaldi began to maintain that if he had not read Servetus, he would never have known who Christ was.[75]

One of the ideas of Servetus that most resonated with Gribaldi was that Christ possessed only a single nature. He is reported to have claimed that Servetus's ideas were the same as beliefs he had held since childhood.[76] It is easy to imagine that, as a boy, prior to his formal religious education, Gribaldi had believed that Christ possessed a single nature, for this was a simpler idea than what was taught by the Church. To an adult, burdened by a millennium and a half of Christology, no statement about Christ was simple or uncontroversial. The idea that Christ had a single nature, and was fully human, led almost inevitably to the Arian conclusion that Christ was a separate being from God the Father, lesser and subordinate and with a different substance and nature.[77] Like Servetus, Gribaldi denied being an Arian, on the rather unconvincing ground that "Arius foolishly thought the Son unlike the Father, and totally unfit for the glory of Jesus Christ."[78] If Gribaldi believed in a Son who was an entirely separate being, but possessing the power and glory of God, then perhaps he was, as George Huntston Williams described him, a ditheist.[79] He would, of course, have denied this as well. It may be that the insight that allowed him to avoid admitting either Arianism or ditheism, while retaining his belief in the single nature of Christ, was Servetus's suggestion that we should think about the unity of the deity in the same way that we do about people who are united in one faith and for a single purpose. Accordingly, Gribaldi, like Servetus, thought that the Father and the Son could be considered a unity because of their "agreement and harmony of spirit."[80]

The theology that Gribaldi adopted after reading *De Trinitatis Erroribus* was, however, noticeably different from that of Servetus. Servetus's theology worked on Gribaldi in the way that it has continued to work on many others to this day: even those who are most sympathetic to his ideas read his works selectively, emphasizing the features that harmonize best with what they already believe. There is so much varied antitrinitarian argument in Servetus that many kinds of heretical thinkers see their cherished ideas reflected in his works. As Jerome Friedman wrote, "Since Servetus related the Word, Christ, and the Son at the very same time that he drew sharp distinctions between them, virtually every Christological position might conceivably be found in his writings."[81]

Gribaldi took Servetus's reservations about the use of arcane theological terms — such as person, hypostasis, and subsistence — and went a step further, rejecting them altogether. He built his major theological statement, *Declarationis Jesu Christi filii Dei*, on passages selected from *De Trinitatis Erroribus*, choosing those with a more Arian slant, while neglecting those that expressed Servetus's modalism. And, unlike Servetus, Gribaldi was not very interested in formulating doctrines about the Word and the Holy Spirit. The Word, he thought, was mentioned in Scripture only to show that Christ had a divine, not a human, origin. He thought of the Holy Spirit as a name given to the activity of God in the world, such as the begetting of the

Son, the anointing of Christ, and the inspiration of the apostles. It is not a third God, a person, or even a disposition, but only a way of describing what God does.[82]

It is in Gribaldi's doctrine of humanity and in his understanding of the drama of atonement that the difference between his theology and that of Servetus stands out most clearly. Unlike Servetus, Gribaldi believed in the centrality of the doctrine of original sin. Although he shared Servetus's conviction that human beings could become the adopted children of God through correct belief, he thought that salvation also depended upon the satisfaction of God's justice through Christ's sacrifice on the cross. That the Son of God was a man with a single nature was what made his sacrifice efficacious. According to Gribaldi, Christ was called the mediator because he was a being intermediate between God and humanity.[83]

In spite of his enthusiasm for what he thought of as Servetus's theology, until the time of the Servetus's trial, Gribaldi was cautious about sharing his new, more radical views. This caution, and his formidable reputation as a scholar and lecturer, helped to keep him out of serious trouble in Padua. He was much sought after by other universities, and his presence in Padua elevated the status of the law school and attracted wealthy students from all over Europe. When he eventually left for Tübingen, many of his students departed with him. Thus it was a serious step to dismiss Gribaldi, one that the university authorities were reluctant to take. After all, even if he was a Protestant, he was no more heretical than many of his students.

Gribaldi's delicately balanced life — as an honored member of the Italian Protestant community in Geneva and as a celebrated law professor in Italy, where his religious opinions were suspect but not felt to be dangerous — was disrupted by his reaction to the arrest and trial of Servetus. Gribaldi found that he could not remain a silent observer of such injustice. Nor could he confine his public protest, as nearly all others had done, to expressing disapproval of the execution of heretics in general. Instead, while in Geneva during the trial, he debated Servetus's Christology with anyone who would listen to him. Because he was a citizen of Bern, it would have been awkward for Calvin to have attempted to discipline him. Gribaldi's Genevan acquaintances, however, were in danger of being brought before the Consistory. Alarmed at his openly heretical views, they began to avoid him. At this point, Gribaldi tried to arrange for a public discussion of Servetus's theology, or, failing that, to obtain an audience with Calvin himself. This Calvin refused, claiming that Gribaldi was dishonestly hiding his own heretical views in an appeal for religious toleration: "For if he had frankly admitted that he was a follower of Servetus, I would have heard him out."[84] This, however, was an offer that Gribaldi, even with his Bernese passport, had to refuse. With the time for the resumption of his academic duties approaching, Gribaldi departed Geneva, while Servetus's fate was still undecided.

Gribaldi did his best, however, to make his voice heard elsewhere. Upon being rebuffed by Calvin, he wrote a letter to the anabaptists in Vicenza.[85] He complained to the Zurich Reformer Heinrich Bullinger and, while in Chur, persuaded Vergerio that Servetus ought not to be executed.[86] He probably also talked to his friends and acquaintances in Basel — Celio Curione, Martin Borrhaus, Boniface Amerbach, and Sebastian Castellio — when he stopped there to collect Boniface Amerbach's son Basil, whom he took back with him to study in Padua.[87] Upon his return there, Gribaldi championed Servetus in his lectures, telling his students that the persecuted Spaniard was appropriately named, because the Latin verb *servare* means to protect or preserve and Servetus had preserved the true doctrine.[88]

Pietro Perna arrived in Padua from Basel in late November, bringing news of the later stages of the trial in Geneva and the execution of Servetus. There he found Lelio Sozzini staying with Gribaldi.[89] It seems quite possible that the conversations and deliberations of an intriguing group of dissidents then assembled in Padua — Gribaldi, Sozzini, Perna, and Gribaldi's students, Peter Gonesius, Michael Zaleski, and Orazio Curione — gave rise to a plan for preparing a pseudonymous protest, *Apologia pro Michæle Serveto*, against the recent judicial proceedings in Geneva.[90] Credited to the fictitious Alphonsus Lyncurius Tarraconensis, *Apologia* was composed by Gribaldi in early 1554.

In the late summer of 1554 Gribaldi returned to Farges for his annual vacation. As usual while he was there, he attended the religious services of the Italian community in Geneva. The minister of the congregation, Celso Martinenghi, challenged him to explain to the congregation his unorthodox views on the unity of God. Gribaldi's presentation was poorly received, and he complained that it was difficult to find the proper words to express his beliefs before such a hostile audience. Invited to make a written presentation, he wrote a letter to the congregation before he left Farges, in which he outlined his principal ideas.[91]

At this time Vergerio was beginning to wonder if his friend Gribaldi had "fallen away" from the Reformed faith. He confided to Bullinger that Gribaldi was obsessed with introducing others to the thinking of Servetus.[92]

But the patient and relatively tolerant Bullinger was not prepared to think the worst of a distinguished Italian Protestant. Despite his concern about what appeared to be Gribaldi's apostasy, Vergerio remained loyal to his old comrade-in-arms, and during the following year he worked hard to extricate Gribaldi from the increasingly dangerous situation he faced in Italy.

The time was rapidly approaching when Gribaldi could no longer safely remain in Venetian territory, even in the relative sanctuary of the University of Padua. In 1550 Pope Julius III had threatened the Venetian Senate with excommunication if they did not cooperate more fully with the Roman Inquisition. In the diplomatic communication between the Vatican and Venice, Gribaldi was identified as a particularly flagrant source of heresy.[93] In 1551 Peter Manelfi, a leader of the Venetian anabaptists, was examined by the Inquisition in Rome and disclosed the names of many Italian Lutherans and anabaptists.[94] In this atmosphere of fear and betrayal, Gribaldi was for a time protected by his Bernese citizenship and the reluctance of the chief magistrate in Padua to carry out the orders of the Inquisition. However, by early 1555 Gribaldi knew that he faced dismissal from the University of Padua if he did not recant his Protestant beliefs.[95]

In February 1555 Gribaldi traveled to Germany for an interview that he had obtained, thanks to Vergerio, with the Lutheran Duke Christoph of Württemberg, who was seeking to attract a distinguished legal scholar to the University of Tübingen. Gribaldi obtained the position and, after winding up his affairs in Padua, went to Zurich in May to meet Vergerio, who then escorted him to Tübingen. That same month, Giovanni Pietro Carafa, who had re-established the Roman Inquisition, was elected Pope Paul IV, a clear indication that Gribaldi had departed Italy none too soon.

While Gribaldi was in Zurich, Bullinger convinced him to write a confession of faith. This document looks orthodox on the surface, but it is so carefully worded that an Arian interpretation is possible.[96] Although Vergerio and Bullinger were still willing to grant Gribaldi the benefit of the doubt, Calvin and Theodore Beza were not.[97] Around this time Calvin wrote to Melchior Wolmar, a celebrated classical scholar who had many years earlier taught Calvin Greek and who, as a Protestant, had influenced Calvin's early religious development. Calvin warned Wolmar, who was currently a professor of law in Tübingen, about Gribaldi, whom he described as reckless, arrogant, and boastful. "Although he admits that Christ is God," Calvin wrote, "he denies that [Christ] and the Father are a single essence.

Tübingen

Thus, if [as we believe] God is from God, then it follows [according to Gribaldi's view] that there are two Gods. A fanatic with delusions of this kind does not hesitate to throw the church into turmoil — although he cannot even correctly spell the name Christ!"[98] (Gribaldi sometimes spelled *Christus* as "Cristus," reflecting Italian spelling.)

In the early summer of 1555 Gribaldi was back at his family home in Farges. While he was there, Calvin invited him to meet "fraternally" with himself and several of the other ministers of Geneva, assuring him that there would be no danger in coming. Accompanied by a few Italian friends, Gribaldi entered the room and asked to be introduced to Calvin. He extended his hand, but Calvin declined to take it. "It would not be right for me to shake your hand," he told Gribaldi, "until we reach an agreement about doctrine. We should certainly not begin with such a ceremony."[99] Thus rebuffed, Gribaldi immediately left.[100]

Having failed to deal with the heretic in an informal way, Calvin then had Gribaldi summoned to an official inquiry held at City Hall. At this meeting Gribaldi complained that Calvin had refused to grant him a private audience, when even princes and kings consented to converse with him. Calvin answered, "I do not boast of having talked with great lords. I can only say that every day I speak to anyone who has business with me, even to the humble and poor." Of Gribaldi he said, "Because I had good evidence in his own handwriting that he was a man who promoted errors regarding the principal articles of our faith, I did not wish to engage in dialogue with him without the presence of witnesses. That would have been a waste of time, for I know what such people are like. But he, on his part, has refused to speak to me in the company of others."[101]

After this unpromising beginning, the conversation that followed was unsatisfactory to both parties. When describing his beliefs, Gribaldi tried to choose his words carefully, but was quickly caught saying something Calvin and the others present thought was heretical. They then scolded him on his theological shortcomings and told him that if he did not give up his heresy he would no longer be allowed to come into the city. Gribaldi protested that this was a severe punishment for mere religious dissent. He was advised that there were far more severe penalties for heresy at the disposal of the government of Geneva, and that only his status as a foreigner protected him.[102]

After he returned to Tübingen, Gribaldi tried to rehabilitate himself in the eyes of the Italians in Geneva by writing them another seemingly orthodox confession. In this confession Gribaldi described the Son, in moderate Arian language, as "similar in every way" to the Father.[103] He also subscribed to the Apostles' and Nicene Creeds, but only "according to the true and evangelical sense."[104]

It was likely around this time that Gribaldi began to write *Declaratio*, his major contribution to antitrinitarian literature. It may have been his intention to write such a book from the time he first assumed the name of Alphonsus Lyncurius for *Apologia*. Perhaps in an attempt to distance himself personally from the work, Gribaldi chose to have *Declaratio* circulated by some of his Polish students in their native land. This strategy had already been pioneered by his friend Curione, who was distributing his own heretical book, *De Amplitudine*, exclusively in Poland and the east. The means for this kind of distribution would soon be available to Gribaldi, for in late 1556 Michael Zaleski, who had studied with him in Padua, arrived in Tübingen. He was the first of a number of young Eastern Europeans who would obtain part of their education there.[105]

While the Swiss reformers were working to establish the Reformed Church in Poland, they worried that the antitrinitarian and other heresies they had managed to contain at home might escape and become widespread in Eastern Europe. When they learned that Gribaldi's former student, Peter

Gonesius, was preaching antitrinitarian heresy in Poland, they immediately concluded that Gribaldi was the source.[106] Then, in March 1556, Vergerio was shown a copy of Curione's *De Amplitudine*, which the Duke of Württemberg had received from Poland.[107] Vergerio, who had long detested Curione for having opposed his attempts to gain a leadership role in the Italian expatriate community, now saw an opportunity to punish his old enemy.[108] While in Poland in early 1557 he demanded that the Protestant leaders there have Curione and *De Amplitudine* condemned.[109] In this he had no success, but on this journey Vergerio observed the influence that the heterodox theology of Gribaldi was having in Eastern Europe. On his return to Württemberg, he therefore felt compelled to apologize for having brought Gribaldi into the Duke's employ. A month later, after having made a short trip to visit the cities of Switzerland, Vergerio realized that he could no longer help or protect Gribaldi. He thereupon informed the Duke, "My conscience compels me to admit frankly that on this journey I have learned a lot about Gribaldi which I did not know before. I am now convinced that he is infected with some of the very worst beliefs."[110]

Vergerio's discussions with the Duke set in motion a formal investigation into Gribaldi's beliefs and his attempts to spread them. Duke Christoph delegated his uncle, Count George of Mümpelgard (Montbéliard), a member of the Reformed Church, to send letters of inquiry to Geneva. He was answered both by the Genevan Council and by Calvin himself. Their replies detailed the frustrating encounters between the Genevan ministers and Gribaldi in 1555.[111] Along with his letter, Calvin sent Gribaldi's "Religionis Christianæ." The Duke showed it to the eminent law professor in Basel, Boniface Amerbach, who acknowledged that the piece contained blasphemies.[112]

On his return to Germany from Switzerland, Vergerio escorted Gribaldi back to face the Senate of the University of Tübingen. When he arrived in Bern, he found the jurist recovering from a stab wound. Gribaldi had been attacked on the street in the center of Bern by an agent of Jean de Grammont, who contested his wife's right to her inheritance.[113] Although Gribaldi soon recovered from the physical injury, his life and reputation were now in danger from another quarter. It is unlikely, however, that he was as yet aware of the powerful forces arrayed against him or the amount of evidence that his foes had collected. Nor was he probably aware that most of his friends, including Vergerio and Amerbach, had turned against him or that Curione, who was now under suspicion himself, was powerless to aid him.

During the course of a two-day hearing before the senate of the University of Tübingen, July 17-18, 1557, Duke Christoph repeatedly pressed Gribaldi to counter the numerous reports circulating about his unorthodoxy by publicly assenting to all the official statements of faith, including the Athanasian Creed.[114] He and his advisors knew that Gribaldi could not do this without denying his own theology.[115] Thus far Gribaldi had designed all the ostensibly orthodox confessions to which he had subscribed — including those written out for Bullinger and for the Italian Church — to leave room for his heterodox beliefs. This time, however, Gribaldi's proposed formulation was rejected because it was worded "with too much obscurity."[116] The Duke then presented Gribaldi with an incriminating document in his own handwriting and asked him to acknowledge it. In this document (no longer extant) Gribaldi is said to have declared his intent to publish a book called *De filio Dei hactenus incognito* (The Hitherto Unknown Son of God). Surprised and taken aback, Gribaldi was forced to admit that he was the author of the document and that he held the views expressed in it. The Duke then urged him "to cast away his erroneous opinions and to embrace the true faith expressed by the Church of God in the creeds." Although the Duke, the Senate, and all the legal and theological advisors present thought that Gribaldi's beliefs were "heretical and extremely dangerous," they granted him a space of three weeks, during which the Duke hoped that Gribaldi might come to acknowledge correct doctrine.[117] Early one morning, a few days before the grace period expired, Gribaldi fled Tübingen on foot.[118]

Immediately after Gribaldi's escape, Duke Christoph had his house searched. Among other things, the Tübingen authorities found a manuscript written in Italian, known to us only by its Latin title, "De vera cognitione Dei" (On the True Knowledge of God), which, according to the Duke, contained "many blasphemies against the Son of God." This document also implicated Curione — already under suspicion for having written *De Amplitudine* — because his handwriting was identified in numerous annotations and marginal notes.[119] After being given this information, the University of Basel formed a commission, including Borrhaus and Amerbach, to investigate their colleague Curione. In part because Curione was a more cautious man than Gribaldi, and in part because his interrogators included individuals who were kindly disposed toward him, the Basel commission returned a more favorable result than did the hearing in Tübingen.[120]

Curione successfully argued that his additions were merely stylistic and that the marginal notes were meant to show Gribaldi where he had made the most serious errors. He claimed that his friendship with Gribaldi had been based upon their shared nationality and the memory of their common cause against the papists. Furthermore, Curione claimed that, after reading "De vera cognitione Dei," he realized that Gribaldi was indeed a heretic. But because Curione was a decent man, he chose not to inform on his friend, but instead hoped that he could do something to save him. He claimed that he and Gribaldi had argued bitterly, in the presence of Pietro Perna, and had not spoken to one another since. He also told the interrogators that he had withdrawn his son Agostino from Gribaldi's tutelage.[121]

In arguing that he had not known of Gribaldi's theological views until after his friend left Italy, Curione was being disingenuous. He had known Gribaldi for at least a decade. Gribaldi had regularly visited him in Basel on his journeys between Padua and Farges. Curione had sent his son Orazio to Padua to study with Gribaldi. Another son, Agostino, had been staying with Gribaldi as a student in Tübingen and acting as Gribaldi's secretary since late 1555. Gribaldi and Curione had often corresponded and Gribaldi had sent Curione other heterodox religious writings — "Theses" and *Declaratio*— for editing and comment. That the witness Curione offered to his purported breakup with Gribaldi was Perna — the man who had introduced Gribaldi to Servetus's ideas — indicates that the event may have been fabricated. Nevertheless, Curione was probably genuinely angry with Gribaldi at the time. He felt compelled to sever his connections with him — not so much because of theological differences, but because Gribaldi's recklessness had brought Curione and other Italian refugees into danger.

Soon after he fled Tübingen, Gribaldi wrote a letter to the university, excusing his flight by claiming that the Duke had hinted, through intermediaries, that it would be best if he were gone.[122] After returning to Farges, he several times visited Bern, where he may have been scouting for news from Tübingen.[123] On August 20, the Council of Bern received a letter from the Duke of Württemberg, in which he reported what he had discovered in his investigation and warned of Gribaldi's openly heretical views. As a result, the Council ordered the local authorities to keep an eye on "the Lord of Farges" and to watch for a pretext to arrest him.[124] When Gribaldi began to distribute a "little book" full of his heretical ideas in the vicinity of Farges, the local Bernese governor rounded up the copies of this publication and

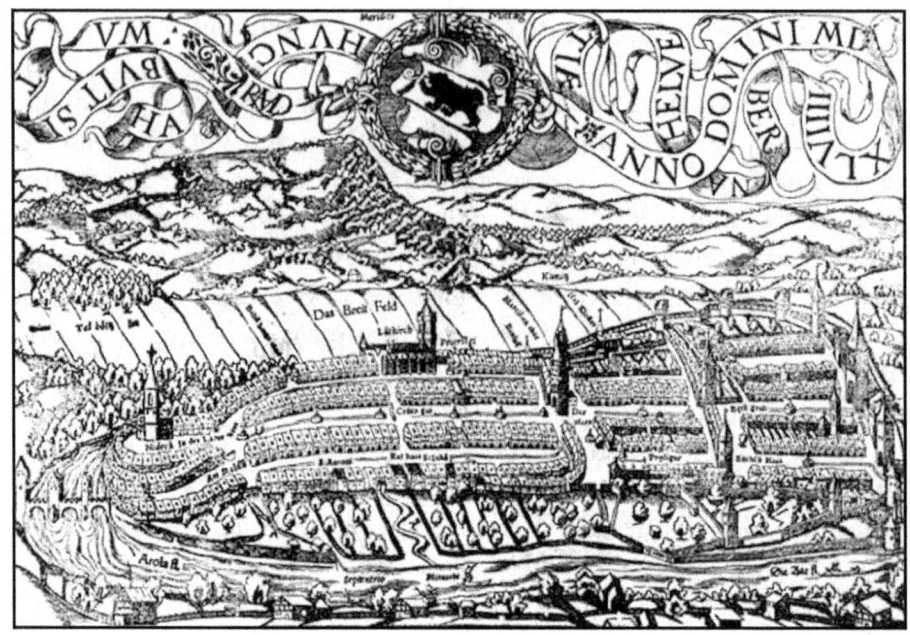
Bern

sent one to the Bernese senate. This led to Gribaldi's arrest on September 6 and the confiscation of his books and papers.[125]

The members of the Bern council, having read the papers and books delivered to them from Tübingen and Farges, were divided into two parties. One recommended that Gribaldi be burned at the stake, while the other favored banishment. For over a week his fate hung in the balance.[126] It was fortunate for Gribaldi that an advocate of religious toleration, Nikolaus Zurkinden, was a leading voice on the council. Zurkinden would have been personally embarrassed by a Bernese decision to execute Gribaldi, for he had boasted to Calvin that the Bernese never used capital punishment to enforce religious conformity.[127] Nonetheless, the final verdict was severe enough: Gribaldi was banished from Bernese territory, including his home at Farges. He was told that he could return after he had gone back to Tübingen and been re-examined and cleared by the Duke of Württemberg. This apparently lenient provision struck fear into Gribaldi. He begged the council not to send him to Tübingen and even warned that such severity might drive him back into the arms of the Catholic Church.[128]

Hoping for permission to return to his estate without having to appear again before the Duke of Württemberg in Tübingen, Gribaldi offered to place himself under the authority of the four parish ministers of Bern.[129] The ministers agreed to this proposed resolution and prepared a confession for Gribaldi to sign, which contained an acknowledgment of the Nicene and Athanasian Creeds and was pointedly designed to force him to disavow the positions expressed in the book they had confiscated from him at Farges.[130] The prepared confession began, "I believe and wholeheartedly confess God to be one in essence, divinity, nature, majesty, power, and glory, although three in person, which the Greeks call hypostases." Among other things he was required to say, "Nor do I in any way believe it acceptable for anyone to say that the eternal Word, acting as the seed of God in the womb of the Virgin, either dissolves or solidifies."[131] Gribaldi attempted, as he had done previously in a similar situation, to find a way to express his views in his own words and thereby avoid a forced recantation of his deeply held beliefs. However, the ministers pushed him hard to sign the confession just as it was. At last, worn out by the constant pressure to recant, and hoping to rejoin his family at Farges, he signed the document. Unfortunately, Gribaldi's efforts to reach a settlement with the ministers, and the humiliation he underwent by denying his faith, were in vain. For the Bern council, having learned with what reluctance Gribaldi had signed the confession, held fast to their original sentence of banishment.[132]

Having managed to avoid Servetus's fate, Gribaldi now found himself in a position similar to that of Francesco Spiera, who, a decade earlier, had wasted away in guilt and despair after being forced to deny his Protestant faith. Unlike Spiera, however, Gribaldi believed that God would forgive even repeated recantations, just as he had pardoned the apostle Peter who, in fear of his life, had denied Christ three times.[133] Gribaldi had already emerged unstricken from several other retractions. He clearly did not believe God would ever give up on him. He anticipated further opportunities to disseminate the ideas that he believed were God's truth. By this time he may have had reason to hope that his pseudo-Servetan work, *Declaratio*, already given into the eager young hands of his Polish and Lithuanian students, might be well on its way towards helping to advance his radical theological ideas in Eastern Europe.

After his wife died in early 1558, Gribaldi wrote to those whom he thought most sympathetic to him in Bern, appealing on behalf of himself as a widower and his seven motherless children. He had no success with the four ministers there, but had better luck with Zurkinden, who, with some difficulty, brokered a deal whereby Gribaldi promised, among other things, to keep silent on the subject of religion. In return the government of Bern agreed that he and his family could go home to Farges. Although Zurkinden feared that he had put his reputation at risk for someone who did not properly appreciate what he had done for him, he "preferred to save Gribaldi rather than to destroy him."[134]

Shortly after presenting his request to the Bernese authorities, and while the negotiations for his repatriation were still going on, Gribaldi wrote to the Rector and Senate at the University of Tübingen, hoping to open the way for recovering his teaching position. Having submitted to the confession imposed on him at Bern, he now presented himself to Tübingen as orthodox and inoffensive in matters of religious faith. He maintained his innocence on the charge of willful heresy. "What would it profit me," he asked, "wretchedly overthrown and oppressed in this world by continual calamities and persecutions, to voluntarily and knowingly cast away the life of the other world for the sake of condemned and impious views?"[135] This is strikingly reminiscent of a passage from *Apologia* in which he defended Servetus on the same charge:

> I believe that there is no one of such dull intelligence, so feeble in understanding, or so lacking in common sense, that he would choose to defend what he knew to be false, when it was obviously not in his interest to do so. Would he seek not only his temporal but also his eternal death on behalf [of a falsehood]? For although many might, for a time, oppose a known truth or deceitfully approve a falsehood in order to gain worldly advantages, nevertheless, no one would knowingly and deliberately choose death and, freely and voluntarily, offer up his soul to eternal destruction for the sake of a false idea.[136]

Gribaldi assured the Senate that none of his creditors would suffer financially because of his recent flight, and asked the Senate to intervene with Duke Christoph on his behalf and secure for him a safe conduct pass.[137] The Duke was willing to permit Gribaldi to visit, as long as he sent his confession of faith ahead for prior approval. Vergerio, who served as both the Duke's counselor and his traveling evangelist, inspected Gribaldi's Bern confession and did not look favorably upon it. "[Gribaldi] is not sincere," he advised the Duke, "and he will not come, even if he has safe conduct."[138] In the end, nothing came of these negotiations. The university chair left open by Gribaldi's departure was filled by another candidate, Johann Hospinian. The unemployed law professor would have to look elsewhere for a situation.

In August 1559 Gribaldi was rehired by the University of Grenoble, which had let him go for financial reasons in 1545. He was once again a popular lecturer on jurisprudence, with students flocking to Grenoble to hear him speak. But soon he was under suspicion by the religious authorities. It could not have helped that he was visited by Valentino Gentile, a friend who had recently been convicted of heresy in Geneva. Nor did Gribaldi endear himself to the local Catholics by staying away from mass, on the excuse that he had to maintain his Protestant credentials in order to keep the Bernese government from confiscating his estate. Calvin's friend Guillaume Farel, who came from that part of France, may have alerted some of his contacts there in order to stir up trouble for Gribaldi. Ultimately, academic jealousy proved to be the immediate cause of his downfall. Friends of a rival professor complained of the unorthodox professor to the governor of Dauphiné, the Duke of Guise, who, together with King Francis II, in November 1560 threatened to close down the university if Gribaldi were not dismissed and expelled from the country. Although it meant an immediate loss of students and of revenue, Grenoble had no choice but to terminate his employment.[139]

Little is known about the last few years of Gribaldi's life in retirement at Farges. It may be supposed that he was not idle, since a correspondent alerted Calvin in late 1563 that "the villain of Farges continues to spread his filthiness and foaming madness, infecting not only men but the very air itself. One of our elders has looked at his most wicked manuscript commentary on the first book of your *Christian Institutes*."[140] In an earlier day, when Servetus had annotated the Geneva Reformer's magnum opus, drastic action followed. But the days were growing short for Calvin. Already a sick man, he died the following spring.

Gribaldi soon followed his old antagonist to the grave. He died of the plague at Farges in September 1564. Beza said of Gribaldi's death, "Swept away by the plague, everyone deserted him, and hardly anyone could be found to bury him."[141] This lonely end represented no particular judgment upon Gribaldi, as Beza implied, for, of course, everyone who could do so shunned a house of plague and its dying inhabitants. There were many such afflicted houses during this epidemic, the worst outbreak of bubonic plague since the Black Death of the fourteenth century. Over 14,000 people died of it in the territory of Bern alone. In Basel, Curione lost three daughters to the plague. In Zurich, Bullinger, who was himself very ill, lost three daughters and his wife as well. Among the other distinguished theologians and scholars taken at this time by the plague were Martin Borrhaus, Theodore Bibliander, and Bernardino Ochino.[142]

Declaratio and the Other Theological Works of Gribaldi

Reassigning *Declaratio*, *Apologia*, "Theses," and *De vera Dei* — works previously attributed to Servetus, Curione, and Sozzini — has resulted in a substantial increase in the hitherto scanty theological *oeuvre* of Gribaldi. We will now be able to study, in greater detail and with better definition, the theology of a man who, for self-protection and for the better promotion of his ideas, chose not to publish his religious writing under his own name. The works described below make it clear that Gribaldi ought to be promoted from a shadowy figure operating in the community of Italian Reformers to a significant theologian in his own right, who had a major influence on the development of antitrinitarianism in the Radical Reformation.

***Apologia pro Michæle Serveto* (1554).** *Apologia* is a legal brief meant to show that the Genevans had no basis upon which to arrest, prosecute, and execute Servetus. Furthermore, Gribaldi argued, even if the charges had substance, Servetus was treated in an extremely unjust manner: he was denied bail, deprived of legal counsel, and not allowed any opportunity to properly arrange his defense. In the midst of this legal and ethically-based protest, Gribaldi's own theological views, modeled, as he thought, after the thinking of Servetus, periodically burst through. It was Gribaldi's position that it was not only evil to condemn Servetus for his beliefs, it was wrong even to accuse him, since he was largely correct in his doctrine. "[Servetus] taught," wrote Gribaldi, "that there is only one uncompounded God, who is neither triple nor three-named, neither divided nor composite, who is undoubtedly the eternal Father and monarch, the author of everything, through whose Word and Spirit all things are arranged; and one Son of God, Jesus Christ, who was born of a virgin of the House of David."[143]

Because Gribaldi offered details about Servetus's career in *Apologia* and because Servetus and Gribaldi had lived in the same region of France during the early 1540s, both having business dealings during that period with the publisher Jean Frellon in Lyons, Uwe Plath contends that Gribaldi must have known Servetus.[144] There is, however, no evidence that they ever met. *Apologia* and the preface to *Declaratio* actually betray a profound ignorance of the details and the important features of Servetus's life. For example, Gribaldi wrote that Servetus was a physician who, when he observed the divisions in the world over religious truth, "turned his attention to sacred literature" and then, "when he believed that he had obtained something that would be useful to the entire Christian flock," published *De Trinitatis*

Erroribus, in which he attacked the Genevan reformers by name.[145] This is incorrect in a number of important ways. Servetus wrote *Erroribus* years before he became interested in medicine. Furthermore, Gribaldi was confusing *Erroribus*, written in 1531, well before the Genevan reformation and before Calvin was a public figure, with *Christianismi Restitutio*, which does contain letters written to Calvin.

Apologia was completed after January 1554, for it contains a clear reference to Calvin's *Defensio orthodoxæ fidei*, issued that month in reply to the mounting criticism of the execution of Servetus.[146] In the spring Gribaldi was occupied in the supervision of students who were preparing a new edition of the fourth part of Justinian's *Corpus Iuris Civilis*, so it is likely that *Apologia* was written early in the year.[147] It was probably finished in February 1554, for in that month Pietro Perna returned from Padua to Basel and may have taken the draft to Curione, who made comments in the margin.[148]

"Theses de filio Dei et Trinitate" (c.1554). After Gribaldi returned to Padua in the autumn of 1553, he frequently talked about Servetus's ideas in his lectures and private conversations. He also tried to organize his thoughts in written form. One such attempt, untitled but subsequently given the name of "Theses de filio Dei et Trinitate," was written in the form of sketchy notes. "Theses" contains arguments, citations of scripture and church authorities, and words and phrases that recur in Gribaldi's later, more developed works. The manuscript has comments, in Latin and Italian, in the hand of Curione.[149] By this time Gribaldi had clearly established a collaborative relationship with Curione, who edited and critiqued his theological works. This continued for several years, until it became dangerous for Curione to associate with him.

***De vera Dei et filii eius cognitione sermo* and other pseudo-Servetan discourses (c. 1554).** By 1554 Gribaldi had almost certainly begun writing a series of short pseudo-Servetan works. In the preface to *Declaratio* he listed the titles of twenty-seven discourses, "most of which [Servetus] kindly shared with me." The title of the surviving discourse, *De vera Dei et filii eius cognitione*, resembles the fourth item in the *Declaratio* list, "De vera unius dei cognitione."[150] Either in manuscript or in printed form, *De vera Dei* survived into the next century and was transcribed by the seventeenth-century historian of Polish antitrinitarianism, Stanislas Lubieniecki, who believed it to be an address made by Servetus just prior to his execution.[151] Nevertheless the eighteenth-century scholar Johann Lorenz Mosheim wrote that *De vera Dei* was "invented by someone who was not at all familiar with Servetus's beliefs."[152]

It may be that Gribaldi had at least one such discourse printed by 1554. The music teacher Francesco Scudieri, hired in Padua to instruct Gribaldi's daughter, reported that, some time between late 1553 and early 1555, Gribaldi handed him a printed booklet, ostensibly by Servetus, but actually, Scudieri claimed, composed by Gribaldi himself.[153] Since this was too early a date for *Declaratio*, it must have been a pseudonymous discourse, similar to those mentioned in the preface to *Declaratio*.

Letter to the Italian Church in Geneva (1554). Gribaldi wrote this letter in Italian and sent it to the Italian congregation in Geneva soon after he spoke before them on September 2, 1554. The theology he professed in the letter is the same as that which he attributed to Servetus in *Declaratio*. This letter, as might be expected, was soon shared with Calvin and other Swiss reformers. A year later, Beza referred to it as "Gribaldi's confession."[154]

"Religionis Christianæ προγυμνάσματα" (c.1554). In his letter to the Italian Church in Geneva, Gribaldi offered to send a more substantial document, including Biblical proof-texts and other authorities, after he returned to Padua. Uwe Plath contends that "Religionis Christianæ," discovered by Delio Cantimori in the Basel University archives, was the promised follow-up document.[155] It was in Calvin's possession in 1557, probably given to him by a member of the Italian community in Geneva. Calvin sent "Religionis Christianæ" to Duke Christoph of Württemberg to encourage him to dismiss Gribaldi from the University of Tübingen.[156] The Duke lent the manuscript to Boniface Amerbach, whose copy survives in Basel. No mention of "Religionis Christianæ" is made in the records of the Tübingen hearing.

"De vera cognitione Dei" (c.1556). This work, which no longer exists, was discovered among Gribaldi's papers after he fled Tübingen. It was written in Italian and addressed to the Italian Church in Geneva. As was his usual practice, Gribaldi had sent the manuscript to Curione for polishing and correction. There were several dozen notes and many marks and pointers in the margin of the manuscript. Curione claimed that he sent it back to Gribaldi and advised him not to send it to Geneva, and that Gribaldi took the advice. As a result, the work lay hidden in a drawer until it was discovered by the Württemberg authorities, who believed that the manuscript looked as if it had been made ready for publication.[157] After learning about the annotations, Vergerio, delighted that he could besmirch his longtime enemy Curione, wrote to Bullinger ecstatically, "Listen! Listen! Celio has been discovered to be Gribaldi's accomplice."[158] Years later, Vergerio referred to "De vera cognitione Dei" as "Gribaldi's book against the Athanasian Creed."[159]

De filio Dei hactenus incognito, and a document announcing it (c.1557). A document announcing the upcoming publication of a book called *De filio Dei hactenus incognito* was presented as evidence in Gribaldi's hearing in Tübingen. Whether the book itself ever existed is unknown.[160]

The "little book" circulated at Farges (1557). We do not know the identity of the "little book" Gribaldi circulated from Farges shortly after his flight from Tübingen. There is, however, a letter written by Johannes Haller, a minister in Bern, in which he summarized and paraphrased some of the content of the book. He said that Gribaldi "sets up three separate gods," including "a supreme Father, who like Jove is chief of the gods," to whom all scripture passages referring to "the ineffable majesty of divinity" apply, and two subordinates, the Son and the Holy Spirit. According to Haller, Gribaldi laughed at the Trinity as a "scholastic delirium" that could not be understood, denied the Nicene and Athanasian Creeds and the doctrine of *communicatio idiomatum*, and misrepresented the ante-Nicene church fathers.[161]

Nearly all of these characterizations of Gribaldi's thought are applicable to Gribaldi's pseudo-Servetan work, *Declaratio*.[162] Even more telling is Haller's description of Gribaldi's account of Christ's conception: "He asserts that the divine seed of the Son of God or Word was solidified into a human being within the virgin mother."[163] This is quite close to what we see in *Declaratio*: "as in the usual way of human reproduction, the father's seed and mother's blood flow together, and from these a body solidifies and a human being is formed."[164] However, if the work Gribaldi was arrested for distributing in the vicinity of Farges bore the name of Servetus as its author, it is hard to imagine that Haller would not have mentioned it. Whatever the "little book" was, it was apparently a work closely related to *Declaratio*, though perhaps in an earlier, shorter form, with Gribaldi named as the author. It might conceivably even have been *Declaratio* itself, without the preface and with a different title page.

Declarationis Jesu Christi filii Dei (c.1557). In March 1559 Gribaldi's major theological work, *Declaratio*, came to light in Tübingen. Michael Zaleski, who had recently completed his studies at the university there, was murdered just as he was about to return home to Poland. A manuscript copy of *Declaratio* was discovered among his personal effects.[165] This led to an investigation into how it came to be there and the extent to which the Polish student community was infected with antitrinitarian heresy.

The initial report made by Vergerio to Duke Christoph of Württemberg, based upon information volunteered by Thomas Drohojowski, blamed everything on Zaleski. According to this account, shortly before his death Zaleski had told his fellow Polish students that *Declaratio* was "the real foundation and the truth of the Gospel." Drohojowski claimed that Zaleski had written the marginal notes and made the underlinings in the text. Zaleski had pressed the students to acknowledge that the contents were sound and consistent with their faith. He also told them that he hoped to have the book printed, but had been unable to find someone who would consent to do the job. When he returned to Poland, he said, he would use his influence with members of his noble family to have it published there.[166]

These initial claims led the Duke to order a full investigation. The report, submitted on May 16, 1559, was a whitewash, minimizing the effect of *Declaratio* on the students and shifting blame away from the deceased Zaleski and the other Polish students present in Tübingen. In this new version, according to the collective testimony given to the interrogators, the manuscript belonged to one Stanislas Kula, who appears not to have been present at all during the investigation. It was he, not Zaleski, who had added the notes and underlining. Zaleski, the students believed, was unlikely to have read it. They were certain that he had not promoted or discussed it. Drohojowski admitted bringing it to Tübingen from Strasbourg, but said that it was at the behest of Kula and as part of a collection of books that had been left in storage with him. He said that the Polish students in Strasbourg had read *Declaratio*, but only to see if it was the source of the heretical Arian doctrines that Peter Gonesius had been condemned for spreading in Lithuania and preaching at the Synod of Secemin in 1556. Some of the Polish students in Tübingen admitted having read the heretical book, but denied that they were propagating its doctrines. One said that *Declaratio* did not hold his interest past page one.[167]

Can any truth be gleaned from these contradictory stories? It is possible, perhaps, to make some reasonable guesses if we inspect closely the motivations of both those investigating and those being investigated. The primary purpose of the Duke's commission was clearly to give the University of Tübingen a clean bill of theological health. Its job was not to stir up trouble, but to minimize and contain it, a task not entirely consistent with finding or reporting the truth. Moreover, the Polish students at Tübingen were largely drawn from the highest strata of Polish society. It would have been a serious matter to accuse or to discipline any of them for unorthodoxy, as they were closely connected to the eminent nobles and churchmen on whom the Protestant leaders in Switzerland and Germany depended for the continued progress of the Reformation in Poland. For example, Thomas Drohojowski, the principal informant in the Zaleski affair, was probably related to the recently deceased Jan Drohojowski, the Roman Catholic bishop of Wladislaw, who wished to reform the Polish Catholic Church and who sympathized with the Reformation. Michael Zaleski was the cousin of Stanislas Lutomirski, a pastor who composed the first Polish Protestant confession of faith.[168] And Lutomirski's father-in-law was Jan Laski (John à Lasco), a Reformer famous throughout Europe and an influence on Anglican and Calvinist liturgy and polity in Great Britain, the Netherlands, and Germany. At this time he was the leader of the Polish Protestants and an important channel for Swiss Reformed influence in Poland. This connection may explain why Zaleski, though conveniently deceased, was not made the scapegoat for the appearance of the *Declaratio* manuscript.

There was at least one other reason why Zaleski's connection to the heretical document was minimized. Besides protecting his beloved university and his own reputation as a Reformer, the Duke wished to shield the people in his employ, in particular Pierpaolo Vergerio. But why was Vergerio, who appeared in an inquisitorial role in the events following the death of Zaleski, himself at risk? The answer lies in the web of Vergerio's personal relationships and loyalties. Vergerio wished to protect the reputation of the Italian Protestant expatriates, many of whom were by this time suspected of antitrinitarian heresy. Though greatly disillusioned with his former friend, he probably had little desire to see the now officially penitent and sufficiently disgraced Gribaldi further harassed. If charges of heresy were to be brought against any of the diaspora Italians, he would probably have preferred that the accused be his enemy Celio Curione. Zaleski did, in fact, have a personal connection to Curione, having stayed with him several times in Basel. But he had an even stronger tie to Gribaldi, since he was one of Gribaldi's students in Padua during the critical period immediately following the trial and execution of Servetus. He was also the first Polish student to follow Gribaldi north to Tübingen.

When Drohojowski first supplied evidence to Vergerio, he did not indicate that *Declaratio* had been brought to Tübingen from elsewhere. The fact that the manuscript was in Zaleski's possession, together with the account of its having originated at University of Tübingen, both strongly pointed to Gribaldi's authorship. Wishing to protect his fellow Italian expatriates, his Protestant contacts in Poland, and the reputation of the University of Tübingen, Vergerio would have been dismayed if the Gribaldi-Zaleski connection became the verdict of the investigation. Accordingly, he did not interfere or suggest that there was any impropriety when, in the later phase of the inquiry, the investigators began to play on the students' sense of self-preservation and elicited a story that deflected the blame onto the absent Stanislas Kula.

The revised account of the presence of *Declaratio* among Zaleski's effects substituted the *Schola argentinensis* in Strasbourg for the University of Tübingen as a point of dissemination of the heretical manuscript. A place of refuge not only for French Protestants, but for many anabaptists and other radicals — including Servetus, who stayed there in 1531 — Strasbourg was a plausible location for the development or exchange of radical ideas.[169] Like Tübingen, it was a city where many Polish students had studied. But it was not a place connected with Gribaldi, nor with Italian Protestants in general. Of course, saying that the book came from Strasbourg left open the possibility that it might have come to Strasbourg from somewhere else. Thus the report left the ultimate origin of the work an open question.

Vergerio, in his private communications, claimed that he knew the true identity of Lyncurius, the "compiler" of *Declaratio*. Writing to Bullinger while the investigation was in progress, he said, "As you can easily guess, the name of the writer of the preface of the book by Servetus is an invention. Who, in fact, would dare to sign his own name to the eulogy of the greatest heretic? We know who has invented this name. We have found it in the papers of the deceased, who was fascinated by this contagious book. All this is certain."[170] Unfortunately, Vergerio did not disclose the identity of Lyncurius in this letter. A few years later, writing to Duke Christoph, he said, "Celio [Curione] is strongly suspected of having compiled several small books 'by Servetus,' together with a preface, as a single volume. These, of course, were the small books found among [the effects] of Michael Zaleski, the Pole murdered here at Tübingen."[171]

The modern rediscoverer of the *Declaratio* manuscript, Stanislas Kot, read these contemporary statements made by Vergerio as proof that Curione was the author of the preface to *Declaratio* and thus was Alphonsus Lyncurius Tarraconensis.[172] Although Vergerio's testimony needs to be taken seriously — he was well acquainted with all of those whom modern scholars have suspected of being Lyncurius — it need not be accepted as conclusive evidence that Curione was the perpetrator of *Declaratio* and *Apologia*. If we trust Vergerio's information, all we can be certain of is this: in 1559 he claimed he knew for certain the identity of Alphonsus; then in 1563 he announced that he "suspected" Curione.

Was Vergerio's certainty downgraded to suspicion because of new evidence? Did he believe it was someone else at first, but later decided that Curione was a more likely suspect? Or, as seems more plausible, were two different identifications made for the benefit of two different recipients? The first letter to Bullinger may have referred to Gribaldi, a man with whom they both had extensive dealings, and whom Bullinger might have identified even without the name being mentioned. The second letter, on the other hand, was written to the Duke of Württemberg — not a friend and colleague, but Vergerio's employer, and a person who had a decided stake in the outcome of the official investigation into the discovery of *Declaratio* at the University of Tübingen. By naming Curione, who may indeed have been guilty of complicity in *Declaratio*, at least in an editorial capacity, Vergerio both maligned an old enemy and shifted blame away from Tübingen.

Vergerio's mysterious hints, which were contained in private communications, led to no disciplinary proceedings against Gribaldi or anyone else. But what Vergerio knew or suspected may have influenced events in the Duchy of Württemberg. At the time of the discovery of *Declaratio*, Gribaldi's application to be restored to his position at the University of Tübingen was still under consideration. It was only later that Hospinian was chosen in his place. Gribaldi might have lost the job in any case; if, however, he was still under consideration by the Duke of Württemberg in the spring of 1559, and Vergerio then suspected Gribaldi of fashioning *Declaratio*, this new manifestation of heresy must have decided the issue in favor of his competitor.

It seems clear that at one time there existed more copies of *Declaratio* than the one discovered in Tübingen and later in Stuttgart. Although none of these have come down to us, Stanislas Lubieniecki possessed a copy, or at least part of one, which he quoted in his *History of the Polish Reformation*, along with the sole surviving short discourse of Gribaldi, *De vera Dei*.[173]

In their guise as writings of Servetus, these two works helped to carry the Arian message of Matteo Gribaldi into Poland.

Gribaldi's Successors

Servetus is commonly considered to have been a tragic, isolated figure in the history of theology, who had no followers and whose ideas died with him. *Declaratio* shows that there was, in the person of Gribaldi, a creative disciple of Servetus, who wished to promote his master's thought, and who personally inspired a group of students and peers, all of whom played a role in spreading and fostering Arianism in Poland.

Peter Gonesius (Piotr of Goniądz). A graduate of the University of Padua, Gonesius left Italy in 1555, shortly after Gribaldi. He immediately journeyed home to Lithuania, where he was engaged as a minister in the domain of Prince Nicholas Radziwiłł. When the Prince heard that Gonesius was spreading the Servetan heresy, he sent him to the Synod of Secemin, which convened in January 1556, where his preaching was monitored for divergences from orthodoxy. Among his recorded remarks, several show how closely he adhered to Gribaldi's unorthodoxy. A summary of the beliefs Gonesius espoused at Secemin is preserved in the "Acts of the Polish Synods":

> He approved of the Apostles' Creed, but rejected the rest — the Nicene and Athanasian Creeds, etc. [He also held that] the Trinity is not God and that the Son of God is certainly God, but lesser than the Father. In addition, he emphasized that the Son of God always paid deference to the Father and pointed out that Christ received all things from the Father ... Likewise he claimed, on the basis of John 17:3, that God the Father is the only true God; that the *Logos*, or invisible, immortal Word, was at the proper time transformed into flesh in the womb of the Virgin; and that the invisible Word was the seed of the incarnate Son. Furthermore, he denied *communicatio idiomatum*, claiming that that there was only one substance or nature in Christ. But he especially attacked the consubstantiality of the Son with the Father. In this regard he said that Christ the man was transformed into God; and that God, or the Word, was transformed into a man.[174]

Although the synod as a whole expressed disapproval of Gonesius's views, many in attendance must have been influenced by his presentation, for nearly half of them later became antitrinitarians.[175]

Gianpaolo Alciati de la Motta. A well-to-do Piedmontese nobleman who was both a physician and a soldier, Alciati joined the Italian Church in Geneva no later than 1552. He concealed his radical thoughts and was so trusted by Calvin that when he revealed himself as an antitrinitarian,

Calvin thought that he had gone mad.[176] Before he fled Geneva, he told Calvin that the Trinity was "three devils, worse than all the idols of the papacy."[177] Although he has been called a disciple of Gribaldi, he was more of an ally and a sympathizer. He identified himself as a "Marian" rather than an Arian — he believed that Christ was born of God and the Virgin Mary, and that he did not exist in another form, such as the Word, before conception. Thus his faith was more similar to Sozzini's than to Gribaldi's. Because of his beliefs, his travels in Eastern Europe (beginning in 1562), and his statement that the Muslims had a better doctrine of God than the Christians, his Calvinist detractors were able to spread the false rumor that he had converted to Islam.[178]

Giorgio Biandrata (Blandrata). Another physician from a noble Piedmont family, Biandrata was a specialist in obstetrics and gynecology. During the 1540s he had been personal physician to Bona Sforza, the Queen of Poland, and her daughter Isabella, the regent of Transylvania. He joined the Italian Church in Geneva around 1556. Not long after settling in Geneva, he engaged Calvin in private debate about the nature of God. He maintained that it was inappropriate to worship a person rather than God, and observed that Christian prayer was commonly addressed to the Father.[179] Calvin found these conversations wearying, for "although [Biandrata] repeatedly pretended to be reconciled, and acquiesced to what I said in reply to him, on the following day he returned as if for the first time, and continued to argue about things to which I had already often heard him agree."[180] Biandrata was reprimanded by the Geneva Consistory and, in May 1558, fled the city.

"[Biandrata] seems to be the same as Gribaldi was," Nikolaus Zurkinden wrote shortly afterwards to Calvin. "For both of them relate the Son to the eternal God, as if he were some kind of lesser god."[181] That summer Biandrata visited the Reformer Peter Martyr Vermigli in Zurich. Vermigli reported to Calvin that Biandrata denied that the Father and the Son were of the same essence, thus creating, after the manner of Gribaldi, a plurality of Gods.[182] Told by Vermigli that he had better move on, Biandrata departed for Poland with Lelio Sozzini. Until 1563, when he became physician to the Transylvanian royal court, Biandrata influenced the development of Polish Protestantism, shepherding it towards Arianism.[183] He went on to become a founder and organizer of the Transylvanian Unitarian Church. Possessing one of the few surviving copies of *Christianismi Restitutio*, he selectively reshaped Servetus's later thought into a new book, *De regno Christi* (1569), to meet the needs of Transylvanian antitrinitarians.[184]

Giovanni Valentino Gentile. Originally from Cosenza in Calabria, Gentile had been a teacher of Latin in Naples before his heretical ideas forced him to flee Italy. When he arrived in Geneva in 1556, he swiftly fell into the orbit of Gribaldi, Biandrata, and Alciati.[185] Hoping to expunge heresy in the Italian Church in Geneva, Calvin called its members to a public meeting in May 1558 and laid before them a confession of faith carefully devised to force them to deny unequivocally the Gribaldian doctrines which were circulating among them.[186] For a few days Gentile managed to withhold his signature from the confession. Then, after signing, because he continued to protest, he was thrown in prison and put on trial. Facing capital punishment, he performed the *amende honorable*, a humiliating public recantation. After he was released he immediately left Geneva and went to Farges. Beginning in 1562, Gentile traveled Poland and elsewhere in Eastern Europe. Not knowing of Gribaldi's death, he returned to Farges in 1566 in hopes of greeting his friend.[187] There he was arrested, taken to Bern, tried, and beheaded for heresy.

Of all the Italian refugees, Gentile was the one whose theology most resembled that of Gribaldi. In Gentile's view, the Father is the one God (God-in-himself, or *autotheos*), while the Son was begotten by the Father as a derivative being possessing a separate substance.[188] The argument that only the Father is *autotheos* is found earlier in Gribaldi's "Religionis Christianæ." Both Gribaldi and Gentile made a real distinction in substance between the Father and the Son. Gribaldi wrote, "By not recognizing the distinction between God and the Son of God, they have impiously confounded the natures of both, which are truly distinct and separate." He dismissed the Trinitarian unity of substance by saying, "If one and the same God, simple and undivided, was made man, then it necessarily follows that the Father and Holy Spirit became incarnate." Similarly, Gentile said, "Unless there is a distinction in substance between God the Logos and the invisible Father, the Logos could not be conceived in the womb of the Virgin, without the Father being incarnated at the same time." Although Gentile thought that there are indeed three spirits — the Father, the Son, and the Holy Spirit — like Gribaldi, who talked of the Father and Son having "an agreement and harmony of spirit," he considered that the unity they share is not one of essence, but rather one of "nature, power, and way of thinking."[189]

The Significance of *Declaratio*

When we first began to suspect that the work we were translating was not, in fact, written by Servetus, we were surprised and somewhat disappointed. However, we quickly realized that removing a book from the list of Servetus's works is not such a setback to our knowledge and understanding of Servetus as it first appears. Because *Christianismi Restitutio* is such a substantial work — taking up three volumes in his complete works — and because we possess *De Trinitatis Erroribus* and several other early theological works, there is no shortage of material upon which to build a detailed and nuanced theological estimate of Servetus. There is actually almost too much material, and few have made themselves masters of the content of these published works. When we believed that *Declaratio* was by Servetus, in addition to having to make sense of the many hard-to-reconcile ideas in *Erroribus* and *Restitutio*, we had also to try to make room for ideas unique to *Declaratio*, including some that are, as we have seen, quite at odds with what Servetus wrote. On the other hand, now that we have removed *Declaratio* from the Servetan canon, and can unreservedly evaluate the differences between it and the genuine works of Servetus, the special characteristics of the theologies of both Servetus and Gribaldi come into much sharper focus.

In the end *Declaratio* serves Servetus — and history — best as a link connecting him, through Gribaldi and his Italian compatriots, to the antitrinitarian Protestant movement in Poland. Declaratio shows that Servetus, through a series of natural transformations, is indeed a father of Arianism and Socinianism in Poland, and an ancestor of the Unitarians and other antitrinitarians in the world today.

Notes on Sources, Transcription, and Translation

The Latin Text of *Declaratio*

Our primary intent has been to produce the first English translation of *Declarationis Jesu Christi filii Dei*. Nevertheless, we decided at an early stage to present it together with an accurate Latin text. This, we hope, will allow readers to engage directly with the original text, and will make it more convenient for other scholars to correct and improve upon our work.

The Latin text of *Declaratio* in this book is our own transcription of the manuscript discovered in Stuttgart by Stanislas Kot in 1953.[1] We have built upon the earlier transcription by Ángel Alcalá and Marian Hillar, which is printed in the landmark Latin/Spanish edition of the complete works of Servetus (*Obras Completas*).[2] In our work we have had the luxury, not available to the original transcribers, of being able to take as much time as we needed. The result is a new, more definitive edition of the Latin text of *Declaratio*. While we cannot guarantee that this edition is without error — and indeed there are several places where our current readings might, and hopefully will, be questioned — we feel confident that we have significantly improved upon the original transcription. We hope that the text is sufficiently accurate that scholars and translators can approach it with almost the degree of confidence they have when dealing with a printed text of the period, such as the 1553 edition of Servetus's *Christianismi Restitutio*.

The Stuttgart manuscript, copied out in the late 1550s, is the work of four copyists, whose handwriting varies in readability and who employed different conventions of abbreviation. Also prevalent in the manuscript are many neo-Latin vagaries of spelling, such as *archana* for *arcana* and *misterium* for *mysterium*. There are a few other orthographic peculiarities. Some of the copyists left out the standard doubling of consonants in words such as *consumatio, Emanuel, agregatus,* and *eclesia* and doubled consonants not normally doubled, e.g. *relligionem, Paull, dessignatio,* and *pateffacta.* We have chosen to leave the variant spellings intact, for they are almost never confusing.

To the extent possible, we have preserved the punctuation from the manuscript. It was often difficult, especially when working from photocopies, to differentiate between commas, periods, and extraneous artifacts, such as stains or specks of dust. Thus there will always be a certain amount of uncertainty insofar as manuscript punctuation is concerned. From a translator's point of view, however, this is not a serious problem. Modern English ideas of punctuation and current sensibilities about proper sentence length and structuring differ so greatly from those of writers of Reformation Latin that any marks provided in the manuscript function as little more than hints to the translator.

A discovery which we made early on in the translation had a significant impact upon the transcription: we realized that large blocks of text, especially in book 2, were copied almost word-for-word from book 3 of Irenaeus's *Adversus Hæreses*. We also found long quotations from Josephus and pseudo-Ignatius, as well as numerous extended quotations from the Bible. Checking *Declaratio* against these texts, and, where necessary, consulting the editions of these works available in the early- and mid-sixteenth century, allowed us to establish or confirm many of our new readings of the manuscript. Nevertheless, because Gribaldi often made slight changes in phrasing, even when plainly quoting and not merely paraphrasing his sources, we never adopted the wording of the source text unless we were completely certain that the manuscript of *Declaratio* bore it out.

All told, our examination and repeated reexamination of the manuscript photocopies, together with our comparative studies of source texts, have led us to make hundreds of changes to the Alcalá/Hillar Latin text. Although many of these changes are of minor importance, a considerable number noticeably affected our translation, and a few resulted in quite different readings of the passages concerned. In several cases the new reading of a single word has introduced an entirely new topic, previously unsuspected, which adds new insight into the history of the document or the ideas of the author. Two examples may be mentioned here. Each of them demonstrates how much depends on the correct reading of a single word.

Page 10

Page 20

Page 70

Page 85

Handwriting samples from the *Declaratio* manuscript

In the first case, the earlier transcription rendered the first two words on manuscript page 55 as *eum abhorrere* [recoil from it]. We had to struggle with this passage over the course of several sessions before a new reading emerged: *cum alcharano* [with the Quran]. Once we realized what was actually written in the manuscript, what had previously been puzzling became clear. The new reading not only made sense of the rest of the sentence, it also revealed Gribaldi's negative attitude towards Islam.

In the second example, on page 93, the earlier transcription read *neotriniti theologi*, which, if correct, was quite an intriguing reading. It certainly seemed worth investigating who Gribaldi thought these neo-Trinitarian theologians were. However, it turns out that the theologians in question were not *neotriniti*, but *neoterici* [contemporaries]. This new reading led us to identify the text that follows as a quotation from a work by John Calvin. This, in turn, gave us a new *terminus a quo* for the dating of *Declaratio*.

The Other Latin Texts

When we determined that *Declaratio* was written by Gribaldi, we decided to expand the scope of the book to include five shorter works by Gribaldi, in order to show how *Declaratio* stands in relation to his other writings. We were able to obtain copies of the manuscripts of three of them. The texts of the other two are taken from printed sources.

The manuscripts of *Apologia pro Michaele Serveto*, "Theses de filio Dei et Trinitate" and "Religionis Christianæ προγυμνάσματα" are in the library of the University of Basel.[3] Although there are published transcriptions of all three,[4] the transcriptions in this book are our own. Because of the fragmentary nature of portions of two of the pages of "Theses," our transcription of some of the words located near the torn sections is conjectural. The manuscript of *Apologia* contains a number of crossings out and corrections. We have used the corrected text, but also show the crossed-out text (if legible).

The text of the **Letter to the Italian Congregation in Geneva** is taken from the transcription in *Calvini Opera*.[5] We compared this transcription with one made by Friedrich Trechsel and included in an appendix to his *Lelio Sozini und die Antitrinitarier Seiner Zeit* (1844).[6] The variations between the two are numerous, but of little significance. The *Calvini Opera* text appears to be the more accurate of the two, since it contains Latin spellings often found in the Italian of that time, such as such as *et* for *e*, *cum* for *con*, and *gratia* instead of *grazia*. Both transcriptions omit many of the accents used in modern Italian. We have inserted accents only where they are needed to distinguish between two different words, such as *ne* and *né*.

De vera Dei et filii eius cognitione sermo was preserved by Stanislas Lubieniecki in his *Historia Reformatoris Polonicæ* (1685).[7] There is no surviving manuscript. We know that what remains to us is not complete, since at one point Lubieniecki notes, "Here something is missing from the manuscript from which this is taken."[8] It was reprinted by Henrik van Allwoerden in *Historia Michælis Serveti* (1727) and Johann Lorenz Mosheim in *Anderweitiger Versuch einer vollständigen und unpartheyischen Ketzergeschichte* (1748). We have taken the Latin text from Lubieniecki. Allwoerden's copy contains variations in punctuation and capitalization, a few corrections, and some new errors, including the omission of two lines of the Lubieniecki text. We have adopted four of Allwoerden's corrections, but otherwise retained the idiosyncrasies of the original transcription.

The Translation

In translating *Declaratio* and the other works in this book, our aim has been to convey the full theological force of Gribaldi's arguments. We made our translation not merely as a gloss on the original Latin, but to convey our best judgment as to what these texts mean. While we have made every effort not to move beyond the boundaries established by the Latin text, we have vowed never to "sit on the fence," offering a merely literal translation that leaves the author's meaning unclear.

The style of these works is often concise and occasionally elliptical. Its author had certain expectations about what his readers would know and be able to fill in themselves. Even well-educated modern readers will find themselves deficient by sixteenth-century standards. For this reason modern translators must often convey an author's thoughts in a somewhat more expanded way. Accordingly, we have occasionally added words or phrases for which there is no explicit justification in the Latin, but which are required in order to complete sentences or thoughts, fill in quotations only alluded to, or supply missing information. We have, where necessary, replaced pronouns with nouns, representing our best judgment about who the often indefinite "he" or "they" might be. These additions are marked so that readers can question our choice of words or information, or supply their own.

Paragraphing and punctuation in the translation are our own. We have started a new paragraph whenever we detected a change in subject or when we felt that the Latin guide words (e.g. *item*) indicated the introduction of a new topic. In order to fashion a clear and readable English version, we have had to break up the sonorous periods of Reformation Latin prose into shorter sentences more in keeping with modern English style.

In presenting the technical philosophical terms of the church fathers and the scholastics, which appear with great frequency in these works, we have followed the common scholarly practice and left words and phrases such as *supposita, communicatio idiomatum,* and *hypostasis* in Latin (or latinized Greek), providing notes to help elucidate their meaning. It should be noted, as well, that Gribaldi frequently trots out philosophical jargon merely to illustrate what he pictures as the deplorable tendency of "theological sophists" to obfuscate and conceal the simplicity of the Gospel message. The obscurity and complexity of the technical terms is precisely his point.

The Translation in a Larger Context

Although *Declaratio* was not written by Servetus, we consider this book to be part of our larger project of translating the works of Servetus. The goal of the project is to produce an integrated set of translations that will reveal the complex relationships among the various works in which Servetus fashioned and refashioned his ideas throughout his lifetime. With the addition of *Declaratio* — about a third of which is copied or adapted directly from Servetus's *De Trinitatis Erroribus* — and the other works by Gribaldi, we can see how the reworking and development of Servetus's thought continued in the years after his death.

Accordingly, when a passage in *Declaratio* is the same or similar to one from *Erroribus* in the original Latin, it will be the same or similar in our translation. Where Gribaldi has misunderstood or reinterpreted a passage, we indicate this by using different words in English. The similarities and differences are further pointed out by the use of marginal notes and underlining to mark the text in *Declaratio* that is drawn from *Erroribus*.

Two of the documents in this book have been previously translated into English. In the case of *De vera Dei*, there are two translations into English prior to our own, the first by Richard Wright, in *An Apology for Dr. Michael Servetus* (1806) and the second by George Huntston Williams, in his translation of Lubieniecki's *History of the Polish Reformation* (1995).[9] There is a previous translation of *Apologia*, by David Pingree (1965).[10] But even where other translations exist, we felt it was important to translate all of these works afresh so that they might be consistent with our translation of *Declaratio*.

Translating and Citing Gribaldi's Source Texts

We have made an effort to identify quotations and references to the Bible, the church fathers, and other sources. To help the reader get a sense of how these works are pervaded by the language of scripture, Biblical language is presented in italics. Like Servetus, Gribaldi often stitched together several phrases from a particular chapter, adding some connecting words of his own. It should also be remembered that Latin-writing theologians of the Reformation period knew large parts of the Latin Bible by heart and that their confidence in the faithfulness of their memory may sometimes have led them inadvertently to produce slightly different wordings from those found in the standard texts. We have therefore made it our practice to translate quotations from the Bible directly from Gribaldi's Latin rather than uncritically accepting existing translations of the Bible. Our word choices, however, are informed by familiar translations such as the Revised Standard and New American Standard versions.

In verifying and translating Bible quotations and paraphrases we have often referred to the various modern editions of the Latin Vulgate Bible, including Nestle-Aland, *Novum Testamentum: Græce et Latine* (2002) and *Biblia Sacra iuxta vulgatam versionem* (1984). When we discovered differences between the Biblical quotation in *Declaratio* and the standard Vulgate text, we compared these passages from *Declaratio* with two versions of the Vulgate available in the early Reformation era, the Latin of the *Complutensian Polyglot* and the Bible text published with the *Glossa Ordinaria*, as well as with two works of Erasmus, his Latin New Testament and his *Annotations on the New Testament*. We found that, for New Testament Bible texts, Gribaldi often favored the Erasmus translation over the Vulgate.

We have occasionally gone back to the Greek in order to understand some of the decisions made by Gribaldi in his presentation of a Latin Bible text. For this we have used the Greek text established by Erasmus for the New Testament, the Septuagint, and the Nestle-Aland *Novum Testamentum*. In the case of controversial passages, such as 1 John 4:3, we have consulted biblical textual scholarship for the history of the textual variants and their interpretation. Bruce Metzger, *A Textual Commentary on the Greek New Testament* (1994) and some of the volumes of the Anchor Bible have been useful in this regard. By consulting Erasmus's *Annotations* and Calvin's Bible commentaries, we were able to get a sense of how these passages were perceived in the early sixteenth century.

In referring to the books of the Bible we have adopted the names commonly used in English Protestant Bibles. In particular, the four books called 1-4 Kings in the Vulgate are called 1-2 Samuel and 1-2 Kings. There are also differences in the numbering of some chapters and verses, especially in the Psalms. In our notes we refer the reader to the standard English Protestant divisions and numeration.

When the interpretation of a Bible text quoted or cited by Gribaldi turns upon a wording found only in a particular Latin version, we specify the version following the chapter and verse citation in the footnotes. In cases where the particular version is the Vulgate, we also give the chapter and verse numbers used in the Vulgate.

In our notes on references to church fathers, we direct the reader to the nineteenth-century *Patrologia Græca* (PG) and *Patrologia Latina* (PL) edited by Jacques-Paul Migne, even though these do not, of course, represent the latest or best versions of these texts. These two collections, PG and PL, have two distinct advantages. First, they are widely available in libraries and can be accessed on the Internet. Secondly, they are comprehensive, standardized collections. Thus we can send the reader to PG and PL using a simple system of volume and page numbers, rather than having to employ a haphazard collection of editions, many of which the reader might find it difficult or impossible to locate. In some cases, when we felt that a particular Migne text might be misleading, we studied the patristic quotations using other editions, including editions of Irenaeus prepared by Erasmus, Adolphus Stieren, and W. Wigan Harvey. These were particularly helpful in converting the chapter and section numbers used by Servetus and Gribaldi to those found in PG.

We trust that our corrected version of the Latin text of *Declaratio*, and our translation of this set of interrelated works, will serve to introduce readers to an important but undervalued antitrinitarian theologian, Matteo Gribaldi.

Declarationis Jesu Christi Filii Dei

A Revelation of Jesus Christ, the Son of God

Incerta et occulta sapientiæ tuæ manifestasti mihi.
You have revealed to me the obscure and hidden things of your wisdom.

Psalms 51:6 (Vulgate 50:8)

Alphonsi Lyncurii Tarraconensis,
pio lectori salutem

Non possum (amice lector) non vehementer dolere de morte pii et docti viri michælis serveti, alias Revves patriotæ mei, cum quo et vitæ et studiorum non mediocris erat mihi coniunctio, cui tanta inerat ingenii acrimonia, iudicii perspicacia, spiritus sublimitas, ut vel antiquorum vel recentiorum theologorum nemini cederet. Is cum multa aput gallos passus esset, ac etiam aput germanos. In italiam transire decreverat, et in libera venetorum civitate degens, universum antiquum Testamentum, quam brevissimis commentariis illustrare ubi (ut idem mihi sæpe, et præsens et absens indicaverat) se facile demonstraturum pollicebatur nullam esse (sic enim loqui solebat) syllabam quæ hominem illum divinissimum Iesum christum redemptorem non præfiguraret, sermones insuper multos ad cognitionem veritatis cum primis utiles editurus erat quorum maximam fere partem sua mecum benignitate communicaverat sub iis (ni fallor) titulis

    De vera scripturarum intelligentia
    De origine deffectus ab apostolica doctrina
    De potentia veritatis
    De vera unius dei cognitione [4]
    De errore Triadis
    De verbo, et spiritu sancto
    De exaltatione hominis Iesu
    De natura et ministerio Angelorum
    De zelo et scientia
    De efficatia fidei
    De vi charitatis

*Greetings to the pious reader
from Alphonsus Lyncurius Tarraconensis*

I cannot, dear reader, but bitterly mourn the death of that pious and learned man, Michael Servetus (also known as Revés), my compatriot, with whom I had no ordinary association in life and studies, in whom there was such vigor of intellect, clearness of judgment, and sublimity of spirit, that he would yield place to no theologian either of antiquity or of more recent days. Having endured much among the French, and among the Germans as well, he planned to cross into Italy, to settle in the free city of the Venetians, and, by means of concise commentaries, to elucidate the Old Testament. As he often mentioned to me, both in person and when we were apart, he promised to demonstrate easily that there is not a single syllable [in the Old Testament] (as he was wont to say) which does not prefigure that most divine man, Jesus Christ the redeemer. He also planned to publish many discourses — most of which he kindly shared with me — which are of the foremost usefulness in understanding the truth. Unless I am mistaken, the titles are:

    On a true understanding of the scriptures
    On the origin of the falling away from apostolic teaching
    On the power of truth
    On a correct understanding of the one God
    On the error of the Triad
    On the Word and the Holy Spirit
    On the elevation of the man Jesus
    On the nature and duties of angels
    On zeal and knowledge
    On the efficacy of faith
    On the power of love

De corpore, anima et spiritu
De natis et regenitis
De vocatione et electione
De præscientia et prædestinatione
De humanis operibus et ceremoniis
De baptismo aquæ et spiritus
De cœna domini
De peccato et satisfactione
De iustificatione
De timore et amore dei
De vera ecclesia
De capite et membris
De dormitione sanctorum
De Resurrectione mortuorum et viventium immutatione
De die Judicii
De beatitudine electorum

et pleraque alia, quæ vir ille indefessus, stilo non satis culto paraverat, in quo non multam sane curam adhibuit, utpote, qui in reconditis scripturæ sensibus et misteriis dei interpretandis totum studium collocaret.

Sed alto dei consilio effectum est, ut tantus vir, violenta morte in transitu interruptus extingueretur, vivus genevæ allobrogum [5] pro heresiarcha combustus, quod ab aliorum opinionibus recessisset, palpabiles de deo et eius filio modernis Theologis quos Theosophistas et philosophos vocat errores obiiciens. Unum tantum natura deum patrem scilicet omnium conditorem, et unum dei filium Iesum hominem crucifixum ostendens, deorum triplicitatem cerberum vocans, in qua opinione constantissime mori voluit nequaquam dubitans quin verissimam de deo et eius filio fidem ex scripturis in quibus omnem suam ætatem studiose consumpserat, assecutus esset præsertim ex libris sanctorum virorum, Irenæi Ignatii et tertulliani qui de filio dei omnino aliter et multo verius senserunt quam moderni theologi, utpote qui apostolis propinquiores, adhuc illorum doctrinam integram conservassent, et scripturæ simplicitatem secuti, nihil sophisticum aut philosophicum miscuissent, horum igitur dogmata iam a Modernis obliterata michæl noster in memoriam reducere cupiebat et veram relligionem ac pietatem quasi sepultam revocare.

On body, mind, and spirit
On birth and regeneration
On vocation and election
On foreknowledge and predestination
On human works and ceremonies
On baptism with water and spirit
On the Lord's Supper
On sin and reparation
On justification
On the fear and love of God
On the true Church
On the head and the members
On the sleep of the saints
On the resurrection of the dead and the transformation of the living
On the day of judgment
On the blessedness of the elect

and many other [works] which that tireless man prepared. [He wrote] in an insufficiently cultivated style, to which he certainly did not pay enough careful attention, for he applied himself entirely to studying the hidden meanings of scripture and interpreting the mysteries of God.

Yet God's lofty plan caused so great a man to be destroyed, his journey interrupted by a violent death. He was burned alive as an arch-heretic in Geneva of the Allobroges[1] because he had departed from the opinions of others, objecting to the glaring errors about God and his Son held by modern theologians, whom he called theological sophists and philosophers. He called the triplication of gods a Cerberus[2] and showed beyond a doubt that there is by nature only one God the Father, the creator of all things, and one Son of God, Jesus, the man who was crucified. Absolutely steadfast in his belief, he was willing to die, never doubting that he was adhering to the truest faith in God and his Son. This faith was based on writings to which he had studiously devoted his life, especially the works of those saintly men, Irenaeus, Ignatius, and Tertullian, who had very different and far truer ideas concerning the Son of God than do modern theologians.[3] These writers, closer in time to the apostles, still preserved intact the [original] doctrine, and, adhering to the simplicity of scripture, mixed nothing sophistical or philosophical into it. Our Michael strove to remind us of the apostles' teachings, which modern theologians have caused us to forget, and to revive, as from the grave, true religion and piety.

Ego igitur ex eius fragmentis, quæ plurima aput me extant, hanc Iesu christi filii dei declarationem ad ipsorum gloriam et piorum utilitatem publicare volui simul cum quatuor sermonibus eiusdem de vera scripturarum intelligentia, de errore triadis, de verbo, et spiritu sancto, et de exaltatione hominis Iesu, ut agnoscat pius lector quantum ille, in dei ecclesia profecisset si ad suam naturalem metam pervenisset. Sed [6] voluntas patris fuit ut evangelicam veritatem suo sanguine confirmaret, neque enim ad martirium cum tali constantia et fervore frustra eum vocavit.

Quod autem eam triplicitatem cerberum appellaret et hypostases medicorum ad id magno in deum patrem et Jesum eius filium zelo impellebatur sibi conscius tantum errorem et divinæ Maiestati valde contumeliosum in quo Theologi fere omnes tam profunde obdormivissent, posse quovis monstruosæ rei nomine appellari veluti nos dialectici quodlibet falsum sophisma sphingem hydram chimeram nuncupare solemus. Sic etiam plerique evangelii professores symbolicum panem qui usque ad hæc ferme tempora pro vero numine cultus fuit deum panarium vel furfuraceum non sine maximo aliorum offendiculo libere appellitarunt.

Tanta est inveteratæ consuetudinis vis et authoritas, ut omnino horrendum ac blasphemum videatur ipsam falsitatem etiam palpabilem minus honestis nominibus dedecorare verum si illius græcanicæ triadis ex huius doctissimi viri libellis licet incultis falsitas detegatur non amplius piaculum videbitur illam et cerberum et alio quovis turpiori vocabulo nuncupare et quod consuetudinis pessimi tyranni potentia tam horrendum et intractabile facere videbatur cognita demum veritate et contrario usu paulatim invalescente facile mitescet ac cicurabitur.

Vale pie lector et sincero spiritu lege ac diiudica.

Therefore, for the glory of [God and Christ], and for the use of the pious, from fragments [of his work], many of which are in my possession, I wish to publish this Revelation of Jesus Christ, the Son of God, along with four more of [Servetus's] discourses—"On a true understanding of the scriptures," "On the error of the Triad," "On the Word and the Holy Spirit," and "On the elevation of the man Jesus"— so that the pious reader may recognize how much he would have accomplished for the Church of God if he had [been allowed to] come to a natural end. But it was the will of the Father that [Servetus] should confirm the gospel truth with his blood. And he, who was possessed of so much steadfastness and fervor, was not summoned to martyrdom in vain.

Conscious of a grave error, greatly insulting to divine majesty, into which almost all theologians had fallen, as into a deep sleep, he was driven by enormous zeal for God the Father and his Son Jesus to call their triplication a Cerberus, and to say that [the word] "hypostasis" belongs to the physicians.[4] [A serious error] may be given any monstrous name, for as logicians we are accustomed to label any spurious sophism a sphinx, a hydra, or a chimera. So too, many teachers of the gospel, have been accustomed to freely call the symbolic bread, which has been commonly worshipped as the actual divine presence down to this day, the bread-basket God or the bran God, not without considerable offense to others.[5]

So great is the power and authority of deep-rooted custom, that it seems quite dreadful and blasphemous to discredit even an obvious falsity with less than respectable names. However, if the falsity of the Greekish Triad is exposed in the little books, however unpolished, of this most learned man, it does not seem to be very sinful to call it a Cerberus, or even to use a more shameful term. What the power of that worst of tyrants, custom, has made to appear so horrendous and intractable, will certainly grow gentler and become tame as the truth is finally recognized and as the opposing point of view grows gradually stronger.

Farewell, pious reader. May you read and form your judgment with an open mind.

[7] *Declarationis Jesu Christi Filii Dei Authore Michæle Serveto alias Revves Tarraconensi liber primus*

Err. 2a In scrutandis æterni dei sacrosanctis misteriis, quatenus scripturæ permittunt ab homine adeo exordiendum putavi, quia quam plurimos video parum aut nihil homini tribuere et verum christum non agnoscere quibus tamen ego ad memoriam quis sit ille christus quem obliti sunt deo bene faciente reducere conabor. Cæterum quid quantumque ipsi christo tribuendum sit ecclesia iudicabit.

Quoniam igitur de homine illo nato ex virgine et a Judæis crucifixo nobis sermo habendus est cum in eo veræ pietatis ac religionis fundamentum omne consistat hæc tria de Jesu illo homine verissimo dicimus et confitemur primo Jesum illum hominem esse christum, secundo Jesum illum ut hominem esse filium dei, tertio Jesum illum hominem esse deum.

In primis hominem illum ex Maria virgine natum et a Judæis crucifixum dici Jesum nemo unquam negavit id enim nomen

Err. 2b proprium, illius est, quod ei adhuc puero iussu angeli ipso die circumcisionis impositum fuit, sicut tibi petrus, et illi Johannes, est enim Jesus (ut ait tertulianus) nomen proprium viri, et cognomen christus. Judæi illum Mariæ filium esse Jesum omnes concedebant, sed christum esse negabant, et alienos a synagoga eos faciebant qui Jesum esse christum faterentur, unde paulus conversus magno et [8] aperto animo Judæis testificabatur Jesum esse christum. Similiter apollo ille Alexandrinus incredibili fervore spiritus Judæos publice revincebat, ostendens per scripturas quod Jesus esset christus seu Messias, nec de ulla re vel persona invisibili erat illorum disputatio, sed de Jesu homine quod is a deo genitus unctus et missus fuisset.

A Revelation of Jesus Christ, the Son of God by Michael Servetus, also known as Revés, of Tarraconensis
Book 1

In investigating the holiest mysteries of the eternal God, I intend, as far as the scriptures permit, to begin with the man [Jesus], since I see that so many pay little or no attention to the human being, and thus do not acknowledge the true Christ. With God's help, I shall endeavor to remind them about the Christ whom they have forgotten. Beyond this, what and how much should be attributed to Christ, the Church will decide.

Since, therefore, our discussion will be about the man born of a virgin and crucified by the Jews, and since the entire foundation of genuine piety and religion rests on him, we declare and profess these three things about the very real human being Jesus: first, the man Jesus is the Christ; second, Jesus, as a man, was the Son of God; third, the man Jesus is God.

To begin with, no one has ever denied that the man born of the Virgin Mary and crucified by the Jews was named Jesus. Indeed, that is his proper name, given to him by the angel's command while he was a child, on the day of his circumcision.[a] Just as your name, for instance, is Peter, and his, John, so too Jesus (as Tertullian[1] says) is a man's proper name. Christ, on the other hand, is a title.[b] The Jews all admitted that he was Jesus, the son of Mary, but denied that he was the Christ. And they *put out of the synagogue* all who *confessed* Jesus *to be the Christ*.[c] For this reason Paul the convert, publicly and with great zeal, *testified to the Jews that Jesus was the Christ*.[d] Likewise Apollos of Alexandria,[2] with tremendous fervor, *confuted the Jews in public, showing by the scriptures that Jesus was the Christ*,[e] or the Messiah. This was not a debate about an invisible person or being; rather it was about the man Jesus, who was begotten by God, anointed by God, and sent forth by God.

---

[a] Luke 1:31, 2:21. [b] Tertullian, *Adversus Praxean* 28 (PL 2 192B). [c] John 9:22. [d] Acts 18:5.
[e] Acts 18:28.

Err. 2b-3a   Christus enim unctum significat et de Jesu homine uncto scriptura loquitur cum dicit iste est puer sanctus tuus quem unxisti, hic est ille sanctus sanctorum quem ungendum prædixit daniel et quem propheta dicit a deo unctum præ consortibus suis et petrus de Jesu homine loquens tanquam rem expeditam dixit ipsi nostis, nam de Jesu sermo omnibus est notus, ut scilicet Jesum a nazareth unxerit deus spiritu sancto et virtute, quoniam deus erat cum illo et ipse est qui constitutus est iudex vivorum et mortuorum. Item petrus in actis, certissime sciat universa domus israël quod hunc Jesum quem crucifixistis fecit deus et dominum et christum. Quidam tamen per illa pronomina rem aliam demonstrare nituntur, sed Johannes mendacem eum dicit qui negat hunc Jesum esse a deo unctum et qui concedit Jesum esse christum, ex deo natus est.

Err. 3a   Tertulianus quoque adversus praxeam hanc vocem Christus naturæ humanæ vocabulum esse dicit et adversus Marcionem facta diligenti de hoc vocabulo Christus inquisitione, nihil de illa secunda persona seu hypostasi (quam isti Christum faciunt) meminit, sed [9] ait quis est filius hominis? nisi homo ipse, natus ex homine, corpus ex corpore, nam hebraico idiotismo filius hominis, filius adam, nihil aliud significat quam homo. Item ipsius vocabuli ratio illud infert nam esse unctum non nisi ad naturam humanam referri potest si ergo (ut idem ait) ungi corporis passio est, quis negabit hominem esse unctum?

Err. 3a-b   Item petrus in recognitione clementis lib. primo rationem vocabuli explicat quoniam reges ab unctione eis facta Christi vocari solebant ut psal. 104 nolite tangere christos, et primo regum 24. Nam faciam rem hanc domino meo Christo? et 26. quis enim extendet manum suam in christum domini? non custodistis dominum nostrum christum, ideo Jesus ipse ab excellentia unctionis præ cæteris christus vocatus est,

Christ, indeed, means "anointed," and scripture is speaking about the anointed human being Jesus when it says, he is *your holy servant, whom you have anointed.*[a] He is the *holy of holies*, whose anointing was predicted by Daniel,[b] and whom the Prophet[3] says *God has anointed above his fellows.*[c] Peter, speaking about the man Jesus, said, *"You know"* – as if it were something obvious, for what was said about Jesus was common knowledge – *"how God anointed Jesus of Nazareth with the holy spirit and with power, for God was with him*, and that *he is the one ordained to be judge of the living and the dead."*[d] Likewise in Acts, Peter says, *"Let all the house of Israel know assuredly that God has made him both Lord and Christ, this man Jesus, whom you crucified."*[e] Nonetheless, some use those pronouns [*illo*, him; *ipse*, he; and *hunc*, this man] to indicate another being, even though John says that *whoever denies that Jesus* is God's anointed is a *liar*, while whoever accepts *that Jesus is the Christ is a child of God.*[f]

Tertullian, in *Against Praxeas*, also says that this word "Christ" is a term pertaining to a human nature.[g] And in *Against Marcion*, having carefully investigated the term "Christ," he mentions nothing about the second person or hypostasis, which some suppose to be Christ. On the contrary, he asks, who is the Son of man, if not a man himself, born of a human being, "flesh born from flesh"?[h] For the Hebrew expression "Son of man," like "son of Adam," means nothing other than a human being. The way the word [Christ] is used implies the same thing, for "to be anointed" can only refer to a human nature. If, therefore, as he says, "to be anointed is an experience of the body,"[i] who will deny that it was a human being who was anointed?

Peter explains the meaning of the word [anointed] in the first book of Clement's *Recognitions*:[4] "because kings, having been anointed, were commonly called Christs" (as in Psalm 104: *Touch not my anointed ones*;[j] and in 1 Samuel 24: *For I should do this thing to my lord, the anointed*;[k] and also in 1 Samuel 26: *Who will put forth his hand against the Lord's anointed? You have not kept watch over our anointed lord*[l]) "therefore, Jesus, on account of the superior nature of his anointing, above all others, is called Christ."[m]

---

[a] Acts 4:27. [b] Dan. 9:24. [c] Ps. 45:7. [d] Acts 10:36,38,42. [e] Acts 2:36. [f] 1 John 2:22, 5:1.
[g] Tertullian *Adversus Praxean* 29 (PL 2 194A). [h] Tertullian, *Adversus Marcion* 4.10 (PL 2 380B).
[i] Tertullian, *Adversus Marcion* 3.15 (PL 2 342B). [j] Ps. 105:15. [k] 1 Sam. 24:6. [l] 1 Sam. 24:10, 26:16.
[m] Pseudo-Clement, *Recognitiones* 1.45 (PG 1 1233B).

nam cæteri reges ab hominibus extrinsecus ungebantur sic saul et david in reges uncti fuerunt. Regum primo et secundo. At Jesus ipse longe excellentius a deo patre suo unctus est oleo sanctificationis et benedictionis internæ de qua unctione Jesu christi loquitur propheta psal. 44. quare unxit te deus deus tuus oleo lætitiæ præ consortibus tuis et psal. 88. oleo sancto meo unxi eum nam sicut deus angelis angelum et sideribus sidus præfecit, ita et hominibus hominem principem et regem constituit Jesum christum et de Jesu loquens, Matheus ait ex qua natus est Jesus ille qui dicitur christus, nota nomen articulum, [10] et cognomen. Intelligenda enim simplicis verba et pronomina illa rem sensu præceptam demonstrantia, et Luce 2. natus est nobis hodie salvator qui est christus dominus et Judæi admirantes opera et sermones Jesu dicunt ei quo usque animam nostram tollis? si tu es christus dic nobis palam Io. 10. et tamen non de re invisibili sed de ipso Jesu homine interrogabant et Luce 23. hunc invenimus dicentem se christum regem esse unde Io. baptista dicebat non arbitremini me Christum esse, sed plane ridicula fuisset, Joannis admonitio si christi nomen seu vocabulum ad hominem referri non posset, quorsum etiam admonuisset christus ut eos homines evitemus qui se dicerent christos Mat. 24. Marci 13. Luce 21. Absurda quoque fuisset Jesu interrogatio et petri responsio, cum dixit quem me dicunt homines esse filium hominis respondit petrus, tu es ille christus filius dei viventis, nam ad hominem loquens debuisset potius dicere christus in te est, filius dei tecum est, non autem, tu es ille similiter quando præcepit Jesus ne cui dicerent quod ipse esset christus quid aliud quam seipsum hominem demonstrabat, nostri vero teologi seu verius Theosophistæ non erubescunt Christi nomen ab ipso Jesu visibili ad rem invisibilem transferre et ei inauditum nomen imponere humanitatem dumtaxat eum vocantes velut rem quamdam sophisticam et inutilem

All other kings were anointed externally by men, as Saul and David were anointed kings (1 Samuel and 2 Samuel).ᵃ But Jesus, in a far superior way, was anointed by God his Father with the *oil of* inward *sanctification*ᵇ and blessing. The Prophet speaks about the anointing of Jesus Christ in Psalm 44: *Therefore your God has anointed you with the oil of gladness above all your fellows*,ᶜ and in Psalm 88: *With my holy oil I have anointed him*.ᵈ For "as God set an angel over all the angels, and a star over all the stars, so too did he establish Jesus Christ as first among men, and their king."ᵉ

Speaking about Jesus, Matthew says: [Mary] *of whom* that [man] *Jesus was born, who is called Christ.*ᶠ Note the name [Jesus], the article [*ille*, that man], and the title [Christ]. Indeed these same words and also the pronouns [*hic* and *ille*] are to be understood in the simplest way as referring to something perceived by the senses.⁵ And in Luke 2: *To us is born this day a savior, who is Christ the Lord.*ᵍ The Jews, wondering at the deeds and words of Jesus, say to him, "*How long will you keep us in suspense? If you are the Christ tell us plainly*" (John 10).ʰ They were inquiring about the man Jesus and not about an invisible being.

In Luke 23, it says *that he himself is Christ, a King*.ⁱ John the Baptist said, "Do not *suppose that I am* the Christ."ʲ John's admonition would have been plainly ridiculous if the name or word "Christ" could not refer to a human being. Furthermore, why has Christ cautioned us to avoid people who call themselves Christs? (Matthew 24, Mark 13, Luke 21).ᵏ Jesus's question and Peter's answer would have been absurd as well [if the word "Christ" could not refer to a human being], when [Jesus] *said, "Who do men say that I, the Son of man, am?"*ˡ and *Peter replied, "You are the Christ, the Son of the living God."*ᵐ For, in speaking to a man, [Peter] ought to have said, "Christ is in you; the Son of God is with you," rather than "*You are* [the Christ]." Likewise, when Jesus instructed [*the disciples*] *to tell no one that he himself was the Christ*,ⁿ what else did he mean but that he was a human being? Truly our theologians, or rather theological sophists, are not ashamed to transfer the name "Christ" from the visible Jesus to an invisible being and impose on him an unheard-of name, calling him merely "a human nature,"⁶ as if he were something sophistical and unprofitable.

ᵃ 1 Sam. 10:1, 2 Sam. 2:4.   ᵇ Exod. 37:29.   ᶜ Ps. 45:7.   ᵈ Ps. 89:20.   ᵉ Pseudo-Clement, *Recognitiones* 1.45 (PG 1 1233A-B).   ᶠ Matt. 1:16 (Erasmus).   ᵍ Luke 2:11.   ʰ John 10:24.   ⁱ Luke 23:2.   ʲ Acts 13:25, John 1:20.   ᵏ Matt. 24:23-24, Mark 13:21-22, Luke 21:8.   ˡ Matt. 16:13,15.   ᵐ Matt. 16:16.   ⁿ Matt. 16:20.

Err. 4a et tamen clarissimum est, ipsius Jesu christi testimonium se hominem [11] esse dicentis quæritis me interficere hominem veritatem vobis locutum, et paulus Mediator dei et hominum homo christus Jesus.

Err. 4a-b Sed quia illa vox homo (si Communicationem illam impiam Idiomatum admittas quæ omnem scripturam obscuravit) violari potest, accipe illam vocem vir et audi petrum dicentem Christum fuisse virum aprobatum et Lucam de Jesu Nazareno qui fuit vir potens opere et sermone et iudicaturus est deus per eum virum et Joannem post me veniet vir cuius non sum dignus solvere calciamenta et Esai Novissimum virorum virum dolorum, et Zacharaiam ecce vir cuius nomen germen. Noli igitur scripturam dei cavillari nec aliquod tuum phantasma proponere sed verum hominem visibilem recognoscere et naturam illorum pronominum demonstrativorum (quibus tota pæne scriptura referta est) diligenter perpende, nam Jesu illo homini ad oculum demonstrato sæpissime dicebatur hic est ille Christus, Tu es Christus ille dei filius, ipse erat Christus, hic est agnus dei qui tollit peccata mundi, hic est filius meus dilectus, hunc audite, vere hic filius dei erat, et infinita similia quæ omni vere et proprie et immediate ad Jesum illum hominem visum palpatum mortuum et suscitatum referebant.

Err. 4b-5a Similiter cum dixit quærentibus Jesum Nazarenum, ego sum et quemcunque osculatus fuero ipse est ait alibi ego ipse sum palpate et videte, et petrus hunc Jesum quem vos interemistis suscitavit deus cuius omnes nos testes sumus, quid per talia pronomina [12] ut sit oculare testimonium demonstrabis? numne longe deterioris conditionis sumus quam mulier illa samaritana quæ dixit venite et videte hominem qui dixit mihi omnia quæcunque feci nunquid hic est christus? nec mirum quod mulier super christo fundata ita dixerit, nam cum ipsa quæreret messiam venturum, qui dicitur Christus, respondit ei Jesus, ego sum qui loquor tecum ego inquit non res illa invisibilis quam isti secundam personam vel hypostasim vocant, sed ego qui loquor tecum.

However, the testimony of Jesus Christ, calling himself a human being, is exceedingly clear: "*You seek to kill me, a man who has told you the truth.*"ª And Paul calls him the *Mediator between God and men, the man Christ Jesus.*ᵇ

If you accept that impious *communicatio idiomatum* [sharing of attributes][7] which has rendered the whole of Scripture obscure, the meaning of the word *homo* [human being] is distorted. Therefore, accept instead the word *vir* [man],[8] and listen to what Peter says: Christ was "*a man attested [to you by God].*"ᶜ And also what Luke says: *concerning Jesus of Nazareth, who was a man, mighty in deed and word.*ᵈ Also: God will *judge* [*the world*] *by a man.*ᵉ In John, [John the Baptist says,] "*After me comes a man, the thong of whose sandal I am not worthy to untie.*"ᶠ In Isaiah: *the most rejected of men, a man of sorrows.*ᵍ In Zechariah: *Behold the man whose name is the Branch.*ʰ Do not therefore quibble with the scripture of God or propose some phantasm of your own devising. Rather recognize the real, visible man.

Consider carefully the nature of the demonstrative pronouns,[9] which fill nearly all of scripture. For so often, when the man Jesus Christ was pointed out, it was said, "*This is the Christ,*"ⁱ or "*You are the Christ, the Son of God,*"ʲ or *He himself was the Christ,*ᵏ or "*This is the Lamb of God who takes away the sin of the world,*"ˡ or "*This is my beloved son; listen to him,*"ᵐ or "*Truly this was the Son of God,*"ⁿ along with a large number of like examples. All of these truly, properly, and immediately refer to the man Jesus, who was seen and touched, who died and rose again. Similarly, to those seeking Jesus of Nazareth, [Jesus] replied, "*I am he.*"ᵒ Also [Judas said], "*Whomever I kiss is the one.*"ᵖ Elsewhere [Jesus] says, "*It is I myself, touch me and see.*"ᑫ And Peter says, "*This Jesus whom you killed, God raised up, of that we all are witnesses.*"ʳ

What can you point out, using such pronouns, that would be [as good as] visual evidence? Are we not in a far worse condition than the Samaritan woman who said, "*Come, see a man who told me all that I ever did. Can this be the Christ?*"ˢ It is no wonder that the woman, on the basis of [her experience with] Christ, would have spoken in this way. For when she asked about the Messiah to come, *he who is called Christ*, Jesus answered, "*I who speak to you am he.*"ᵗ I, he said, not that invisible being they call the second person or a hypostasis, but *I who speak to you*.

ª John 8:40. ᵇ 1 Tim. 2:5. ᶜ Acts 2:22. ᵈ Luke 24:19. ᵉ Acts 17:31. ᶠ John 1:27,30. ᵍ Isa. 53:3.
ʰ Zech. 6:12. ⁱ John 7:41. ʲ John 11:27. ᵏ Matt. 16:20. ˡ John 1:29. ᵐ Mark 9:7. ⁿ Mark 15:39.
ᵒ John 18:5. ᵖ Matt. 26:48, Mark 14:44. ᑫ Luke 24:39. ʳ Acts 2:32, 5:30. ˢ John 4:29. ᵗ John 4:25-26.

Err. 5a   Item de quo homine intelligitur illud dictum apostoli? sicut unius hominis delicto ita per gratiam unius hominis Jesu christi, et sicut per hominem mors ita per hominem resurrectio mortuorum, vides quod scriptura non capit hominem connotative, nec hominem tantum, sed adam eum vocat, nostri vero Theosophistæ hominem connotativum et sophisticum, volunt esse nostræ religionis fundamentum, tolle (obsecro) istam græcanicam philosophiam de hypostasibus et idiomatum Communicatione et suppositis connotativis et videbis lucem magnam, tolle quæso has sophisticas imposturas et vocum novitates, et Jesum christum vere atque aperte cognosces, Christi enim sermones sunt fundamenta ecclesiæ et plani ac simplicissimi sunt, unde petrus eloquia dei eloquia casta cum simplicitate sunt accipienda et paulus non in sublimitate sermonum annunciandum est testimonium Christi [13] sed de plano, et quasi parvuli, facti et quasi nihil aliud scientes nisi Jesum Christum et hunc crucifixum. Nota verba pauli qui nihil aliud scire vult nisi Christum crucifixum, certe aliquid hic de hypostasibus et connotativis et communicatione idiomatum meminisset. Sequamur ergo morem et doctrinam apostolorum qui spiritu sancto illustrati non arte humana compositis verbis aut rhetorico colore depictis sed purissime ac simplicissime Jesum christum crucifixum prædicabant.

Err. 5a-b   Quæ enim fraternitas nobis esset cum christo, si christus homo non esset? Qualis esset comparatio Mosis et christi per apostolum dicentem amplioris enim gloriæ iste præ mose dignus habitus est cum Moses tanquam famulus, Christus vero tanquam filius? quorsum in tota illa epistola ad hebræos tantopere insistit paulus qui ostendendo Christum Jesum etiam supra angelos fuisse exaltatum nisi ut hominis exaltationem sublimitatemque demonstret, nam quod illa secunda hypostasis seu natura dei sit plusquam angeli et Moses exaltata satis ridicule probare contenderet nec eius intentio ad illud adaptari potest ex sentential enim prophetæ loquitur apostolus admirantis tantam Christi gloriam, quod cum homo sit omnia fuerint illi subiecta, ita et non ab angelis adoretur,

About what man is this statement of the Apostle[10] to be understood: As *by one man's trespass*, so by *the grace of that one man, Jesus Christ*?[a] And as *by a man came death, by a man has come also the resurrection of the dead*.[b] Observe that scripture does not use the word "man" connotatively.[11] It calls him not only a man, but Adam as well.[c] Truly, our theological sophists prefer a connotative and sophistical man as the foundation of our religion. Away, I implore you, with that Greekish philosophizing about hypostases and *communicatio idiomatum* and connotative *supposita*,[12] and you will see *a great light*.[d] Take away these sophistical impostures and strange new expressions and you will come to know Jesus Christ clearly, as he truly is.

Indeed, the words of Christ, plain and of the utmost simplicity, are the foundation of the church. Hence Peter says[13] *the words of God are pure words*,[e] to be received simply. And Paul says *the testimony of* Christ is *not proclaimed in lofty words*,[f] but plainly and like *little children*,[g] and as if *knowing nothing except Jesus Christ and him crucified*.[h] Note well these words of Paul, who wished to know nothing except Christ crucified. Certainly he might have mentioned something here about hypostases, connotatives, and *communicatio idiomatum* [if he had wanted to]. Let us therefore follow the manner and teaching of the apostles, who, illuminated by the Holy Spirit, did not use words *fashioned by human artifice*[i] or daubed with rhetorical color, but rather in the purest and simplest way proclaimed Jesus Christ crucified.

Indeed, what brotherhood with Christ could there be for us if Christ were not a man? What comparison could the Apostle make between Moses and Christ, when he said that [Christ] is *worthy of greater glory than Moses*, since *Moses was [faithful] as a servant, but Christ truly as a son*?[j] Why does Paul, who points to Jesus Christ as being exalted even higher than the angels, so insist on this throughout the Epistle to the Hebrews,[k] unless to show the exaltation and sublime nature of a man? For it would be ridiculous for him to attempt to prove that the second hypostasis or nature of God is more exalted than the angels and Moses; nor can his meaning be construed in that way. For the Apostle made use of the words of the Prophet,[14] who marveled at the greatness of Christ's glory because, while [Christ] was a man, and thus not worshipped by angels, *all things were made subject to him*.[l]

---

[a] Rom. 5:15.   [b] 1 Cor. 15:21.   [c] 1 Cor. 15:45.   [d] Isa. 9:2.   [e] Ps. 12:6.   [f] 1 Cor. 2:1.
[g] 1 Thess. 2:7 (Vulgate).   [h] 1 Cor. 2:2.   [i] 2 Peter 1:16.   [j] Heb. 3:3-6.   [k] Heb. 1:4, 1:13, 2:9.   [l] Heb. 2:8.

præterea numne veritas ipsa testificata est quod oportuit christum pati et ita intrare in gloriam suam, et petrus Christus pro [14] peccatis nostris mortuus est, et paulus pro omnibus mortuus est christus et ad Timotheum Jesus christus venit in mundum, peccatores salvos facere, homini ergo qui vere unctus et passus est, Christi nomen proprie convenit non rei invisibili, seu hypostasi incorporeæ, ut Theosophistæ falso docuerunt, et ideo Josephus Historicus De Jesu Nazareno loquens libro 16 cap. 9 sic ait, fuit autem iisdem temporibus Jesus sapiens vir, si tamen virum eum nominare phas est, erat enim mirabilium operum effector, et doctor omnium eorum hominum qui libenter audiunt veritatem, et multos quidem Judæorum, multos etiam ex gentibus sibi adiunxit, Christus hic erat hunc accusatione primorum nostræ gentis virorum. Cum pilatus in crucem agendum decrevisset non deseruerunt ii, qui ab initio eum dilexerunt, apparuit enim eis tertia die, iterum vivus secundum quod divinitus inspirati prophetæ, et hæc, et alia de eo innumera miracula futura esse prædixerant. Sed et in hodiernum diem Christianorum, qui ab ipso nuncupati sunt, et nomen perseverat, et genus hæc Josefus ex prædictis igitur iam tibi pro baptismo esse puto primum illud enuntiatum scilicet Jesum illum hominem esse verum christum, et Christi vocabulum ad solam naturam humanam pertinere neque secundæ personæ vel hypostasi convenire, quæ a deo uncta dici non potest et consequenter, Judæos frustra alium Christum vel Messiam expectare, cum de Jesu illo Nazareno homine passibili viro dei christo, et filio, plenissima [15] sint omnium scripturarum testimonia, quæ unicuique pio et fideli magis facienda sunt quam omnes hominum opiniones et inutiles traditiones, ad laudem dei qui est benedictus in sæcula.

Furthermore, does not truth itself[15] bear witness that it was *necessary that the Christ should suffer and enter into his glory*?[a] Peter says that *Christ died for* our *sins*.[b] Paul says that Christ *died for all*,[c] and, in the Epistle to Timothy, *Jesus Christ came into the world to save sinners*.[d] Thus the name "Christ" most suitably fits a human being who was actually anointed and suffered, not some invisible being or incorporeal hypostasis, as the theological sophists have falsely taught.

The historian Josephus,[16] speaking of Jesus of Nazareth in book 16, chapter 9 [of *Antiquities of the Jews*], writes as follows,[17] which I believe serves as [Josephus's] own baptism:

> About this time lived Jesus, a man of wisdom, if indeed it is proper to call him a man. For he accomplished miraculous feats and was a teacher of people who willingly hear the truth. Indeed he won over to himself many Jews and many gentiles as well. He was the Christ. When Pilate, on the basis of the accusations of the foremost leaders of our nation, condemned him to be crucified, the ones who loved him from the start did not forsake him. On the third day, he appeared to them, restored to life. For the prophets inspired by God had foretold this, and countless other miraculous deeds about him. And to this day the name and tribe of Christians, who are named after him, continue to exist.[e]

All this means that the man Jesus truly is the Christ, and that the word "Christ" pertains solely to a human nature. It does not fit a second person or hypostasis, which cannot be spoken of as anointed by God. Consequently the Jews wait in vain for another Christ or Messiah. For there is abundant testimony in scripture about Jesus of Nazareth the human being, the man who suffered, the man of God, the Christ, and the Son. And the testimony of the scriptures is of far greater weight than all the opinions of men and their injurious traditions. To the glory of *God, who is blessed forever*.[f]

---

[a] Luke 24:26. [b] 1 Peter 3:18. [c] 2 Cor. 5:14,15. [d] 1 Tim 1:15. [e] Josephus, *Antiquities of the Jews* 18.63. [f] 2 Cor. 11:31.

Declarationis Jesu Christi per Michælem Servetum liber secundus

Err. 6a Nunc ad secundam propositionem devenio manifestissime probaturus eundem ipsum Jesum Christum hominem, visibilem, et passibilem, ex maria virgine natum, esse verum, proprium et unigenitum altissimi dei filium et quia In hoc potissimum articulo totus christianæ pietatis, ac veræ religionis cardo consistit, altius exordiendo meram tibi de filio dei veritatem apertissime demonstrabo.

Deus igitur æternus, immutabilis, et incomprehensibilis admirabiles suæ infinitæ potentiæ sapientiæ et bonitatis divitias ac thesauros manifestare volens, filium hominem sibi generare decrevit, per quem, et perceptibilis fieret et omnem suam voluntatem adimpleret per quem, et propter quem omnia alia deus ipse pater fecit atque creavit, hunc filium suum unigenitum pro redemptione humani generis miserrime perditi, divinæ, et immutabili iustitiæ satis facientem acerbissime pati ac mori voluit, immensam benignitatem erga creaturas suas ostendens, facta per filium suum unigenitum redemptione atque reconciliatione qui patri obedientissimus velut agnus immaculatus pro peccatis hominum hostiam voluntariam se ineffabili charitate exhibuit quod misterium neque per angelos, neque per ullam aliam creaturam, peragi [16] poterat, nisi per eum qui esset Christus dei, ab ipso deo naturaliter et immediate genitus, et ab æterno sanctificatus nulla enim mundi creatura neque etiam angeli ipsi in conspectu dei mundi sunt, hunc ergo hominem purissimum et sanctissimum deus in filium proprium per generationem sibi peculiariter elegit, per quem omnia fecit et in quo sibi bene complacuit.

A Revelation of Jesus Christ by Michael Servetus
Book 2

I come now to the proof of my second proposition: that this same man, Jesus Christ, who was visible, suffered, and was born of the Virgin Mary, is the true and only begotten *Son of God the Most High*.[a] All of Christian piety and true religion hinges on this article of faith. And by setting it forth in greater detail, I shall clearly demonstrate to you the plain truth about the Son of God.

Since the eternal, unchanging, and inconceivable God wished to reveal the awesome wealth and treasure of his infinite power, wisdom, and goodness, he chose to beget a human son of his own, in whom he would be perceptible, and who would carry out all his will. *Through him and by him*, God the Father made and created all other things.[b] God willed that his only begotten Son should suffer most cruelly and die to redeem a lost and miserable humanity, satisfying divine and inalterable justice. Thus God displayed his boundless goodwill toward his creatures. This redemption and reconciliation was accomplished by means of his only begotten Son, who, absolutely obedient to the Father, out of ineffable love, like *a spotless lamb*,[c] offered himself up as a willing sacrifice for the sins of humanity. For this mystery could not be accomplished by angels or by any other creature, but only by the one who was the anointed of God.

He was begotten by God, naturally and without any intermediary, and sanctified from eternity. For no creature in the world, not even an angel, is pure in the sight of God. Therefore, by begetting this most pure and holy man, God chose him exclusively as his own Son, *through whom* he *made all things*[d] and *with whom he was well pleased*.[e]

---

[a] Luke 1:32.   [b] Heb. 2:10.   [c] 1 Peter 1:19.   [d] John 1:3.   [e] Matt. 3:17.

Breviter hic homo dei filius unigenitus, fuit Implementum finis et Consumatio omnium operum et consiliorum dei patris super omnes creaturas sublimatus etiam ad patris æqualitatem omni virtute potentia, gloria, et deitate repletus, quo modo autem hic

Err. 6a   homo a deo patre genitus fuerit apertissime lucas declarat referens verba angeli dicentis virgini Mariæ, Spiritus sanctus superveniet in te et altissimi virtus obumbrabit tibi ideoque quod ex te nascetur sanctum, filius dei vocabitur, quo modo autem christus ex dei semine incorruptibili conceptus sit, declarat Johannes quia verbum dei quod fuit apud ipsum deum, ante omnem creationem per quod omnia facta sunt, quasi ipsius dei semen patris in uterum virginis dessignato tempore illapsum est et spiritu sancto cooperante homo factum est, non quod deus ille pater hominum more de se genitale semen emiserit aut aliquam essentiæ suæ particulam [17] decerpserit, ex eaque Christum Jesum progenuerit, sed cum ea sit divini numinis virtus ac fecunditas, ut quæ velit ex quorumque velit ea esse faciat, quia non est impossibile apud Deum omne verbum, quæ virtus in creando mundo pateffacta est Logon illum suum quod verbum vel oraculum dei interpretamur in utero virginis hominem esse fecit, ut Ioa. manifeste testatur. Ut enim ad hominem humano ritu generandum patris semen et sanguis matris concurrunt, et ex his coagulatur corpus homoque conflatur, sic ad Jesum Christum generandum Maria virgo Logon seu verbum, illud dei per quod omnia facta sunt, quasi semen quoddam a deo missum accepit, ex quo in eius utero spiritu dei agente caro Christi totusque homo Jesus Christus factus est, sic enim ipsi virgini de semine viri investiganti respondit angelus, spiritus sanctus in te veniet, et altissimi virtus inumbrabit te. Idcirco vel quapropter sanctus iste partus dei filius erit, sic enim significat nominari, et ad hanc similitudinem petrus dixit, nos renatos ex semine immortali per vivum sermonem dei, Christus enim verus homo ex cœlesti et immortali sermone natus est, ideoque et dei filius per naturam deus nos vero eius consortes, participes et cohæredes ex cœlesti semine verbi

In short, this man, the only begotten Son of God, was the fulfillment, goal, and consummation of all the works and plans of God the Father. He was far above all creatures, equal to the Father, and filled with every excellence, power, glory, and divinity.

Luke explains clearly how this man was begotten by God the Father, recounting the words of the angel to the Virgin Mary: "*The Holy Spirit will come upon you, and the power of the Most High will overshadow you; therefore the child to be born will be holy, and will be called the Son of God.*"[a]

John reveals the way in which Christ was conceived from the incorruptible seed of God: how the *Word of God*, that *was with God* before all creation and *through whom all things were made*,[b] acting as God's seed, flowed into the womb of the Virgin at the appointed time, and, with the help of the Holy Spirit, was made man. Not that God the Father actually emitted generative semen as men do. He did not remove a particle of his own essence and from that particle beget Jesus Christ. Rather the power and fecundity of the divine godhead is such that he can bring into existence whatever he wishes from whatever he wishes. "*For with God nothing is impossible.*"[c]

God's power was made manifest, as John clearly testifies, when he formed his *Logos* (which we translate as the Word or utterance of God) into a human being in the Virgin's womb. For, as in the usual way of human reproduction, the father's seed and mother's blood flow together, and from these a body solidifies and a human being is formed,[d] so, in the begetting of Jesus Christ, the Virgin Mary received the *Logos*, or Word of God, *through whom all things were made*,[e] as a kind of seed sent from God. By the working of God's spirit in her womb, Christ's flesh and the whole man Jesus Christ were made. Indeed this is how the angel answered the Virgin, when she asked about the need for male seed: "*The Holy Spirit will come upon you, and the power of the Most High will overshadow you; therefore* (or because of this), *the child to be born will be holy, and will be* (this is what is meant by "*called*") *the Son of God.*"[f]

It was by analogy that Peter said we are *born anew of imperishable seed through the living word of God*.[g] For Christ was a man who was born from the heavenly and everlasting Word. Thus he is the Son of God, and is by nature God. We, however, are his companions, sharers with him, and his co-heirs.

---

[a] Luke 1:35.   [b] John 1:1-3.   [c] Luke 1:37.   [d] See Aristotle, *On the Generation of Animals* 2.4.739.
[e] John 1:3.   [f] Luke 1:35.   [g] 1 Peter 1:23.

renati sumus et filii dei per adoptionem vocamur. Ille enim uterque et naturalis dei filius [18] origo est nostræ filiationis, et potestatem dedit hominibus filios dei fieri quicumque crederent in nomen eius Jo. 1.

Err. 6a   Deus igitur respectu Christi vere et proprie dicitur pater, quia deo vicem humani patris supplente genitus est non autem ex homine Joseph, ut Judæi falso putabant, et Carpocrates Cerintus Ebion et Photinus impie mentiti sunt, et novissime miseri Anabaptistæ. Potentissima in dei virtus vice viri ex verbo suo (ut iam dictum est) Mariam virginem foecundavit ac replevit agente in ea spiritu sancto qua vi illa dei filium peperit.

Err. 6a-b   Nota vocem illativam quapropter, aut idcirco, et collige rationem illationis, quare filius dei partus ille vocetur, nimirum, quia ex deo, et virgine natus est, eadem filiationis ratio de homine Jesu Christo apud Danielem exponitur qui eum vocat lapidem sine manibus abscisum, item apud Matth. cum dicit quod virgo facta est gravida a spiritu sancto, et quod in ea conceptum est, a spiritu sancto profectum est, et is erit salvator Emanuel hoc est nobiscum deus; Nota igitur quod potestas illa in utero virginis genita, et concepta, quæ filius dei, et deus dicitur, est homo ille Jesus Christus.

Nota etiam diligente quod dicit Lucas. Is filius quem tu concipies, et paries, filius dei vocabitur, et erit magnus apud deum, et dabit illi deus sedem David patris sui. Unde Irenæus li. 3. ca. 18. Angelus inquit Evangelizans Mariæ eum qui sit filius altissimi, eundem et David filium confitens. David autem secundum matrem, sed quia filiatio principaliter [19] ad patrem refertur. Ideo David non audet eum filium suum apellare: sed dominum, sic enim in spiritu de ipso Christo ait, Dixit Dominus domino meo sede a dextris meis. An igitur illa secunda illa persona vel Hypostasis quam isti filium vocant sit facta magna, et acceperit a deo sedem patris sui David, et a deo dictum sit ei, sede a dextris meis, hæc autem omnia de vero filio dicuntur qui est homo ille Jesus Christus.

We are born anew from the celestial seed of the Word and are called the children of God by adoption. He is both the natural son of God and the source of our own adoptive sonship. *He gave to all who believed in his name the power to become children of God* (John 1).[a]

Thus, God is truly and properly called the Father of Christ, because, when Christ was begotten, God took the place of a human father. Christ was not begotten by the man Joseph, as the Jews mistakenly believed, and as the impious Carpocrates, Cerinthus, Ebion and Photinus falsely claimed,[1] and as, lately, the wretched Anabaptists have also claimed.[2] God's consummate power, operating in place of a man, by means of his Word (as I just said), fertilized the Virgin Mary and brought her to fullness through the action of the Holy Spirit within her. By this power she gave birth to the Son of God.

Note the inferential word *quapropter* [because of this] or *idcirco* [therefore], and you will grasp the meaning of the inference whereby the child is called the Son of God.[3] Undoubtedly, this was because he was born from God and a virgin. The same understanding of the sonship of the man Jesus Christ is set forth in the book of Daniel, which calls him *a stone cut by no human hand*.[b] And likewise, Matthew explains that a virgin was made *pregnant by the Holy Spirit*, and that *what was conceived in her came from the Holy Spirit*. He would be the Savior, *Emmanuel, which means God with us*.[c] Note, therefore, that the power that was begotten and conceived in the Virgin's womb, which was the Son of God and is called God, was the man Jesus Christ.

Also note carefully what [the angel] says in Luke: "The son whom *you will conceive and bear will be called the Son of* God and *he will be great* in the sight of God; *and God will give him the throne of his father David*."[d] Thus Irenaeus[4] says in [*Against Heresies*], book 3, chapter 18:[5] "The angel, announcing the good news to Mary, says that he who is *the Son of the Most High* is also the *son of David*."[e] He is the son of David, however, through his mother. But, since sonship is principally defined with reference to the father, David does not presume to call him his son, but rather his Lord. Thus, in the spirit of prophecy, he says about Christ, "*The Lord said to my Lord, sit at my right hand*."[f] Can the second person or hypostasis, whom [theologians] call the Son, *be made great* and receive from God *the throne of his father David*?[g] Would God say to it, "*sit at my right hand*"? In truth, however, all these things are said about the real Son, the man Jesus Christ.

---

[a] John 1:12. [b] Dan. 2:34,45. [c] Matt. 1:18-23. [d] Luke 1:31-32. [e] Irenaeus, *Adv. Hær.* 3.16.3 (PG 7a 923A), quoting Luke 1:32, 3:31. [f] Ps. 110:1. [g] Luke 1:32.

Err. 6b   Aliqui verba angeli pervertere conantes vocem sanctum ibi cavillantur, quasi primogenitus Christus non sit ea dignus, cum quidem Lucas paulo post declaravit, quare sanctum dixerit, quia omne primogenitum sanctum deo vocabitur, et petrus: Convenerunt enim vere adversus sanctum filium tuum Jesum, et psalmista, non dabis sanctum tuum videre corruptionem.

Err. 6b-7a   Item considera quod Lucas non dicit illam virtutem Altissimi quæ virginem inumbravit filium vocari, sed id quod ab illa virtute genitum est, ideo filius dei vocabitur, quoniam illa dei virtus vice viri fuit, et humani patris vicem supplente, quod enim cæteri hominum filii a matre deducunt, Christus accepit a virgine, quod autem a patre accipiunt Christus a deo altissimo vero eius genitore desumpsit. Nam vera omnino ac naturalis est apud deum et Christum Jesum paternitas et filiatio, nec mirum aut absurdum cuiquam videri debet, si deus qui dat omnibus generationem pater quoque generans esse advenit, et hominem filium sibi generare ut scriptura aperte testatur.

Err. 7a   Isti vero non advertunt quid Christus sit verbum dei, et quare [20] lata sint huius divini verbi et seminis archana a cuius similitudinem dicitur quod semen seminantis est verbum dei, et sicut ex verbo dei, tanquam ex divino semine natus est Christus. Ita verbo dei nos renascimur, differt autem Christi generatio ab aliis rebus factis vel creatis, quia omnia per verbum facta sunt, Christus autem ex ipso verbo convertibiliter factus est. Nam ipsum verbum dei per quod omnia constant incorporeum et invisibile, in utero virginis factum est corporeum visibile, et passibile, et Joannes vere, et proprie dixit, et verbum caro, id est homo factum est, non per unionem sicut idiomatum communicationem, ut nostri Theosophistæ male opinantur, sed proprie et convertibiliter, Christus igitur nihil aliud est, quam verbum dei ipsum corporeum, et homo factum, et Joannes hanc conversionem recte exposuit, cum dixit quod erat ab initio, quod audivimus, quod vidimus oculis nostris, quod perspeximus, et manus nostræ contrectaverunt de verbo vitæ, quæ manifestata est nobis, hoc et testamur et annuntiamus.

Some, in an effort to distort the words of the angel, quibble about the word "holy," as if Christ, the firstborn, were not worthy of it. Although, indeed, a little later, Luke shows why he had said "holy":[a] because every firstborn will be called holy to God.[b] Peter says, *"Truly they were gathered together against your holy Son Jesus."*[c] And the Psalmist: *"You will not allow your holy one to see corruption."*[d]

Note that Luke does not claim that the power of the Most High which overshadowed the Virgin will be called the Son, but rather that he who was begotten by the power *therefore will be called the Son of God.*[e] For the power of God was acting as a man and taking the place of a human father. What all other sons of men obtain from their mothers, Christ received from the Virgin, and what they receive from their fathers, Christ took from God the Most High, his actual begetter. The father-son relationship of God and Jesus Christ is entirely real and natural. It should not seem at all marvelous or strange that God, who begets all things, also becomes a father who procreates and begets a human son for himself, as scripture clearly testifies.

In truth, [the theologians] do not perceive that Christ is the Word of God, nor do they comprehend how wide the mysteries are of this divine Word and seed. On this subject, the parable says that *the seed of the sower is the Word of God.*[f] Just as Christ was born from the Word of God as from divine seed, so by the Word of God we are born again. But Christ's begetting differs from that of other beings that are made or created. For all things are made through the Word, but Christ was formed from the Word itself, by a process of transformation. In the Virgin's womb, the incorporeal and invisible Word of God, by which all things exist, became corporeal, visible, and capable of suffering. And John, employing words in their usual way, correctly says, *the Word became flesh*[g] – that is, a human being – not by means of a union, or by *communicatio idiomatum*, as our theological sophists falsely assert, but in reality and by a process of transformation. Therefore, Christ is nothing other than the Word of God itself, made corporeal and human. John accurately explains this transformation when he says, *That which was from the beginning, which we have heard, which we have seen with our eyes, which we have looked upon, and touched with our hands, concerning the word of life made manifest to us, and we testify to it and proclaim it.*[h]

---

[a] Luke 2:23. [b] Exod. 13:2,13:12, 34:19, Num. 8:17. [c] Acts 4:27 (Erasmus). [d] Ps. 16:10, quoted in Acts 2:27, 13:35. [e] Luke 1:35. [f] Luke 8:11. The parable is in Luke 8:4-15, Matt. 13:18-23, and Mark 4:14-20. [g] John 1:14. [h] 1 John 1:1-2.

Nostri vero Theologi tenebris palpabilibus immersi et Jesum Christum ignorantes illum dividunt ac solvunt in duas naturas distinctas, et separatas, duos christos aut filios introducentes, alium quidem invisibilem, et impassibilem, quem dicunt esse dei filium sine carne, et alium visibilem ac passibilem, quem dicunt filium virginis sine patre, contra quos exclamat Joannes. Omnis spiritus qui solvit Jesum ex deo non est, sed Antichristus est, nam [21] verbum adhuc invisibile, et incorporeum divinant, et ab ipso Jesu visibili distinguunt Christum solventes, quæ fuit Hæresis Valentini, contra quam quinque libris scripsit sanctus Irenæus præsertim in toto libro tertio, ubi intra cætera dicit, hoc autem factum est ut adimpleretur quod dictum est, a domino per prophetam, Ecce virgo concipiet in utero et pariet filium et vocabunt nomen eius Emanuel, quod interpretatum nobiscum deus, manifeste significans eam promissionem quæ fuerat ad patres impletam ex virgine natum filium dei, et hunc ipsum salvatorem Christum: quem prophetæ prædicaverunt non sicut ipsi dicunt Jesum quidem ipsum esse qui ex Maria sit natus, Christum vero qui desuper descendit, et paulo post inquit Simeon autem ille qui accepit responsum a spiritu sancto se non moriturum nisi prius videret Christum dei, infantem accipiens de manibus virginis, laudavit deum confitens ipsum esse christum filium dei, quem ipse suis oculis viderat, et manibus contrectaverat, et paulo post, Non ergo alterum filium hominis novit Evangelium nisi hunc qui ex Maria qui et passus est, sed neque Christum avolantem ante passionem ab Jesu, sed hunc qui ex Maria natus est, novit dei filium, et eundem hunc passum resurrexisse, quemadmodum Joannes dei discipulus confirmat dicens, Hæc autem scripta sunt, ut credatis, quoniam Jesus est Christus filius dei, et ut credentes vitam æternam habeatis [22] in nomine eius, providens has blasphemas regulas quæ dividunt dominum quantum in ipsis est, ut ex altera et altera substantia dicentes eum factum, et paulo post, Unus igitur deus pater, et unus Christus Jesus dominus noster, sermo dei visibilis factus, et incomprehensibilis factus comprensibilis, et impassibilis passibilis factus, et verbum homo, universa in semetipsum recapitulans

Truly our theologians, immersed as they are in such palpable darkness[a] and ignorant of Jesus Christ, divide him up and split him into two distinct and separate natures, producing two Christs or two sons. They say one Son of God is invisible, incapable of suffering, and without flesh. The other is visible and suffering, the son of a virgin and fatherless. Against them John exclaims, *Every spirit which divides Jesus is not of God but is the Antichrist.*[b] They conjure up a Word which remains invisible and incorporeal, and distinguish it from the visible Jesus, tearing Christ asunder. This was the heresy of Valentinus, against whom Saint Irenaeus wrote five books.[6] [He discusses the nature of Christ], especially throughout Book 3, where, among other things, he says:

> *All this took place to fulfill what the Lord had spoken by the prophet: behold a virgin shall conceive and bear a son, and they shall call his name Emmanuel, which means God with us.*[c] This clearly shows that the promise made to the patriarchs had been fulfilled, that the Son of God was to be born of a virgin, and that he was the Savior, Christ, whom the prophets had foretold, and not, as [the Valentinians] claim, that Jesus was born from Mary, while Christ descended from on high.[d]

A little further on [Irenaeus] says:

> Simeon was told by the Holy Spirit that he would not see death before he had seen God's Christ. Receiving the infant from the hands of the Virgin, he praised God, proclaiming the child to be Christ, the Son of God, whom he had seen with his own eyes and touched with his own hands.[e]

Yet a little further on:

> Therefore the Gospel did not know of another Son of man, other than the one who was of Mary and who suffered. Neither did it know of a Christ spirited away from Jesus before the passion, but was only aware of the one who was born of Mary: the Son of God, the same one who suffered and was resurrected. John, God's disciple, affirms this, saying, *but these are written that you may believe that Jesus is the Christ, the Son of God, and that believing you may have eternal life in his name.*[f] For he foresaw these blasphemous schools of thought which divide up the Lord as best they can, claiming him to be of one substance and then another.[g]

Shortly after that [Irenaeus says]:

> Therefore, *there is one God the Father, and one Jesus Christ our Lord,*[h] the Word of God made visible, the incomprehensible made comprehensible, the non-suffering made capable of suffering, and the Word made man, recapitulating all things in himself.[7]

---

[a] A possible reference to Exod. 10:21: "a darkness to be felt." [b] 1 John 4:3 (Vulgate). [c] Matt. 1:22-23, quoting Isa. 7:14. [d] Irenaeus, *Adv. Hær.* 3.16.2 (PG 7a 921B-C). [e] Condensed from Irenaeus, *Adv. Hær.* 3.16.4 (PG 7a 923B), based on Luke 2:26-32. [f] John 20:31. [g] Irenaeus, *Adv. Hær.* 3.16.5 (PG 7a 924C-925A). [h] 1 Cor. 8:6.

ut sicut in supercœlestibus spiritalibus et invisibilibus princeps est verbum dei, sic et in visibilibus et corporalibus principatum habeat, in semetipsum primatum assumens, et apponens semetipsum caput Ecclesiæ, universa attrahat ad semetipsum, apto in tempore, præcognita sunt enim hæc omnia a Patre, perficiuntur autem a filio, sicut congruum est apto tempore, sed et Paulus ait, Cum autem venit plenitudo temporis misit deus filium suum, per quod manifestum est, quoniam omnia quæ præcognita erant a patre ordine et tempore, et hora præcognita, et apta, perfecit dominus noster unus quidem et idem existens, dives autem et multus, diviti et multæ patris voluntati deserviens, cum sit ipse salvator eorum qui salvantur, et dominus eorum qui sunt sub domino,[*] et deus eorum quæ constituta sunt, et unigenitus patris et Christus qui prædicatus est, et sermo dei incarnatus cum advenisset plenitudo temporis in quo filium hominis fieri oportebat filium dei.

Igitur omnes extra dei dispositionem sunt qui sub obtentu agnitionis alterum quidem Jesum intelligunt alterum autem Christum et unigenitum, erroris quidem discipuli qui a foris oves per [23] eam quam habent extrinsecus loquellam, similes nobis eadem nobiscum loquentes intrinsecus vero lupi, sententia enim eorum homicidialis deos quidem plures confingens, et patres multos simulans, comminuens autem et per multa dividens filium dei, quos et dominus nobis cavere prædixit, et discipulus eius Joannes in prædicta Epistola fugere eos præcepit, multi seductores exierunt in hunc mundum qui non confitentur Jesum Christum in carne venisse, hic est seductor et Antichristus, et multi pseudoprophetæ exierunt de sæculo, sed in hoc cognoscite spiritum dei, Omnis spiritus qui confitetur Jesum Christum in carne venisse ex deo est, omnis spiritus qui solvit Jesum Christum non est ex seo sed ex Antichristo est, hæc autem sunt similia illi quod in Evangelio eiusdem dictum est quoniam verbum caro factum est et habitavit in nobis et vidimus gloriam eius, propter quod rursus in epistola clamat, omnis qui credit quod Jesus est Christus ex deo natus est unum et eundem sciens Jesum Christum cui apertæ sunt portæ cœli propter carnalem eius assumptionem in carne enim assumptus est in cœlum, qui etiam in eadem carne in qua passus est, veniet revelans gloriam patris,

---

[*] Editions of Irenaeus since 1596 have *dominio* [dominion] instead of *domino* [Lord].

Just as in the heavens above, among spiritual and invisible beings, the Word of God is foremost, so too among visible and corporeal beings [Christ] should occupy the highest place, assuming primacy in himself and placing himself at the head of the church, in order to draw all things to himself at the proper time. For all these things were known in advance by the Father, but accomplished, as was appropriate, by the Son at the suitable time.[a]

Paul also says, *But when the time had fully come, God sent forth his son.*[b] From this it is clear that our Lord brought to perfection, in their fitting order, season, and hour, all the things that were known beforehand by the Father – our Lord being indeed one and the same [with the Father], abundant and powerful. For he serves the abundant and powerful will of his Father, in that he is the Savior of those who are saved, the Lord of those who are under the Lord, the God of those things which have been established, the only begotten son of the Father, and the Christ who was foretold. And he is the Word of God, made flesh *when the time had fully come* when it was necessary for the Son of God to become the Son of man.[c]

All, therefore, are outside of God's dispensation who, based on pretended knowledge, make a distinction among Jesus, Christ, and the only begotten. These are the disciples of error, who, based on their public professions, seem to be sheep, who appear similar to us and say the same things we do; *but who inwardly are really wolves.*[d] Their homicidal idea conjures up a multitude of gods, multiplying a host of fathers, fragmenting and dividing the son of God in a multitude of ways. These are the ones the Lord warned us about, and in the aforementioned epistle his disciple John instructed us to shun them, saying, *Many deceivers have gone out into the world, who do not acknowledge the coming of Jesus Christ in the flesh; such a one is the deceiver and the Antichrist.*[e] Also: *Many false prophets have gone out into the world, but by this you know the Spirit of God: every spirit which confesses that Jesus Christ has come in the flesh is of God, every spirit which divides Jesus Christ is not of God but is of the Antichrist.*[f] These words are similar to what is said in the gospel of John: *the Word became flesh and dwelt among us, {and we beheld his glory}.*[g] This is also why he proclaims in his epistle, *Everyone who believes that Jesus is the Christ has been born of God*,[h] knowing one and the same Jesus Christ, for whom the gates of heaven were opened because he took on flesh. {For in the flesh he was taken up into heaven} and, in the same flesh in which he suffered, he shall also come to reveal the glory of the Father.[i]

---

[a] Irenaeus, *Adv. Hær.* 3.16.6-7 (PG 7a 925C-926A).   [b] Gal. 4:4.   [c] Irenaeus, *Adv. Hær.* 3.16.7 (PG 7a 926B-C).   [d] Matt. 7:15.   [e] 2 John 1:7.   [f] 1 John 4:1-3.   [g] John 1:14. The text in {braces} is not in Irenaeus.   [h] 1 John 5:1.   [i] Irenaeus, *Adv. Hær.* 3.16.8 (PG 7a 926C-927C).

et paulus consentiens ad Romanos, multo magis hi qui abundantiam gratiæ et Justitiæ accipiunt in vitam, regnabunt per unum Jesum Christum. Nescit ergo apostolus eum qui evolavit Christum ab Jesu, neque eum novit salvatorem, qui sursum est quem impassibilem dicunt; Si enim alter quidem passus est alter autem impassibilis mansit, et alter quidem [24] natus est, alter vero in eum qui natus est descendit et rursus reliquit eum, non unus sed duo monstrantur, quoniam autem unum eum, et qui natus est, et qui passus est, Christum Jesum novit apostolus in eadem epistola iterum dicit, An ignoratis, quia quodquod baptizati sumus in Christo Jesu, in morte Jesu baptizati sumus, ut quemadmodum resurrexit a mortuis, sic et nos in novitate vitæ ambulemus, rursus autem significans Christum passum eundem ipsum filium dei qui pro nobis mortuus est, et sanguine suo redemit nos in præfinito tempore, ait, ut quid enim Christus, cum adhuc essemus infirmi secundum tempus pro impiis mortuus est? commendat autem suam dilectionem deus in nobis, quoniam cum adhuc essemus peccatores, pro nobis Christus mortuus est, multo magis nunc iustificati in sanguine eius salvi erimus per ipsum ab ira, si enim cum essemus inimici reconciliati sumus deo per mortem filii eius, multo magis reconciliati salvi erimus in vita ipsius, hunc eundem qui apprehensus est, passus est, et effudit sanguinem suum pro nobis, hunc Christum, hunc filium dei manifestissime annuntians qui etiam surrexit, et assumptus est in cœlum, quemadmodum ipse ait simul autem Christus mortuus, immo qui et resurrexit, qui est in dextera dei, et iterum scientes quoniam resurgens a mortuis iam non moritur, prævidens enim et ipse per spiritum, subdivisiones malorum magistrorum, et omnem ipsorum dissensionis occasionem volens abscindere ait, quæ prædicta sunt.

    Si autem spiritus eius qui suscitavit [25] Jesum a mortuis habitat in nobis, qui suscitavit Christum a mortuis vivificabit et mortalia corpora nostra. Nolite ergo errare unus et idem est christus Jesus filius dei, qui per passionem suam reconciliavit nos deo, et resurrexit a mortuis, qui est in dextera patris, et perfectus in omnibus, qui cum vapularet, non percutiebat, qui cum pateretur non est minatus, et cum Tyrannidem pateretur rogabat patrem, ut ignosceret his qui se crucifixerant. Ipse enim vere salvavit. Ipse enim verbum dei. Ipse unigenitus a patre Christus Jesus deus noster.

And in his Epistle to the Romans, Paul agrees: *Much more will those who receive the abundance of grace and righteousness reign in life through the one Jesus Christ.*[a] Consequently, the Apostle knew nothing of the Christ who flew away from Jesus, nor of that savior on high, whom they say is not subject to suffering. For if, in truth, there was one who suffered and another who remained incapable of suffering; one who was born, while the other actually descended into him who was born, and in turn abandoned him; then this means that not one, but two [Christs] are taught.[b]

But since the Apostle knew him to be one, namely Jesus Christ, who was born and who suffered, he again says in the same epistle, *Do you not know that all of us who have been baptized in Christ Jesus, are baptized into the death of Jesus, that in the way he arose from the dead, we too might walk in newness of life?*[c] And again, showing that the Christ who suffered was himself the Son of God, who died for us and redeemed us with his blood at a predestined time, he says, *For how is it, that Christ, while we were still weak, at the right time died for the ungodly? But God shows his love for us, in that, while we were yet sinners, Christ died for us. Much more, then, being now justified by his blood, shall we be saved by him from wrath. For if, while we were enemies, we were reconciled to God by the death of his Son; much more, now that we are reconciled, shall we be saved by his life.*[d] He declares unmistakably that the same one who was arrested, suffered, and shed his blood for us, was both Christ and the Son of God, who also rose again and was taken up to heaven. As Paul says, *But, likewise, it is Christ that died, yes indeed, that is risen again, who is at the right hand of God.*[e] And again: *We know, because he rose from the dead, he now will never die.*[f] Paul says this, foreseeing, by means of the spirit, the partitions of these evil teachers, and wishing to prevent opportunity for dissension.[g]

If, however, the spirit of him who raised Jesus from the dead dwells in us, he who raised Jesus from the dead will give life to our mortal bodies also.[h] Therefore, make no mistake: Jesus Christ, the Son of God, is one – the same one who by his suffering reconciled us to God and *rose from the dead*, who *is at the right hand of the Father,*[i] who is perfect in all things, *who when he was beaten, did not strike back, who when he suffered, did not threaten.*[j] And when he suffered at the tyrant's hands, he asked his father to forgive those who had crucified him. It was he who truly brought about salvation, since he is the Word of God, the only begotten of the Father, Jesus Christ, our God.[k]

---

[a] Rom. 5:17. [b] Irenaeus, *Adv. Hær.* 3.16.8-9 (PG 7a 927A-928A). [c] Rom. 6:3-4. [d] Rom. 5:6, 8-10.
[e] Rom. 8:34. [f] Rom. 6:9. [g] Irenaeus, *Adv. Hær.* 3.16.9 (PG 7a 928A-C). [h] Rom. 8:11. [i] Rom. 8:34.
[j] 1 Peter 2:23 (a variant reading known in the time of Irenaeus). [k] Irenaeus, *Adv. Hær.* 3.16.9 (PG 7a 928C-929A).

Hæc Irenæus Adversus Valentinum lib. III, cap. XVIII, postea in sequenti cap. subiungit, etenim potuerunt dicere Apostoli Christum descendisse In Jesum, aut eum qui ab invisibilibus est, in hominem visibilem, sed nihil quidem tale neque scierunt, neque dixerunt, si enim scissent dixissent utique quod autem erat hoc, et dixerunt, et paulo post ait subdivisiones excogitaverunt qui spiritum quidem interimunt alium autem Christum, et alium Jesum intelligunt, et non unum christum, sed plures fuisse docent, et si unitos eos dixerint, et iterum ostendunt eum passum esse, alterum autem impassibilem perseverasse.

Item in cap. 20. ait ostenso manifeste quod sermo in principio existens apud deum per quem omnia facta sunt, his novissimis temporibus secundum præfinitum tempus a patre passibilis homo factus est, et paulo post quoniam non christus impassibilis descendit in Jesum, sed ipse Jesus cum esset christus passus est pro nobis et Petrus cum respondisset tu es Christus filius dei vivi manifestum fecit quoniam filius hominis hic est Christus filius dei viventis, si quis autem quasi duorum existentium iudicium [26] de his faciat invenietur multo melior et patientior et vere bonus qui in vulneribus ipsis et plagis et reliquis in se commissis beneficus et nec memor in se commissæ malitiæ eo qui avolavit nec ullam iniuriam neque opprobrium passus est, sed quoniam solus vere magister dominus noster est bonus vere filius dei, et patiens verbum dei patris, filius hominis factus, luctatus est, et vicit, erat enim homo, pro patribus certans et per obedientiam inobedientiam persolvens. Si enim homo non vicisset inimicum hominis, non iuste victus esset inimicus, rursus nisi deus donasset salutem non firmiter haberemus eam, et nisi homo coniunctus fuisset deo nostro non potuisset particeps fieri incorruptibilitatis

Thus Irenaeus wrote in *Against Valentinus*, book 3, chapter 18. Later, in the following chapter, he adds:

> Certainly the apostles could have said that Christ descended into Jesus, or that he who was from the invisible realm {descended into a visible man}, but they neither knew nor said anything of the kind. For if they had known it, they would certainly have said it. They mention only what actually happened.[a]

And a bit further on, he says:

> They have concocted divisions which destroy the Spirit. They understand one who is Christ and another who is Jesus, and teach that there was not one Christ, but many, even if they speak of them as a unity. They try to show that while one suffered, another actually remained untouched by suffering.[b]

Also, in chapter 20 he says:

> It has been clearly demonstrated that the Word existing *in the beginning with God, through whom all things were made*,[c] in these latter days, at a time ordained by the Father, became a man capable of suffering.[d]

And shortly thereafter, he says:

> A non-suffering Christ did not descend into Jesus, but, rather, Jesus himself, because he was the Christ, suffered for us.[e] And when Peter answered, *You are the Christ, the Son of the living God*,[f] he made it clear that this man, the Son of man, is Christ, the Son of the living God.[g]
>
> But if anyone who supposes that there are two beings were to compare them, the [Christ] who remained benevolent amidst the wounds and blows and other cruelties inflicted on him, and paid no heed to the wrong done him, will be found to be much better, more long-suffering, and truly good, than he who took flight and suffered neither injury nor insult.[h]
>
> But since our Lord alone is truly Master, truly the good and long-suffering Son of God, the Word of God the Father made the Son of man, when he struggled, he overcame. For he was a man, contending on behalf of his forefathers, and by his obedience paying in full the debt of their disobedience.[i] For unless a man had conquered the enemy of man, the enemy would not have been be fairly defeated; unless God had granted us salvation, we could never really have possessed it; and unless a man had been joined with God, he could never have shared in incorruptibility.[j]

---

[a] Irenaeus, *Adv. Hær.* 3.17.1 (PG 7a 929B). [b] Irenaeus, *Adv. Hær.* 3.17.4 (PG 7a 931B). [c] John 1:2-3.
[d] Irenaeus, *Adv. Hær.* 3.18.1 (PG 7a 932A). [e] Irenaeus, *Adv. Hær.* 3.18.3 (PG 7a 934A). [f] Matt. 16:16.
[g] Irenaeus, *Adv. Hær.* 3.18.4 (PG 7a 934 B-C). [h] Irenaeus, *Adv. Hær.* 3.18.5 (PG 7a 936B).
[i] Irenaeus, *Adv. Hær.* 3.18.6 (PG 7a 936C-937A). [j] Irenaeus, *Adv. Hær.* 3.18.7 (PG 7a 937A-B).

qua enim ratione filiorum adoptionis eius particeps esse possemus? nisi per verum filium eam quæ est ad ipsum recepissemus ab eo communionem nisi verbum eius communicasset nobis caro factum igitur qui dicunt eum putative manifestatum, neque incarnatum, neque vere hominem factum adhuc sub veteri sunt damnatione opportebat enim eum qui inciperet occidere peccatum et mortis reum redimere hominem id ipsum fieri quod erat ille, id est hominem, si igitur sermo dei homo factus est ut Moses: autem vera sunt opera dei, si autem homo factus non est, sed quasi caro apparebat non erat verum opus eius.

 Hæc et alia permulta de veritate unius Christi filii dei passi mortui et suscitati [27] copiose scribit sanctus Irenæus cuius verba si diligenter inspexeris facile cognosces quantum hodierni nostri Theologi ab apostolorum doctrina recesserint et ab evangelica veritate deviarint docentes filium dei non esse passum pro nobis neque mortuum et suscitatum, item et Jesum illum hominem ex virgine natum qui redemptionem fecit in sanguine suo verum et proprium dei filium esse negantes quæ blasphemiæ et impietates universam christi ecclesiam et relligionem polluerunt, et ut illam divisionem quam de unico Christo faciunt verbo tenus consolidarent quandam Idiomatum Communicationem adinvenerunt quam Apostoli nunquam scriverunt vel cogitaverunt. Omnis enim scriptura tam antiqua quam nova de filio dei loquens semper ad Jesum illum hominem respexit semper ad Christum illum visibilem et passum se proprie, et simpliciter retulit, nullum alium dei filium faciens preter illum Jesum crucifixum verbum dei corporatum visibile, et passibile factum, virum et hominem dici filium ipsa vocabuli natura nos docet, sicut enim propria passio corporis est ungi sic propria passio carnis est nasci. Caro igitur (inquit Tertullianus) nata est, et caro erit filius dei, nam filius dei natus est, nec prius verbum dei apud nos filius dici cœpit quam in utero virginis corporeum, et visibile, et sic homo factum est quamvis apud deum in lumine suæ æternitatis [28] filius semper fuerit, ut infra clarius explicabitur.

Err. 7a

For how could we be included in the process of God's adoption of sons, unless we had received fellowship with him through the true Son; unless his Word, made flesh, had entered into communion with us? Therefore, those who say that he only seemed to appear, and neither became incarnate nor was truly man, remain under the old condemnation.[a]

For he who was undertaking to destroy sin and to redeem man under sentence of death, had to become the what he was, that is, a man. Therefore, the Word of God was made a man. Moreover, as Moses says, *The works of God are true*.[b] If, however, he had not been made man, but only seemed to be flesh, his work would not have been true.[c]

Saint Irenaeus writes at length about these and many other things concerning the truth of the one Christ, the Son of God, who suffered, died and was raised from the dead. If you carefully examine what he wrote, you will easily comprehend how far our current theologians have fallen away from the teaching of the apostles and deviated from the gospel truth, by teaching that the Son of God did not suffer for us, did not die, and was not raised from the dead. In the same way, they deny that the man Jesus, born of a virgin, who brought about redemption by his blood, was the true and proper Son of God. These blasphemies and impieties have polluted the entire church of Christ and all religion. In an attempt to mend with words the division they have made in the one Christ, they have invented *communicatio idiomatum*, which the apostles never contemplated and about which they never wrote. All of scripture, both the Old and New [Testaments], always speaks of the Son of God in terms of Jesus the man and always refers simply and straightforwardly to the visible and suffering Christ, portraying no other Son of God except Jesus crucified, the Word of God which became visibly incarnate and capable of suffering.

The nature of the word ["son"] teaches us that the Son is to be called a man and a human being. Indeed, as being anointed is a condition characteristic of the body, so being born is a condition characteristic of the flesh. "Therefore," Tertullian says, "it was flesh that was born, and that flesh will be the Son of God."[d,8] For the Son of God was born. We did not begin to call the Word of God the Son until, in the womb of the Virgin, it was made corporeal and visible, and thus was made a man. Nonetheless, in God's terms, in light of his eternity, the Son has always existed, as will be made clearer below.

---

[a] Irenaeus, *Adv. Hær.* 3.18.7 (PG 7a 937C). [b] Deut. 32:4. [c] Irenaeus, *Adv. Hær.* 3.18.7 (PG 7a 938A-B).
[d] Tertullian, *Adversus Praxean* 27 (PL 2 190C).

Err. 7a   Dic mihi cuius est ille filius de quo toties fit mentio apud Mathæum quem Joseph ille iustus assumebat, ducebat, et reducebat, numne puer ille est filius ab Ægypto vocatus, an vere filius ille est illa secunda hypostasis quæ tamen in Ægyptum translata non fuit metu Tyranni nec ex Ægypto post illius mortem revocata, certe nullus scripturæ locus de filio loquens huic secundæ personæ aut hypostasi, invisibili et impassibili convenit, oportuit enim per filium dei fieri redemptionem, ut Sathan Mors, et peccatum potentissime superarentur, et in triumphum ante patrem adduceretur, et hæc omnia per verum hominem fieri oportuit, ut ex Irenæo supra docuimus, quare necessario sequitur hominem filium dei, esse pro nobis passum mortuum, et suscitatum ut etiam sic patiendo perfectam apud patrem gloriam consequeretur regnum illi cum triumpho restituens.

Tu autem quod sanctissimum illum virum ex virgine natum, sine patre esse contendis, et simpliciter humanitatem vocas dic quæso numne ille homo erat? quod si homo, et genitum esse, et genitorem habuisse necesse est, alioqui homo natus dici non potest, ergo et filium esse oportet eius qui illum genuit, Adam primus homo proprie filius dici non potest quia natus non est, [29] sed ab ipso deo de limo terræ formatus unde genitus dici
Err. 7a-b   non potest, nec genitorem seu patrem habens. At homo Jesus Christus, et natus, et filius est. Sic enim ubique scriptura testatur, filiatio autem ad patrem seu genitorem refertur, nec quisquam filius dici potest nisi patrem ostendat. Cæterum non alium patrem seu genitorem illius hominis Jesu Christi reperies quam ipsum deum, nisi forte vel Jesum, phantasma esse credas aut cum Ebionitis, et Anabaptistis Joseph illi patrem constituas. Sed non minor est impietas eorum, qui ex uno filio duos faciunt, aut ex duobus filiis et duabus naturis distinctis et separatis unum agregatum seu compositum philosophantur.

O miseram Theologiam immo verius sophisticam philosophiam, hæc ne est apostolica doctrina? hæc ne veritas evangelica? de Jesu Christo unico dei filio impudenter philosophari?

Tell me, who is that son so often mentioned in Matthew, whom the upright man Joseph accepted, led forth [into Egypt], and brought back?[a] Was that child not the *son called out of Egypt*?[b] Or is the Son really the second hypostasis, which was not taken to Egypt out of fear of the tyrant nor called back from Egypt following [Herod's] death? Certainly, no reference to the Son in scripture is applicable to the second person or the invisible and non-suffering hypostasis.

Redemption through the Son of God was necessary, in order to defeat Satan, death, and sin, and bring the Son in triumph before the Father. And all these things had to be done by a real human being, as we have just shown on the authority of Irenaeus. It necessarily follows that the Son of God is a man who suffered for us, died, and was brought back to life; so that, by his suffering, he might achieve perfect glory with the Father, and triumphantly restore the kingdom to God.

You, however, contend that this holiest of men was born from a virgin, without a father, and disingenuously call that "a human nature." Tell us, I implore you, whether or not he was a man. If he was a man, and was born, he must have had a begetter. Otherwise, he cannot be said to have been born a man. Therefore, he must be the son of the one who begot him.

Adam, the first man, cannot properly be called a son, because he was not born, but was formed by God himself from the mud of the earth. Thus he cannot be said to have been begotten, having had neither a procreator nor a father. But the man Jesus Christ was born and was a son. All of scripture bears witness to this. Sonship is defined in terms of a father or procreator. Nor can anyone be called a son, unless someone can point to a father. You will find no other father or begetter of the man Jesus Christ than God himself, unless perchance you believe that Jesus was a phantasm or, with the Ebionites and Anabaptists, you propose Joseph as his father. But as for those who make two sons from one, or those who, on the basis of two sons and two distinct and separate natures, philosophize about a single aggregate or composite, their impiety is no less.

O wretched theology – or, to put it more precisely, sophistical philosophy! Is this the teaching of the apostles? Is this the gospel truth, to philosophize shamelessly about Jesus Christ, the only son of God?

---

[a] Matt. 2:13-15.   [b] Matt. 2:15, referring to Hosea 11:1.

Err. 7b-8a Sophisticare quantum velis in filiationis ratione ut ex illis duobus natis, genitis vel filiis unum facias agregatum vel suppositum connotativum, nunquam persuadebis, ut secundum scripturæ sinceritatem unicus dei filius esse credatur, cum re ipsa duos filios, duos genitos, et duos natos ante oculos videas, sed tales versutias nunquam scripturæ cogitaverunt, quæ simplicissime, et sincerissime de Jesu illo visibili unico, atque unigenito dei filio loquuntur, nullamque aliam rem personam vel naturam, præter ipsum hominem natum commemorat, et ita Ignatius de una, et eadem re loquens de Jesu christo inquit [30] filio dei qui est vere natus ex deo et virgine, nunc igitur ex scripturis hoc tibi misterium sic explicabo ut etiam mulierculæ, lippi et tonsores Jesum illum hominem Christum esse verum dei filium luce clarius intellegant, et in hoc sit radix totius intentionis nostræ et perpetuum fundamentum christianæ pietatis ac relligionis Christus enim se etiam mulieribus verum Messiam, et dei filium prædicabat hoc idem Apostoli omnibus gentibus simpliciter annuntiarunt hæc erat una illorum intentio Jesum illum crucifixum dei filium christum persuadere. Sed quomodo muliercula filium illum Methaphysicum, seu hypostaticum intelliget ubi quam plurimi etiam subtilissimi heresiarchæ lapsi sunt, et adhuc hodie labuntur.

 Agamus igitur scripturis et apertissima illarum testimonia proferamus.

Wax sophistical all you wish about the nature of sonship, so as to make those two children, offspring, or sons into a single aggregate or connotative *suppositum*, you will never persuade me to believe that this [aggregate] is the only Son of God, as plainly described in scripture. For, in fact, you can see before your very eyes two sons, two offspring, and two children.

But the scriptures never conceived of such contrivances! They speak in the simplest and most straightforward way about Jesus, the visible, unique and only begotten Son of God, and never mention any other being, person, or nature except the man who was born. Thus when Ignatius[9] said, "About Jesus Christ, the Son of God, who was truly born from God and from the Virgin,"[a] he was speaking of one and the same being.

Now, therefore, I will explain this mystery from scripture, so that even uneducated women, half-blind men, and barbers[10] will understand, as clear as day, that the man Jesus Christ is the true Son of God. Herein lies the root of my undertaking and the eternal basis of Christian piety and religion. Christ, indeed, proclaimed, even to women, that he was the true Messiah and the Son of God. And the apostles unambiguously preached the same thing to all the nations. This was their sole intention: to persuade people that the crucified Jesus was the anointed Son of God. But how could an ordinary woman understand the metaphysical or hypostatical Son, when so many arch-heretics, even the most cunning, have erred, and continue to err to this day?

Now, therefore, let us delve into the scriptures and draw forth their testimony, which is absolutely clear.

---

[a] Ignatius, *Epistola ad Smyrnæos* 1 (PG 5 707B); *Epistola ad Ephesios* 7 (PG 5 738D).

Declarationis Jesu Christi, per Michælem Servetum, liber tertius

Ut igitur Jesum illum visibilem verum dei Altissimi filium tibi comprobemus arripiamus primum testimonium ipsius patris. Mathæus tertio Marci primo et Lucæ tertio. Nam cum Jesus in Jordane baptizaretur a Ioanne, descendit spiritus sanctus corporali specie quasi columba super eum, et vox de cœlo facta est, hic est filius meus dilectus in quo mihi bene complacitum est [**31**] hoc idem testificatus est pater in transfiguratione ipsius filii Math. 17. Marci 9. Lucæ 9. Hic est filius meus dilectus ipsum audite.

Err. 8a Idem testificatus est Ioannes Baptista Io. 1. dicens vidi spiritum descendentem in speciem columbæ de cœlo, et mansit super eum, et ego non noveram eum sed qui misit me ut baptisarem aqua is mihi dixit super quem videris spiritum descendentem ac manentem hic est qui baptisat spiritu sancto, et ego vidi et testificatus sum hunc esse filium dei, nota quæso patentissima verba sine circumloquio, nam secundum opinionem Theosophistarum deceptus fuisset Ioannes ab oraculo dei, et ipse quoque falsum dixisset testificans illum quem vidit, et de quo audivit esse filium dei nec credibile est Ioannem de re illa separata et invisibili cogitasse nec per communicationem idiomatum locutum fuisse quando quidem nulla adhuc erat tunc triadis personarum vel hypostasum apud sanctos viros cognitio sed solius hominis Christi vel Messiæ visibilis expectacio quem dei filium vere, et simpliciter credebant ac fatebantur

A Revelation of Jesus Christ by Michael Servetus
Book 3

To prove that the visible Jesus was the true Son of God the Most High, let us first turn to the testimony of the Father himself, in Matthew chapter 3, Mark chapter 1, and Luke chapter 3. When Jesus was baptized by John in the Jordan, the Holy Spirit descended on him bodily in the form of a dove, and *a voice from heaven said, "This is my beloved Son, with whom I am well pleased."*[a] The Father also bears witness to this at the transfiguration of his son, saying *"This is my beloved Son, listen to him"* (Matthew 17, Mark 9, and Luke 9).[b]

John the Baptist also bore witness to this at John 1, saying,

I saw the Spirit descend in the form of a dove from heaven, and it remained on him. I myself did not know him; but he who sent me to baptize with water said to me, "He on whom you see the Spirit descend and remain, he is the one who baptizes with the Holy Spirit." And I have seen and have borne witness that this is the Son of God.[c]

Pray consider these extremely plain words, spoken without circumlocution. For, according to the theological sophists, John was deceived by the voice of God and also spoke falsely when he bore witness about the one whom he had seen, whom he had been told was the Son of God. It is not credible that John was thinking about a separate and invisible being, or that he was speaking of *communicatio idiomatum*. For among those saintly men [the evangelists] there was as yet no conception of a triad of persons or hypostases, but only of the man Christ, or of the expectation of the visible Messiah, whom they truly and simply believed and proclaimed to be the Son of God.

---

[a] Matt. 3:17, Mark 1:11, Luke 3:21.   [b] Mark 9:7, Matt. 17:5, Luke 9:35.   [c] John 1:32-34.

Err. 8a-b nec deus signum aliquod dederat de re invisibili cognoscenda, sed de homine visibiliter demonstrato, hic est filius meus vel tu es filius meus, quod si deus per illud pronomen hic est rem aliam latentem et Metaphysicam designabat, non dedisset patens testimonium de filio suo sed populum seduxisset, quod absurdissimum est dicere [32] vel cogitare nisi cum nostris philosophis sophisticando dicamus deum demonstrando Jesum visibilem pro filio suo semper locutum fuisse per communicationem idiomatum, similiter et ipsum Jesum semper improprie, et abusive locutum quando se ipsum dei filium esse dicebat, et deum sibi patrem palam fatebatur. Sed certe impium est, ipsi veritati loquenti tales improprias, et abusivas locutiones ascribere, nec talis Communicatio Idiomatum simplicitati, et sinceritati divinæ scripturæ convenit, sed ex græcanica philosophia defluxit, nec utique apud hebræos cognita fuit, vel in usum recepta, quæ si ad intelligentiam misteriorum dei et evangelicæ veritatis necessaria fuisset, utique Apostoli de illa prius aliquod monuissent, ne aliud pro alia prædicantes semper auditorum fidem fefellissent, et credentes in erroribus detinuissent, quod a puritate evangelii alienissimum est.

Err. 8b Item cum interrogasset Jesus cæcum illuminatum, credis in filium dei? et ille respondisset quis est domine, ut in eum credam, dixit ei Jesus, et vidisti eum, et qui loquitur tecum ipse est, quid quæso clarius et simplicius dici potuit se ipso ad oculum demonstrato. Considera quod Christus qui est ipsa veritas, nec unquam loquendo fefellit manifeste mentitus esset dicens, et vidisti eum, et ipse est qui loquitur tecum, cum tamen filius dei secundum istos omnino invisibilis, et incorporeus sit, immo graviter a Christo seductus [33] fuisset homo ille si virum visibilem pro filio dei incorporeo, et invisibili simpliciter adorasset nec etiam putandum est Christum ei tunc sophistice per communicationem idiomatum fuisse locutum.

Err. 8b Item quam personam demonstrabat centurio ille quando dixit vere filius dei erat iste, erat ne milles ille Methaphisicus vel sophista? ut per Communicationem Idiomatum loqueretur. Nondum enim græcanicam illam de tribus hypostasibus, et suppositis connotativis philosophiam didicerat, sed de Jesu Nazareno crucifixo simpliciter loquens

God did not give any indication of an invisible being that had to be pursued mentally, but rather a man visibly revealed: "*This is my Son*,"[a] or, "*You are my Son.*"[b] If, by the pronoun "this," God had meant some other, hidden and metaphysical being, he did not give clear testimony about his son, but, rather, led people astray. This is an utterly ridiculous thing to say or think, unless, like our philosophers, we sophistically say that, when God pointed to the visible Jesus as his Son, he always spoke in terms of *communicatio idiomatum*, and that Jesus likewise always spoke peculiarly and deceptively when he called himself the Son of God and publicly proclaimed that God was his father. It is certainly impious to ascribe such inappropriate and deceptive language to the sayings of the truth itself [that is, Christ]. *Communicatio idiomatum* does not accord with the simplicity and sincerity of holy scripture, but has seeped in from Greekish philosophy. Such concepts were neither known nor used by the Hebrews.

If [those concepts] had been needed in order to comprehend the mysteries of God and the truth of the gospel, the apostles would have taught about them earlier. They would not have betrayed the trust of their listeners, nor entangled believers in error, by proclaiming one thing [the visible man] instead of another [the invisible being], something which is completely alien to the purity of the gospel. When Jesus asked the blind man who had regained his sight, "*Do you believe in the Son of God?*" and he answered, "*Who is he, master, that I may believe in him?*" Jesus said to him, "*You have seen him, and it is he who is speaking with you.*"[c] How, I ask you, could he have expressed it more simply and clearly, than by pointing to himself? If, as [the theologians] would have it, the Son of God is entirely invisible and incorporeal, then Christ, who is truth itself and never spoke deceptively, would clearly have been lying when he said, "*You have seen him, and it is he who is speaking with you.*" In that case the man [whose sight was restored] would have been led astray by Christ, since he naively worshipped the visible man instead of the incorporeal and invisible Son of God, and never imagined that Christ was speaking to him in terms of a sophistical *communicatio idiomatum*.

What "person" was the centurion talking about when he said, "*Truly this was the Son of God*"?[d] Was that soldier a metaphysician or a sophist that he should speak in terms of *communicatio idiomatum*? For he had never received instruction in the Greekish philosophy about the three hypostases and connotative *supposita*. But, speaking simply about Jesus of Nazareth crucified,

---

[a] Matt. 3:17.   [b] Mark 1:11, Luke 3:22.   [c] John 9:35-37 (Vulgate).   [d] Matt. 27:54, Mark 15:39.

verum dei filium confessus est quod tamen theologi nostri impiissime negant.

Err. 8b Item Audi paulum qui illico atque visum recepit ingressus synagogas Iudeaorum predicabat Jesum crucifixum quoniam hic est filius dei nec sermo, hic, de secunda persona seu hypostasi intelligi potest, verbum enim seu logos ille dei ex post facto a Ioanne declaratus est ad hanc doctrinam confirmandam tantum abest ut ei repugnet. Nam Johannes divinam, et cœlestem Jesu Christi originem ex verbo idest dei semine productum demonstrare voluit, et quomodo a deo exiisset ut impiam et perversam illorum hæresim refelleret qui Jesum illum ex virgine natum dei filium esse negabant, sed ex virili semine conceptum asserebant velut Carpocrates Cerinthus Ebion, et photinus contra quos præcipue Johannes ab ecclesiis Asiæ rogatus stupendum et divinum illud elogium scripsit in quo nihil aliud intendit nisi Jesum illum virum sanctissimum cuius [34] gloriam ipse Johannes viderat verum dei filium ex divino non humano semine genitum demonstrare et sic, nota causam quare Johannes longo tempore post alios evangelistas illud scripserit, et nota effectum de quo et ad quem finem scripserit ut et infra latius declarabitur.

Err. 8b Item Considera si summus sacerdos de secunda hypostasi cogitabat quando dixit es tu filius dei benedicti, et respondit ei Jesus ego sum, utique et interrogatio et responsio de Jesu illo homine visibili fuit, unde pro maxima blasphemia reputabant quod homo se dei filium faceret nec fuisset tam difficile vel odiosum Judæis si Jesus non dixisset se esse dei filium, sed potius dixisset filius dei mecum est vel in me loquitur quod sane fuisset ipsi Christo (secundum Theologos nostros) et verius et tollerabilius nec tantam sibi apud Judæos Conflasset Invidiam, sed certe in tota scriptura antiqua et nova nunquam inventa fuit hæc locutio quod filius dei esset in Christo, sed ipse christus visibilis semper se ipsum dei filium vere et simpliciter annuntiabat et hoc crediderunt omnes pii et Apostoli per universum orbem prædicarunt, et in hac confessione consistit fides nostra, ecclesiæ fundamentum et vita æterna.

he acknowledged the true Son of God. This our theologians impiously deny.

Furthermore, hear what Paul says: as soon as he recovered his sight, he went into *the synagogues* of the Jews and *proclaimed Jesus* crucified, *saying that he is the Son of God*.[a] His words cannot be understood as referring to a second person or hypostasis.

The Word, or *Logos*, of God, was introduced by John, after the fact, to support the doctrine [that Jesus is the Son of God]. Thus he was far from being opposed to it. For John wished to demonstrate the divine and celestial origin of Jesus Christ from the Word – how he was produced from the seed of God and came forth from God – in order to refute the wicked and perverse heresy of those who denied that Jesus, born of the Virgin, was the Son of God and who, like Carpocrates, Cerinthus, Ebion, and Photinus, asserted that [Jesus] was conceived from the seed of a man.[1] Against these John, mainly at the behest of the churches of Asia [Minor],[2] wrote that wondrous divine paean, in which he undertook to demonstrate that no one else but Jesus, the holiest of men, whose glory John himself had seen, was the true Son of God, born of divine, not human, seed. Note what led John to write [his gospel], long after the other evangelists [wrote their gospels].[3] Note the effect of it, and to what end he wrote it. I will speak about this passage in greater detail below.

Consider whether the high priest had in mind the second hypostasis when he asked, "*Are you the Son of the Blessed God?*" and Jesus answered, "*I am*."[b] Assuredly, both the question and the reply were about Jesus, the visible man. That is why [the Jews] took [Jesus's reply] as the greatest blasphemy: that of a human being making himself out to be the Son of God. For it would not have been so difficult [to accept], or so odious to the Jews, if, instead of saying that he was the Son of God, Jesus had said, "the Son of God is with me," or "is speaking in me" – which was what happened, according to our theologians. That would have seemed more true and tolerable, and would not have stirred up such resentment among the Jews. But certainly that manner of speaking – that the Son of God was in Christ – is never found in all of scripture, in either the Old or New [Testament]. Rather, the visible Christ always announced, truly and simply, that he himself was the Son of God. All [the faithful] believed this, and the pious apostles proclaimed it throughout the world. On this confession we base our faith, the foundation of the church, and life eternal.

---

[a] Acts 9:20.   [b] Mark 14:61-62.

Err. 8b-9a

Item de qua persona intelligebat Martha cum dixit Ego credo quod tu sis Christus ille filius dei vivi, qui in hunc mundum venturus erat? Utique de illo Jesu visibili suo hospite et magistro simplicissime loquebatur, rogo [35] tecum paulisper consideres si Martha et aliæ personæ piæ quæ crediderant Jesum illum virum sanctissimum esse dei filium non ab ullo terreno patre, sed ab ipso deo vere genitum fuerant ab aliquo instructæ de istis tribus personis aut hypostasibus aut idiomatum communicatione aut suppositis connotativis et huiusmodi subtilitatibus quæ nunc ad Intelligendum Christum a nostris Theologis obtruduntur.

Porro olim tempore christi et Apostolorum nulla alia fides nulla alia Confessio ad salutem exigebatur nisi simplicissima illa fides et confessio quod Jesus ille vir potens opere et sermone esset verus Christus et summi dei filius et pauci admodum huc credere poterant quod homo passibilis esset proprius et naturalis dei altissimi filius nec mirum quod tam arduum et admirabile misterium filiationis a paucis tunc crederetur cum etiam hodie illi qui quotidie scripturarum testimonia ante oculos habent et sapientiores aliis reputantur hominem a deo singulariter genitum credere nolint aut certe non possint, nemo enim credit nisi qui ab ipso deo trahitur et illuminatur. Nam sicut deus pater non nisi per Jesum filium cognosci potest, ita nec filius ipse cognoscitur nisi per divinam patris revelationem. Nota et ideo Christus hac potissimum ratione petri Confessionem laudavit quia neque caro neque sanguis illud ei revelaverant, sed pater ipse cœlestis ut loco suo plenius ostendetur.

[36] Item, audi Nathanalem virum simplicem et sine dolo quam recte de Jesu illo visibili testificatus fuerit dicens Rabbi tu es ille filius dei, tu es ille rex israël, ecce quomodo simplex ille homo simpliciter vocat Jesum et regem Israël, et filium dei confessionem suam ad hominem referens qui cum eo loquebatur nullam aliam personam extrinsecus considerans neque de his hodiernis subtilitatibus quidquam intelligens. Nam omnes patriarchæ prophetæ et viri sancti spiritu dei illustrati semper crediderunt eum hominem qui futurus erat Christus seu Messias, et rex Israël facturus redemptionem humani generis a deo patre exiturum, et ipsius naturalem ac proprium filium esse quod et Simeon in suo cantico declaravit et in hac fide ac spe euntes obdormierunt in domino.

What "person" was Martha thinking of when she said, "*I believe that you are the Christ, the Son of the living God, he who is coming into the world*"?[a] Certainly, she was simply speaking about the visible Jesus, her guest and teacher. I ask you to consider for a moment whether Martha and those other pious individuals who believed Jesus, that most holy man, to be the Son of God – truly begotten by God himself and not by any earthly father – ever received instruction about the three persons or hypostases or *communicatio idiomatum* or connotative *supposita* and subtleties of this sort, which our theologians have imposed upon our understanding of Christ.

Moreover, in the time of Christ and the apostles, no faith or confession was needed for salvation other than this most uncomplicated one: that the man Jesus, *powerful in deed and word*,[b] was the true Christ and the Son of the highest God. At that time very few were able to believe that a man capable of suffering could be the very own, natural Son of God the Most High. It is not surprising that this difficult and wondrous mystery of sonship was believed by few at that time, when even now those who have the testimony of the scriptures daily before their eyes, and are reputedly wiser than others, refuse to believe in a man uniquely born of God – or, at least, are incapable of believing it. No one really believes unless he is drawn [to belief] and enlightened by God. For as God the Father cannot be comprehended except through Jesus the Son, neither can the Son be understood except through the divine revelation of the Father. That is why Christ praised Peter's very powerful confession, *for flesh and blood had not revealed it to him, but the heavenly Father*,[c] as I will [presently] show more fully.

Hear how precisely Nathaniel, a simple and guileless man, bore witness to the visible Jesus, saying, "*Rabbi, you are the Son of God; you are the king of Israel*."[d] See how this plain man simply calls Jesus both the king of Israel and the Son of God. His confession referred to the one who was speaking to him. He did not consider any other "person" or have in mind any of these modern-day subtleties. For all the patriarchs, prophets, and holy men, illumined by the spirit of God, always believed [Christ] to be a man, and always believed that he who was the Christ, or Messiah to come, and the king of Israel, who was going to redeem humanity, would issue forth from God the Father and be his very own, natural son. This also is what Simeon declared in his canticle.[e] Relying on this faith and hope, [the believers] slept in the Lord.

---

[a] John 11:27 (Vulgate). [b] Luke 24:19. [c] Matt. 16:16,17. [d] John 1:49. [e] Luke 2:29-35.

Audi aliud evangelicum testimonium, porro qui erant in navi accesserunt omnes ad Jesum, et adoraverunt eum dicentes vere filius dei es, forte illi rudes, et idiotæ quidquam de hypostasibus aut connotativis intellexerant, vel per communicationem idiomatum loquebantur nec Christus ipse hunc titulum ab errantibus sibi atribui sustinuisset quemadmodum et bonitas titulum a se reiiciens, omnem patri gloriam reservavit, Luce 18.

Nunc etiam Thomas eum vidit et palpavit, credidit illum sic visum et palpatum esse filium dei et deum suum dicens dominus meus et deus meus, et tum respondit illi Jesus, quia vidisti thoma credidisti, ecce quomodo hominem visibilem et palpabilem credidit esse, et dominum et deum suum non aliter crediturus nisi vidisset et palpasset. Sed beatos dixit Jesus eos qui etiam non videntes [37] credidissent. Nostros tamen Theologos beatos dicere non possumus qui nec ipsi credere volunt nec alios credere patiuntur, sed suis philosophicis imposturis a vera fide, plenis et inflatis voluminibus abducere conantur, quibus tamen filius ipse dei Jesus Christus mundum iudicaturus iusta aliquando præmia rependet et tunc videbunt quem negarunt et transfixerunt.

Err. 26a-b   Accedat nunc egregia illa petri confessio super qua fundata est vera ecclesia et christiana religio quæ nunquam deficiet ut Christus ipse promisit. Cum enim post multa signa, et multas cum Judæis habitas concertationes Christus cum discipulis suis in partes Cæsareæ venisset interrogavit eos dicens quem me dicunt homines esse filium hominis. At illi responderunt, alii quidem dicunt te esse Joannem baptistam alii vero heliam, alii vero hiieremiam aut unum de numero prophetarum, dicit illis Jesus at vos quem me esse dicitis? respondens autem simon petrus dixit, tu es Christus ille filius dei viventis, tunc dixit illi Jesus, beatus es Simon bar Iona quia caro et sanguis non revelavit tibi sed pater meus qui est in cœlis, et ego verissime dico tibi quod tu es petrus et super hanc petram ædificabo ecclesiam meam et portæ inferorum non prævalebunt adversus eam et tunc edixit discipulis ne cui dicerent quod ipse esset Christus.

Hear another Gospel witness: *And those in the boat all approached Jesus and worshipped him, saying, "Truly you are the Son of God."*[a] Could it be that these rough-hewn, uneducated men knew anything about hypostases and connotatives, or talked in terms of *communicatio idiomatum*? Christ would not have allowed the title [Son of God] to be given to him in error. In the same way he refused to accept the title, "Good," reserving all glory for the Father.[b]

When Thomas saw and touched [Jesus], he believed that he whom he had seen and felt was the Son of God, his God. He said, *"My Lord and my God."* Jesus answered him, saying, *"Because you have seen, Thomas, you have believed."*[c] Behold how [Thomas] believed him to be a visible and palpable man. Thomas was not prepared to believe that Jesus was his Lord and God, unless he saw and touched him. But Jesus called those blessed who believed even when they had not seen.[d] However, we cannot call our theologians blessed, who neither wish to believe, nor allow others to believe, but strive, by means of their padded and pumped-up volumes of philosophical humbug, to seduce people from the true faith. Jesus Christ, the Son of God, who will judge the world, will one day justly repay them. Then they will see who it was that they denied and pierced [with nails and a spear].

Now let us turn to Peter's remarkable confession, on which are founded the true church and the Christian religion, which, as Christ promised, will never cease.[e] Now when, after many signs and wonders, and disputes with the Jews,[f]

> [When] Christ had come with his disciples into the district of Caeserea, he asked them, "Who do men say that I, the Son of man, am?" They answered, "Some, indeed, say that you are John the Baptist, others however Elijah, others however Jeremiah or one of the prophets." Jesus said to them, "But who do you say that I am?" Simon Peter replied, "You are the Christ, the Son of the Living God." Then Jesus said to him, "Blessed are you, Simon Bar-Jona! For flesh and blood has not revealed this to you, but my Father who is in heaven. And I tell you truly, you are Peter, and on this rock I will build my church, and the gates of hell shall not prevail against it." And then he charged the disciples to tell no one that he was the Christ.[g]

---

[a] Matt. 14:33. [b] Luke 18:19. [c] John 20:27-29. [d] John 20:29. [e] Matt. 16:16-18. [f] Miracles in Matt. 14 and 15 and discussion of signs with the Pharisees in Matt. 16:1-4. [g] Matt. 16:13-20.

Audi Christiane nota perpende et considera omnia supradicta verba, primo interrogationem christi de homine. Item responsionem discipulorum [38] etiam de homine. Mox responsionem petri de ipso Jesu loquente item ipsius christi aprobationem et deinde inhibitionem. Nota pronomina ipsius Jesu loquentis demonstrativa quem me dicunt filium illum hominis et vos quem me esse dicitis et tu es ille. Numquid ista omnia de Jesu homine an vero de secunda illa persona vel hypostasi sunt intelligenda? Dicite mihi super quam petram fundavit dominus ecclesiam suam nisi super hac fide et confessione quod ipse homo passibilis et mortalis, esset verus dei Christus et filius, sed ab hac petra Theologi nostri misere defecerunt nec Jesum illum filium hominis cum petro et apostolis filium dei fateri voluerunt unde nescio super quam petram agnoverint quam potius reprobarunt.

Sed iam et ad alia scripturæ testimonia procedamus quando enim philippus Eunuchum illum baptizavit et de Jesu nazareno instruxit qui velut ovis ad occisionem pro expiatione peccatorum virorum ductus fuerat ut prædixerat Esaias audi simplicem et sinceram ipsius eunuchi confessionem, credo (inquit) filium dei esse Jesum christum, nota causam huius confessionis quia eunuchus legebat Esaiam loquentem de christo passo et sic de homine illo Messia qui erat redempturus Israel quod ille non intelligens, rogavit philippum ut ei locum prophetæ declararet de quo homine diceretur tunc philippus non de tribus personis vel hypostasibus vel communicatione idiomatum vel suppositis connotativis [39] eum instruxit nihil enim horum sciebat philippus, quæ longo post tempore a græcis philosophis seu Theosophistis inventa fuerunt, sed simpliciter et sincere de Jesu illo Nazareno viro dei, potente in operibus et sermone Magistro suo instruxit, docens quod esset verus dei filius, quem oportuerat pati pro redemptione humani generis, ut voluntatem patris et omnem de seipso scripturam adimpleret, et hæc omnia narranti philippo credidit eunuchus, nimirum sancto dei spiritu afflatus, et insignem illam suæ fidei credidit confessionem, scilicet Jesum illum passum esse dei filium.

Listen, Christian. Note, weigh, and consider all the words spoken above: first, Christ's question about a man; next, the answer of the disciples, also about a man; soon after, the reply of Peter speaking about Jesus; then, the approval of Christ and the prohibition. Note the demonstrative pronouns used by Jesus when he said, *"Who do they say that I, the Son of man, am?"* *"Who do you say that I am?"* and [Peter replied], *"You are the [Son of the Living God]."* [a] Should all these pronouns be understood as applying to Jesus the man, or are they really about the second person or hypostasis? Tell me, upon what rock did the Lord found his church, other than this faith and confession, that the very man who suffered and was subject to death was truly Christ and the Son of God? But our theologians have shamefully abandoned this rock. Unlike Peter and the apostles, they do not want to say that Jesus, the Son of man, is the Son of God. For that reason, I wonder whether, instead of recognizing the *cornerstone*, they have *rejected* it.[b]

Let us now proceed to further testimony from scripture. For example, listen to the simple and sincere confession of the eunuch, when Philip baptized him and taught him about Jesus of Nazareth,[c] who, as Isaiah foretold, had been *led like a sheep to slaughter*[d] for the expiation of mankind's sins. He said, *"I believe that Jesus Christ is the Son of God."* [e,4]

Consider the reason for this confession of faith. The eunuch was reading in Isaiah about the suffering Christ – the man, the Messiah who was to redeem Israel – and because he did not understand it, he asked Philip to clarify the passage and tell him what man was being described.[f] Philip did not teach him about three persons or hypostases, *communicatio idiomatum*, or connotative *supposita*. Indeed, Philip knew nothing of such things, which were invented much later by Greek philosophers, or rather theological sophists. Instead he taught him simply and truthfully about his Master, Jesus of Nazareth, the man of God, *powerful in word and deed*;[g] explaining that he was the true Son of God, who was meant to suffer for the redemption of humanity in order to carry out the will of the Father and fulfill everything that had been written about him in scripture. And, doubtless inspired by God's Holy Spirit, the eunuch believed all that Philip told him and fully believed in that notable confession of faith: that the Jesus who suffered was the Son of God.

---

[a] Matt. 16:13, 15-16   [b] Ps. 118:22, quoted in Matt. 21:42, Mark 12:10, Luke 20:17, Acts 4:11, 1 Peter 2:7.   [c] Acts 8:27-38.   [d] Isa. 53:7, quoted in Acts 8:32.   [e] Acts 8:37.   [f] Acts 8:27-34.   [g] Luke 24:19.

Quam vero aliam (christiane fidelis) quæris theologiam quam philippi prophetam declarantis? quam aliam fidem habere aut confessionem facere debes quam Eunuchi? quorsum tot sophismata et questiones inutiles in doctrina et relligione christi suscitatæ? quæ tota uno et quidem apertissimo testimonio continentur. Nempe Jesum illum christum crucifixum esse verum et unicum dei filium quæ potest esse in hac confessione difficultas? tot oraculis et testimoniis divinis comprobata.

Sed iam audiamus paulum Ad Hebræos scribentem, Multiphariam locutus est deus olim per prophetas, novissime vero per filium suum. Constat autem Jesum hominem, non illam secundam hypostasim sermo nos dei in terris locutum esse, et quid aliud agit paulus toto illo primo capite? nisi ut ex antiquæ [40] scripturæ testimoniis Jesum illum hominem crucifixum, verum et proprium dei filium esse demonstret, super Angelos et omnes creaturas exaltatum. Cui unquam Angelorum dixit deus, filius meus es tu, ego hodie genui te, Ego ero illi pater, et ille erit mihi filius, qui per semetipsum purgatione facta peccatorum, consedit in dextra maiestatis dei. Item ad quem unquam Angelorum dixit sede a dextris meis.

Nempe hæc omnia de filio dei vere dicuntur et tamen non ad illam secundam hypostasim, sed ad ipsum Jesum hominem necessario referuntur, quem hebræi pro dei filio agnoscere noluerunt, ut paulus aperte demonstrat, cum quibus etiam Theologi nostri omnino conveniunt negantes filium dei passum esse, et ad eius dextram sedere, sed hæc omnia filio hominis tribuentes Jesum christum redemptorem nostrum unicum dei et virginis filium solventes et dividentes, hinc videri potest quomodo scripturas intelligant et quod perverse a recto, et manifesto sensu detorqueant.

Err. 5b Audi etiam Joannem, signa fecit ut credamus quod Jesus est ille christus filius dei. Nota quod de Jesu signum faciente manifestum erat aput omnes, sed in hoc misterium fidei consistebat, ut crederent quod Jesus ille signa faciens esset verus christus et dei filius, qui a solo patre genitus et unctus erat,

What theology do you require, faithful Christian, other than Philip's exposition of the words of the prophet? What faith ought you to have, what confession should you profess, other than the one the eunuch made? Why have so many sophisms and useless questions been raised about the teaching and religion of Christ? This [teaching] is all contained in that one very clear testimony, namely, that the Jesus who was crucified was the true Christ and the only Son of God. What difficulty can there be in this statement of faith, confirmed by so many divine prophecies and witnesses?

Now hear what Paul wrote in the Epistle to the Hebrews: *In various ways God spoke of old by the prophets, but in these last days he has spoken through his Son.*[a] It follows from this that Jesus the man, not the second hypostasis, was the Word of God speaking to us on earth. What was Paul doing, in this entire first chapter, except demonstrating, by means of ancient scriptural testimony, that Jesus, the man who was crucified, was the true and only Son of God, exalted above the angels and all creatures? For to what angel did God ever say, "*You are my son. Today I have begotten you. I will be his Father and he will be my son*"?[b] [What angel], having *made purification for sins, sat down at the right hand of the Majesty of God*?[c] To what angel did [God] ever say, "*Be seated at my right hand*"?[d]

Without a doubt, as Paul clearly demonstrates, all these things are truly spoken about the Son of God – not the second hypostasis – Jesus the human being. The Hebrews refused to recognize him as the Son of God, and our theologians entirely agree. [The theologians] deny that the Son of God is capable of suffering and that, [having suffered,] he sits at God's right hand. They attribute all these things to the Son of man. They divide and partition our redeemer Jesus Christ, the only son of God and the Virgin. From this, it can be seen how they understand scripture. They have perversely distorted its correct and obvious meaning.

Hear also what John says: *He performed miracles so that we may believe that Jesus is the Christ, the Son of God.*[e] Note that when Jesus performed a miracle, it was obvious to everyone. But the miracle of faith consisted in this: that they were able to believe that the Jesus who performed these miracles was the true Christ, the Son of God, he who was begotten and anointed by the one Father.

---

[a] Heb. 1:1-2. [b] Heb. 1:5, quoting Ps. 2:7. [c] Heb. 1:3. [d] Heb. 1:13. [e] John 20:30-31.

Err. 5b-6a haec autem non conveniunt illi secundae hypostasi, quae ex signis et miraculis cognosci non poterat, nam externa illa signa non arguunt interiores illas philosophias et latentes [41] hypostases. Christus enim Jesus palam de seipso testabatur quod opera quae ipse faciebat satis declarabant eum a patre missum, et eum se filium dei dixisset Judaeis Indignantibus dixit si mihi non creditis saltem operibus credite, illa de me testificantur sic Nathanahel ex signo externo, quia Jesus dixit vidi te sub ficu fatetur eum esse illum dei filium qui mitendus erat rex israel, sic etiam discipuli ex eo quod Jesus ventos fugavit et sedavit procellam maris, accesserunt ad eum et adoraverunt dicentes vere filius dei es, nec puto quod illi per communicationem idiomatum loquerentur, cum nihil aliud praeter illum Jesum visibilem magistrum summum agnoscerent, et adorarent. Similiter petrus ex signis quae Jesus fecit et ex sermonibus ipsius infert dicens Domine ad quem ibimus verba vitae aeternae habes et nos credimus et cognovimus quod tu es christus filius dei vivi, et tamen petrus qui magistrum suum verum dei filium toties confessus fuerat, graecanicam illam philosophiam de hypostasibus et communicatione idiomatum penitus ignorabat sed vere proprie et simpliciter ut res erat loquebatur.

Accedamus nunc ad ipsiusmet Jesu christi testimonia et argumenta qui est magister veritatis. Nam ad Judaeos inquit, vos dicitis me blasphemare quia dixerim filius dei sum, si non facio opera patris mei nolite mihi credere, sin vero facio, etsi mihi non creditis, saltem operibus credite, ut cognoscatis [42] quod pater in me est, et ego in patre, haec verba sunt adeo clara ut nihil evidentius de Jesu homine dei filio dici possit. Nam Jesus ipse visibilis, non hypostasis illa invisibilis, opera patris faciebat et sygna quae nullus alius homo facere poterat, et in ipso Jesu homine pater erat, per spiritum suum, ut declarat Joannes In hoc cognoscimus quod in eo manemus et ipse in nobis, quoniam de spiritu suo dedit nobis.

Such things, however, do not fit the second hypostasis, which cannot be understood on the basis of *signs and wonders*.[a] For outward signs do not prove esoteric philosophies and hidden hypostases. Jesus Christ openly bore witness that the works he performed were sufficient proof that he was sent by the Father.[b] He said to the outraged Jews that he was the Son of God. He said, "*If you do not believe me, at least believe my works.*"[c] "*They bear witness to me.*"[d]

On the basis of an outward sign, Jesus saying to him, "*I saw you under the fig tree*," Nathaniel confessed that [Jesus] was the Son of God, who was sent to be the king of Israel.[e] Because Jesus dispersed the winds and calmed the tempest on the sea, the disciples approached and worshipped him, saying, "*Truly, you are the Son of God.*"[f] I do not believe that they were speaking in terms of *communicatio idiomatum*, when they acknowledged and worshipped none other than the visible Jesus, the supreme teacher. Peter came to the same conclusion, because of the miracles that Jesus performed and the words he spoke, saying, "*Lord, to whom shall we go? You have the words of eternal life; and we have believed, and come to know that you are the Christ, the Son of the living God.*"[g] But Peter, who so often proclaimed that his teacher was truly the Son of God, was completely unaware of Greekish philosophizing about hypostases and *communicatio idiomatum*. Instead, he very simply and straightforwardly spoke of things as they really were.

Let us now consider the testimony and proofs of Jesus Christ, the teacher of truth. He said to the Jews, "*Do you say that I blaspheme since I would say, 'I am the Son of God?' If I am not doing the works of my Father, then do not believe me. But if, in truth, I do them, even though you do not believe me, at least believe the works, that you might understand that the Father is in me and I am in the Father.*"[h]

These words are so plain that nothing clearer can be said about the man Jesus, the Son of God. For the visible Jesus, not the unseen hypostasis, was doing the work of the Father and performing miracles, which no other man could do. The Father was in Jesus by means of his Spirit, as John declares: *By this we know that we abide in him and he in us, because he has given us of his own Spirit.*[i]

---

[a] Rom. 15:19.　[b] John 5:36.　[c] John 10:38.　[d] John 10:25.　[e] John 1:48-49.　[f] Matt. 14:33.　[g] John 6:68-69, Matt. 16:16.　[h] John 10:36-38.　[i] 1 John 4:13.

Christus autem spiritum dei sine mensura accepit, et ideo pater in eo et ipse in patre manebat, per obœdientiam charitatem et spiritus veritatem, non autem dicit scriptura quod in ipso Jesu esset filius dei, vel ipse Jesus in filio, nec quod prima hypostasis esset in secunda vel secunda in prima, sed relatio semper fit inter deum patrem invisibilem, et filium eius visibilem, Jesum christum, nec aliter in tota scriptura invenies, nec mirum quia ipsemet Jesus homo visibilis et passibilis, erat unicus dei filius, item pater verba quæ dedisti mihi dedi eis et ipsi acceperunt, et cognoverunt vere quod a te exivi, et crediderunt quod tu me misisti, sanctifica eos per veritatem tuam, sermo tuus veritas est, sicut tu me misisti in mundum, ita et ego misi eos in mundum non pro eis te autem rogo tantum, sed et pro iis qui per sermonem eorum credituri sunt in me ut omnes unum sint, et sicut tu pater in me, et ego in te, ita et ipsi in nobis unum sint, hæc omnia ab ipso Jesu homine, et de ipso [43] non de alio filio vel alia persona dicuntur, nec usquam loquitur quod credentes sint unum cum prima et secunda persona vel quod pater sit in verbo, aut verbum in patre, quemadmodum de Jesu christo homine recte dicuntur nec unquam invenitur quod verbum illud invisibile vel secunda persona patrem rogaverit, quia (secundum istos) idem deus seipsum rogaret et tamen ubique legimus filium rogasse patrem, immo hæc est propria natura filii, rogare patrem, nec ullæ preces magis efficaces et penetrantes inveniuntur, quam filiorum ad parentes et ideo christus ut verus filius rogavit patrem ne deficeret fides petri, rogavit pro credentibus, rogavit pro persequentibus rogavit pro seipso, ut a patre clarificaretur, et si possibile fuisset calix ille supplicii transiret, proinde magna est cæcitas et impietas dicere quod Christus non rogabat patrem ut filius dei sed ut filius hominis, semper scripturam improprie et abusive intelligentes, ac falsis interpretationibus depravantes, quæ nec divinis misteriis conveniunt, nec ulla ratione possunt verificari.

Christ received *the spirit* of God *without measure*.[a] For that reason *the Father* was *in* him, *and* he *in the Father*,[b] in obedience, love, and the truth of the spirit. Nevertheless, Scripture does not say that the Son of God was in Jesus or that Jesus was in the Son. Nor does it say that the first hypostasis was in the second, or the second hypostasis in the first. Rather it says that a relationship always exists between the unseen God the Father and his visible son Jesus Christ. You will not find it otherwise in the whole of scripture. And no wonder, since Jesus himself, the visible and suffering human being, was the only Son of God.

> "Father, I have given them the words which you gave me, and they have received them and know in truth that I came from you, and they have believed that you sent me." "Sanctify them in your truth. Your word is truth. As you sent me into the world, so I have sent them into the world." "Yet it is not for these alone that I ask, but also for those who believe in me through their word, that they may all be one, and, just as you, Father, are in me and I in you, that they also may be one in us."[c]

All these things were said by the man Jesus Christ about himself, and not about some other son or some other "person." He never meant that those who believe would be one with the first or the second person, nor that the Father would be in the Word or the Word in the Father. These words are correctly said only about the man, Jesus Christ.

The invisible Word, or second person, never asked anything of the Father. For then, according to [the theologians], God would have been asking something from himself. However, we read everywhere that the Son appealed to the Father. Indeed, it is the special nature of the Son to appeal to the Father. No entreaties are more effective and compelling than those of children to parents. Thus Christ, as a true son, prayed to his father that Peter's faith might not waver, and appealed to [the Father] on behalf of his persecutors and those who believed in him.[d] On his own behalf he prayed that he might be glorified by the Father and that, if possible, the cup of affliction might pass from him.[e] Hence, it is great blindness and impiety to say that Christ did not pray to the Father as the Son of God but [only] as the Son of man. [Those who say this] consistently interpret scripture improperly and erroneously, and distort its meaning with false interpretations which do not conform to the divine mysteries and which cannot possibly be verified.

---

[a] John 3:34. [b] John 10:38, 14:10-11, 17:21. [c] John 17:8, 17-18, 20-21. [d] Luke 22:32, Luke 23:34, John 17:20-21. [e] John 17:5, Luke 22:42.

Jesus igitur redemptor noster ad Altissimum deum patrem suum in omni opere suo semper et immediate se retulit tamque verus naturalis et unicus ipsius dei filius et qui aliter credit iam iudicatus est.

Item nonne christus rogavit patrem pro iis qui eum cognoverunt, et crediderunt quod a patre exivisset, et in mundum [44] missus esset; sed quid aliud est exire a patre, quam ab eo gigni et produci, ut aput prophetam ex te enim exibit mihi dux qui regat populum meum, ut aput Joa. ex nobis exierunt, sed non erant ex nobis, item virtus de illo exibat, sic christus dixit exivi a patre, et veni in mundum. Item sciens Jesus quod a deo exisset, et ad deum iret, similiter venire in mundum idem est quod nasci ut aput Jo: Illuminat omnem hominem venientem in hunc mundum, et in hunc sensum dixit Jesus pilato, ego in hoc natus sum et ad hoc veni in mundum ut testimonium perhibeam veritati.

Similiter mittere in mundum est officium aliquod apud homines exequendum committere, sic missus fuit Gabriel Angelus ad Mariam, sic Jo. Baptista ad Judæos, ut pararet viam christo, sic etiam christus dei filius missus est ab ipso deo in mundum, ut omnem voluntatem patris adimpleret, sic ab eodem christo Missi sunt apostoli in mundum, ut omni creaturæ evangelium prædicarent hæc sunt, omnes dei altissimi dispositiones. Nostri autem Ebioniti negantes christum illum qui patrem rogabat esse dei filium, et a deo exivisse in eius oratione partem habere nolunt, quia non credunt. Christus autem pro credentibus tantum rogavit et ideo recte illis dici potest in peccato vestro moriemini.

Audi nunc argumentum ipsius christi inevitabile, [45] cum enim videret Iudæos non recte sentire de origine Messiæ, quem expectabant promissum in lege, ut qui non crederent ipsum Messiam seu Christum esse filium dei, et ex deo genitum, sed potius ex virili semine nasciturum, prout adhuc hodie tenent, et obstinato corde tuentur, ut illorum falsam opinionem ex scriptura convinceret, interrogavit eos, cuius dicunt christum esse filium? at illi responderunt, davidis,

For, in everything he did, our savior Jesus, the true, natural, and only Son of God, always went directly to his father, God the Most High. He who believes otherwise, now stands judged.

Did not Christ appeal to the Father on behalf of those who acknowledged him and believed that he had *come forth from the Father*[a] and been sent into the world? What else does it mean to *"come forth from the Father,"* other than to be begotten and brought forth from him? As the prophet says, *From you shall come forth for me a ruler, who will govern my people.*[b] As John says, *They went out from us, but they were not of us.*[c] Similarly, *power came forth from him.* And Christ said, *"I came from the Father and have come into the world."*[d] Jesus, knowing that he came from God, knew that he was going back to God.[e] Thus to come into the world is the same as to be born, as it says in John: *He enlightens every person coming into the world.*[f] And it was with this meaning that Jesus spoke to Pilate: *"For this I was born, and for this I have come into the world, to bear witness to the truth."*[g]

Similarly, "to send into the world" is to entrust a duty to be carried out among humankind. Thus, the angel Gabriel was sent to Mary,[h] and John the Baptist was sent to the Jews to prepare the way for Christ.[i] Christ, the Son of God, was sent by God himself in order to fulfill the whole will of God. And the apostles were sent into the world by Christ to preach the gospel to all creation. These things were all done according to the dispensation of God the Most High. Our Ebionites,[5] however, can have no part in his prayers because they do not believe: for they deny that the Christ who pleaded to the Father was the Son of God, and *came forth from God.*[j] But Christ prayed on behalf of believers only. For that reason it can justly be said of [the unbelieving "Ebionites"], *"You will die in your sin."*[k]

Listen now to the irrefutable argument made by Christ when he saw that the Jews did not have a correct understanding of the origin of the Messiah, whom they were awaiting as promised in the Law. They did not believe that the Messiah, or the Christ, was the Son of God, begotten by God, but rather that he was to be born from a man's seed (and even to this day they hold and maintain this with obstinate hearts). To refute their false opinion on the basis of scripture he asked them: *"Whose son,* do you say, *is Christ?"* And they replied, *"David's."*

---

[a] John 16:28. [b] Micah 5:2, quoted in Matt. 2:6. [c] 1 John 2:19. [d] Luke 6:19. [e] John 16:28.
[f] John 1:9 (Vulgate). [g] John 18:37. [h] Luke 1:26. [i] John 1:6. [j] John 13:3. [k] John 8:21.

tunc Jesus sic retorsit, si christus (ut dicitis) filius Davidis est. Quomodo david ipse in spiritu vocat eum dominum suum? Dixit dominus domino meo sede a dextris meis, quis pater unquam vocavit filium dominum suum? Plane hoc esset nimis præposterum, et abusivum, igitur necesse est vos fateri christum seu Messiam alium habere patrem quam davidem, nempe ipsum deum qui quidem deus pater, et filius eius Christus, ipsius davidis domini sunt, et nemo ad hoc respondere poterat.

Collige ergo ex prædictis tria inevitabilia contra nostros Theosophistas, primo, quod Christus seu Messias ut homo (nam tota quæstio de Messia seu Christo homine fuit nec unquam de re invisibili inter Iudæos controversia fuit) vere est dei filius, nec alium habet patrem quam ipsum deum, qui genuit illum, nec david ad Christum pertinet nisi ratione matris ut declarat Irenæus lib. III cap. 9. et 18. Paternitas autem tota ex deo est, et eo tendebat argumentatio et inductio Jesu christi, quia cum de filiatione alicuius simpliciter [46] quæritur non ad matrem sed ad patrem generantem relatio fit, cum enim ad filium producendum, et pater et mater concurrunt, principalis tamen et agens dispositio patris est non matris, et ideo tota filiatio patri simpliciter ascribitur, et necessarium filii correlativum est pater, non mater, unde mirandum est de istorum cæcitate qui Jesum christum filium sine patre esse concedunt.

Secundo quod Christus ut homo vere dicitur filius, ex patre deo et matre homine genitus, quod tum isti negant quia filiationem soli verbo simplici et incorporeo tribuunt, seu hypostasi invisibili de quo vel unum iota in tota scriptura non invenies.

Tertio quod Jesus christus ut verus dei filius, et non davidis sedet ad dexteram sui patris quod etiam isti negant, dicentes Christum sedere in cœlis ad dexteram dei patris, non ut filium dei sed ut filium hominis tantum, cum tamen in hoc actu sessionis universa scriptura de verbo dei filio et vero patre loquatur, ut ex hoc argumento Christi concludenter evincitur, et ex dicitis pauli per totum illud primum caput Ad hebræos.

Jesus then retorted, "If Christ, as you say, is the Son of David, *how is it that David, inspired by the Spirit, calls him Lord, saying, 'The Lord said to my Lord, sit at my right hand'*? What father ever called his son, my Lord?"[a] Obviously such a statement would be exceedingly preposterous and perverse. Therefore, you must admit that Christ, or the Messiah, has a Father other than David. In truth, God himself – who is indeed God, the Father – and his Son, Christ, are both lords of David. *And no one was able to answer that.*[b]

From what has been said, you now have three irrefutable arguments in reply to our theological sophists. First, that the Christ, or the Messiah, as a man (for, among the Jews, the whole dispute about the Messiah, or the man Christ, was never a controversy about an invisible being), is truly the Son of God, and does not have any Father other than God himself, who begot him. As Irenaeus says in Book 3, chapters 9 and 18, David is not related to Christ except through his mother.[c] His paternity is wholly from God, and this is where the logic of Jesus Christ's argument leads, since a person's filial status is defined not in terms of the mother, but of the father who begets him. Even though a father and a mother join together to produce a son, the primary and directing force belongs to the father, not to the mother. And for this reason the entire filial relationship is ascribed to the father. The necessary correlative of a son is not a mother, but a father [i.e. father and son are only defined relative to each other]. Hence, the blindness of those who maintain that Jesus Christ was a son without a father is to be marvelled at.[6]

Secondly, that Christ, as a man, is rightfully called a son, born from God the Father and a human mother. This [the theological sophists] deny, since they assign sonship only to the uncompounded and incorporeal Word, or to an invisible hypostasis, about which you will find not a single iota in all of scripture.

Thirdly, that Jesus Christ, as the true son, not of David, but of God, sits at the right hand of his Father. This they also deny, saying that in heaven Christ sits at the right hand of God the Father, not as the Son of God, but only as the Son of man. Nevertheless, whenever scripture speaks of being seated [at the right hand of God], it mentions the Son of God, who is the Word, and his true Father. This is conclusively proven by Christ's argument [with the Jews in Matthew 22], and also by the entire first chapter of Paul's Epistle to the Hebrews.[d]

---

[a] Matt. 22:42-45.   [b] Matt. 22:46.   [c] Irenaeus, *Adv. Hær.* 3.9.2, 3.16.3 (PG 7a 870B, 922B).
[d] See Heb. 1:3, 1:13.

Sed huius erroris tam palpabilis evidens causa fuit quia patrem deum et dei filium nunquam distinguere didicerunt, sed utrumque pro eadem substantia et natura et pro eodem deo re et numero temere assumpserunt, non considerantes, quod universa scriptura pro expeditissimo fundamento [47] veritatis, hoc unum nobis proponit. Unum tantum esse deum simpliciter et per naturam, a quo sunt omnia, qui est pater ille invisibilis, deus deorum, et unum dominum Jesum christum, filium eius visibilem, per quem sunt omnia dominum et deum a patre super omnia constitutum, ut in sequente libro plenius demonstrabitur ubi de filii deitate copiose tractabimus.

Vis adhuc clarius et apertius testimonium ipsius christi de seipso loquentis, hæc est autem voluntas eius qui misit me patris, ut omnis qui videt filium, et credit in eum, habeat vitam æternam, quid hic respondebunt nostri Theologi, qui dicunt filium dei esse invisibilem, forte arguent christum de mendacio, aut dicent illum per communicationem improprie esse locutum. O Miseram Theologiam, Audi Irenæum de visibili filio dei sanctissime loquentem, lib. III. cap. 9. Unus igitur et idem deus est pater domini nostri, qui et præcursorem per prophetas missurum se promisit et salutare suum idest verbum suum visibile effecit omni fieri carni, incarnatum et ipsum, ut in omnibus manifestus fieret rex eorum, etenim oportebat ea quæ iudicantur suum videre iudicem, et ea quæ gloriam consequuntur oportebat scire eum qui munus gloriæ eis donat et ideo scriptum est videbit omnis caro salutare dei nostri, quod cum vidisset [48] Simeon, obdormivit in pace, quod et Thomas vidit ac palpavit.

Rursus hunc dei filium visibilem et palpabilem clarissime attestatur Johannes cuius verba cavillari non possunt, quod erat ab initio, quod audivimus, quod vidimus oculis nostris, et manus nostræ palpaverunt, de verbo vitæ ut societas nostra sit cum patre et filio eius Jesu christo, cuius sanguis emundat nos ab omni peccato, ecce quomodo Johannes vere audivit vidit et palpavit filium dei passibilem, qui est verbum vitæ, unde et paulo post ait

The obvious cause of so palpable an error is that [the theologians] never learned to distinguish between God the Father and the Son of God, but rashly assumed that each had the same substance and nature. They took both to be the same God, in being and number, not realizing that the whole of scripture sets forth one thing as the most satisfactory foundation of truth: that there is by nature only *one* indivisible *God, from whom all things are*, the invisible Father, God of gods. *And* that there is *one Lord Jesus Christ, through whom all things are*,[a] his visible Son, established by the Father as Lord and God over all things. This will be more fully demonstrated in the following book, where we will discuss the divinity of the Son more extensively.

Would you like to hear, more clearly and more plainly, Christ's own testimony about himself? *"For this is the will of the Father who sent me, that everyone who sees the Son and believes in him should have eternal life."*[b] What will our theologians, who say that the Son of God is invisible, reply to this? Perhaps they will argue that Christ was lying, or that he had spoken idiosyncratically by means of *communicatio* [*idiomatum*]. O wretched theology! Listen to Irenaeus, in book 3, chapter 9, speaking in the saintliest manner about the visible Son of God:

> The Father of our Lord, therefore, is the one and the same God who, through the prophets, promised to send a forerunner[c] and also made his salvation – that is, his Word – visible to all flesh. [The Word] itself was incarnate, so that in all things their king would be revealed. For it is necessary for those who are going to be judged to see their judge, and for those who attain glory to know who gives them the gift of glory.[d]

Thus it was written, *All flesh shall see the salvation of our God*.[e] When Simeon beheld this, he died in peace.[f] Thomas also saw and felt this.[g]

This [is the] visible and palpable Son of God, whom John most clearly attests, at whose words [the theologians] cannot quibble:

> *That which was from the beginning, which we have heard, which we have seen with our eyes, and touched with our hands, concerning the word of life* – that *our fellowship is with the Father and his Son, Jesus Christ,* whose *blood cleanses us from all sin*.[h]

See how John truly heard, saw, and felt the suffering Son of God, who is the word of life. Whence a little later he says:

---

[a] 1 Cor. 8:6. [b] John 6:39-40. [c] John the Baptist. See John 3:28. [d] Irenaeus, *Adv. Hær.* 3.9.1 (PG 7a 869B-870A). [e] Luke 3:6, referring to Isa. 40:5. [f] Luke 2:29. [g] John 20:27. [h] 1 John 1:1,3,7.

in hoc aparuit charitas dei in nobis, quod filium suum unigenitum misit deus in mundum, ut vivamus per eum, in hoc est charitas non quod nos dilexerimus deum, sed quod ipse dilexerit nos et misit filium suum propitiationem pro peccatis nostris. Deum nemo vidit unquam, sed ex hoc cognoscimus quod in eo manemus et ipse in nobis quoniam de spiritu suo dedit nobis, et nos vidimus, et testamur quod pater misit filium servatorem mundi, et quisque confessus fuerit, quod Jesus est filius dei, deus in eo manet, et ipse in deo. Nota diligenter O christiane omnia supradicta verba Joannis et manifestissime cognosces eum loqui de filio dei visibili passibili Jesu christo servatore, et miraberis quomodo Theologi nostri tam apertas scripturas tam manifesta testimonia de Jesu redemptore negaverint, qui tum omnia fecit omnia meruit [49] omnia confirmavit, extra quem non est salus. Sed quid plura, numne etiam demones ipsi hanc veritatem aperte fateri coacti sunt? quid tibi et nobis Jesu filii dei, venisti ante tempus torquere nos, item si filius dei es, dic ut lapides isti panes fiant, sciebat enim sathan Messiam venturum, esse filium dei, sed quisnam esset ignorabat, et de Jesu plusquam de ullo alio homine dubitavit, ac timuit, et ideo accessit ad eum ut tentaret et periculum faceret, si aliquo modo, aut ratione, posset expertis indiciis cognoscere, illum esse, sed ita prudenter a Christo reiectus et elusus fuit, ut nihil certi de illo tunc expiscari aut assequi potuerit.

 Pudet iam me in re tam clara et indubitata, tot rationibus et argumentis insistere, sed ingens raritas et ignorantia seu potius protervia, et obstinatio, nostrorum temporum ad hoc me compellit.

 Aplicabo igitur adhuc figuram abrahæ, et isaac ad immolandum oblati, quis enim dubitat quin deus, in persona Isaac filii abrahæ unigeniti, sacrificium et immolationem dilectissimi sui unigeniti præfigurare voluerit, quorsum attinebat tentare Abraham de immolando unico filio, quem deus iam in omni opere et consilio promptum ac fidelem invenerat nisi ut misterium redemptionis in Jesu christo filio designaret, quem pater ipse clementissimus, volentem et obsequentem, hostiam obtulit mundam et immaculatam, pro mundi reconciliatione, et expiatione omnium peccatorum,

BOOK 3

In this the love of God has appeared to us, that God sent his only begotten Son into the world, so that we might live through him. In this is love, not that we loved God but that he loved us and sent his Son to be the expiation for our sins. No one has ever seen God; but by this we know that we abide in him and he in us, because he has given us of his own Spirit. And we have seen and testify that the Father has sent his Son as the savior of the world. And whoever confesses that Jesus is the Son of God, God abides in him, and he in God.[a]

Note carefully, Christian, all the words of John [above], and you will undoubtedly recognize that he is speaking about the visible, suffering Son of God, the savior, Jesus Christ.

You will wonder at how our theologians have rejected such clear statements and such obvious testimony about Jesus Christ, the redeemer, who accomplished everything, gained everything, and secured everything, outside of whom there is no salvation. But why say more? Were not the demons themselves compelled to openly acknowledge this truth? *"What have you to do with us, Jesus, Son of God? Have you come to torment us before the time?"*[b] Likewise, *"If you are the Son of God, command these stones to become loaves of bread."*[c] For Satan knew that the Messiah to come was the Son of God, although he did not know precisely who he was. He was more anxious and fearful about Jesus than any other man. For that reason, he approached him in order to tempt him and put him to the test, to see if, by some means, he might be able to recognize him by reliable evidence. He was, however, so skillfully rebuffed and frustrated by Christ that he was unable to elicit anything useful from him.[d]

Now, I am ashamed to go on and on with so many arguments and so much reasoning in a matter so clear and indisputable. However, the extreme oddity and ignorance, or rather, the impudence and obstinacy, of our times, forces me to do so.

I shall, therefore, touch here on the allegorical figure of Abraham, and [his son] Isaac, who was offered as a sacrifice.[e] Who doubts that, in the person of Isaac, the only son of Abraham, God wished to prefigure the sacrifice and offering up of his best beloved and only begotten son? What was God's purpose in testing Abraham, whom he had already found to be ready and loyal in every thought and deed, [by commanding] the sacrifice of his only son, unless it was to indicate the mystery of redemption in Jesus Christ the Son [of God], whom the most merciful Father offered as a willing and obedient sacrificial victim, pure and *without blemish*, for the reconciliation of the world and the atonement of all sins?[f]

---

[a] 1 John 4:9-15.   [b] Matt. 8:29.   [c] Matt. 4:3.   [d] Matt. 4:1-11.   [e] Gen. 22:1-18.   [f] Lev. 1:3-4.

neque hinc armare se possunt hæretici dicentes filium dei passum [50] non esse, sed aliud corpus pro eo, a patre inssertum, velut in Isaac præmonstratum fuit, sed miræ nugæ sunt oportuit enim filium dei pati, Isaac autem pati non oportebat, sed sacrificium filii præfigurando deus bonam voluntatem Abrahæ pro sancto reputavit.

Ad idem argumentum accipe manifestam parabolam Jesu christi, paterfamilias plantavit vineam, et locavit agricolas, postea misit servos ut fructus suos acciperent, illis vero occisis, tandem misit filium suum unigenitum, quem velut heredem similiter occiderunt, et cognoverunt Judæi quod de se diceret, ecce quoniam christus aperte se filium dei significavit, et se post prophetas et servos occisos ut filium et heredem ab eis occidendum prænuntiavit. Nostri vero Theologi dicunt filium dei non esse passum, sed filium virginis tantum. O stulti et tardi nunc indurati corde ad credendum, nonne oportuit christum idest dei filium pati, et ita intrare in gloriam suam. Numne agnus dei occisus est, et nos per sanguinem suum redemit, quid aliud commemorat scriptura, quam admirabile illud clementissimi dei erga nos beneficium, et ineffabilem charitatem, ut filium suum proprium et unigenitum pro nobis dederit, et sic filio proprio ut paul inquit non pepercit sed pro nobis omnibus tradidit illum quomodo non omnia nobis cum illo donabit. Item gratias agentes patri qui eripuit nos a potestate tenebrarum et transtulit in regnum filii sibi dilecti per quem habemus redemptionem per [51] sanguinem suum remissionem peccatorum.

Et petrus Astiterunt reges terræ et principes convenerunt in unum adversus dominum, et adversus christum eius, convenerunt enim vere adversus sanctum filium tuum Jesum quem unxeras, Herodes simul et pontius pilatus cum gentibus et populis isræl ad faciendum quæcumque manus tua, et consilium tuum prius decreverat ut fierent. Item paulus: qui semel fuerunt illuminati et sancti spiritus participes facti si prolabantur denuo sibi ipsis filium dei crucifigunt, et Johannes sanguis filii dei emundat nos ab omni peccato infinita hic adduci possent quæ passim occurrunt, quid igitur dicemus?

The heretics cannot defend themselves by saying that the Son of God did not suffer, and that instead some other body was substituted in his place by the Father, as was foreshadowed in the story of Isaac. This is utter nonsense. It was indeed necessary for the Son of God to suffer. It was not, however, necessary for Isaac to suffer, for, in prefiguring the sacrifice of his [own] son, God credited Abraham's willingness to sacrifice his son as a pious act.

Carrying the argument further, consider this straightforward parable of Jesus Christ. *A landowner planted a vineyard and left it in the charge of tenant farmers. Afterwards he sent his servants to collect his fruit*, but [the tenants] killed them. *Finally he sent his* only *son. But, since he was the heir, they killed him* as well.[a] Then the Jews *perceived that* Christ *was speaking about them*.[b] See how he made it plainly known that he was the Son of God, and foretold that, after *the prophets and servants* [of the Lord] had been slain,[c] he himself, as the son and heir, would be killed by them. But our theologians say that it is only the son of the Virgin who suffers, not the Son of God. O you slow-witted dullards, whose hearts are hardened in disbelief!

Was it not *necessary that Christ* – that is, the Son of God – *should suffer and enter into his glory*?[d] Was not the Lamb of God killed, and did he not *redeem us by his blood*?[e] What else does scripture record but the most merciful God's wondrous gift to us: that *he gave his* own *only begotten Son for us.*[f] *He did not spare his own Son*, as Paul says, *but gave him up for us all. Will he not also give us all things with him?*[g] Also, *giving thanks to the Father, who has delivered us from the power of darkness and brought us into the kingdom of his beloved Son, through whom we have redemption through his blood, the forgiveness of sins.*[h]

Furthermore Peter said,

"*The kings of the earth rose up, and the rulers were gathered together, against the Lord and against his Anointed* [Christ]," *for truly Herod and also Pontius Pilate, along with the Gentiles and the peoples of Israel, were gathered together against your holy Son Jesus, whom you anointed, to do whatever your hand and your plan had decreed to take place.*[i]

And Paul: *Those who have once been enlightened and have become partakers of the Holy Spirit, if they should fall away again, they crucify the Son of God in themselves.*[j] And John: *The blood of the Son* of God *cleanses us from all sins.*[k] Innumerable examples, scattered throughout the Bible, could be mentioned. What more need we say?

---

[a] Matt. 21:33-39. [b] Matt. 21:45. [c] 2 Kings 9:7. [d] Luke 24:26. [e] Rev. 5:9. [f] John 3:16. [g] Rom. 8:32.
[h] Col. 1:12-14. "Through his blood" is an ancient interpolation to match Eph. 1:7.
[i] Acts 4:26-28, quoting Ps 2:2. [j] Heb. 6:4-6. [k] 1 John 1:9.

Nugatur ne scriptura persuadens nobis deum filium suum proprium et unigenitum pro maximo beneficio et dilectionis argumento donasse ut pro peccatis nostris moreretur, si revera filius eius non fuit sed virginis tantum, quod beneficium? quæ charitas? quæ dilectio fuisset? alienum filium pro suo tam acerbis supliciis exponere. Numne hoc esset nobis imponere et arietem pro Isaac substituere quam vero gratiam fidem vel honorem filio dei deberemus? Si in passione avolavit solum filium hominis in angustiis derelinquens ut inquit Irenæus, O impias filosophorum traditiones O nefandas scripturarum interpretationes Sic ne Theosophistæ purissima eloquia depravarunt? Sic ne sacrosancta illius misteria nobis explicarunt, ut nihil tuti nihil certi [52] nihil vere aut proprie ex scripturis habere possit, sed omnia improprie sophistice et abusive intelligentes, ita ut universa scriptura de deo, de patre, de filio, de christo, loquens semper nobis imponat, semper unum dicens et aliud intelligi volens, i enim scriptura simpliciter et diserte testatur, deum misericordem proprium et unigenitum filium suum pro nobis morti destinasse et ex hoc immensa eius in nos benignitas commendatur, quæ blasphemia et impietas est tam apertam scripturam pervertere, et sophisticis interpretationibus tantum dei beneficium obscurare, si scriptura aperte dicit Christum filium dei esse et oportuisse christum pati quæ temeritas tam sinceram et expeditam locutionem cavillari quorsum attinebat verbum dei incarnari, nisi ut visibile et passibile fieret, et pro miserrimo homine divinæ iustitiæ satisfaceret, immo neque redemptio neque reconciliatio, inter hominem et deum fieri potuisset, neque ullo modo divinæ iustitiæ satisfieri nisi per sanguinem et mortem filii dei qui solus fuit, agnus ille sanctus mundus et immaculatus et hostia acceptabilis in conspectu sui patris, cum tamen nulla creatura mundi neque etiam angeli ipsi in conspectu dei mundi sint, et adeo neque per angelos aut aliam creaturam tale ac tantum misterium redemptionis peragi potuisset, cum noxa esset infinita et infinitem requireret satisfactionem, [53] quæ non nisi a dei filio præstari potuit.

Is scripture talking nonsense when it persuades us that God gave his own only begotten son to die for our sins, as the greatest act of kindness and proof of his love? If in truth [Jesus] was not his son, but only the Virgin's, where was the kindness shown? Where was the love? What kind of love would it have been to expose somebody else's son to such bitter punishment in the place of his own? Would not this have been deceiving us, like substituting a ram for Isaac? What gratitude, faith, or honor should we owe the Son of God, if in the Passion he took flight, leaving behind the Son of man alone in dire straits, as Irenaeus says?[a] What impious philosophical teachings! What wicked interpretations of the scriptures! Have not the theological sophists distorted the purest of words? Have they not so explained these most holy mysteries to us that nothing is secure or certain, that nothing can be truly and correctly obtained from scripture? Instead they understand everything peculiarly, sophistically, and perversely, so that all of scripture is always deceiving us when it speaks of God, the Father, the Son, and Christ, forever saying one thing and meaning another.

If, indeed, as scripture simply and eloquently bears witness, our merciful God destined his own only begotten Son to die for us, thus showing his boundless kindness toward us, it is blasphemy and impiety to pervert such clear scriptural testimony and to obscure so great a blessing from God with sophistical interpretations. For if scripture plainly calls Christ the Son of God and says that it was necessary for Christ to suffer, it is rash to take issue with such sincere and uncomplicated speech.

What purpose did it serve for the *Word* of God to be *made flesh*,[b] unless it became visible, capable of suffering, and able to satisfy divine justice on behalf of wretched man? Indeed, neither redemption nor reconciliation between man and God was possible, nor could divine justice be satisfied, except through the blood and death of the Son of God, who alone was the holy *lamb, pure and spotless,*[c] and *a victim acceptable* in the sight of his Father.[d] Since no creatures on earth, not even the angels themselves, *are clean in the sight of* God,[e] such a great mystery as redemption could not have been accomplished by the angels or by any other creature. For the degree of sin was infinite and required an infinite degree of satisfaction, which could only be provided by the Son of God.

---

a Paraphrase of Irenaeus, Adv. Hær. 3.18.6 (PG 7a 936B-C).   b John 1:14.   c 1 Peter 1:19.
d See Lev. 22:20, 1 Peter 2:5.   e Job 15:15.

Ego quidem neque redemptum neque deo reconciliatum me esse crederem, nisi per verum dei filium redemptio et reconciliatio facta fuisset, et in hoc solo articulo fides nostra et æterna vita consistit. Quid profuisset Petro Marthæ et aliis apostolis ac discipulis Jesu christi, credere et confiteri eum esse verum dei filium nisi etiam credidissent eundemmet dei filium misterium redemptionis peregisse, sed audi hic ridiculam nostrorum Theologorum expositionem dicunt enim dei filium passum esse per communicationem idiomatum, sed longe aliter sensit ipse dei filius qui rogabat patrem ut calix ille a se transiret, et dicebat animam suam, tristem et mestam esse usque ad mortem. Dico igitur quod verus dei filius vere et proprie passus est in corpore suo acerbissimos dolores et cruciatus horrendæ mortis, ut omnis scriptura testatur, immo fortius dicere audeo quod iustissimus deus nunquam alium filium pro satisfactione aliorum ad tam crudele supplicium destinasset nec unquam alienum filium tanta sibi charitate obsequentem invenisset suum igitur verum proprium et unigenitum filium non alienum nobis donavit iustissimus et clementissimus pater.

Err. 4a   Circa vero hunc articulum de Jesu christo visibili et passibili dei filio qui est vere fidei et relligionis fundamentum, non tantopere institissem neque in re tam clara et aperta tot authoritatibus, rationibus, argumentis, et exemplis, laborassem, sed quia quorundam mentes adeo corruptas video ut [54] etiam ad radios solis caligent et veritatem neque audire neque intelligere velint, quorum damnatio iusta est atque utinam soli ipsi delirarent nec alios secum in præcipitium traherent sua perversa dogmata et inventiones pro Christi evangelio obtrudentes et hoc est mirabile in oculis nostris quoniam græcanica illa philosophia statim a tempore Apostolorum tantum invaluerit et ita nostrorum Theologorum mentes fascinaverit ut relicto penitus fundamento evangelicæ veritatis, quod est Jesus christus dei filius crucifixus ad nescio quas hypostases et deorum multitudinem sine scriptura diverterint quæ nunquam ab ullo intelligi vel explicari potuerunt.

Indeed, I could not believe that I was either redeemed or reconciled to God unless that redemption and reconciliation had been brought about by the true Son of God. Our faith and eternal life depend upon this single article of belief. What good would it have done Peter, Martha, and the other apostles and disciples of Jesus Christ, to believe in him and confess him to be the true Son of God, unless they also believed that that same Son of God had accomplished the mystery of redemption?

Now hear the ridiculous explanation of our theologians. They claim that the Son of God suffered by means of *communicatio idiomatum*. However, the Son of God himself felt quite differently. *He prayed* to his *Father* that *the cup would pass from* him and said that his *soul was sorrowful*, saddened *even unto death*.[a] I say, therefore, that the true Son of God himself really suffered the bitterest of pains in his own body and was crucified – a horrible death – as the whole of scripture testifies. Furthermore, I am prepared to maintain firmly that the infinitely just God would never have intended another son to suffer such cruel punishment in order to pay the penalty for others, nor could he ever have found another son so loving and obedient to him. Thus, the most just and merciful Father gave us his true and only begotten son, and no one else.

I would not have so insisted on this article of faith about Jesus Christ being the visible and suffering Son of God, which is truly the foundation of faith and religion, nor labored on a matter so clear and obvious, using so many authorities, reasons, arguments, and examples, if I had not seen that the minds of certain people are so corrupted that they are blind, even to the rays of the sun, and wish neither to hear nor to understand the truth. Their damnation is justified – would that they were alone in their madness, and not dragging others with them over the precipice, pushing forward their own perverse dogmas and inventions in place of the gospel of Christ!

It seems amazing that, ever since the time of the apostles, this Greekish philosophy has grown so powerful and has so fascinated the minds of our theologians that, having thoroughly abandoned the foundation of gospel truth, which is Jesus Christ, the Son of God crucified, they have turned away from scripture to I know not what hypostases and a multitude of gods. No one has ever been able to comprehend or explain these things.

---

[a] Matt. 26:38-39, Mark 14:34,36, Luke 22,42.

Quid aliud sonat universa scriptura? quid aliud prophetæ et apostoli annuntiarunt quæ est alia vita æterna quam cum paulo vase electionis, credere unum solum Deum æternum invisibilem qui est pater ille a quo omnia et unum dei filium dominum Jesum christum crucifixum per quem omnia. Numne et ipsa veritas hoc idem expressit, hæc est vita æterna ut cognoscant te pater solum deum verum et quem misisti Jesum Christum quid clarius? quid sincerius? et explicatius? per quam aliam doctrinam vel prædicationem tot millia hominum quotidie ab apostolis ad veram fidem et relligionem convertebantur? forte per prædicationem de tribus personis seu hypostasibus vel idiomatum communicatione aut de naturis et suppositis connotativis similibusque nugis sophisticis quæ tam comune habent cum evangelio quam evangelium [55] cum alcharano? An vero magis de uno illo Jesu Nazareno crucifixo viro sanctissimo, quod is esset verus Christus dei filius servator mundi et redemptor humani generis verbum dei incarnatum visibile et passibile factum.

Quod si Jesus ille visibilis (ut isti dicunt) filius dei non erat, sed logos ille invisibilis qui ei assistebat cum scriptura nunquam ad logon seu verbum illud incorporeum filiationem retulit nec unquam dixit patrem verbi nec verbum filium dei, sed ad Jesum hominem semper retulit filiationem, dicens deum patrem Jesu christi et Jesum Christum filium dei qui immo Johannes ut omnem tolleret de filiatione hominis dubitationem signanter dixit quis est qui vincit mundum nisi qui credit quod Jesus est filius dei, Jesum simpliciter dixit quod est proprium nomen hominis verbo invisibili nequaquam conveniens, proinde nescio qua ratione Theologi nostri hanc interpretationem communiter et mordicus acceperint quod scilicet scriptura semper improprie et abusive loquatur numne saltem semel de patre et filio loquens vere et proprie dicere potuisset deum patrem verbi et verbum filium dei. Numne Christus qui est ipsa veritas saltem semel vel cum Judæis vel cum discipulis suis loquendo, vel tunc maxime cum a pontifice fuit adiuratus, ut diceret si ipse erat filius dei viventis, hanc communicationem idiomatum aperuisset et vere ac proprie dixisset filius dei qui in me est aut mecum est aut verbum dei, quod in me loquitur, aut filius quem pater ad me misit et [56] similes locutiones quæ fuissent veræ, propriæ et apertæ,

What does scripture as a whole mean – what did the prophets and apostles proclaim – and what is eternal life, except to believe, with Paul, the *chosen vessel*,[a] that *there is only one* unseen eternal *God, the Father, from whom all things are, and one* Son of God, the *Lord Jesus Christ* crucified, *through whom all things are*?[b] Has not truth itself [Christ] expressed this very thing: "*This is eternal life, that they know you, Father, the only true God, and Jesus Christ, whom you have sent.*"[c] What could be clearer? What could be more truthful? By what other doctrine or preaching were so many thousands of people daily converted to the true faith and religion? Was it perhaps by preaching about three persons or hypostases, or about *communicatio idiomatum*, or about natures, connotative *supposita*, and such sophistical trifles, which have as little in common with the gospel as the gospel has with the Quran? Or was it not truly about that holiest of men, the one Jesus of Nazareth crucified? He is the true Christ, the Son of God, the Savior of the world, the redeemer of the human race, and the Word of God incarnate, made visible and capable of suffering.

How can they claim that it was not the visible Jesus, but rather the invisible *Logos* standing beside him, that was the Son of God? For scripture never refers to the *Logos* or the Word as a different, incorporeal sonship, nor ever speaks of the Father of the Word, or the Word as the Son of God, but always refers to sonship in terms of Jesus the human being, saying, God the Father of Jesus Christ and Jesus Christ, the Son of God. In order to remove all doubt about the sonship of the man, John distinctly said, *Who is it that overcomes the world but he who believes that Jesus is the Son of God?*[d] He simply said Jesus, which is a man's proper name and completely unsuited to an invisible Word.

Furthermore, on the basis of I know not what reasoning, our theologians have on the whole tenaciously maintained this interpretation, by which it would seem that scripture always speaks in a twisted and inappropriate way. But would not [scripture] at least once, when talking about the Father and the Son, have truly and properly said that God is the Father of the Word, and that the Word is the Son of God? And would not Christ, who is truth itself – either when speaking to the Jews or to his own disciples, and, most of all, when the high priest solemnly asked him if he was the Son of the living God[e] – have revealed this *communicatio idiomatum* at least once, by truly and correctly stating, "the Son of God who is in me" or "with me," or "the Word of God which speaks in me," or "the Son whom the Father sent to me," or similar phrases, which in that case would have been true, accurate, and clear?

---

[a] Acts 9:15. [b] 1 Cor. 8:6. [c] John 17:3. [d] 1 John 5:5. [e] Matt. 26:63, Mark 14:61.

non autem seipsum visibilem palam et simpliciter dei filium appellare improprie et abusive loquendo et et veri filii titulum sibi usurpando a quo (secundum istos) sustentabatur ac rogabatur, homo enim loquebatur et homo filium dei se esse dicebat quis autem tales scripturas abusivas sophisticas et fallaces unquam probaret?

Iam igitur vides quantum Theologi nostri propter suam inanem philosophiam ab apostolorum doctrina et evangelica luce recesserint universam scripturam suis erroneis commentis penitus obscurantes, quæ tamen per se planissima est etiam mulierculis patens unum tantum misterium salutis complectens et id quidem simplicissime scilicet, Jesum illum Nazarenum hominem visibilem palpabilem et crucifixum vere Christum et dei filium esse, redemptorem nostrum dominum et deum nostrum et beatus qui hoc crediderit et in hac petra firmus permanserit in qua scio non permansuros omnes qui suas falsas et impias opiniones contra Jesum christum conceptas et radicatas indurato corde et pertinaci spiritu defendere conabuntur, nam dei veritas et sana Jesu christi notitia non ambitione spiritus, sed humilitate cordis acquiritur præsertim ab iis qui non suam sed domini sui gloriam quærunt.

Relicta igitur hac secundaria ecclesia suis philosophicis inventionibus turgida, sanctam et apostolorum illam [57] primitivam sequamur quæ nihil de istis hypostasibus idomatibus aut connotativis sciebat sed solum Jesum Christum dei filium crucifixum in cuius nomine et non alterius filii vel personæ vitam æternam sperabat. Si enim nos homunciones per fidem in Jesum Christum crucifixum filii dei efficimur et nominamur, quid amplius quam nos haberet ipse Jesus Christus, homo sanctissimus et electissimus nisi esset verus et naturalis dei filius qui est author nostræ filiationis in deo, igitur quando de ipso Jesu filio fit mentio proponi solet articulus et dicitur hic est ille filius dei ad denotandum eum non generali et communi appellatione filium dici ut nos, sed peculiari quadam et magis propria ratione

Err. 9a

Instead, according to them, speaking in a twisted and inappropriate way, he plainly and simply called his visible self the Son of God. And he would also have been usurping the title of the true Son for himself, from [the Word] which employed and sustained him, because it was a man who spoke and a man who said that he was the Son of God. But who would prove such scriptures to be false, sophistical, and perverse?

Now, therefore, you can see how far our theologians, with their empty philosophy, have fallen away from the teaching of the apostles and the light of the gospel, and utterly obscured the whole of scripture with their erroneous fabrications. Nonetheless, [what scripture teaches] is, in itself, most plainly apparent, even to ordinary women. Although it encompasses so great a mystery as salvation, it is as simple as can be: that Jesus of Nazareth crucified, visible and palpable, is truly the Christ and the Son of God, our redeemer, *our Lord and our God*.[a] Whoever believes this and remains steadfast on this rock is blessed. However I am convinced that all those who stubbornly attempt to defend their false and impious opinions, conceived and rooted in their hardened hearts, in opposition to Jesus Christ, will not remain on [this rock]. For God's truth and a sound understanding of Jesus Christ is gained, not through spiritual ambition, but in humility of heart, and especially by those who seek not their own glory, but the glory of their Lord.[b]

Leaving behind the second-rate church [of the present day], with its turgid philosophical inventions, let us follow the holy, primitive church of the apostles, which knew nothing about those hypostases, [*communicatio*] *idiomatum*, or connotatives, but only about Jesus Christ crucified, the Son of God, in whose name, and not in that of another son or person, it hoped for eternal life. If indeed, through our faith in Jesus Christ crucified, diminutive creatures like us are made and called sons of God, what more would Jesus Christ, that holiest and most chosen of men, have us believe, but that he is the true and natural Son of God and the one responsible for our own sonship in God?

Therefore, when Jesus himself, the Son of God, is mentioned, the [definite] article is usually placed before [his name], as in, "This is the Son of God."[7] Thus he is not called by the ordinary and generic term "son" as we are, but must be denoted in a certain special and more appropriate way.

---

[a] Rev. 4:11.   [b] A possible reference to Ps. 115:1 and the Latin hymn based on it, *Non nobis*.

Err. 9a-b siquidem nos non naturales filii neque filii originis dicimur, sed filii dei efficimur per adoptionem, ipsum vero Christum facere adoptivum impietas est Bonosianorum nam de Jesu non legitur talis adoptio, sed vero a deo patre generatio ideoque verus proprius et naturalis dei filius est et verus hæres, caput et deus ipse non minus proprie dicitur patrem immo magis proprie deus pater Jesu dicendus est quam alii quia ipse in aliorum omnium generatione sua admirabili providentia et virtute concurrit in generatione autem Jesu christi filii sui ipse solus deus operatus est citra alterius patris aut genitoris concursum. Si igitur Altissimus deus pro beneplacito [58] voluntatis suæ ac implemento æterni consilii sui filium sibi

Err. 9b visibilem generare voluit et in eius generatione solus operatus est quare non æque proprie illius filii pater dicetur sicut terreni patres filiorum suorum, nunquid ego qui generationem aliis tribuo ipse sterilis ero dicit dominus, deus ergo qui solo verbo mundum ex nihilo creavit et primum hominem ex luto fecit, non potuit alium hominem ex verbo suo et divino semine sibi generare? Immo in hoc admirabile suæ potentiæ, virtutis et perfectionis thesauros patefecit quos creavit, fecit, et genuit quorum enim effectuum excellentissimus omnium fuit filii hominis generatio qui fuit complementum et consumatio omnium operum et consiliorum dei patris in quo deus ipse sibi bene complacuit per quem et propter quem omnia alia facta et creata sunt.

Unus est ergo deus qui est pater ipse et unus dei filius Jesus Christus crucifixus ipsius dei verbum corporatum visibile et passibile factum cui sit honor et gloria in sempiterna sæcula.

For we ourselves are not called natural sons, or sons by direct descent, but are made sons of God by adoption. To say that the true Christ himself was adopted is the impiety of the Bonosians.[8] For we do not read that Jesus was adopted in such a way, but rather that he was truly begotten by God the Father. Therefore the true, very own, and natural Son of God is the true heir, the head. And God himself is no less properly called the Father.

Certainly God is more properly said to be the father of Jesus than of others, because, although he plays a role in the begetting of everyone else through his wonderful providence and power, in the begetting of his son Jesus Christ, God was acting alone, without the cooperation of any other father or begetter. If, therefore, God the Most High, according to the gracious purpose of his will and in fulfillment of his eternal plan, wished to beget a visible son for himself, and acted alone in begetting him, why should he not be called the father of that son just as properly as earthly fathers are of their sons? *"Can it be that I, who grant procreation to others, shall myself be sterile?" says the Lord.*[a] Was God, who created the world out of nothingness by the Word alone and made the first man from clay, not able to beget for himself another man by means of his Word and his divine seed? In this wondrous way he revealed the treasures of his potency, might, and perfection. And the most outstanding accomplishment of all was the begetting of the Son of man, in whom God himself was well pleased, *through whom and by whom all* other *things* were made and created,[b] and who was the fulfillment and consummation of all the works and plans of God the Father.

There is, therefore, *one God*, who is *the Father, and one* Son of God, *Jesus Christ* crucified,[c] *the Word* of God *made flesh*,[d] visible and capable of suffering, to whom *be honor and glory for ever and ever.*[e]

---

[a] Isa. 66:9 (Vulgate). [b] Heb. 2:10. [c] 1 Cor. 8:6. [d] John 1:14. [e] 1 Tim. 1:17, Rev. 5:13.

Declarationis Jesu Christi, per Michælem Servetum, liber quartus

Nunc venio ad tertiam conclusionem initio huius operis, propositum scilicet Jesum illum christum visibilem dei filium verum deum nostrum esse, et primo ut clare ostenditur.

Err. 9b-10a

Nam cum sit dei filius et [59] ab ipso deo genitus rationem deitatis ab ipso accepisse palam est. Est enim deus de deo, lumen de lumine deus verus de deo vero. Etenim Christus secundum hominem interiorem sonat quid divinum ex interna divinitus sibi facta unctione. Unde Esaias de christo loquens et requiescet super eum spiritus domini spiritus sapientiæ et intellectus, spiritus consilii et fortitudinis, spiritus scientiæ et pietatis et replebit eum spiritus timoris domini, et iterum ecce servus meus suscipiam eum, electus meus complacuit sibi in illo anima mea, dedi spiritum meum super eum, et David etiam de Christo loquens propterea unxit te deus, deus tuus oleo lætitiæ præ consortibus tuis, item Esa. Spiritus domini super me eoque unxerit me evangelizare pauperibus et mansuetis, et Daniel Septuaginta hebdomades abreviatæ sunt super populum tuum et super urbem sanctam tuam ut consummetur prævaricatio et finem accipiat peccatum et deleatur iniquitas et adducatur justitia sempiterna et impleatur visio et prophetia et ungatur sanctus sanctorum, et petrus in actis Convenerunt vere adversus sanctum filium tuum quem unxisti. Item anuntians pacem per Jesum Christum, hic est omnium dominus ipsi nostis post baptisma quod prædicabat Joannes ut Jesum Nazarenum unxerit deus spiritu sancto,

A Revelation of Jesus Christ by Michael Servetus
Book 4

I come now to the third proposition, advanced at the outset of this work, namely, that Jesus Christ, the visible Son of God, is our true God. I will now show this clearly.

As he is the Son of God, and begotten by God, the nature of the divinity he received from [God] is obvious. He is indeed "God of God, light of light, true God of true God."[a] For, *in terms of his inmost self,*[b] "Christ" means something divine, the result of an internal anointing by God. Wherefore Isaiah, in speaking of Christ, says, *And the Spirit of the Lord shall rest upon him, the spirit of wisdom and understanding, the spirit of counsel and might; the spirit of knowledge and piety. And the spirit of the fear of the Lord will fill him.*[c] And also, *Behold my servant, I will uphold him, my chosen. My soul has delighted in him. I have put my spirit upon him.*[d]

Likewise David, speaking of Christ, says, *Therefore God, your God anointed you with the oil of gladness, above your fellows.*[e] And Isaiah says, *The Spirit of the Lord is upon me, and therefore [the Lord] has anointed me to preach the good news to the* poor and the meek.[f]

Daniel says, *Seventy weeks are decreed concerning your people and your holy city, to finish the transgression, to put an end to sin, and to erase iniquity, to bring in everlasting righteousness, to fulfill the vision and the prophecy, and to anoint the holy of holies.*[g]

In Acts Peter says, "*Truly they were gathered together against your holy Son, whom you have anointed,*"[h] and also, "*preaching peace through Jesus Christ (he is Lord of all), you know what John* [the Baptist] *preached after the baptism* [of Jesus], *that God anointed Jesus of Nazareth with the Holy Spirit.*"[i]

---

[a] From the Nicene Creed.   [b] Rom. 7:22.   [c] Isa. 11:2-3 (Vulgate).   [d] Isa. 42:1.   [e] Ps. 45:7.   [f] Isa. 61:1.
[g] Dan. 9:24.   [h] Acts 4:27.   [i] Acts 10:36-38.

LIBER QUARTUS

Err. 9b-10a

Jesus ergo secundum Tertullianum [60] inventus est deus per virtutem et spiritum et homo per carnem quia quod natum est ex spiritu spiritus est et spiritus est deus et hac ratione idemmet Christus visibis* et indivisus vere homo est, sed virtute et spiritu deus. Communicata sibi a patre deitatis gratia, unde propheta dixit

Err. 10a, 11b, 13a

puer natus est nobis vocabitur nomen eius deus fortis vide quam perspicue et dei nomen et fortitudo illi puero nato tribuantur, item aput Esaiam et Matheum puer ille natus ex virgine vocatus est Immanuel idest nobiscum deus, et Thomas appellavit eum dominum et deum suum, et paulus vocat eum deum in omnibus laudandum et benedicendum, et Johannes ad differentiam deorum manium et simulachrorum eum verum deum appellat. Scimus inquit quod filius dei venit, et dedit nobis mentem ut cognoscamus illum qui verus est, et sumus in vero filio eius Jesu Christo hic est verus deus et vita æterna, filioli cavete vobis a simulacris.

Err. 10a

Præterea in multis scripturæ locis ostenditur eius divinitas quoniam de deo exaltatus fuit ut acciperet plenitudinem divinitatis et nomen super omne nomen, in quo omne genu curvetur cœlestium terrestrium et infernorum et adorent eum omnes alii dii et angeli dei. Data est enim illi a patre omnis potestas in cœlo et in terra et Thronus in sæculum sæculi et eum ad dexteram suam sedere fecit.

Err. 11b

Nam dignus est agnus qui occisus est accipere omnem divinitatem hoc est potentiam [61] divitias sapientiam fortitudinem honorem gloriam et benedictionem et repleri spiritu sancto gratia et veritate, Apocalip. 5 et Jo. 1. et in eo omnis divinitas a patre infusa corporaliter inhabitat, Collo. 2. qui declaratus fuit filius dei cum potentia secundum spiritum sanctificationis ex eo qui resurrexit a mortuis

Err. 11b

Jesus Christus dominus noster, Rom. 1. Quod si scriptura dicit Mosen fuisse factum deum pharaonis et Cyrum deum Israëlis per potentiam et superioritatem a Deo illis concessam quanto magis Jesus Christus verus dei filius factus erit et Thomæ et omnibus creaturis deus ac dominus, et ideo Petrus in actis, certo sciat tota domus Israhel quod dominum et Christum fecerit deus hunc Jesum quem vos crucifixistis,

---

* Should read *visibilis*.

Now, according to Tertullian, Jesus was found to be "God by virtue of [his] power and spirit," and "a man by virtue of [his] flesh."[a] Since *what is born of the Spirit is spirit*,[b] and *God is spirit*,[c] therefore Christ, visible and indivisible, although truly a man, is God in terms of his power and his spirit. The gift of deity was communicated to him by the Father, which is why the prophet said, *Unto us a child is born, his name will be called mighty God*.[d] See how both the name of God and his strength are manifestly bestowed on the newborn child. Again, in Isaiah and Matthew, the child born of a virgin is called *Emmanuel, that is, God with us*.[e] Thomas also called him his Lord and his God.[f] And Paul calls him *God to be* praised and *blessed in all things*.[g,1] John, differentiating him from idols and gods of the underworld, calls him the true God. *And we know*, he says, *that the son of God has come and has given us understanding so that we may know him who is true; and we are in his Son Jesus Christ. He is the true God and eternal life. Little children, keep yourselves from idols.*[h]

Furthermore [Christ's] divinity is revealed in many other passages in scripture: *Because he was exalted by God* that he might receive *the fullness of deity* and *the name which is above every name, to whom every knee should bow, in heaven and on earth and under the earth*,[i] and *let all the* other *gods* and *God's angels worship him*.[j,2] *All power in heaven and on earth has been given to him by the Father*,[k] and a *throne for ever and ever*;[l] he also *seated* him at his *right hand*.[m] For *worthy is the lamb who was slain to receive* all divinity, that is, *power and riches and wisdom and strength and honor and glory and blessing* (Revelation 5).[n] [He was] *filled* by the Holy Spirit with *grace and truth* (John 1).[o] And *in him the whole deity*, poured in by the Father, *dwells bodily* (Colossians 2).[p] He was *designated Son of God in power, according to the Spirit of holiness by his resurrection from the dead, Jesus Christ our Lord* (Romans 1).[q]

If scripture says that Moses was *made a god to Pharaoh*[r] and Cyrus *the God of Israel*,[s,3] through the power and superiority granted them by God, how much more will Jesus Christ be made the true Son of God, the God and Lord of Thomas[t] and of all creation. And thus Peter, in Acts, says, "*Let all the house of Israel know assuredly that God has made him both Lord and Christ, this Jesus, whom you crucified.*"[u]

---

[a] Tertullian, *Adversus Praxean* 21 (PL 2 181B).   [b] John 3:6.   [c] John 4:24.   [d] Isa. 9:6.   [e] Matt. 1:23, Isa. 7:14.
[f] John 20:28.   [g] Rom. 9:5.   [h] 1 John 5:20-21.   [i] Phil. 2:9-10, Col. 2:9.   [j] Heb. 1:6, quoting Ps. 97:7 (Septuagint).   [k] Matt. 28:18.   [l] Heb. 1:8.   [m] Eph. 1:20, Col. 3:1, Heb. 8:1, 10:12, 12:2, etc.   [n] Rev. 5:12.
[o] John 1:14.   [p] Col. 2:9.   [q] Rom. 1:4.   [r] Exod. 7:1.   [s] Isa. 45:3.   [t] See John 20:28.   [u] Acts 2:36.

sed Theologi nostri, non admittentes Jesum illum visibilem virum dei sanctissimum redemptorem nostrum esse dei filium et deum vocari, dixerunt hæc esse hypostasis illius invisibilis nomen, sed ratione unionis etiam ipsi Jesu Christo filio virginis communicari et ad hunc finem communis philosophorum scola illam communicationem idiomatum adinvenit egregiam sanæ totius scripturæ interpretationem quam nemo apostolus unquam scivit vel cogitavit.

Err. 10b

Audi eorum Theologiam Constituunt in christo duos filios et duplicem naturam distinctam alterum quidem invisibilem et impassibilem, scilicet verbum [62] illud dei incorporeum et hunc dicunt esse filium patris et eundemmet deum cum ipso patre licet sit diversa ab eodem persona aut hypostasis, et hic filius invisibilis secundum eos descendit in hominem adiungens et uniens se illi atque illum regens et sustentans.

Alterum vero purum hominem dicunt filium virginis tantum visibilem et passibilem qui ab invisibili regitur et sustentatur et cum scriptura dicit Jesum hominem esse filium dei vel deum non proprie loquitur, sed per quandam communicationem idiomatum et proprietatum ratione unius compositi seu agregati vel suppositi connotativi qui dicitur Christus similiter cum scriptura, dicit filium dei locutum, passum, mortuum et suscitatum, aiunt non proprie dici sed per eandem idiomatum communicationem, et sic filius dei sua nomina et proprietates filio virginis communicat et contra filius virginis sua nomina et passiones quo ad modum loquendi filio dei communicat et talis est inter eos unio et societas quomodo autem hi duo filii duplicis naturæ distinctæ in uno supposito vel agregato simul iungantur.

Item, quomodo et qua ratione sua prædicata sibi invicem communicent et quomodo unus et idem Christus indivisus ex duobus filiis aut duabus naturis distinctis constare dicatur. Item quomodo filius sit diversa [63] hypostasis a patre et tamen unus et idemmet deus cum patre intelligatur, nec explicare sciunt nec ullo scripturæ testimonio probant, fingunt autem quandam novam impositionem in illo termino homo ut æquipollent huic toti orationi sustentans naturam humanam et illam dictionem Christus a prophetis et apostolis assumptam dicunt ad significandam secundam personam seu hypostasim connotative idest connotando quod sustentet humanitatem et Jesum hominem verum et perfectissimum humanitatem tantum appellare non erubescunt. O miseram et impudentem Theologiam.

Err. 10b

TE11a

But our theologians, not allowing that the visible Jesus, that most holy man of God, our redeemer, is to be called the Son of God and God, have claimed that these are names of that invisible hypostasis, which, by means of a "union" was communicated to Jesus Christ, the son of the Virgin. And to this end the prevailing school of philosophers invented *communicatio idiomatum*, an egregious interpretation of sound scripture, which no apostle ever knew or thought about.

Listen to their theology! They set up two sons in Christ and a twofold distinct nature, the second of which is invisible and non-suffering – that is, the incorporeal Word of God. They say that, although [the Word] is a separate person or hypostasis from [the Father], it is the Son of the Father, and the very same God as him. According to them, this invisible son descends into the man, joining and uniting itself to him, as well as directing and sustaining him.

[The theologians] say that there is actually another [son], a purely human son of the Virgin, who alone is visible and suffers, and who is controlled and sustained by the invisible [son]. Thus [they say] when scripture says that the man Jesus is the Son of God, or God, it is not speaking in a normal way, but in terms of *communicatio idiomatum* and the properties of a single composite or aggregate [being] or connotative *suppositum*, which is called Christ. Similarly, when scripture says the Son of God spoke, suffered, died and rose again, they claim that this is not said in a normal way, but by means of that same *communicatio idiomatum*, by which the Son of God shares his titles and properties with the son of the Virgin, while, conversely, the son of the Virgin "communicates" his names and his suffering to the Son of God. And such, moreover, is the unity and fellowship between them, that these two sons, with two distinct natures, are joined together in a single *suppositum* or aggregate.

How and by what means do they communicate to each other what is predicated of [each of] them? How is one and the same indivisible Christ said to consist of two sons or two distinct natures? They do not know how to explain how the son can be a separate hypostasis from the Father and nevertheless is to be understood as one and the same God as the Father, nor do they prove this by any testimony of the scriptures. Instead, they contrive a new definition for the word "man," making it equivalent to the entire expression, "sustaining a human nature." And they say that the word "Christ" was used by the prophets and apostles to signify the second person or hypostasis connotatively, that is, by connoting "that which sustains a human nature." They are not ashamed to call Jesus, the true and most perfect man, just "a human nature." O wretched and impudent theology!

Err. 11a   Sed quid dicerent? si in omnibus bibliis latinis loco illius vocis Christus poneretur unctus quæ est propria et latina Christi significatio an pure et sincere loquendo secundam personam esse unctam, dicerent et eam accepisse spiritum et veritatem dei ut de vero Christo dicitur, ecce puer meus quem elegi dilectus meus ponam spiritum meum super illum quæ verba non ad illam secundam personam, sed ad verum Christum Jesum aput evangelistam relata invenies, Mathæ. 12.

Err. 11b-12a   Præterea quid communicare de suo potest homo ipsi deo aut de novo tribuere? Nam aut id atributum est perfectio et deum argueret imperfectum aut est imperfectio et rationem imperfectionis deo convenire concedes, quod sane impium et absurdum est. Quod autem deus homini [64] aliquid tribuat vel communicet hoc non est diminutio dei, sed exaltatio hominis nec ulla in deo mutatio, sed in homine deus enim altissimus et invisibilis semper idem, æternus et immutabilis est natura sua perfectissimus, igitur concedentes deum homini communicare dona sua dicimus Jesum Christum per

Err. 12a   dei gratiam et largitionem esse dominum et deum nostrum, deum magnum deum fortem, deum verum, deum benedictum, servatorem, iustificatorem, et redemptorem nostrum, iudicem vivorum et mortuorum.

Cæterum non concedentes hominem aliquid suum ipsi deo communicare perhorrescimus dicere deum æternum et invisibilem esurisse flevisse passum mortuum et suscitatum nec unquam scriptura tali modo loquendi velut priore usa est. Proinde eam apertissime tibi liquere puto quo nam modo et qua ratione scriptura appellet Jesum christum deum, nimirum quoniam filius dei est, per gratiam seu naturam gratuitam omni deitatis, potestatis et gloriæ plenitudine decoratus, rex dominus et deus super omnes creaturas a Deo Patre consti-

Err. 12b   tutus, ut docet Irenæ. lib. III. cap. 12. Verum contra prædicta instabunt Theologi si christus illo modo sit deus ergo plures deos esse concedis et tamen unum esse deum omnis scriptura vere et firmiter attestatur, istud fuit argumentum farisæorum, ad quod tamen respondit ipsa veritas. Nonne scriptum est in lege vestra, ego [65] dixi dii estis

But what would they have said if the word *unctus* [anointed], which is the correct Latin rendering of [the Greek word] "Christ," had been used instead of the word *Christus* throughout the entire Latin Bible? Speaking honestly and candidly, could they really have said that the second person was anointed and had received *the spirit* and the truth *of God*, as is said of the real Christ?[a] *Behold my servant whom I have chosen, my beloved; I will put my Spirit upon him.*[b] You will find, in the Evangelist (Matthew 12), that these words do not refer to the second person, but to the real Christ.[c]

What of his own can a man communicate to God, or what new thing can he bestow? For either what is given is perfection, and this proves that God is imperfect, or it is an imperfection, and you thereby grant that the idea of imperfection is appropriate to God, which is utterly impious and absurd. However, the fact that God bestows or "communicates" something to a man does not diminish God, but only elevates the man. God does not change at all; only the man does. For the most high and invisible God, forever the same, eternal and unchanging, is in nature absolutely perfect. Therefore, granting that God communicates his gifts to the man, we say that Jesus Christ, by the grace and generosity of God, is *our Lord and our God, mighty God, true God, blessed God,* our *savior,* justifier, and *redeemer, the judge of the living and the dead.*[d]

Moreover, as we do not allow that a man can communicate anything of his own to God, we are loath to say that the eternal and invisible God felt hunger, wept, suffered, died, and rose again. Scripture never speaks in this way. Consequently, I believe it is patently clear in what manner and for what reason, scripture calls Jesus Christ God. Doubtless it is because the Son of God, by means of grace or a freely-given nature,[4] was adorned with *all the fullness of deity,*[e] power, and glory, and established by God the Father as "King, Lord, and God over all creation," as Irenaeus teaches in book 3, chapter 12.[f]

The theologians will certainly argue against what has just been said, [claiming] that if Christ were God in this way, one would then have to grant that there is more than one god, although all of scripture truly and firmly attests that there is [only] one God. That was the argument of the Pharisees, to which truth itself [Christ] replied, *Is it not written in your law: I said you are gods?*

---

[a] Acts 10:38. The reference to Acts 10 is made explicitly in the parallel passage from *Erroribus*. [b] Isa. 42:1.
[c] Matt. 12:18, quoting Isa. 42:1. [d] Rev. 4:11, Isa. 9:6, 1 John 5:20, Rom. 9:5, Isa. 49:26, Acts 10:42.
[e] Col. 2:9. [f] Irenaeus, *Adv. Hær.* 3.12.9 (PG 7a 902B-C).

Err. 12b   si illos dixit deos ad quos sermo dei factus est quanto magis deus dicendus est filius hominis quem pater sanctificavit et misit in mundum. Nota argumentum et nota responsionem. Cum enim argueretur Jesus a Judæis quod cum homo esset, faceret se deum asserens se dei filium, et propterea dicerent illum blasphemavit, respondit se esse deum, eo modo quo propheta deos dixit eam sibi rationem deitatis atribuens quæ ab ipso deo hominibus concederetur, non enim applicavit illis rationem Triadis nec personarum sive hypostasum neque sibi unius altissimi et invisibilis dei patris nomen et naturam vindicavit sed se deum a patre per gratiam et sanctificationem potius demonstravit.

    Filius enim deus factus est et in carne manifestatus unigenitus patris plenus gratiæ et veritatis, Io. 1. Cæterum unum tantum dici simpliciter et absolute per naturam deum scilicet patrem illum a quo omnia sunt satis iudicat scriptura ubique deum ab ipso filio distinguens ut infra suo loco plenissime ostendemus pro quo sufficere nobis deberet verus ille pauli tam apertus Ad Corinth. 8. Nam et si sunt qui dicantur dii sive in cœlo, sive in terra, quemadmodum sunt dii multi et domini multi nobis tamen unus est deus qui est pater ille ex quo omnia et nos in illum et unus dominus Jesus Christus per quem omnia, et nos per illum. Item hæc est vita æterna ut cognoscant te solum deum verum et quem misisti Jesum Christum. Item omnis viri caput Christus est caput autem mulieris vir, caput vero Christi deus. Item Ephe. 1. deus domini nostri Jesu Christi pater gloriæ det vobis spiritum sapientiæ et revelationis. Item Ad Ephe. 4. unus dominus, una fides unum baptisma, [66] unus deus et pater omnium qui est super omnia et per omnia et in omnibus nobis. Item Ad Corinth. 15. Cum autem subiecta fuerint illi omnia tunc et ipse filius subiectus ei qui illi omnia subiecit ut sit deus omnia in omnibus. Item vado ad patrem meum et patrem vestrum, Deum meum et deum vestrum

If he called them gods to whom the word of God came, how much more must the Son of man be called God, *whom the Father consecrated and sent into the world*?[a] Note their accusation and then note his rebuttal. For the Jews argued that *even though he was a man*, by claiming to be the Son of God, Jesus *made himself out to be God*.[b] Thus they said that he blasphemed. He answered that he was a god in the way in which the Prophet spoke of gods, ascribing to himself that meaning of deity, which was granted to human beings by God. He did not propose to them the idea of a triad, nor the ideas of persons or hypostases, nor did he claim for himself the name and nature of God the Father, but demonstrated instead that he was God, by means of grace and consecration by the Father.

The Son, indeed, became God and was revealed in the flesh as *the only begotten Son of the Father, full of grace and truth* (John 1).[c] Furthermore, only one can be called God, simply and absolutely, by nature – *the Father, from whom are all things*,[d] as scripture everywhere amply attests, distinguishing God from the Son. In the proper place, below, we shall make this abundantly clear. For the moment that truth so clearly expressed by Paul in Corinthians 8 should suffice: *For although there may be so-called gods in heaven or on earth – just as there are many "gods" and many "lords" – yet for us there is one God, who is the Father, from whom are all things, and for whom we exist, and one Lord, Jesus Christ, through whom are all things and through whom we exist.*[e] And again: *This is eternal life, that they may know you, the only true God, and Jesus Christ whom you have sent.*[f]

Likewise, *the head of every man is Christ, while the head of a woman is the husband. The head of Christ, of course, is God.*[g] And in Ephesians 1 [Paul prays that] *the God of our Lord Jesus Christ, the Father of glory, may give you a spirit of wisdom and of revelation.*[h] And in Ephesians 4: *one Lord, one faith, one baptism, one God and Father of all, who is above all and through all and in all of us.*[i] And in Corinthians 15: *When all things are subjected to him, then the Son himself will also be subjected to him who put all things under him, that God may be all in all.*[j] And *I go to my Father and your Father, my God and your God.*[k]

---

[a] John 10:35-36, quoting Ps. 82:6. [b] John 10:33. [c] John 1:14. [d] 1 Cor. 8:6. [e] 1 Cor. 8:5-6.
[f] John 17:3. [g] 1 Cor. 11:3. [h] Eph. 1:17. [i] Eph. 4:5-6. [j] 1 Cor. 15:28. [k] John 20:17.

et paulus semper et ubique deum a Christo distinguit, gratia et pax vobis a deo patre nostro et domino Jesu Christo. Item ecclesia semper oravit deum per filium eius Jesum Christum.

Possim huc infinita alia adducere quæ suo loco plenius adducentur ex quibus cuicunque tunc clarius patebit solum patrem simpliciter et per naturam dici deum de quo dicitur, Audi Israhel dominus deus noster, unus deus est et ipse est deus deorum æternus invisibilis et immutabilis a quo omnia alia sunt et dependent etiam ipse filius qui semper omnem suam potestatem gloriam et divinitatem ab ipso patre recognovit, data est mihi a patre omnis potestas in cœlo et in terra, pater clarifica me ea gloria quam habui aput te prius quam mundus fieret. Item propter quod deus summe extulit illum et dedit illi nomen supra omne nomen, ut in nomine Jesu Christi omne genu curvetur cœlestium terrestrium et infernorum. Item qui credimus secundum efficatiam roboris et fortitudinis eius quam exercuit in Christo cum suscitaret eum ex mortuis et sedere fecit ad dexteram suam in cœlestibus supra omnem principatum ac potestatem et virtutem ac dominum et omne nomen quod nominatur non solum in sæculo hoc verum etiam in futuro et omnia subiecit sub pedes illius et eum dedit caput super omnia ipse eclesiæ quæ est corpus illius [67] complementum eius qui omnia in omnibus adimplet Ephe. 1. Ecce quomodo manifeste scriptura dicit solum patrem simpliciter esse deum et esse caput ac deum filii sui solum autem esse caput et deum nostrum qui est medius inter deum et nos et a patre velut a capite et deo suo omne donum recognoscit.

Err. 13a-b   Quid si dixero patrem filio maiorem? ut ipsemet filius aperte fatetur, vado ad patrem quia pater maior me est, numquid propterea me Arrianum iudicabis. Nam arrius cum de filio diversum a patre stultissime sentiret et Jesu Christi gloriæ incapacissimus esset novam quandam creaturam homine excellentiorem introduxit quam patrem maiorem dicebat cum tamen ea seclusa et omni distinctione personarum seu hypostasum remota potuisset vere et pie concedere patrem filio maiorem

And Paul always and everywhere distinguishes God from Christ, saying, *Grace and peace to you from God our Father and the Lord Jesus Christ*.[a] Also note that the church has always prayed to God through his Son Jesus Christ.

Here I could mention countless other texts, which will be introduced more fully in their proper place. Then it will be more clearly apparent to anyone that the Father alone is called God, simply and by nature. About whom it is said: *Hear, O Israel: The Lord our God, is one God*.[b] And he is *God of gods*,[c] *eternal, invisible*[d] and unchanging,[e] *from whom all other things are* and on whom they depend.[f] Furthermore, the Son, who always recognized that all his power, glory, and divinity were from God, said, "*All authority in heaven and on earth has been given to me* from the Father"[g] and "*Father, glorify me with that glory which I had with you before the world was made*."[h] Also, *Therefore, God has highly exalted him, and given him a name above every name, that at the name of Jesus Christ, every knee should bend, in heaven, on earth, and under the earth*.[i] Also:

> *We who believe, according to that working of his strength and power, which he administered in Christ when he raised him from the dead and made him sit at his right hand in the heavenly places, far above all rule and authority and power and dominion, and above every name that is named, not only in this age, but truly that which is to come; and he has put all things under his feet and has made him the head over all things of the church, which is his body, and the completion of him who fulfils all in all* (Ephesians 1).[j]

Behold how scripture plainly says that the Father alone is purely God, and is alone head and God of his Son, while [the Son] is our head and God, the *mediator between God and* ourselves.[k] [The Son] acknowledges that all things are given by the Father as his head and God.

What if I say that the Father is greater than the Son? As the Son himself clearly confesses, *I go to the Father, for the Father is greater than I*.[l] How can you, for this reason, judge me to be an Arian?[5] For since Arius foolishly thought the Son unlike the Father and totally unfit for the glory of Jesus Christ, he introduced a new creature, superior to a human being, but which he said was inferior to the Father. Nevertheless, leaving that aside and removing every distinction of person or hypostasis, he could have claimed, truly and piously, that the Father is greater than the Son.

---

[a] Rom. 1:7, 1 Cor. 1:3, 2 Cor. 1:2, Gal. 1:3, Eph. 1:2, Phil. 1:2, 2 Thess. 1:2, Philem. 1:3. This was a common formula at the beginning of epistles.   [b] Deut. 6:4.   [c] Deut. 10:17.   [d] 1 Tim. 1:17. See also Rom. 1:20.   [e] The Latin Bible does not use the word *immutabilis* (unchanging) to describe God, but uses various synonyms e.g. eternal (Dan. 6:26), incorruptible (Rom. 1:23), immoveable (Heb. 6:17), enduring (1 Peter 1:23).   [f] 1 Cor. 8:6.   [g] Matt. 28:18   [h] John 17:5.   [i] Phil. 2:9-10.   [j] Eph. 1:19-23.   [k] 1 Tim. 2:5.   [l] John 14:28.

ut ex prædictis facile constat nec me movet vana istorum interpretatio quo omnem scripturam pervertant dicentes Christus semper loqui non ut filium dei, sed ut purum hominem et filium hominis tantum vocando deum patrem suum improprie et per communicationem idiomatum quæ nova blasphemia est paulus enim dicit Christum ut filium dei novissime locutum et patri subiectum qui illi omnia subiecit nec alium filium agnoscit vere illhic communicatio idiomatum locum habet nisi nugas et imposturas philosophorum manifeste sequaris præterea Christus non potest dici caput ecclesiæ sanctæ nisi ut filius dei et tamen huius capitis pater ipse et caput et deus est Ephe. 1.

Err. 13b   Arrius ergo in pluralitate rerum separatarum et invisibilium philosophari volens fedissime lapsus est **[68]** cum nec ipse verum deum patrem et verum dei filium Jesum crucifixum agnoverit, sed et in chimera triadis permanserit diverso tum ab aliis theologis modo qui sub unius dei natura tres personas seu hypostases re et numero differentes coæternas et coæquales introducebant sine ullo prorsus scripturæ fundamento, unde tot hæreses sectæ et opiniones inter homines fluxerunt, ut totum mundum a multo iam tempore erroribus et false a te* repleverunt.

Err. 13b   Et ut erroris causam plane intelligas, scire debes omnia quæ de Jesu Christo scripta sunt in iudea contigisse et hæbreorum lingua ut plurimum adnotata fuisse qua excepta in omnibus aliis linguis mira est penuria nominum divinitatis Græci enim solam vocem theon habent et Latini deum Hæbrei autem copiosis nominibus inter deum, et deum distinguere possunt habent enim pro formidabili nomine dei invisibilis vocem Iova, item pro omni alio nomine divini potentiæ et superioritatis, et pro eo qui divina unitate ac potestate præditus sit habent hæc nomina Eloim et Adonai, et secundum hæc nomina Christus dei filius dicitur deus,

---

* Should read *falsitate*.

As is readily apparent from what I have just said, I am not impressed by the vacuous interpretation of those who pervert the whole of scripture, saying that Christ was always spoken of, not as the Son of God, but purely as a man and the son of a man, and that God is to be called his Father only in a special way and in terms of *communicatio idiomatum*. This is a new blasphemy! For Paul calls Christ the *Son* of God who *has spoken to us in these last days*,[a] and says that he is subject to the Father[b] who *puts everything in subjection to him*.[c] He does not recognize any other son. Does *communicatio idiomatum* really apply here? Clearly not, unless you chase after the nonsense and impostures of the philosophers! Furthermore, Christ cannot be called the head of the holy church except as the Son of God, but the Father is both head and God of this head [that is, Christ] (Ephesians 1).[d]

Therefore Arius, preferring to philosophize about a multitude of separate and invisible beings, fell into the most shameful error, because he recognized neither the true God the Father, nor the true Son of God, Jesus crucified. He persisted in the chimera of a triad, though in a manner different from other theologians. They introduced, contained within the nature of one God, three co-eternal and coequal persons or hypostases, differing in being and number, all without any scriptural foundation. So many heresies, sects, and opinions have poured out among men from this, that for a considerable time now the whole world has been filled with errors and falsehood.

In order to clearly understand the cause of this error, you must keep in mind that all the events that have been recorded concerning Jesus Christ happened in Judaea. Also, as has often been noted, in all other languages, with the exception of Hebrew, there is a surprising scarcity of names for the Divine. For Greek has only the word *theos*, and Latin, *deus*. Hebrew, on the other hand, can distinguish between God and God by means of an abundance of names. Indeed, for the formidable name of the invisible God, they have the word *Jehovah*. For every other divine name of power and superiority, and for him who is endowed with the divine unity and power, they have the names *Elohim* and *Adonai*. And it is in accordance with these names that Christ, the Son of God, is called God.

---

[a] Heb. 1:2.   [b] 1 Cor. 15:28.   [c] Heb. 2:8.   [d] Eph. 1:22.

Err. 14a   et hanc deitatis rationem in Jesu Christo facile ex veteri testamento cognosces si diligenter animadvertas quæ vox aput hæbreos ponatur quando Christus vocatur deus, et hinc poteris perspicuam colligere differentiam inter proprium nomen dei patris qui solus est a se et natura deus Gal. 4. et alia nomina Christo atributa qui **[69]** est deus a patre per gratiam vel gratuitam naturam. Nam quando thomas Jhesum dominum et deum suum appellavit non dixit Iova, sed Adonai et Eloim, similiter Eloim dixit apostolus heb. 1. de filio dei loquens et quod iuxta vocem Eloim sit factus nobis deus non aliud significat quamquod sit factus dominus noster, rex noster et iudex noster.

         Dei enim nomen potentiam et superioritatem significat igitur Christo nomen dei vere convenit quia pater in regem et dominum unxit eum et ei principatum dedit supra omnes creaturas. Nam datum est ei regnum et omne iudicium et omnis potestas in cœlo

Err. 13b-14a   et in terra quumne etiam Cyrum regem qui veri Christi idest regis erat typus scriptura Eloim vocat deum Isrælis Esa. 45. Dabo inquit tibi thesauros absconditos ut scias quod ego sum deus qui novi nomen tuum deum Isrælis similiter moses constitutus fuit a deo deus pharaonis per potestatem et superioritatem quam dederat illi deus in pharaonem. Igitur longe magis ipsi filio Jesu Christo, dei nomen convenit qui a patre super omnes creaturas sublimatus fuit omni potestate deitate gratia et benedictione repletus, unde Esaias vocabitur inquit deus fortis et Emmanuel id est nobiscum deus.

Err. 14a   Theologi autem qui tam impie et indigne de Christi humanitate sentiunt non considerant istud fuisse omnium divinorum operum excellentissimum ministerium quod et gentibus stultitia et hæbreis scandalum fuit. Deum scilicet voluisse ex verbo suo hominem sibi filium producere visibilem **[70]** passibilem et mortalem et illum supra omnes creaturas extollere et in omni gloria et sublimitate ad dextram suam collocare omnia illi subiciens qui esset consumatio et implementum omnium operum et consiliorum dei patris, dominus et deus noster visibilis per quem et propter quem omnia facta sunt

You will easily learn from the Old Testament the kind of deity that is in Jesus Christ, if you pay close attention to which Hebrew word is used when Christ is called God. You will also be able to comprehend the clear difference between the proper name of God the Father, who alone is God, by himself and by nature (Galatians 4),[a] and the other names that are given to Christ, who is God by means of grace or a nature freely given by the Father. For when Thomas called Jesus his *Lord* and his *God*, he did not say *Jehovah*, but *Adonai* [Lord] and *Elohim* [God].[b] Similarly, speaking of the Son of God in Hebrews 1, the Apostle says *Elohim*.[c,6] According to the meaning of the word *Elohim*, [to say] that he became God over us means nothing other than that he became our *Lord, our king*, and *our judge*.[d]

Indeed, the name [*Elohim*] signifies the power and superiority of God. Therefore, the name God is truly appropriate to Christ, since the Father anointed him king and Lord, and gave him rule over all creatures. For kingship and all judgment and all power in heaven and on earth was bestowed on him. Did not scripture also call King Cyrus, who was a type of the true Christ (that is, the King), *Elohim*, the God of Israel (Isaiah 45): "*I will give you hidden treasures*, he said, *that you may know that I am the God who knew your name, the God of Israel.*"[e] Similarly, God made Moses *a God to Pharaoh*[f] because of the power and superiority which God had given him over the Pharaoh. Therefore, the name God is far more suited to the Son, Jesus Christ, whom the Father raised above all creatures, and filled with all power, divinity, grace, and blessedness. For this reason Isaiah says: *He will be called Mighty God*[g] and *Emmanuel, which means, God with us*.[h]

The theologians, however, who think so impiously and unjustly about the human nature of Christ, do not consider that this, which was *folly to Gentiles and a stumbling-block to Jews*,[i] was the most excellent of all the works God performed: that God wished to bring forth from his Word a human being as his Son – visible, capable of suffering, and subject to death – to raise him up above all creatures, and, in all glory and sublimity, to place him at his *right hand*, making all things *subject to him*.[j] [Christ] was the consummation and fulfillment of all the works and plans of God the Father. He was our visible Lord and God, *through whom and by whom all things* were made.[k]

---

[a] Gal. 4:8.   [b] John 20:28, quoting Ps. 35:23.   [c] Heb. 1:8, quoting Ps. 45:6.   [d] Isa. 33:22.
[e] Isa. 45:3. See book 4, note 3.   [f] Exod. 7:1.   [g] Isa. 9:6   [h] Matt. 1:23, quoting Isa. 7:14.
[i] 1 Cor. 1:23.   [j] 1 Peter 3:22.   [k] Heb. 2:10.

Err. 14a	sed adhuc hoc parum est ut de cristo integre sentias donec verbi archana noveris et diceris* hunc sanctissimum hominem Jesum dei filium iam ab æterno ante omnia sæcula deum fuisse aput ipsum
Err. 53a	deum patrem cui omnia ab æterno sunt presentia et quæcumque aput nos in tempore fuerunt sunt, vel erunt, immutabili suæ æternitatis lumine ut iam facta videt ac dispensat et mille anni aput eum tanquam dies externa quæ preteriit et hac ratione verbum seu logos dei qui erat ipse Christus prædestinatus ante omnem creationem erat aput patrem et deus verus de deo vero ut Joannes
Err. 14a-14b	describit de quo tamen fusius infra disseremus, et ideo Apostolus ipsum Christum Eloim vocat Heb. l. Immo etiam Solomon iuxta historiam dicitur Eloim est enim locus ille ex psalmo 44. desumptus nec tamen Apostolus in ea voce Eloim robur suæ probationis in totum ponit, sed in eo quod dixit Thronum et regnum eius in sæculum sæculi. Nam ex sola voce Eloim non probasset Christum maiorem angelis vel aliis principibus terræ quia etiam ipsi eodem nomine [71] nuncupantur, et dii a propheta dicuntur similiter ubi dicitur et adorent eum omnes angeli item minuisti eum paululum ab angelis utrobique ponitur Eloim iam igitur te luce clarius videre
Err. 15b	puto quomodo ignorantia hebraicæ, phrasis græcos philosophos in re tam seria et fundamentali mire decepit dum divinitatis nomina distinguere nescierunt et patrem ac filium diversas ut aiunt personas ac subsistentias pro uno et eodem deo acceperunt patris et filii naturam et substantiam confundentes contra sensum aposto. heb. 1. qui aperte dicit filium esse splendorem gloriæ et expressam imaginem substantiæ dei et Coll. 1. vocat filium visibilem imaginem invisibilis dei, unde ad denotandum differentiam Jesu Christi ab aliis diis particularibus cum ipse sit filius et per naturam gratuitam deus et hæres additur ipsi Christo deus omnis terræ deus magnus, deus verus, deus fortis, admirabilis et super omnia benedictus quam rem

---

* Should read *disceris*.

However, even this is insufficient for a complete knowledge of Christ. For this you must come to understand the mysteries of the Word, and become acquainted with that most holy man Jesus, the Son of God. *Before all the ages*[a] and from eternity, he was already God with God the Father, to whom all things are eternally present. In the unchanging light of his eternity, he sees and arranges, as already accomplished, those things which, among us in time, were, are, or will be. *A thousand years* with him *are but as an outward*[7] *day when it is past.*[b] Thus, the Word, or *Logos*, of God, which was Christ, predestined before all creation, was with the Father, as John relates,[c] and was "true God of true God."[d] We will discuss this at greater length below.

Thus in Hebrews 1 the Apostle calls Christ *Elohim*. Indeed, according to tradition, Solomon is also called *Elohim* (this passage is taken from Psalm 44). The Apostle does not, however, place the force of his argument on the word *Elohim*, but on the statement that *his throne* and *kingdom* are *for ever and ever.*[e,8] For, from the word *Elohim* alone, he could not have proved Christ greater than other rulers of the earth or angels, since even they are called by the same name and are called gods [*Elohim*] by the Prophet.[f] Similarly, where it says, *Let all the angels worship him*,[g] or *You have made him a little lower than the angels*,[h] in both places *Elohim* is used.

Therefore, I believe that you can now see more clearly how, in so serious and fundamental a matter, ignorance of Hebrew phraseology has so wildly deceived Greek philosophers that they have not been able to distinguish the different names for divinity, both Father and Son. They say that they think of persons and subsistences[9] as one and the same God, thereby confusing the nature and substance of the Father and the Son. However this is contrary to the meaning of the Apostle, who, in Hebrews 1, says clearly that the Son is *the splendor of the glory and the very stamp of the substance of God.*[i] Also, in Colossians 1, he calls the Son the visible *image of the invisible God.*[j]

Thus, in order to convey the difference between Jesus Christ and other, partial gods, since he is the Son and heir, and, by a nature freely given, God, Christ is also called God of *all the earth, great* God,[k] true God, *mighty God, wonderful*,[l] and *blessed above all things.*[m]

---

[a] 1 Cor. 2:7. [b] Ps. 90:4. [c] See John 1:1. [d] From the Nicene Creed. [e] Heb. 1:8, quoting Ps. 45:6.
[f] Ps. 82:6. [g] Heb. 1:6, quoting Ps. 97:7. [h] Heb. 2:7, 9, quoting Ps. 8:5. [i] Heb. 1:3. [j] Col. 1:15.
[k] Ps. 47:2. [l] Isa. 9:6. [m] Rom. 9:5.

Err. 15b   propter penuriam nominum divinitatis non aliter quam per vocem Theos Apostoli græcis declarare potuerunt, sed tamen perraro ea voce de Christo loquentes utuntur quinimo fere semper domini vocem assumunt. Nam in scriptura pater dicitur deus et filius dominus quæ omnia sunt diligenter adnotanda, nec tantum nobis fecissent negotii si hæbraica græci didicissent.

 Nunc ergo clare perpendas unde primum ille error græcorum tam perniciose [72] defluxit de triade seu tribus hypostasibus unum deum et et de uno deo tres personas distinctas facientibus nec non de communicatione idiomatum de duabus naturis et duobus filiis de suppositis connotativis de agregatis et similibus nugis de quibus nunquam Apostoli cogitarunt nec in tota scriptura vel unus apex reperitur. Illi enim significationem huius vocis deus et divinorum nominum differentiam iuxta phrasim hebraicam ignorantes et videntes Christum aliquando in scriptura deum appellari et tamen unum tantum deum nobis colendum proponi coacti sunt tres personas sive hypostases in una deitate constituere et unam ex illis pro Christo assumere et consequentius duos Christos et duos filios facere unum filium dei alterum filium hominis unum visibilem et passibilem alterum invisibilem et impassibilem et quando scriptura vocat Christum deum de invisibili intelligunt qui homo non est et sic Jesum Christum redemptorem nostrum et caput ecclesiæ, unicum mediatorem dei et hominum, filium dei et deum esse negant cum tamen universa scriptura nihil aliud evidentius exprimat et loquatur, sed forte timent ne duos deos faciant cum tamen ipsi revera et in effectu in sua triade tres nobis deos per

Err. 32b   naturam et coæquales obtrudant et [73] tamen contra omnem rationem concedunt quod unus imperet alteri et alter mittatur ab altero nescientes quod inter æquales non cadit dominium neque superioritas et ab æquali potentia non fit actio et quod concursu se invicem impederent propter quod necesse est fateri omnia ad unum simplicissimum deum referenda esse qui est pater ille omnium conditor voluntarius qui etiam filium voluntarie genuit cui omnia obœdiunt et subiciuntur etiam ipse filius ut aperte testatur apostolus Corinth. 8. et 15.

Due to the dearth of divine names [in Greek], the apostles could only express [divinity] to the Greeks by using the word *theos* [god]. Nevertheless, when speaking of Christ, they use this word very rarely, almost always employing the word *kyrios* [Lord]. For in Scripture the Father is called God, and the Son, Lord. All this needs to be considered carefully. For the Greeks would not have caused us so much trouble if they had learned Hebrew.

Now, therefore, you can clearly judge the source of the Greeks' pernicious error about the triad or three hypostases forming one God – and also their creating three separate persons out of one God, not to mention *communicatio idiomatum*, two natures and two sons, connotative *supposita*, aggregates, and similar nonsense, about which the apostles never gave a thought, and concerning which there is not even a single jot in all of scripture. Indeed they are ignorant of the meaning of the words for God and of the various divine names in the Hebrew language. Because they see that in scripture Christ is sometimes called God – although there is only one God that we should worship – they are compelled to establish three persons or hypostases in one deity and to maintain that one of them is Christ.

A greater consequence is that they are compelled make two Christs and two sons, one of whom is the Son of God and the other the Son of man, one visible and capable of suffering, the other invisible and incapable of suffering. Furthermore when scripture calls Christ "God," they understand this to mean an invisible being who is not a man, thus denying that Jesus Christ, *our redeemer*[a] and *the head of the church*,[b] the *one mediator between God and men*,[c] is the Son of God and God, when, nevertheless, the whole of scripture says and expresses nothing more clearly. Is it perhaps because they are afraid of creating two gods, even though, with their triad, they are in effect foisting on us three gods, equal in nature? And yet, contrary to all reason, they accept that one god can command the other, and that one can be sent forth by the other, not understanding that dominance and superiority do not happen among equals, that decisive action does not arise from an equality of power, and that, in combination, equals would impede one another. Because of this, one must admit that all things originate in one pure and simple God, who is the Father, by virtue of his own will the founder of all that is, who willingly begot the Son. All things obey and are subject to him, even the Son himself, as the Apostle plainly testifies (Corinthians 8 and 15).[d]

---

[a] Isa. 47:4. [b] Eph. 1:22, 5:23; Col. 1:18. [c] 1 Tim. 2:5. [d] 1 Cor. 8:6, 15:27-28.

Vide igitur quantum valeat parvus error in principio alicuius disciplinæ vel doctrinæ ut ex inde tot blasphemiæ et impietates fuerint consecutæ. At quanto melius et fidelius fecissent simplicissimam nobis ex scriptura fidem proponere in unum solum deum patrem solum natura deum, infinitum, invisibilem, immutabilem, qui est omnium deorum deus lucem habitans inaccessibilem et unius eiusdem dei filium verum et naturalem dominum Jesum Christum crucifixum verbum dei incarnatum visibile et passibile factum, deum visibilem de deo invisibili, quem sic pati oportuit ut omne consilium decretum et voluntatem patris adimpleret et gloriam suam cum victoria et triumpho de omnibus inimicis plenissime consequeretur, hic est verus deus noster, filius sibi dilectus in quo pater sibi bene complacuit et cui tantum gratiæ, virtutis, spiritus, potestatis, honoris et divinitatis contulit quantum omnipotentissimus pater dilectissimo [74] atque unigenito filio dare et conferre potest ut in eo sit omnis spes nostra et fidutia nostra et ei sit omnis laus honor gloria et benedictio in sæcula sæculorum amen.

Hæc est vera pura simplex et sincera doctrina christiana, hæc est mera sacrosancti evangelii prædicatio in tota scriptura tam antiqua quam nova clarissime explicata nec aliam fidem vel doctrinam annuntiarunt prophetæ, prædicarunt Apostoli, et martires sanguine confirmarunt. Tu autem pie et fidelis christiane qui nullius hominis autoritatem duceris et in nullius verba iurasti, sed simplicitatem spiritus et scripturæ sinceritatem sequi desideras perpende obsecro et in corde tuo semota omni ambitione diligenter considera utra tibi verior, purior, sincerior et explicatior doctrina relligionis videatur et Christi evangelio conformior an ea quam tibi proxime declaravi de uno deo patre et uno eiusdem dei filio domino Jesu Christo crucifixo. An vero illa quam ab aliquo tempore græcanica tibi philosophia hebrais semper prorsus ignara tot voluminibus et commentariis tibi inculcavit de tribus personis seu hypostasibus de duabus naturis et duobus filiis de idiomatum communicatione et suppositis connotativis sine quibus dicunt misteria Christi recte intelligi non posse nec evangelium tute prædicari.

Observe, therefore, how a small error at the outset of a teaching or doctrine grows more powerful until it leads to a great many blasphemies and impieties. How much better and more faithful would it have been if they had propounded, based on scripture, a pure and simple faith in only *one God, the Father*,[a] who alone is God by nature, infinite, invisible, and unchanging, God of all gods, who *dwells in inaccessible light*;[b] and in the true and natural Son of this one God, the Lord Jesus Christ crucified, the Word of God incarnate, made visible and capable of suffering, visible God from invisible God,[c] who was required to suffer in order to fulfill every plan, decree, and purpose of the Father,[d] and to achieve his glory to the fullest degree in triumphant victory over all his enemies. This is our true God, the *beloved Son, in whom* the Father was *well pleased*,[e] and on whom he bestowed as much grace, *might*, spirit, *power, honor, and divinity*,[f] as the most omnipotent Father is capable of giving and conveying to his most loved and only begotten Son, *so that* all our *hope and faith might be in him*,[g] and to him *let there be* all praise, *honor, glory, and blessing for ever and ever. Amen.*[h]

This is the true, pure, simple and genuine Christian doctrine. This is the unadulterated proclamation of the holy gospel set forth most plainly in all of scripture, in both the Old and New [Testaments]. The prophets did not proclaim, the apostles did not preach, nor did the martyrs preserve with their blood any faith or doctrine other than this. You, indeed, pious and faithful Christian, you who follow the authority of no man and swear by the words of none, but seek rather to obey the simplicity of spirit of genuine scripture, weigh carefully, I beseech you, and, setting aside all outside influence, diligently consider in your heart which doctrine of religion seems to you truer, purer, more authentic, clearer, and more in line with the gospel of Christ: the one which I have just set forth, about one God the Father and the only Son of that same God, the Lord Jesus Christ crucified, or the one which Greekish philosophy – utterly unknown to the Hebrews – has for so long been forced upon you, in so many volumes and commentaries, about three persons or hypostases, two natures and two sons, the *communicatio idiomatum* and connotative *supposita*, without which they say that the mysteries of Christ cannot be rightly understood nor the gospel soundly proclaimed.

---

[a] 1 Cor. 8:6. [b] 1 Tim. 6:16 [c] See Col. 1:15. [d] See Luke 24:26-27. [e] Matt. 3:17. [f] Rev. 5:12.
[g] 1 Peter 1:21. [h] Rev. 5:13.

O miseros christianos si vanam et impostorem græcorum philosophiam pro sincera fide, pro [75] castissimis dei eloquiis et purissimo Jesu, Christi evangelio recipere compellantur quos Hæbrei Scythi Turci et omne infidelium genus merito ridet subsannat, proferant isti philosophi et tota scriptura saltem unum apicem qui illas sophisticas ipsorum voces confirment. Numne aliquando paulus vas electionis qui nihil omnino prætermisit quod ad veræ fidei et Christianæ relligionis declarationem pertineret semel tantum de talibus hypostasibus, naturis, et communicatione idiomatum meminisset, sed talia penitus ignoravit et si paulus ignoravit quis hominum scivit? aspice quam brevibus tota est resoluta Chimera quam nullus unquam intelligere neque explicare potuit et si forte aliquis sublimis spiritus evangelicæ veritatis avidus se explicare volens huius Triadis misterium seu verius philosophiam sibi ab eis explicari desideret statim audit non esse de misterio tam arcano et recondito ultra querendum in quo scrutando et explicando Augustinus omnem fere ætatem consumpsit et tamen nihil magis proficere potuit et ideo oportere capturare intellectum nec plus sapere quam oporteat ne oprimatur a gloria. Sed sanctorum patrum ac Theologorum fidem qui hæc nobis per manus tradiderunt simpliciter et sine alia investigatione sequendam. O ridiculam pietatem, et cur non etiam de votis purgatorio, [76] eucharistia, libero arbitrio, invocatione divorum et huiusmodi traditionibus, antiquorum patrum dogmata secuti sunt ad veritatis ergo diligentius investigarunt? Sed utinam verum dixissent quod Christiana religio de hac Metaphisica Triade nihil unquam scrivisset vel investigasset. Numne bene præmonuerat Paulus ne Christi fideles huic philosophiæ et vocum novitatibus aures accomodarent nec se talibus sophisticis deliramentis involvi et seduci permitterent quod tamen non multo post miserabiliter secutum est cum gravissimo totius Christianæ relligionis detrimento,

O Christians, how miserable you are, if you are compelled to accept an empty and deceitful Greek philosophy – which the Hebrews, Scythians, Turks, and infidels of every kind[10] rightfully ridicule and mock – in place of the genuine faith, the holy utterances of God, and the untainted gospel of Jesus Christ. Let the philosophers produce, from anywhere in scripture, even a single speck of support for their sophistical pronouncements. Did Paul, the *chosen vessel*,[a] who left out nothing pertaining to the revelation of the true faith and the Christian religion, at any time even so much as mention hypostases or natures, or such a thing as *communicatio idiomatum*? He was totally unfamiliar with such things. And if Paul was unfamiliar with them, who, of all mankind, knew about them? See how rapidly this entire chimera, which no one has ever been able to understand or explain, evaporates!

If a spirit eager for the gospel truth, wishing to distentangle the mystery – or, more correctly, the philosophy – of this triad, asks some eminent person to explain it to him, he immediately hears that he should inquire no further about so arcane and abstruse a mystery. Augustine spent nearly his entire life investigating and trying to explain [the triad] but was unable to make any progress. For that reason, we are told that we must restrain our intellects and not trouble ourselves any more about the matter, lest we should be overcome by vainglory. Instead, we [are instructed] simply to follow the faith of those holy fathers and theologians who have handed these things down to us, and not to pursue any further investigation.[11]

What a ridiculous kind of piety! And why have [these eminent persons] not also sought out the truth, and more carefully investigated the teachings of the [church] fathers on prayer, purgatory, the Eucharist, free will, the invocation of the saints, and [other] traditions of this kind? If only [the fathers] had told the truth! For then the Christian religion would never have needed to have written anything about or investigated this metaphysical triad. Did not Paul do well to forewarn Christ's faithful not to pay heed to philosophy or to listen to strange new expressions, nor to permit themselves to become entangled and led astray by such sophistical nonsense?[b] Unfortunately, however, shortly thereafter, this is precisely what occurred, to the grave detriment of the entire Christian religion.

---

[a] Acts 9:15.   [b] Col. 2:8. See also 1 Cor. 2:1-5.

dic quæso quem fructum aut ædificationem fecit unquam in Christianismo talium sophismatum prædicatio quem unquam ex hæbreis a mille annis et citro Christo lucrifecerunt, cum tamen Apostoli per sinceram unius dei patris, et unigeniti eius filii Christi Jesu crucifixi prædicationem uno die tot milia Judæorum converterunt et in dies credentium numerus tam ex gentibus quam Judæis mirum in modum cresceret ac multiplicaretur. Sed illi tunc non tres deos vel hypostases neque duos filios prædicabant quis unquam Judæorum hanc numinum triplicitationem seu verius hunc cerberum credidisset aut nunc etiam crederet. Cum unum tantum deum æternum invisibilem omnium conditorem simplicissime sibi colendum agnoscant et deorum pluralitatem merito nobis obiiciant et [77] irrideant. Verum ab apostolis unum tantum deum patrem audiebant, et unum tantum dei filium Jesum Christum illum pro redemptione Israel mortuum, suscitatum, et glorificatum, hanc fidem facile agnoscebant et nunc etiam agnoscerent et converterentur si hæc fides ac relligio ab hodiernis Theologis sicut olim ab apostolis simplicissime et purissime annuntiaretur nec dubito cessaturas omnes hæreses et contentiones inter Christianos si de Christo dei filio bene sentirent.

Sed mirabilia sunt Altissimi dei iuditia nec sine consilio hunc tantum errorem vagari permisit cum alios etiam non leves errores in æclesia usque ad hæc tempora perseverasse. Nec non Macometanam sectam tam impiam falsam et abhominabilem per universum fere orbem grassari et invalescere videamus, solus deus et dei sermo palpabilis verax est, omnis homo mendax conclusit deus omnes sub errore et peccato ut omnes a filio qui solus patris est veritas, iudicentur, sapientes stulti facti sunt quia in inventionibus suis ambularunt non dei gloriam querentes, sed suam et ideo sicut palea sine tritico inventi sunt.

Err. 15b   Nunc venio ad argumentum de pluralitate deorum, quod manifeste contra illos retorqueo. Nam illi statuunt tres personas re et numero distinctas nec concedunt eas [78] esse qualitates seu dispositiones unius Dei secundum proprietatem latinæ vocis, sed dicunt esse tres subsistentias quas græce hypostases vocant, egregiam sane vocem etiam medicis admodum familiarem,

Tell me how Christianity has ever grown or been strengthened by the preaching of such sophistries. Which Jews have they won over to Christ, during the last thousand years or more? The apostles, however, converted many thousands of Jews in one day[a] by their straightforward preaching of one God the Father and his only begotten son, Christ Jesus crucified. The number of believers, from among the gentiles as well as the Jews, daily multiplied and increased wondrously.[b] However, they were not then preaching about three gods or hypostases, nor about two sons. What Jew could ever have believed in such triplication of divinities – or, in truth, this Cerberus – or could believe in it now? For [the Jews] realize that they ought to worship, in the simplest way, only one eternal, invisible God, the creator of all things. Thus they rightfully throw this multiplicity of gods in our faces and scoff at it. For then [the Jews] heard from the apostles about only one God, the Father, and only one Son of God, Jesus Christ, who died for the redemption of Israel and was resurrected and glorified. They easily understood this faith, and would also understand it now and be converted, if today's theologians proclaimed that faith and religion as the apostles did, most simply and purely, in the early days. Nor do I doubt that all the heresies and contentions among Christians would cease if they had a correct understanding of Christ, the Son of God.

But wondrous are the judgments of God the Most High. He did not allow so great an error to spread for no reason. (And there are other errors, by no means trivial, which also persist in the church to this day.) Otherwise, we would not see the Mohammedan sect, so impious, false, and abominable, prowling about and gaining strength throughout the world. For only God and the palpable Word of God are true; *every man is false*.[c] God has confined everyone in error and sin, so that all may be judged by the Son, who alone is the Truth of the Father. *The wise have become fools*, because they follow their own contrivances, seeking their own glory, not *the glory of God*.[d] Thus they are found to be like chaff without wheat.[e]

I will now decisively turn the argument about a plurality of gods against [the theologians]. They set up three persons, distinct in being and number, while not granting, according to the meaning of the Latin word [*persona*], that these [persons] are qualities or dispositions of one God. Instead, they say that there are three "subsistences," which, in Greek, they call "hypostases" – certainly an uncommon word, although one quite familiar to physicians.

---

[a] Acts 2:41. [b] Acts 2:47. [c] Rom. 3:4, Ps. 116:11 (Vulgate 115:11). [d] Rom. 1:22, 3:23.
[e] Matt. 3:12, Luke 3:17.

et volunt unam quamquam harum personarum seu hypostasum esse deum, et tamen unum tantum deum, et unam naturam, et unam substantiam esse dicunt proponunt nobis tres subsistentias distinctas et persuadere volunt unam esse substantiam nescio unde hanc subtilem diferentiam inter substantiam et subsistentiam hauserint. Item proponunt nobis tria entia seu tres res existentes, et unam naturam esse dicunt, et sic in effectu volunt unum esse tria et tria unum quis spiritus hæc intelligeret?

Si enim volunt deum, quod est nomen substantiale et appellativum, de tribus substantiis re et numero distinctis æqualiter prædicari, videamus quomodo hanc chimeram dissolvere possunt quia et in effectu tres æquales deos natura constituant, ut recte etiam perpendit vir in omni disciplina præsertim in sanctis literis conspicuus Laurentius Valla lib. 6 Elegantiarum cap. 450, ubi de persona et eius propria significatione disserit contra Bœthium videant (inquit) qui personas non qualitates sub* substantias esse volunt, quomodo tres deos non constituant, quod certe et impium et blasphemum est.

Err. 15b-16a His igitur sophisticis commentis procul reiectis, pro <u>solutione argumenta</u>. Dicamus Christum Jesum esse deum <u>eo modo quo</u> ipsemet Iudæis exprobantibus se deum esse declaravit nec alium magistrum vel interpretem exquiramus. Ille enim, cum <u>de eius deitate ageretur</u>, non negavit se esse deum, sed aperte per largitionem [79] et gratiam super abundantem plus quam in omnibus aliis a deo electis et divinitate illustratis quos scripturæ deos appellant, qua Christus est filius et per naturam gratuitam deus, non sicut alii homines terreni et dii particulares.

Prætterea <u>licet Christus sit deus</u>, est tamen unum cum deo patre unitate spiritus, voluntatis et charitatis, ideo non sequitur illa pluralitas quam ipsi prætendunt, quæ potius sequeretur si essent duo vel tres dii per naturam æquales, ut ipsi constituunt, quia unus ab alio mitti vel dispensari non posset ut supra docuimus.

---

* Should read *sed*.

But although they wish each of these persons or hypostases to be God, they nevertheless say there is only one God, one nature, and one substance. For they propose to us three distinct subsistences and want to persuade us that these are all a single substance. I do not see from what source they have derived this subtle distinction between substance and subsistence. They likewise presume three entities or three existing beings, and say that they are one nature, so that, in effect, they want one to be three and three, one. What mind could understand this?

They want "God," which is a substantive and appellative noun, to be predicated equally of three substances, distinct in being and number. Let us see if they can vanquish this chimera! As Lorenzo Valla,[12] a man preeminent in all disciplines, especially in sacred literature, has also rightly judged, they have in effect set up three gods, equal in nature. In book 6 of *De Elegantiis*, chapter 450,[a] where he writes about *persona* and its proper meaning, he argues against Boethius,[13] saying that those who wish persons to be not qualities, but substances, should consider the possibility that they have thereby set up three gods,[14] which is doubtless both impious and blasphemous.

Having, therefore, cast aside such sophistical inventions, let us examine those arguments that offer a solution. Let us say that Jesus Christ is God in the way that he revealed himself as God to the Jews who rebuked him. Let us not seek any other teacher or interpreter. When pressed about his divinity, he did not deny that he was God. But clearly, due to the generous gift of superabundant grace, Christ, unlike other earthly men and partial gods, is the Son, and, by his freely-given nature, God. This grace was given to him in a greater degree than [it was given to] all the others who were chosen by God and divinely illumined, whom scripture calls gods.

Besides, although Christ is God, he is nevertheless one with God the Father in a unity of spirit, will, and love. Thus, the plurality which [theologians] see is not there, but rather results if, as they would have it, there are two or three gods equal in nature. In that case, as we have shown above, it would be impossible for one of them to be dispatched or sent forth by the other.

---

[a] Lorenzo Valla, *De Elegantiis Latinæ Linguæ* 6.34.

Err. 16a At vero Christus est deus communicata sibi a patre deitatis ratione, ideo una et eadem est ratio deitatis Christi cum patre et sic in effectu unus cum patre deus dici potest. Nulla enim maior unitas omni respectu inveniri potest quam inter patrem et filium licet re et natura distinguantur. Item hac ratione dixit Christus Ego et pater unum sumus, qui videt me, videt et patrem, pater in me est, et ego in patre, pater in me manens, ipse facit opera. Et huiusmodi nec mirum cum filius sit visibilis imago, patris invisibilis et omnis virtus ac spiritus dei patris in filio visibili Jesu Christo reluceat et ita ex admirandis operibus et sermonibus patrem in filio esse cognovimus et hæc est unitas illa de qua scriptura loquitur non autem de unitate seu identitate naturæ ut male docuerunt.

Lege et percurre universam scripturam. Numquam invenies filium dei pro eodem deo naturaliter [80] accipi, sed semper dei filium pro eo qui ab ipso deo æterno invisibili re et natura distinguitur. Nempe quia solus pater a se ipso et natura deus, æternus, invisibilis et immutabilis, nunquam filius nunquam genitus, nunquam homo, nunquam missus, nunquam passus, nunquam visus, nunquam mortuus et suscitatus fuit, sed semper idem, æternus, invisibilis, incomprehensibilis et immutabilis mansit, et aliter dicere vel sentire horrenda blasphemia est. Filius autem dei vere homo, vere genitus, vere natus, vere missus, vere visus et palpatus, vere passus, mortuus et suscitatus, et hoc credere et confiteri

Err. 15b-16a; 21b (the word *Tritoitæ*) vita æterna est. Fingant igitur isti Tritoitæ sibi quotquot voluerint per naturam deos æquales. Nobis cum Paulo unus sufficit deus summus et invisibilis qui est pater ille a quo omnia, et nos in illum, et unus dominus Jesus Christus redemptor noster per quem omnia et nos per illum, qui est filius benedictus in sæcula.

On the other hand, Christ is truly God because of the nature of the divinity shared with him by the Father. Thus, the nature of the divinity in Christ and the Father is one and the same. So, in effect, he can be called one God with the Father. For, no matter how you look at it, no greater unity can be found than that of the Father and the Son, even though they are distinct in being and nature. This is why Christ said, "*I and the Father are one*";[a] "*who sees me sees also* the Father";[b] "*the Father is in me and I in* the Father";[c] "*the Father who dwells in me, he does the works.*"[d] This being the case, there is no [cause for] wonder, for since the Son is the visible image of the invisible Father, all the power and spirit of God the Father shines forth in the visible Son Jesus Christ, and thus we recognize, from his wondrous deeds and words, that the Father is in the Son. This is the unity about which scripture speaks. It does not, however, speak about a unity or identity of nature, as [the theologians] have erroneously taught.

Read and examine all of scripture. You will never find that "Son of God," naturally understood, means the same thing as God. Instead you will find that "Son of God" is always used for one who is distinct in being and nature from the eternal, invisible God. Of course, the Father alone in his very self and nature is the eternal, invisible, and unchanging God. He was never a Son, never begotten, never a man, never sent, never suffered, never seen, never dead and restored to life, but has ever remained the same, eternal, invisible, incomprehensible, and unchanging. It is a terrible blasphemy to say or think otherwise. However, the Son of God was truly a man, truly begotten, truly born, truly sent, truly seen and touched, truly suffered, died and was restored to life. To believe and to confess this is eternal life. Let those tritoites [tritheists],[15] therefore, contrive for themselves as many gods, equal in nature, as they like. For us, as for Paul, *one God* is enough: the most high and invisible Father, *from whom all things are and in whom we are, and one Lord Jesus Christ*, our redeemer, *through whom all things are and through whom we exist*,[e] who is the blessed Son forever.

---

[a] John 10:30.   [b] John 12:45.   [c] John 17:21.   [d] John 14:10.   [e] 1 Cor. 8:6.

[81] *Declarationis Jesu Christi Filii Dei.*
Per Michælem Servetum,
liber quintus

His sic iactis veræ relligionis et fidei evangelicæ fundamentis, superest aliquot locos scripturæ diligenter explicare qui prima facie aliquam difficultatem facere videntur ex quorum declaratione prædicta omnia clarius et verius elucessent.*

Err. 22b

Primus locus est Io. 1. In principio erat verbum aput deum et deus erat illud verbum et verbum illud homo factum est, quæ verba videntur munire quod deus ille unicus, esset verbum et idemmet carnem assumpserit et consequenter idememet deus et pater et filius sit in utero virginis incarnatus.

Secundus locus est Io. 8. Antequam abraham fieret Ego sum.

Tertius in Epistola Io. Tres sunt qui testimonium dant in cœlis pater verbum et spiritus sanctus et hii tres unum est.

Quartus. 17. Io. Pater, glorifica me ea gloria quam habui aput te prius quam hic mundus fieret.

Quintus. Christus primogenitus omnis creaturæ. Collo. 1.

Sextus. Phillip. 2. Non rapinam arbitratus est se esse æqualem deo quibus locis multi allii conformes murmurantur quos christo ipso benefaciente statim explicatos accipies.

Primus igitur locus Io. 1 de deo et verbo sic explicatur verbum idest, oraculum dei patris erat aput ipsum deum idest reconditum [82] nondum patefactum nec creaturis manifestatum cuius prima manifestatio fuit in creando mundo nam per ipsius verbi potentiam omnis creatio peracta est dixit enim deus fiat et factum est.

---

* Should read *eluxissent*.

A Revelation of Jesus Christ the Son of God
by Michael Servetus
Book 5

Having thus laid the foundations of true religion and gospel faith, we now need to thoroughly elucidate several scriptural passages, which at first glance appear to present difficulties [for the argument I have presented]. Once these are explained, all that I have previously said will stand out more clearly and accurately.

The first passage is from John 1: *In the beginning was the Word, [and the Word was] with God, and the Word was God*,[a] and *the Word became* a man.[b] These words appear to bolster the argument that God alone was the Word, that he himself assumed flesh, and consequently that the same God, who was both the Father and the Son, was incarnate in the Virgin's womb.

The second passage is from John 8: "*Before Abraham was, I am*."[c]

The third is from the Epistle of John: *There are three who bear witness in heaven – the Father, the Word, and the Holy Spirit – and these three are one.*[d,1]

The fourth is from John 17: "*Father, glorify me with the glory which I had with you before the world was made.*"[e]

The fifth is from Colossians 1: Christ *the firstborn of all creation.*[f]

The sixth is from Philippians 2: *He did not consider it theft to be equal to God.*[g]

With Christ's blessing, I will quickly elucidate for you these passages, and many others like them, which are often the subject of discussion.

The first passage, from the first chapter of John, on God and the Word, can be explained as follows: *the Word*, that is, the utterance of God, *was with God* himself,[h] that is, hidden away and not yet revealed to his creatures. It was first manifested during the creation of the world. For it was through the power of the Word that all creation was brought about. God said "*Let it be*", and it was done.[i]

---

[a] John 1:1. [b] John 1:14. [c] John 8:58. [d] 1 John 5:7-8. [e] John 17:5. [f] Col. 1:15. [g] Phil. 2:6.
[h] John 1:1. [i] Gen. 1:3,6-7, etc.

Postea subdit et deus erat illum verbum hæc clausula diligenter adnotanda est quia duplicem habet sensum. Nam uno modo intelligi potest quod ipse deus pater esset illudmet verbum suum nondum patefactum et sensus erit quod antequam illud dei verbum sive oraculum et decretum caro fieret et in hominis formam transiret qui postea locutus est et voluntatem manifestavit atque adimplevit, ipsemet deus erat verbum suum idest per se ipsum invisibiliter loquebatur non per filium post vero incarnationem sui verbi non amplius per se ipsum invisibiliter sed visibiliter per filium locutus est, Heb. 1. Et sic verbum quæ est quædam ipsius dei dispositio ipsummet deum simpliciter esse non dicimus quia vera religio docet omnia quæ ab ipso deo sunt et essentiam atque initium ab eo sumpserunt ab eodem patre æterno et invisibili per naturam esse distincta alioquin si omnis dei dispositio ipsemet deus esse dicatur sequitur illa subiecti repugnantia et perplexitas a deo maxime aliena quod scilicet Deus æternus sit idemmet disponens et dispositum proferens et prolatum creans et creatum faciens et factum quæ secundum naturam et substantiam dici non possunt licet aliquo modo interpretative deus de sua dispositione prædicari possit ut hic Deus ipse est verbum suum quod fecit. Deus est sapientia quam ipse creavit, ab initio et ante sæcula creata [83] sum, Ecle. 1. et 24. et ita dictum Joannis recte intelligi potest. Sed dummodo semper inteligamus Joannem hoc loco de verbo dei incorporeo loquitur prout aput ipsum deum reconditum erat nec dum homo factus aut filius, ut supra late declaravimus et infra adhuc latius demonstrabitur.

Vel et secundo modo intelligi potest quod verbum illud dei esset deus scilicet a deo patre per communicationem deitatis. Nam cum sermo ille dei esset aput ipsum deum cui omnia præsentia sunt, iam ut christus homo et filius benedilectus designatus postea nobis in tempore revelandus nimirum erat etiam deus de deo benedictus et gloriosus iam ergo aput ipsum patrem qui solus per naturam deus est, erat ille logos suus, ut Christus Jesus eius filius deificatus, plenus omni potentia gloria et divinitate.

To this John adds: *and the Word was God*.[a] The last part of the verse is worth noting carefully, since it has a double meaning. In one sense, it can be understood to mean that God the Father was himself his Word, not yet revealed. In other words, before the Word, or utterance and decree of God, became flesh and passed into human form, which afterwards spoke, manifested, and fulfilled his will, God himself was his Word; that is, he spoke through himself, invisibly, and not through the Son. But after the incarnation of his Word, he no longer spoke invisibly through himself, but visibly through his Son (Hebrews 1).[b] And so we do not say that the Word, which is a kind of disposition of God, is exactly the same thing as God himself, since true religion teaches that all things which are from God take their essence as well as their beginning from him, and are by nature distinct from the eternal and invisible Father. Otherwise, if every disposition of God is said to be God himself, then there follows a contradiction and a confusion of subject [with object] which is utterly alien to God. For then the eternal God would be both the disposer and the thing disposed, the bringer forth and the thing brought forth, the creator and the created, the doer and what is done. Such things cannot be said about nature and substance, although, looking at it in a certain way, God can be predicated of his own disposition, so that God himself is his Word, which he himself created.

God is the wisdom which he created: *I* [wisdom] *was created from the beginning and before time* (Ecclesiasticus 1 and 24).[c] This is the way in which John can be correctly understood – provided that we always keep in mind that in this passage John is speaking of the incorporeal Word of God, exactly as it was when hidden within God, and not when it was made a man or a son, as we have stated at length above and as will be further demonstrated below.

This passage can also be understood in another way: that the Word of God was God, that is, it was from God the Father by means of a sharing of deity. For when the Word of God was with God, to whom all things are present, [the Word was] already designated to be the man Christ and [God's] well-beloved Son, who was later to be revealed to us in time. [The Word] was then, without a doubt, God from God, blessed and glorified. It was, therefore, already with the Father, who alone is God by nature. It was his *Logos*. As Jesus Christ, [the Word] was the deified Son, filled with all power, glory, and divinity.

---

[a] John 1:1.   [b] Heb. 1:1,2.   [c] Ecclesiasticus (Sirach) 1:9, 24:9 (Vulgate 24:14).

Ut ipsemet deus Jesus redemptor noster, cum in hoc mundo patrem oraret apertissime declaravit, Pater ego te glorificavi super terram, opus consummavi quod dedisti mihi ut facerem. Et nunc glorifica me tu pater aput temet ipsum, gloria quam habui aput te, prius quam hic mundus fieret.Vides ergo quomodo filius in angustiis mundi positus orabat Patrem se glorificari ea gloria quam iam habuerat aput patrem cum pater per illum et propter illum omnia crearet et omnia creata illi subiiceret, et hoc est quod dicit, paul, Corinth. 2. Loquor sapientiam dei in mysterio, quæ est recondita, quam præfinierat deus ante sæcula in gloriam nostram, quam nemo principium huius sæculi cognovit, nam si cognovissent dominum gloriæ non crucifixissent.

Et ita [84] Joannes dixit verbum illud esse deum, idest deitate atque potentia et gloria repletum, ad diferentiam omnium aliarum rerum conditarum, quæ licet a deo patre prodierunt multam tamen rationem deitatis obtinuerunt, sicut logos ipse christus Jesus quod primo principatitum ante omnia et super omnia a deo per deitatem deus de deo lumen de lumine deus verus de deo vero, et hac ratione Christus etiam dicitur primogenitus omnis creaturæ quia in spiritu et dispositione dei omnia creata præcessit. Et omnia ad ipsum accesorie facta sunt.

Sed ne videatur tibi dura et conversa interpretatio. Exponendo deum demum prædicatio ipsius verbi sequentis, cum natura prædicati sit ut suo subiecto post ponatur. Et ideo potius dicendum fuit, Et verbum illud erat deus, dico quod hic modus loquendi in scriptura frequenter inveniatur. Præsertim aput Joannem Cap. 4. Spiritus est deus et eos qui eum adorant spiritu ac veritate oportet adorare. Nam illa vox spiritus anteposita stat in vim prædicati et deum in vim subiecti. Deus enim est spiritus et ideo spiritu adorari vult nemo enim novit ea quæ sunt dei nisi spiritus dei, Corinth. 2. Omne enim simile suo simili facilius comprehenditur et detestatur,

Jesus our redeemer openly revealed himself as God when in this world he prayed to the Father: "*Father, I glorified you on earth. I have completed the work which you have given me to do. And now, Father, glorify me in your own presence, with the glory which I had with you, before the world was made.*"[a] Here you see how the Son, in the midst of the troubles of this world, prayed to the Father that he might be glorified with that glory he already possessed in the Father, when the Father, through him and for his sake, created all things and subjected all created things to him. This is what Paul says in 1 Corinthians, chapter 2: *I tell a secret and hidden wisdom of God, which God determined before the ages, for our glory. None of the princes of this world were aware of this, for if they had been, they would not have crucified the Lord of glory.*[b]

And so John calls the Word "God" – that is, filled with divinity, power, and glory, in a way unlike all other created things. Although these [created things] possess a considerable degree of divinity, in that they came forth from God the Father, Jesus Christ, as the *Logos*, was the first of the heavenly beings, *before all things*[c] and *over all things*.[d] By means of his divinity from God, he is "God of God, light of light, and true God of true God."[e] Christ is always called *the firstborn of all creation*,[f] since according to the spirit and dispensation of God, he preceded all created things. And all things were made as an appendage to him.

But lest this interpretation [of the relationship between God and the Word] seem to you harsh and twisted – to explain "God" only as the predicate of "the Word," which follows it [in the Greek and Vulgate text of John 1], when it is the nature of a predicate to be placed after its subject – it should rather be said, "and the Word was God" [with "the Word" preceding "God."][2]

I say that this manner of speaking is often found in scripture. For example, in John, chapter 4: *Spirit is God, and those who worship him must worship in spirit and truth.*[g] For the word "spirit," although placed first, has the force of a predicate, while "God" acts as the subject. Indeed, *God is spirit*, and, for that reason, he wishes to be worshipped in spirit: *For no one knows what belongs to God, except the Spirit of God* (Corinthians 2).[h] For all things are more easily confronted and comprehended by their like.

---

[a] John 17:1-5.   [b] 1 Cor. 2:7-8.   [c] Col. 1:17.   [d] Eph. 1:22.   [e] From the Nicene Creed.   [f] Col. 1:15.
[g] John 4:24.   [h] 1 Cor. 2:11.

ex his habes locum Joannis aperte declaratum quia Theologis nostris male perceptus multorum errorum præbuit ocasionem hinc, in illam pluralitatem personarum seu hypostasum temere [85] derivarunt dum hæbraicam phrasim ignorantes, et inter deum ac dei filium distinguere nescientes, utriusque naturam vere distinctam et separatam, satis impie confuderunt.

Err. 67b   Secundus offert se locus, Io. 8. Antequam Abraham fieret ego sum, pro cuius declaratione adnotandum est, quod non dixit Christus, Ante Abraham ego natus sum sed simpliciter ego sum, referens se ad suum esse originale, velut verbum illud dei simplex et incorporeum, antequam ex virgine nasceretur et corporeum ac visibile fieret, Cum igitur Christus Jesus sit logos ille dei corporatus, et homo factus qui logos ante omnia sæcula. Et ante omnem creaturam fuit, utique ratione suæ essentiæ potuit vere dicere, Ante adam et Abraham sum, et hac ratione Io. Baptista de eo testificans ait, hic est de quo dicebam, qui cum me sequeretur antecesit me, quia prior me erat, loquebatur autem Io. de Jesu illo visibili filio dei sanctissimo, qui aput deum prior omnibus fuit, licet aput mundum post ipsum Joannem fuerit in carne manifestatus.

Et Io. Evangelista testatur de verbo vitæ quod erat ab initio et ab ipso postea visum ac palpatum fuit. 1. Io. Et ex prædictis facile potes Theollogorum errorem deprehendere qui dicunt Jesum illum visibilem, non esse filium, nec verbum dei, sed ipsi filio unitum nam ratione talis unionis quæ in tempore facta fuit, Non potuiset Jesus vere et proprie dicere Judæis, Antequam Abraham fieret [86] ego sum, Sed quia Jesus ille visibilis, erat ipsummet dei verbum postea corporatum. Et homo factum, non per unionem sed per conversionem vere potuit dicere, Ante omnes ego sum.

Et hoc modo patet etiam declaratio et resolutio ad quintum de primogenitum omnis creaturæ ad cuius intelligentiam et aliorum similium illud perpetuo adnotandum est unam ex potissimis
Err. 52b   errorum causis fuise quod in dei operibus et misteriis nulli tempori subiectis de prioritate et posterioritate temporum carnaliter iudicamus et ea velut humana metimur.

Thus we have clearly elucidated the passage from John. Since it was understood erroneously by our theologians, this opened the way to a multitude of errors. Due to their ignorance of the Hebrew way of expressing things, they have blindly strayed into this plurality of persons or hypostases. By not recognizing the distinction between God and the Son of God, they have impiously confounded the natures of both, which are truly distinct and separate.

The second passage is in John 8: "*Before Abraham was, I am.*"[a] It should be noted that Christ did not say, "Before Abraham, I was born," but simply "*I am*," referring to his original state of being as the Word of God, pure and incorporeal, before he was born from the Virgin and became corporeal and visible. For, indeed, Jesus Christ is the *Logos* of God, who was the *Logos* before all ages and was given a body and made man. He existed before all creation. And so, on account of his essence, he could truthfully say, "*Before* Adam and *Abraham, I am.*" For this reason, *John* the Baptist, *bearing witness to him*, says, "*This is the one about whom I said, 'although he followed me, he is ahead of me, because he was [made] before me.'*"[b] John was talking about Jesus, the visible, most holy Son of God, who was with God before all things, even though in the world he appeared in the flesh after John himself.

John the Evangelist also *bears witness concerning the word of life, which was from the beginning*, and which he afterward saw and touched (1 John).[c] From what I have just said, you can easily uncover the error of the theologians, who say that the visible Jesus was neither the Son nor the Word of God, but was united to the [invisible] Son. For, on the basis of such a union, which took place in time, Jesus could not rightly and truthfully have told the Jews, "*Before Abraham was, I am.*" However, since the visible Jesus was the Word of God which afterward became incarnate and was made man – not by means of a union but by a transformation – he could truthfully say, "*Before all things, I am.*"

The way is now open to explain and resolve the fifth passage, *the firstborn of all creation.*[d] To understand this and other similar matters, we must always keep in mind that one of the greatest sources of error results from our judging the works and mysteries of God, which are not subject to time, and judging them, according to the flesh, in terms of past and future time, measuring them as if they were human events.

---

[a] John 8:58.   [b] John 1:15.   [c] 1 John 1:1.   [d] Col. 1:15.

Err. 53a Sed cum æternus deus suæ æternitatis lumine quæcunque fuerunt sunt et erunt velut iam facta et sibi presentissima conspiciat ac disponat, et mille anni, ante ipsum tanquam dies externa quæ preteriit vere de filio suo Jesu Christo, dixit ego hodie genui te, quia ab initio mundi usque ad Christum natum una est dies qua Christi generatio agitur, et nullam esse in deo temporum distinctionem arguit mos loquendi in prophetis qui ex ore dei futura pro posteribus annunciant.

Nam ante mundi creationem ratio temporum non deo sed homini necessaria fuit, quibus distinguendis luminaria cœlestia disposita sunt: Erunt inquit in tempora dies et annos ergo nec tempus habuit ante tempus qui fecit tempus nec initium ante initium qui initium constituit nec deus se tempori subiecit mundum

Err. 53b creando. Nunc esset reiecto velamine temporis consideres horam generationis et nativitatis Jesu christi fuise in ipso mundi initio deo præsentem facile concedes deum tunc et ante omnia [87] verbum suum protulisse et ita ex eo filium hunc Jesum genuisse qui novissimis diebus et definito tempore nobis manifestatus est et hoc est quod cum magna admiratione dicit Esai, Antequam veniret tempus partum masculum peperit, tempus enim pariendi, et ipsa nativitatis hora, sed antequam hoc fieret iam ab initio et ante luciferum genuit eum ecce ergo quomodo deus filium quem sibi ab æterno generare decreverat, magnifice genuit, sic enim cum magnifice generari oportuit qui constituendus erat rex et dominus omnium et iudex viventium ac mortuorum, et si tu dicas fateor quod deus ante sæcula verbum illud invisibile protulit sed non genuit, ante sæcula Jesum illum invisibilem* qui sub Augusto cæsare ex virgine natus est. Nunne dixi tibi quod ea quæ in tempore hominibus revelantur et patefiunt apud ipsum deum iam facta sunt et in æternitatis lumine comprehenduntur. Cum enim de misteriis dei loquimur et suæ immutabilis voluntatis æternique decreti efectus contemplamur ad ipsum deum iuxta eius naturam omnis actio referenda est non ad homines distinctioni temporum subiectos

---

* Should read *visibilem*.

But since the eternal God observes and ordains, in the light of his eternity, all things that have been, are, and will be, as if already done and entirely present to him, and since *a thousand years* to him *are but as an outward day when it is past*,[a] he spoke truthfully when he said about his Son, Jesus Christ, *Today I have begotten you.*[b] For from the beginning of the world until the birth of Christ is a single day [to God], the one in which he begot Christ. The way the prophets speak proves that there are no distinctions of time with God. For from the mouth of God, they announce things to come as having already occurred.

Before the creation of the world, a system of time was not needed by God. It was, however, needed by man [after the creation]. To measure [time] the lights of heaven were arrayed: *"They will be,"* [God] *said, "for seasons, days, and years."*[c] Therefore, the creator of time did not possess time before the beginning of time, nor did he who set the beginning have a beginning before the beginning. By creating the world, God did not make himself subject to time. Now, having lifted the veil of time, you can see that the hour of the begetting and birth of Jesus Christ was present to God at the very beginning of the world. You will then readily allow that God spoke his Word before all things, and thus, by means of [the Word], begot [his] son Jesus, who, in these latter days, at a definite hour, was revealed to us.

For in wonderment Isaiah said: *Before the time for her delivery* – the time of labor and the hour of nativity – *she gave birth to a male child.*[d] But before this happened, even from the beginning and *before the dawn* [of time], *he begot* him.[e] Behold, therefore, how magnificently God begot his Son, whose begetting he had decreed from all eternity. For it was fitting that he who was established as the king and Lord of all, and *the judge of the living and the dead*,[f] should be thus magnificently begotten. But perhaps you might say, "I acknowledge that before all the ages God brought forth his invisible Word, but not that before the ages he begot the visible Jesus who was born of a virgin in the time of Augustus Caesar." Have I not told you that what is revealed and disclosed to humanity in time, is already accomplished in God, and is thus to be apprehended in the light of eternity? For when we speak about the mysteries of God and his immutable will, and when we contemplate the effects of his eternal decrees, every act must be referred to God, according to his nature, and not to human beings, who are subject to the distinctions of time.

---

[a] Ps. 90:4. [b] Heb. 1:5, Ps. 2:7. [c] Gen. 1:14. [d] Isa. 66:7. [e] Ps. 110:3 (Vulgate 109:3). [f] Acts 10:42.

deinde dicimus deum ante omnem creationem et creaturam Jesum Christum hominem ex verbo suo genuisse et ipsum proprium filium elegisse, per quem et propter quem omnia alia creavit et creata illi subiecit et sic in spiritu et dispositione dei patris omnium conditoris omnem creaturam prædiscit.

Err. 54a Et vere primogenitus fuit, ita Paul, Ad Collo. 1. et hoc misterium nobis declarat sapientia. Nam quia ab initio cum sermone facta primogenitam inter creaturas se vocat hoc sacramentum adnotans. Paulus Christum quem dei sapientiam ac potentiam esse dicit primogenitum vocat hoc idem confirmat, Ad Roma. 8. dicens quod deus præfinivit electos quos et vocavit confortes* fieri imaginis filii sui ut ipse sit primogenitus inter multos fratres, dicuntur enim electi ad eius similitudinem vocari cum ipse vere a deo genitus sit et alii ad eius imaginem per spiritum et sermonem dei regeniti, Io. 1.Et 1 Pet. 1. Præterea christus Jesus etiam dicitur primogenitus quia primus omnium a mortuis resurexit. [88] Et in hoc sensu accepit Paull, Collo. 1. et in actis Cap. xiii, dicens nimirum nobis resuscitato Jesu sicut in psalmo primo scriptum est, filius meus es tu, ego hodie genui te et sic omni respectu Jesus christus omnium creaturarum vere primogenitus est.

Err. 22a Tertius est Io. locus. Tres sunt qui testificantur in cœlis, pater sermo et spiritus sanctus et hii tres unum sunt, et hæc verba nihil aliud sonant quam tres esse in cœlis qui de ipso Jesu homine testimonium perhibuerunt quod sit filius dei.

Et primo pater qui semel atque iterum dixit, hic est filius meus dilectus in quo mihi bene complacui, ipsum audite, item jesus ipse qui est ipsemet sermo dei incarnatus et visibilis factus, de se ipso testificans. Io. 5. et 8. cum enim Judæi obiicerent ipsi christo quod diceretur esse lucem mundi, et quod de se ipso testificaretur, Respondit jesus, Et si ego perhibeam testimonium de me ipso verum est testimonium meum, quia scio unde veni et iudicium meum verum est quia solus non sum sed ego et qui misit me pater, quin et in lege vestra scriptum est quod duorum hominum testimonium verum est. Ego sum qui testimonium fero de me ipso. Et testimonium fert de me pater qui me misit.

---

* Should read *conformes*.

Therefore we say that God, before all creation and every creature, begot the man Jesus Christ from his Word, and chose him as his own Son, *through whom and for whom* he created all other things[a] and, once they were created, made them subject to him. Therefore, according to the spirit and by the disposition of God the Father, the author of all things, [Christ] has prior knowledge about every created thing.

Truly, as Paul says in Colossians 1, he was *the firstborn*,[b] and wisdom proclaims this mystery to us.[c] Noting this mystery, [Paul] calls [Christ] *the firstborn among creatures* because he was made with the Word from the beginning. Paul calls Christ, whom he says is *the wisdom and the power of God*,[d] the firstborn. [Paul] supports this in Romans 8, saying that God predetermined the elect, *whom he also summoned to conform to the image of his Son, so that he might be the firstborn among many brothers.*[e] The elect are said to be in his likeness, since he was truly begotten by God, while others are reborn in his image through the Spirit and Word of God (John 1 and 1 Peter 1).[f] Jesus Christ is also called the firstborn since he, before anyone else, rose again from the dead.[g] And this is how Paul understands it in Colossians 1 and in Acts 13, where he clearly says, *Jesus was raised for us, as it is written in the first Psalm, "You are my son, today I have begotten you."*[h,3] Thus, in every respect, Jesus Christ is truly *the firstborn of all creatures*.

The third passage is in John: *There are three who bear witness in heaven – the Father, the Word, and the Holy Spirit – and these three are one.*[i] These words mean nothing other than that there are three in heaven who have borne witness that the man Jesus is the Son of God.

The first is the Father, who more than once said, *"This is my beloved Son, with whom I am well pleased. Listen to him."*[j]

The second is Jesus, *the Word* of God *made flesh*[k] and visible, who, in John 5 and 8, bore witness to who he was. For when the Jews objected that Christ was calling himself *the light of the world*[l] and that he was bearing witness to himself,[m] Jesus replied, *"Even though I bear witness to myself, my testimony is true, because I know where I came from. And my judgment is true, for it is not I alone [who testify], but I and the Father who sent me. Indeed it is written in your law that the testimony of two men is true: I bear witness to myself, and the Father who sent me bears witness to me."*[n]

---

[a] Heb. 2:10. [b] Col. 1:15. [c] Ecclesiaticus (Sirach) 1:9, 24:9 (Vulgate 24:14). [d] 1 Cor. 1:24. [e] Rom. 8:29. [f] John 1:12-13, 1 Peter 1:23. [g] Col. 1:18. [h] Acts 13:33 (Erasmus), quoting Ps. 2:7. [i] 1 John 5:7. [j] Matt. 3:17, 17:5. [k] John 1:14. [l] John 8:12. [m] John 5:31, 8:13. [n] John 8:14-18. See also John 5:31-37.

Prætterea sermo dei cœlestis quem christus ipse loquebatur testimonium reddebat de eo quod esset filius dei et a deo missus, et ideo dicit sermonem quem audistis, non est meus, sed patris mei et verba quæ loquor vobis spiritus et vita sunt. Et beati qui audiunt verbum et custodiunt illud, et sermo eius veritas est, et si terrena dicenti non creditis, quomodo si dixero vobis cœlestia inteligetis. Verba igitur christi divina et cœlestia eum de cœlo esse testificabantur, item trinum testimonium est spiritus sancti qui in specie columbæ Jesum primo esse illum dei filium demonstravit Io. 1. quem ante per prophetas annuntiaverat et novissime in specie ignearum testificatus per os apostolorum, quod Jesus ille crucifixus esset dei filius, et hi tres testes. Pater et ipse filius Jesus et spiritus sanctus unum sunt, non quidem unitate naturæ, vel identitate substantiæ. Ut teologi male interpretantur sed unitate finis et consensus quia ut verissimi testes in unum finem et misterium simul [89] concordant non ut testes dissoni qui unum non erant cum diverso modo ac varie de eodem actu testificarentur nec ut testes Caiphæ contra Christum perducti, quorum testimonia non erant convenientia.

Tres autem prædicti testes cœlestes de Jesu dei filio bene conveniunt et unum sunt sicut etiam tria sunt in terris, idest aput homines testimonia in idem conformia scilicet spiritus electorum a spiritu dei illustratus, Aqua baptismi, Et sanguis martirum qui quotidie pro hac fide et confessione effunditur quæ omnia in ipso Jesu Christo prius fuerunt verificata. Nam pro hac confessione qua se palam dei filium dixerat mortem sustinuit et de corpore suo spiritum, aquam et sanguinem emisit, et ita intelligitur hæc unio testimoniarum seu testium concordia.

Unde apparet quam ridicula sit illorum expositio qui hanc unionem ad naturam vel substantiam rei deducere conantur sicut et illum ego et pater unum sumus quæ expositio tam vera est quam verum est spiritum aquam et sanguinem eandemmet esse substantiam vel naturam:

Furthermore, the words of God from heaven, which Christ spoke, also bore witness that he was the Son of God, sent from God. That is why he says, "*The words you have heard are not mine, but my Father's,*"ᵃ and "*The words that I am speaking to you are spirit and life.*"ᵇ Also, "*Blessed are those who hear the word and keep it,*"ᶜ and "*His word is truth*"ᵈ and "*If I have told earthly things that you do not believe, will you understand if I speak to you of heavenly things?*"ᵉ Thus the divine and heavenly words of Christ bear witness that he was from heaven.

The third witness is the Holy Spirit, which in the form of a dove pointed to Jesus as the Son of God (John 1),ᶠ whom [the Spirit] had previously foretold through the mouths of the prophets. And in the form of [tongues of] flame, it later bore witness, through the mouths of the apostles, that the crucified Jesus was the Son of God.ᵍ

These three witnesses – the Father, the Son Jesus, and the Holy Spirit – are one, certainly not by natural unity or identity of substance, as the theologians wrongly understand it, but by a unity of purpose and a combined harmony of will. For, like the truest witnesses, they agree together about one purpose and mystery, unlike discordant witnesses who do not agree when they give differing testimony about the same event, and unlike the witnesses whom Caiaphas brought against Christ, whose testimony did not concur.ʰ

The aforementioned three heavenly witnesses to Jesus, the Son of God, concur [in their testimony] and are one, just as do the three witnesses on earth, that is, among men: the spirit of the elect, illumined by the spirit of God; the water of baptism; and the blood of martyrs, which is daily shed for this faith and confession. All of these [testimonies] have previously been shown to be true in the case of Jesus Christ. For by that confession in which he openly declared himself the Son of God, he suffered death, and from his body shed spirit, water, and blood. This is the way the unity of testimony and harmony among these witnesses is to be understood.

From this it is obvious how absurd the interpretation is of those who attempt to reduce this unity to the nature or substance of a [single] being, based on, "*I and the Father are one.*"ⁱ This interpretation is like [saying that] spirit, water, and blood have the same substance or nature.

ᵃ John 14:24. ᵇ John 6:63. ᶜ Luke 11:28. ᵈ John 17:17. ᵉ John 3:12. ᶠ John 1:32. ᵍ Acts 2:3.
ʰ Matt. 26:59-60. ⁱ John 10:30.

Imo in scriptura dictio unum numquam pro identitate substantiæ vel naturæ accipitur sed pro convenientia et conformitate spiritus vel consensus ut Io. 17. Pater sancte serva eos per nomen tuum ut sint unum sicut et nos et Corint. 3. cæterum his qui plantat et his qui rigat unum sunt, et hac ratione iussit. Christus omnes credentes <u>baptizari in nomine patris et filii et spiritus sancti</u> nimirum in nomine eorum quorum testimonium ipsi baptizati crediderant accipiendo tamen semper pro ipso Jesu visibili ut Matth. 12. Omne peccatum in patrem vel filium hominis remittetur et quoniam omnia prædicta testimonia in hunc finem conspirant ut Jesum Christum demonstrent et eius contemplatione emanarunt ideo petrus et alii apostoli annunciabant Judæis remissionem peccatorum per Jesum christum crucifixum in eiusdem nomine baptizantes nec legitur in scriptura quod apostoli simpliciter baptizarent, in nomine patris tantum vel spiritus sancti sed in nomine omnium simul et explicite, ut Jesus docuerat vel simpliciter et implicite, in nomine ipsius Jesu christi. Actu. 2. et 8. ad denotandum, quod omnia divina misteria in solo Jesu christo filio consummantur et comprehenduntur [**90**] et id diserte explicatur ab Ireno. adversus Valentinum, lib. 3. cap. 20. dum inquit in christi enim nomine subauditur qui unxit et ipse qui unctus est. Et ipsa unctio quemadmodum per Esaim filius ait spiritus dei super me propter quod unxit me significans et ungentem patrem, et unctum filium, et unctionem qui est spiritus, hæc Irene.

Err. 28b

O christiane notam* elegantissimam et verissimam sanctæ et apostolicæ Ecclesiæ, triadem patris et filii et spiritus sancti in quibus solus pater ungens et natura deus qui filium Jesum unxit spiritu suo sancto, in omni abundantia et plenitudine nec constituas tibi tres deos distinctos, et per naturam æquales æquiparando unctum et unctionem ipsi ungenti qui illa disponit et dispensat, et cognosces te ex palpabilibus tenebris in serenissimam lucem revocatum. Et ideo Joannes spiritum sanctum unctionem frequenter vocat dicens, sed vos unctionem habetis a sancto illo et nostis omnia et unctio quam accepistis ab eo manet in vobis et non necesse habetis ut quisque doceat vos sed sicut ipsa unctio docet vos manete in ea.

---

* Should read *nota*.

However, in scripture the word "one" never means identity of substance or nature, but indicates an agreement and harmony of spirit, as in John 17: "*Holy Father, protect them through your name that they might be one as we are.*"[a] Furthermore, in Corinthians 3: *Those who plant and those who water are one.*[b] For this reason Christ commanded that all believers should be *baptized in the name of the Father, the Son, and the Holy Spirit* [c] – that is, in the name of those whose testimony was believed by those who were baptized.

These [three witnesses], however, are always to be understood as meaning the visible Jesus, as [it says] in Matthew 12: "*Every sin against* God or *the Son of man will be forgiven.*"[d] Since all [three heavenly] witnesses work together toward this end – to reveal Jesus Christ – and all become known by contemplating him, therefore Peter and the other apostles proclaimed to the Jews *the forgiveness of sins* through Jesus Christ crucified, baptizing in his name.[e] We do not read in scripture that the apostles baptized in the name of the Father or of the Holy Spirit alone. Rather [they did so] either explicitly in the name of all [three] together, as Jesus taught, or simply and implicitly in the name of Jesus Christ (Acts 2 and 8),[f] indicating that all the divine mysteries were brought to completion and embraced in Jesus the Son alone. This is set forth eloquently by Irenaeus in *Against Valentinus*, book 3, chapter 20, where he says,

> We are to understand, by the name "Christ," he who anointed, he who was anointed, and the anointing itself. Speaking through Isaiah, the Son says, "*The Spirit of God is upon me, because* he *anointed me,*"[g] signifying the anointing Father, the anointed Son, and the actual anointing, which is the Spirit.

Thus says Irenaeus.[h]

Notice, Christian, this most true and elegant triad of the holy and apostolic church – the Father, the Son, and the Holy Spirit – in which the Father alone does the anointing, and in which he who by nature is God has anointed his Son Jesus with his Holy Spirit in the most plenteous abundance. Do not set up three separate gods who are equal by nature, in order to establish an equivalence among the anointed, the anointing, and the anointer who ordains and arranges [these things] and you will find yourself delivered out of palpable darkness into the fairest light. Thus John often calls the Holy Spirit an anointing, saying, *But you possess anointing from the Holy One and know all. The anointing you have received from him abides in you. It is not necessary that anyone should teach you, as the anointing itself is your teacher. Abide in that [anointing].*[i]

---

[a] John 17:11. [b] 1 Cor. 3:8. [c] Matt. 28:19. [d] Matt. 12:31-32. [e] Acts 2:38. [f] Acts 2:38, 8:16. [g] Isa. 61:1.
[h] Irenaeus, *Adv. Hær.*3.18.3 (PG 7a 934B). [i] 1 John 2:20, 27.

Venio ad aliud argumentum quare scriptura dicit Christum esse ex semine david secundum carnem, quasi tota humanitas Christi sit ipsi virgini tribuenda quæ erat ex stirpe David et sic quod Christus, ut homo non proprie filius dei ita intelligunt Theologi nostri dicentes Christum constare ex duplici natura distincta divina scilicet et humana et respectu humanitatis esse apatora id est sine patre, sed prius quam hoc argumentum disolvam, Volo aliud multo necesarium declarare videlicet, quomodo beata virgo dicatur de stirpe David cum id ex scriptura nova nusquam colligatur et propterea miseri Anabaptisti hanc rationem invenire nescientes impie mentiti sunt Jesum Christum esse filium Joseph quia de Joseph scriptura aperte loquitur quod fuerit de stirpe David ut patet ex genealogia Mattæi et Lucæ quod de Joseph non de maria origine* sortem et propaginem texuerunt. Ad hoc clare respondeo quod evangelisti satis declaraverunt Mariam esse ex stirpe David cum ostendunt virum eius Joseph Ex eadem stirpe progenitum. Nam genealogia ad virum semper refertur tamquam ad caput familiæ et tamen etiam uxor in eadem comprehenditur quia non poterat aliquis per legem Mosis ducere in [91] uxorem nisi de eadem tribu et familia ut est textus apertus quem non viderunt anabaptisti in Cap. ultimo numerorum unde necesse fuit virginem desponsatam viro de domo david Ex eadem domo fuisse progenitam.

Nunc venio ad argumentum quare Christus dicatur ex semine david secundum carnem, ad quod respondeo quod beata virgo quod fuit ex stirpe David, ut ostendimus partem habet filiationis in Jesu christo fillio dei respectu corporis organizati. Nam quod cæteri filii hominum actipiunt a matre, Jesus actepit a virgine sed propterea non negat scriptura eumdem Jesum etiam ut hominem filium dei esse, nec paternam generationem ab ipso deo procesisse ut clarissime Lucas describit oportuit enim filium dei ex matre nasci licet a deo patre exierit. Igitur Jesus ille qui ex virgine natus est vere filius et hominis est indivisus et licet deus ut pater est quo ad humanitatem in generatione Christi concurrerit virtus in altissimo virginem inumbravit et fecundavit ut talem partum conciperet quia non est impossibile aput deum omne verbum.

---

* Should read *origenem*.

I come now to another argument which is based upon the scriptural [passage] which says that Christ is *of the seed of David according to the flesh*.[a] Our theologians understand this to mean that all of Christ's humanity is to be attributed to the Virgin, who was of the lineage of David, so that Christ, as a man, is thus not properly the Son of God. They say that Christ has a nature which is twofold and distinct, divine and human, and claim that, in terms of his humanity, he is *apatora*, that is, "without a father."[4]

Before I refute this argument, I would like to make another crucial point: that the blessed Virgin can be said to be from the line of David, even though this claim is not made explicit in the New Testament. Unaware of this line of reasoning, the wretched Anabaptists have impiously and falsely claimed that Jesus was the son of Joseph,[5] since scripture clearly says that Joseph is of the line of David, as is well-known from the genealogies in Matthew and Luke. [These Anabaptists] have fashioned an ancestry, lineage, and destiny for him based upon Joseph and not upon Mary. My answer to this is clear: the evangelists have sufficiently demonstrated that Mary is of David's line by showing that her husband Joseph was born of that lineage. For a genealogy always refers to the husband as the head of the family. Nonetheless, the wife is also included in it because, according to the law of Moses, one could not take a wife except from one's own tribe and family. The obvious proof of this is found in the last chapter of Numbers, a text which the Anabaptists have overlooked, where [it is written] that a young woman betrothed to a man of the house of David ought herself to be born of that same house.[b]

Now I come back to the argument whereby Christ is said to be *of the seed of David according to the flesh*.[c] My response to this is that the blessed Virgin, since she was, as I have shown, of David's line, has a parental share in the physical body [6] of Jesus Christ, the Son of God. For, what other sons of men receive from their mothers, Jesus received from the Virgin. Scripture does not on that account, however, deny that Jesus, as a human being, is the Son of God, or that his paternal begetting proceeds from God. Luke writes most clearly that it was necessary that the Son of God be born of a mother, even though he came forth from God.[d] Therefore, the indivisible Jesus who is born of the Virgin is truly the Son and belongs to humankind, even though God, as the father, engaged in the begetting of Christ, including his human nature. *The power* [of God] in the highest *overshadowed* the Virgin and caused her to become pregnant,[e] so that she might conceive such a child. *For nothing is impossible with God.*[f]

---

[a] Rom. 1:3.   [b] Num. 36:8.   [c] Rom. 1:3.   [d] Luke 24:26, 1:31-33.   [e] Luke 1:35.   [f] Luke 1:37.

Virgo autem non participavit in Christo quoad spiritualem generationem nam illa soli deo genitori tribuitur qui solus omnia dona spirituali* ipsi filio communicavit. Scriptura igitur dicit Jesum esse filium David secundum carnem ut carnalem generationem quæ sola ex matre est a spirituali distingunt quæ a solo patre est quæ per spiritum sanctificationis et ipsum verbum quod ab æterno est mirifice deducitur. Pater enim cœlestis partum illum virginis oleo leticiæ et spiritu sanctificationis inunxit ut rex et dominus omnium creaturarum nasceretur et hanc unctionem Jesus non a matre sed a solo patre actepit et per communicationem huius unctionis spiritualis nos etiam in Christo regeneramur et renascimur et hoc aput Paullum clarius legitur, Collo. 3. Ubique habentes [92] servos dicuntur domini secundum carnem eo quia per spiritum dei in Christo Jesu non est servus neque dominus sed omnes unum sumus et fratres omnes, sic etiam ad Romanos 9. vocantur cognati secundum carnem ad differentiam eorum qui cognatione spirituali per christi spiritum coniunguimur. Unde Christus dixit quisquis fecerit voluntatem patris mei hic meus et frater et soror et mater est.

Cum igitur Christus ex carne et spiritu constet ex deo et homine vere natus creditur quia deus est spiritus, et quod natum est ex spiritu spiritus est et hinc confunditur opinio perversa Ebionis et Cerinti quod solam in christo carnalem generationem ponebant quæ ex virginali semine deducitur non intelligentes carnalem dici respectu matris cum tamen a patre rationem verbi et spiritus significantis divinam et cœlestem originem acteperit sic etiam carnalem cognationem intellexit Josippus lib. 17. antiquitatum, cap. 8. Ubi de mathia sacerdote loquens inquit sed Josephus Eliimi filius cognatus eius secundum carnem pro eo munere sacerdotali fungitur quod illi ex parte matris coniunctus esset. Unde Irene. lib. III. cap. 27. loquens de filio dei hic est inquit qui ex virgine quæ fuit de genere David generatus est propter hoc enim et de fructu ventris eius regem promisit quod erat proprium virginis prægnantis et non de fructu lumborum vel renum eius quod est proprium viri generantis

---

* Should read *spiritualia*.

The Virgin, however, did not share in the spiritual generation of Christ, for that is solely attributed to God, the Father, who alone shared all his spiritual gifts with his Son. Thus scripture says that Jesus is the son *of David according to the flesh*,[a] in terms of corporeal generation, from the mother alone, which is to be distinguished from spiritual generation, which is from the Father alone. This [generation] is miraculously brought forth from eternity by means of *the Spirit of holiness*[b] and the Word. The heavenly Father *anointed* the Virgin's offspring *with the oil of gladness*[c] and *the Spirit of holiness*, so that the king and Lord of all creation might be born. Jesus received this anointing, not from his mother, but from the Father alone.

By sharing in this spiritual anointing, we too are regenerated and reborn in Christ. This is said quite clearly by Paul, in Colossians 3, where those having slaves are called masters according to the flesh, since through the Spirit of God in Jesus Christ there is neither slave nor master, but we are all one and all brothers.[d] Thus also, in Romans 9, some are called *kin according to the flesh*,[e] to differentiate them from those who are united in spiritual kinship through the Spirit of Christ. And so Christ said, *"Whoever does the will of my Father is my brother, and sister, and mother."*[f]

Therefore, since Christ consists of flesh and spirit, and because *God is spirit*,[g] and *what is born of the Spirit is spirit*,[h] [Christ] is rightly believed to be born from God and from humankind. Thus are refuted the perverse ideas of Ebion and Cerinthus,[7] who propose only a fleshly generation for Christ, derived from the seed of the Virgin. They did not understand that although he was spoken of as flesh in terms of his mother, he nonetheless acquired from the Father a nature derived from the Word and the Spirit, thereby pointing to his divine and celestial origin.

Josephus also understood blood relationship [as meaning kinship through the mother]. Speaking of the priest Matthias in *Antiquities [of the Jews]*, Book 17, chapter 8, he says, "But Joseph the son of Elimus, his kin according to the flesh, discharged the priestly function for him,"[i] since [Joseph] was related to [Matthias] on his mother's side. This is why Irenaeus, speaking of the Son of God in book 3, chapter 27, says,

> This is he who was born of a virgin, who was [herself] of the line of David. On this account, [God] promised that the king would be "of the fruit of [David's] belly,"[j,8] a description which characterizes a pregnant virgin, and not "the fruit of his loins or internal organs," which would indicate a begetting male.[k]

---

[a] Rom. 1:3. [b] Rom. 1:4. [c] Ps. 45:7. [d] Col. 3:11. See also Gal. 3:28. [e] Rom. 9:3. [f] Matt. 12:50. [g] John 4:24. [h] John 3:6. [i] Josephus, *Antiquities of the Jews* 11.6.4. [j] Ps. 132:11. [k] Irenaeus, *Adv. Hær.* 3.21.5 (PG 7a 952A).

igitur cum dicimus Christum esse filium mariæ secundum carnem spiritualem tantum ab ea generationem excludimus quæ ratione verbi æterni et spiritus sanctificantis ex solo patre est non tamen propterea filiationem omnem ab ipso patre excludimus vel separamus est enim dominus Jesus filius dei patris et quo ad carnem et quo ad spiritum quia totus Christus indivisus unicus est altissimi dei filius eius in virtute in utero virginis generatus et de spiritu dei conceptus, et ideo etiam ut homo non adoptivus sed proprius et naturalis dei filius est, et quod cæteri filii hominum a suis patribus accipiunt, [93] accepit Christus a deo et sic verus homo vere filius dei est ut vere centurio confesus fuit dicens, Vere filius dei erat iste de homine illo crucifixo loquens disoluunt et in impiam illam Valentini heresim delabuntur contra quos exclamant Joannes et Irenæus ut fusius supra ostensum fuit breviter in generatione Christi quæ ab æterno et secundum spiritum Virgo non participavit sed in ea quæ est secundum carnem in tempore definito virgo cum dei virtute simul concurit nec tamen propterea dividendus est Christus dicendo passus est ut caro non ut spiritus quia caro et spiritus unum Christum faciunt individuum, quia ex carne et spiritu constat et recte dicimus Christum passum in carne non passum, ut caro prout impii sophisthæ dicunt. Credamus igitur pie ac sincere aptissimis scripturæ testimoniis inherentes Jesum illum Christum visibilem passum et suscitatum esse totum et indivisum dei patris filium cui sit honor et gloria sempiterna.

Superest nunc disolvere illum nodum quem isti obiiciunt, Ex paulo ad Phil. ii. ab* probandum quod christus sit idemmet deus æternus cum patre eadem essentia et natura et hunc locum dicunt quidam Neoterici Theologi quod ne omnes quidem diaboli ei extorquebant et verum dicunt quoniam non diaboli sed veri dei spiritus cum a prava illorum interpretatione facilime extorquebit et vindicabit si nimia illa philantia et ambitio aliquantulum se ponantur,

---

* Should read *ad*.

Therefore, when we say that Christ is the son of Mary, according to the flesh, we merely exclude her from spiritual generation, which, by reason of the eternal Word and Spirit of holiness, is from the Father alone. On this account we do not, however, exclude or separate the Father from any part of the parental relationship. For the Lord Jesus is the Son of God, according to both the flesh and the spirit, since the whole Christ, undivided, is the only son of the most high God, begotten by his power in the Virgin's womb and conceived by the Spirit of God. For that reason, even as a human being, he is not the adopted but the very own and natural Son of God. What other sons of men receive from their fathers, Christ received from God. Thus he is a true man and truly the Son of God, as the centurion rightly acknowledged when, speaking about the crucified man, he said, "*Truly this was the Son of God.*"[a]

[But the theologians] divide him up and sink into the wicked heresy of Valentinus, whom [both] John and Irenaeus decry, as I have shown at greater length above.[9] Briefly, however, the Virgin did not take part in the generation of Christ from eternity, according to the spirit, but acted in conjunction with the power of God in what [took place] at a definite time according to the flesh. Christ, however, must not on that account be divided [in two], in order to claim that he suffered as flesh, not as spirit, because flesh and spirit [together] make one undivided Christ, as he consists of flesh and spirit. Thus we rightly say that Christ suffered in the flesh, and not that he suffered as flesh, as the impious sophists claim. Let us therefore piously and straightforwardly believe, relying on the most appropriate scriptural evidence, that the visible, suffering, and risen Jesus Christ is the whole and undivided Son of God the Father, to whom be *honor and glory forever.*[b]

It now remains to untangle the knot, which [the theologians] present in order to prove from chapter 2 of Paul's letter to the Philippians that Christ is himself the eternal God, and of the same essence and nature as the Father. One of our contemporary theologians says that "not even all the devils that there are could tear [his interpretation of] the passage away from him."[10] He is correct to say that devils could not do this; however, the spirit of the true God could. For [this passage] would be quite easily rescued from such a twisted interpretation and vindicated, if [the theologians] could but for a moment put aside their excessive self-conceit and ambition.

---

[a] Matt. 27:54. [b] 1 Tim. 1:17, Rev. 5:13.

Err. 17a-b inquit enim paulus de domino Jesu Christo non rapinam arbitratus est se esse æqualem deo hæc verba pauli sunt tam varie a theologis distracta ut nullus sanus et perfectus sensus ellici possit [94] et maxime quoniam ipsi ea verba ad filium Invisibilem seu ad secundam illam personam referre conantur cum tum paulum de Jesu homine illo visibili redemptore nostro manifestissime sit primo intelligunt quidam quod illa secunda persona citra rapinam vel latrocinium arbitrabatur se æqualem primæ personæ, rursusque hanc prophanam expositionem ad philosophicas naturas detorquent dicentes quod non est arbitratus esse rapinæ id quod erat naturæ, alii legunt non arbitratus est rapinam æqualitatis dei id est non cogitavit dei æqualitatem rapere et sibi usurpare. Vel numquam cogitavit se deo parem facere hic sensus aliquantum propius accedit literæ quia paulus numquam de illis personis vel naturis cogitavit sed hoc tantum illhic agit ut mirificam Jesu Christi modestiam et humilitatem ostendat ad cuius exemplum alios fratres reformari cupit et primæ expositioni aperte repugnat Natura illius dictionis, Sed, quæ præcedentibus necessario adversatur in hunc modum fratres imitatores estote domini Jesu Christi qui non se exaltavit sed humiliavit non est arbitratus sibi æqualitatem dei in potentia vendicare sed seipsum deiecit et inanivit.

Err. 17b-18a   Verum frustratum in ociosis tempus et operam perdo cum in verbis magistri lateat vera solutio est enim argumentum phariseorum qui Io. 5. mordebant Christum quia faciebat se æqualem deo et Christus eis respondens hanc [95] æqualitatem non negavit. Sed dixit quæcumque pater fecerit hæc itidem et filius ipse facit. Pater enim diligit filium et quemadmodum pater suscitat mortuos et vivificat sic et filius quos vult vivificat et denique pater omne iuditium et omnem potestatem dedit filio in cœlo et in terra ut omnes honorificent filium sicut honorificant patrem,

For Paul says of the Lord Jesus Christ: *He did not consider it theft to be equal to God.*[a] These words of Paul have been so variously pulled apart by theologians that no sound and complete meaning can [now] be elicited from them, especially since [the theologians] attempt to refer these words to the invisible son, or second person, even though Paul was obviously speaking about Jesus, the visible man, our redeemer.

To begin with, some understand [this passage to mean] that the second person, without theft or robbery, considered itself equal to the first person. They even twist this unholy interpretation further, applying it to "a philosophical nature" and saying that he did not consider it theft to take what was his own nature. Others interpret it as meaning that he did not contemplate theft of equality with God, that is, he did not think of stealing equality with God and usurping it for himself. Or even that he never considered making himself the equal of God. This latter meaning approaches somewhat closer to what was actually written, because Paul never thought of such persons or natures, but was only concerned in this [passage] to illustrate the wonderful modesty and humility of Jesus Christ, by whose example he wanted the other brethren to be transformed.

However, the nature of the word "but" – which necessarily stands in opposition to what precedes it – clearly contradicts the first interpretation [above]. [For Paul said,] *Brethren,* thus *be imitators* of the Lord Jesus Christ,[b] who did not exalt himself, but *humbled himself,* and *did not think to claim for himself equality* in power *with God,* but abased and *emptied himself.*[c]

However, I am wasting time and effort on unnecessary things, when the true solution lies in the words of the Master. It is found in Christ's answer to the argument of the Pharisees, who, in John 5, criticized him, because he made himself equal to God. And he did not deny this equality, but said, "*Whatever the Father does, the Son does also. For the Father loves the Son,*" and "*As the Father raises the dead and gives them life, so also the Son gives life to whom he will.*" And, finally, "*The Father gave to the Son all judgment and all power in heaven and on earth, that all may honor the Son as they honor the Father.*"[d]

---

[a] Phil. 2:6. [b] Modeled on Phil. 3:17. [c] Phil. 2:6-8. [d] John 5:19-23, Matt. 28:18.

Err. 18a	ecce quomodo filius sit factus æqualis patri et quomodo forma et species deitatis in eo relucebat quia pater eum sibi in virtute potentia honore et gloria adæquavit ut tot ac tanta signa et miracula in suo nomine et propria virtute operaretur et hoc est quod Paulus ait eum in forma et specie dei constitutum id est ad similitudinem dei altissimi, potentem et gloriosum factum quæ verba nullo modo conveniunt ei qui a se ipso per naturam deus est recte diceretur in forma et specie dei constitutus, sed talia verba dicta conveniunt Jesu christo vero et proprio ipsius dei filio qui omnem deitatis plenitudinem a patre corporaliter accepit Collo. ii. et ab eo in forma et specie dei per gloriam et potentiam constitutus est, dignus est enim agnus accipere omnem divinitatem, virtutem, divitias sapientiam, fortitudinem, honorem gloriam, et benedictionem. Apoc. quinto. Item et vidimus gloriam eius gloriam velut unigeniti, a patre plenum gratiæ et veritatis Io. 1, Item Petrus Acta 2. certo sciat tota domus Israël quod dominum et Christum fecerit deus hunc Jesum quem vos crucifixistis filius ergo [96] a patre et rex et dominus et deus super omnes creaturas constitutus est et ad suæ maiestatis æqualitatem sublimatus qui declaratus est filius dei cum potentia secundum spiritum sanctificationis ex eo quod resurrexit a mortuis Roma. 1. quem deus
Err. 18b	suscitavit a mortuis et sedere fecit ad dexteram suam super omnem principatum potestatem virtutem et dominium et omne nomen quod nominatur non solum in hoc sæculo verum etiam in futuro et omnia subiecit sub pedes illius et eum dedit caput super omnia ipsi ecclesiæ quæ est corpus illius complementum eius qui omnia in omnibus adimplet ephes. 1. Item propter quod deus exaltavit illum et dedit ei nomen super omne nomen ut in nomine Jesu filii sui omne genu flectatur cœlestium terrestrium et infernorum et omnis lingua confiteatur quod dominus sit Jesus Christus ad gloriam dei patris philipp. ii. et hanc æqualitatem filii cum deo suo in virtute
Err. 18b-19a	et potentia adnotavit Daniel Ecce filius hominis veniebat et usque ad antiquum dierum pervenit et data est ei omnis regia potestas et hiieremias de eo admiratur dicens quis est ille qui ita accedit et applicatus est deo ut usque ad æqualitatem sibi propinquet,

Behold how the Son was made equal to the Father and how the form and likeness of divinity shone out from him, because the Father made him equal to himself in *power, strength, honor, and glory*,[a] in order that he might perform so many and such great signs and miracles, in his own name and by his own power. For this reason Paul says that he was created *in the form* and likeness, that is, *in the image of God* the Most High,[b] and made powerful and glorious. Such words, "*in the form* and likeness *of God*," in no way fit one who, in and of himself, is rightfully said to be God by nature. But such words do fit Jesus Christ, the true and proper Son of God, who received *bodily the whole fullness of deity* from the Father (Colossians 2)[c], and, through glory and power, was established by [the Father] in the form and likeness of God.

Indeed, *worthy is the Lamb to receive* all *divinity, virtue, riches, wisdom, strength, honor, glory, and blessedness* (Revelation 5).[d,11] Similarly, *And we beheld his glory, glory as of the only Son from the Father, full of grace and truth* (John 1).[e] Likewise Peter, in Acts 2: "*Let all the house of Israel know assuredly that God made him Lord and Christ, this Jesus, whom you have crucified.*"[f]

The Son of the Father, therefore, was established as King, Lord, and God over all creatures. He was raised to equality with [the Father] in majesty *and designated Son of God with power according to the Spirit of holiness in that he rose from the dead* (Romans 1),[g] he whom God *raised from the dead and made to sit at his right hand, above all rule, authority, power, and dominion, and every name that is named, not only in this age but also in the one to come, and put all things under his feet, and made him the head over all things for the church, which is his body, the fulfillment of him, he who fills all in all* (Ephesians 1).[h] Again, *because God has exalted him and bestowed on him the name above every name, that at the name of his Son Jesus every knee should bow, in heaven, on earth, and under the earth, and every tongue confess that Jesus Christ is Lord, to the glory of God the Father* (Philippians 2).[i] Daniel also noted this equality of the Son with God: *Behold there came the Son of man, and he came to the ancient of days. And to him was given all kingly power.*[j] And Jeremiah, marveling, says of him, *Who is this who* thus *approaches and draws near to God*,[k] so that he comes near to equality with him?

---

[a] Rev. 5:12-13. [b] Phil. 2:6, James 3:9. [c] Col. 2:9. [d] Rev. 5:12. [e] John 1:14. [f] Acts 2:36. [g] Rom. 1:4. [h] Eph. 1:20-23. [i] Phil. 2:9-11. [j] Dan. 7:13-14. [k] Jer. 30:21.

quanquam vere hanc tantam cum deo æqualitatem et potentiam Christus in se esse cognosceret eam tamen non est arbitratus facere rapinam id est non cogitavit neque unquam in animum suum induxit tali [97] æqualitate et potentia abuti et illam in rapinam ac tirannidem vertere quin potius ad instar abiectissimi servi sese ipsum deiecit, inanivit et ad omnem huiusmodi ignominiam exposuit usque ad turpissimam mortis condemnationem ad quam humilitatem et deiectionem Paulus exhortans fratres sic inquit, fratres sic animati esse debetis ut Christus Jesus qui cum In forma dei esset non rapinæ habuit suam cum deo æqualitatem, Sed seipsum eo usque ad nihilum redegit ut sumpta servili forma factus sit hominum similis usque ad mortem crucis ignominiosam. Et hic est verissimus Apostoli sensus et cogitatio tantum abest ut locus hic aliquid de identitate essentiæ aut naturæ concludat cum de forma specie, similitudine et æqualitate loquatur et certe omnis similitudo et æqualitas necessario essentiæ identitatem excludit cum nullum simile sit idem ut patet ad sensum, et ideo divus Ignatius Ioannis evangelistæ discipulus qui pro Jesu christo martirium constantissime tulit hanc identitatem essentiæ seu naturæ inter hereticas sui temporis opiniones recenset et damnat sic scribens <u>ad Tarsenses</u> ex philippis, Agnovi quod quidam ex ministris sathanæ voluerunt vos conturbare quorum quidam dicunt quod Jesus putative natus est et putative crucifixus, quidam vero quod non est filius eius qui fecit mundum. Alii autem quod ipse est <u>ille qui est super omnia deus</u> et paulo post et quia iste qui natus est ex muliere filius est dei et qui crucifixus est omnis creaturæ et deus verbum et omnia fecit iussione patris quod et apostolus corroborat dicens unus deus pater [98] ex quo omnia et unus dominus Jesus Christus per quem omnia, Et iterum unus enim deus et unus mediator dei et hominum homo Christus Jesus qui est imago dei invisibilis primogenitus universæ creaturæ quoniam in ipso creata sunt omnia quæ sunt in cœlo et in terra visibilia et invisibilia et ipse est ante omnes et omnia in ipso constant et quia non est ipse ille qui est super omnia deus sed filius ipsius qui et ascendere se ad eum profitetur dicens ascendo ad patrem meum patrem vestrum deum meum et deum vestrum

Err. 35a

Although Christ certainly recognized in himself his equality with God and his great power, he nevertheless did not consider committing theft. That is, he never considered – it never even entered his mind – abusing such equality and power and transforming it into usurpation and tyranny. Instead, he became like the most humble of servants, emptied himself, and exposed himself to every kind of ignominy, to the point of being sentenced to a most shameful death. Thus Paul, exhorting the brethren to this kind of humility and self-abasement, said: Brethren, *you need to be of like mind with Christ Jesus, who, though he was in the form of God, did not consider his equality with God as theft*, but instead reduced himself to nothing, *taking the form of a servant*, and *was made in the likeness of men, even to the point of* enduring a shameful *death upon the cross*.[a] This is the Apostle's real meaning. Since [Paul] is speaking about form, appearance, similarity, and equality, this passage cannot possibly imply anything about the identity of the essence or the nature [of the Father and the Son]. Surely, to speak of similarity and equality necessarily excludes any talk of identity of essence, since nothing similar can be [exactly] the same, which is obvious to anyone with an ounce of common sense.

And therefore the disciple of John the Evangelist, St. Ignatius, who steadfastly suffered martyrdom for the sake of Jesus Christ, included this identity of essence, or nature, among the heretical ideas of his era and condemned it. Writing to the people of Tarsus from Philippi, he said,

> I understand that certain of the ministers of Satan wished to upset you, some of them saying that Jesus was only supposedly born and only supposedly crucified, some, indeed, saying that he is not the Son of him who made the world. Others maintain that he is God over all things.[b]

A bit further on [Ignatius says]:

> For he who was born of a woman is the Son of God, and he who was crucified is also God of all creation, the Word, and [he who] made everything at the command of the Father. This the Apostle also corroborates, saying, *One God, the Father, from whom all things are, and one Lord, Jesus Christ, through whom all things are.*[c] And again, *One God and one mediator between God and men, the man Christ Jesus,*[d] {who *is the image of the invisible God* and} *the firstborn of all creation,*[e] *for in him were created all things in heaven and earth, visible and invisible. And he is before all things and in him all things hold together.*[f] And since he is not God over all things, but [God's] Son, he [proclaims] that he is ascending to him, saying, "*I am ascending to my Father and to your Father, to my God, and to your God.*"[g]

---

[a] Phil. 2:5-9.   [b] Pseudo-Ignatius, *Ad Tarsenses* 2 (PG 5 890A-B).   [c] 1 Cor. 8:6.   [d] 1 Tim. 2:5.
[e] Col. 1:15.   [f] Col. 1:16-17.   [g] John 20:17.

et quando fuerint ei omnia subiecta tunc et ipse subiectus erit illi qui ei subdidit omnia ut sit deus omnia in omnibus, ergo alius est ille qui filio subiecit omnia et qui est omnia in omnibus, et alius est filius cui subiecta sunt omnia qui et post hæc omnia subiectus erit illi qui ei subdidit omnia et non est homo purus ille per quem et in quo facta sunt omnia, hæc Ignatius ex meris Apostoli verbis.

Err. 19a-b   Et ex prædictis refellitur Theophilacti cæcitas qui de qualitate* naturæ in personis sensit cum Paulus non de natura vel essentia Christi sed de eius forma et specie illic agat. Alioqui deberes etiam concedere quod prima persona est, pater dei et æqualis filio quod tamen scriptura abhorret, item observa sequelam pauli quapropter deus exaltavit illum an ergo secunda persona sit tam mirifice exaltata a prima quia se humiliavit, Ridiculum est enim dicere quod dei natura se humiliaverit. Num ego deus qui non mutor et qui deus æqualem sibi deum exaltaverit et ad hæc non animadverterunt Moderni Theologi [99] qui cum scholasticis simpliciter transierunt et impletum est dictum Jesu Christi si cæcus cæcum ducat ambo in foveam cadunt, Christus ergo licet verus esset rex a deo unctus et supra omnem creaturam sublimatus et omnium hominum atque spirituum dominus et deus constitutus,

Err. 18a non tamen acteptavit illam mundi rapinam quando cognovit quod erant illum rapturi ut regem facerent Io. 6. sed regnum suum de hoc mundo esse noluit, et ad hunc discursum Io. Cap. 5 et 6. respicit paulus.

Err. 18b   Item non cogitavit rapinam facere ut raptis sibi duodecim legionibus Angelorum se contra Judæos violenter armaret, atque defenderet sed tanquam agnus mansuetus humiliter pati voluit.

Err. 19b Item noluit contra patrem rapinam facere abdicando se violenter ab eo opere ad quod pater illum destinaverat aut regiam huius mundi tyrannidem occupando sed semper in humili et abiecto statu vivere voluit non habens ubi caput reclinaret

---

* Should read *æqualitate*.

And *when all things are subjected to him, [the Son] himself will also be subjected to him who put all things under him, that God may be all in all.*[a] Therefore, there is one who made all things subject to the Son and who is all in all, and another who is the Son to whom all things are subject, and following all of this, [the Son] will be subject to him who put all things under him. And this is no mere man, *through whom* and in whom *all things were made.*[b]

So says Ignatius, based wholly on the words of the Apostle.[c]

What has just been said refutes the blindness of Theophylact, who conceived of an equality of nature among the persons.[12] For here Paul is not concerned with the nature or essence of Christ, but with his form and appearance. Otherwise, one would be compelled to admit that the first person is the father of God and is equal to the Son. However, Scripture shrinks from this. Also observe the implications of Paul's [words]: *wherefore God has exalted him.*[d] Could the second person, because it humbled itself, have been so wondrously exalted by the first? It is, indeed, ridiculous to say that the nature of God humbled itself. Can it be that "*I am the God who does not change*"[e] and, [at the same time, the God] who God exalted to be a God equal to himself? But modern theologians, having entirely gone along with the scholastics, have not paid attention to this. Thus are fulfilled the words of Jesus Christ: "*If a blind man leads a blind man, they both fall into a pit.*"[f]

Therefore, although Christ was indeed a true king, anointed by God, raised above every creature, and established as Lord and God of all men and spirits, he nonetheless he refused the theft of the world, when *he realized that* [the people] *were about to seize him to make him king* (John 6).[g] Rather he denied that his *kingdom* was *of this world.*[h] And [in Philippians 2] Paul refers to this discourse [of Christ to the Jews, which is found] in John, chapters 5 and 6. Likewise, he did not consider committing theft by arming and defending himself violently against the Jews by taking command of *twelve legions of angels.*[i] Instead, gentle as a lamb, he preferred to suffer humbly. He refused to commit theft against the Father by violently renouncing the task for which his Father had destined him, or, by acquiring a kingship or tyranny over this world, but, rather, chose always to live in a low and humble state, having *nowhere to lay his head.*[j]

---

[a] 1 Cor. 15:28.   [b] Heb. 2:10. See also 1 Cor. 8:6, John 1:3.   [c] Pseudo-Ignatius, *Ad Tarsenses* 4-6 (PG 5 891B-C).   [d] Phil. 2:9.   [e] Mal. 3:6.   [f] Matt. 15:14. See also Luke 6:39.   [g] John 6:15.   [h] John 18:36.   [i] Matt. 26:53.   [j] Matt. 8:20, Luke 9:58.

utinam ad exemplum Christi se reformarent et viverent qui se nomine evangelicos profitentur non orirentur inter Christianos tot odia dissidia sectæ et contentiones.

Err. 20b-21a

Tandem summa summarum hæc est quod omnis scriptura tam antiqua quam nova, excepto illo unico Joannis verbo incorporeo de Jesu Christo illo visibili loquitur sed illud verbum Joannis 1. non intelligitur de eo quod nunc est sed de eo quod erat, erat enim prius substantia invisibilis incorporea impassibilis quæ postea deffinito tempore in utero virginis facta est visibilis corporea et passibilis. Nam verbum prius non erat homo nunc homo factum est ut Joannes in progressu [100] declarat qui testatur se verbum illud vitæ oculis vidisse suis et manibus contrectasse nec verbum illud dei nunc aliter considerari potest nisi simpliciter et indivisum et verus homo deus vel deus homo naturalis dei et virginis filius visibilis passibilis et redemptor vocatus Jesus Christus non compositus neque divisus de quo omnis scriptura Testimonium perhibet, quod ipse sit principium et complementum seu consumatio omnium operum et consiliorum dei et sine ipso nihil factum est et per ipsum incorporeum omnia facta sunt restituta ac reparata et hæc est vera fides et relligio nostra.

Et ex prædictis refellitur nostrorum Theologorum cæcitas qui ipsum Christum dividunt considerantes eum nunc ut filium dei tantum quem semper invisibilem et impassibilem permansisse dicunt, nunc ut filium hominis sine patre visibilem et passibilem quantum in ipsis est unicum dei filium dissolventes et in effectu duos Christos statuentes etsi unitos eos dicant sententia quidem homicidialis secundum Irenæum, per multa dei filium dividens quod si quasi de duobus iudicium fiat, longe melior invenietur qui in ipsis vulneribus et passione pro persecutoribus suis oravit quam ille qui in passione evolavit, quare unus et idem est dei filius qui et de virgine natus est et pro nobis crucifixus verbum dei visibile et passibile factum et in ligno suspensum hæc Irene.

If only those who call themselves evangelicals[13] would reform themselves according to the example of Christ and live in that way, then such hatred, dissension, schism, and contention would not arise among Christians.

In summary, all of scripture, the Old as well as the New [Testament], speaks of the visible Jesus Christ – with the single exception of the [passage] in John about the incorporeal Word.[a] However, in John 1, the Word is not to be understood as it is now, but as it was. For what was at first an invisible, incorporeal, and non-suffering substance, later, at the appointed time, became, in the Virgin's womb, visible, corporeal, and capable of suffering. For the Word, which earlier was not a man, had now been made a man, as John proceeds to show, testifying that he had *seen the word of life with his own eyes and touched it with his own hands*.[b] Nor can the Word of God now be considered other than simply the indivisible and true man-God or God-man, the natural Son of God and the Virgin, visible, capable of suffering, the Redeemer called Jesus Christ, who is neither composite nor divided. All of scripture bears witness that he is the beginning, end, and fulfillment of all the works and plans of God. *Without him nothing was made, and through him,* [when he was] incorporeal, *all things were made*,[c] restored, and renewed. This is our true faith and religion.

What I have just said refutes the blindness of our theologians who divide up Christ. At one moment they consider him to be the Son of God, so that they say he has always remained invisible and incapable of suffering, and, at another moment, consider him to be the visible and suffering, fatherless Son of man. They do everything in their power to divide up the only Son of God. In fact, they set up two Christs, whom they claim are united.

"This is indeed a homicidal idea," says Irenaeus, "one that divides up the Son of God in many ways."[d] But "if anyone who supposes that there are two beings compares them, the [Christ] who, amidst his wounds and suffering," prayed for those who persecuted him, "will be found to be far better than he who took flight from suffering."[e] Therefore, "the Son of God is one and the same"[f]: he who was born of a virgin and was crucified for us; and the Word of God made visible and suffering, who was hung upon the cross.[g] Thus says Irenaeus.

---

[a] John 1:1-3. [b] 1 John 1:1. [c] John 1:3. [d] Irenaeus, *Adv. Hær.* 3.16.8 (PG 7a 927A).
[e] Irenaeus, *Adv. Hær.* 3.18.5 (PG 7a 936A-B). [f] Irenaeus, *Adv. Hær.* 3.16.9 (PG 7a 929A).
[g] See Irenaeus, *Adv. Hær.* 3.18.7 (PG 7a 938B), 3.16.9 (PG 7a 928B), 3.9.1 (PG 7a 869B), 3.18.1 (PG 7a 932A), 3.12.5 (PG 7a 898B).

Quisquis igitur confessus fuerit quod Jesus ille homo est filius dei in eo manet et ipse [101] in eo, et omnis qui crediderit Jesum esse Christum ex deo natus est et quis est qui vincit mundum nisi qui credit quod Jesus est filius dei, et credentes quod Jesus est filius dei vitam æternam habebitis in nomine eius et hæc scripta sunt ut credatis quod Jesus est Christus filius dei et omnis qui dividit aut solvit Jesum Christum ex deo non est sed anti Christus est. Hæc Io. unde tu pie lector attente considera quorsum Joannes ille apostolus et evangelista toties inculcat Jesum quod est proprium nomen illius viri ex virgine nati esse dei filium et ita credendum esse nisi quia iam suo tempore hæc hæresis vigebat, eorum scilicet qui Jesum illum hominem ex virgine natum verum et proprium dei filium esse negarent quæ hæresis totum mundum postea occupavit et a nostris Theologis in tantum adornata fuit suis subtilitatibus et chimeris ut Christiano gregi hanc impiissimam et execrabilem blasphemiam pro evangelica veritate obtruserint scilicet Jesum illum visibilem ex virgine natum qui sanguine suo mundum patri reconciliavit non esse proprie et simpliciter dei filium neque proprie dei filium dici posse nisi per quandam idomatum communicationem quam nemo unquam Apostolus neque Apostolorum discipulus scivit aut cogitavit.

Quid enim universa scriptura docere contendit nisi ut Jesum illum crucifixum dei filium esse credamus et in eius nomine confidamus. Ad hoc tendebat omnium Apostolorum prædicatio ut hunc Jesum visibilem qui pependit in ligno annuntiarent et persuaderent omnibus esse verum [102] dei Christum et filium super hac fide fundatæ sunt ecclesiæ, super hoc articulo mortuus est ipse Christus quia filium dei se esse dicebat super hac veritate dei vox semel atque iterum audita est hic est filius ille meus dilectus in quo mihi bene complacui ipsum audite, super hoc articulo data est lex fidei et novum testamentum ipsius filii sanguine confirmatum hoc est evangelium illud Apostolis demandatum ut Jesum illum crucifixum verum dei filium omnibus annuntiarent et in eius sanguine remissionem peccatorum et vitam æternam hæc est confessio quam a nobis Christus ipse requirit

Therefore, *whoever confesses that* the man *Jesus is the Son of God abides in [God] and [God] abides in him.*[a] *Everyone who believes that Jesus is the Christ is born of God.*[b] *Who is it that overcomes the world, but he who believes that Jesus is the Son of God?*[c] *Believing that Jesus is the Son of God, in his name you shall have* eternal *life,* and *these things are written that you may believe that Jesus is the Christ, the Son of God.*[d] *Everyone who divides and sunders Jesus Christ is not of God,* but *the Antichrist.*[e] Thus says John.

Therefore, faithful reader, carefully consider why John the apostle and evangelist so often emphasizes that Jesus – which is the proper name of the man born of the Virgin – is the Son of God, and that this is what we are required to believe. The reason must be that in his own time the heresy was already flourishing, that denied that Jesus, the man born of the Virgin, was God's own true Son. This heresy later spread throughout the entire world, and was lavishly adorned by our theologians with their subtleties and chimeras. They have forced this most impious and execrable blasphemy on the Christian flock in place of the gospel truth. For they claim that the visible Jesus who was born of the Virgin, who with his blood reconciled the world to the Father, was not purely and simply the Son of God, and cannot properly be called the Son of God, except through the use of *communicatio idiomatum*, which no apostle or disciple of the apostles ever knew of or contemplated.

For what does all of scripture mean to teach, other than that we should believe that the crucified Jesus is the Son of God, and that we should place our trust in his name? The preaching of every apostle seeks to spread the news about the visible Jesus who was *hung upon the cross*[f] and to persuade everyone that he was the true Christ and the Son of God. It was on this faith that churches were founded. It was for this article [of faith] that Christ died, because he said he was the Son of God. Time and again the voice of God was heard on behalf of this truth: "*This is my Son in whom I am well pleased. Listen to him.*"[g]

Upon this article, the law of faith was established and the New Testament confirmed by the blood of the Son. This was the "good news" that was entrusted to the apostles to proclaim to everyone: Jesus Christ crucified, who is the true Son of God, the remission of sins through his blood, and eternal life. This is the confession that Christ requires of us.

---

[a] 1 John 4:15. [b] 1 John 5:1. [c] 1 John 5:5. [d] John 20:31. [e] 1 John 4:3 (Vulgate). [f] Acts 10:39.
[g] Matt. 17:5.

ut eum dei filium coram hominibus intrepide fateamur ut ipse itidem nos fratres suos coram patre suo confiteatur hoc est fœdus salutis nostræ et in signum et arcam huius fœderis datur nobis spiritus sanctus qui crediderit in me (inquit) flumina de ventre eius fluent aquæ vivæ et hoc dicebat Christus de spiritu sancto quem accepturi erant credentes in eum hoc est evangelii verbum fide corda purificans de quo dictum est qui non crediderit condemnabitur hoc est verbum illud vitæ quod Io. vidit ac palpavit de quo dixit petrus tu es ille Christus filius dei viventis qui in hunc mundum venisti, et alibi præcepit (inquit) nobis ut prædicaremus et testificaremur quod ipse sit ille de quo etiam testificatus est Johannes baptista, ego eum vidi et testificatus sum hunc esse filium dei et Paulus, una cum christo crucifixus sum vitam autem quam nunc in carne vivo per fidem vivo filii dei qui dilexit me et [103] tradidit semetipsum pro peccatis meis et hoc tantum modo promittitur hominibus vita æterna qui credunt hunc Jesum crucifixum esse verum Christum dei filium immo sic deus dilexit et clarificavit filium suum Jesum illum visibilem ut hoc unicum fidei præceptum scilicet credendi in Christum crucifixum sit loco universæ legis surrogatum et longe maior in eius observatione sequatur utilitas quam ex totius antiquæ legis implemento numquam enim facta est promissio vitæ æternæ sicut fidei in Christum Jesum crucifixum.

Ab hoc fidei fundamento defficientes Theologi nostri et interpretes scripturæ nunquam intelligere potuerunt quæ esset vera iustificatio sed eorum cæcitas adeo profunda est ut si christus ipse visibilis iterum prædicaret se esse filium dei iterum eum crucifigerent vel iuxta hodiernum morem accensis flammis concremarent, sed ut palpabiliter eorum errores agnoscas et in media luce caligationem, diligenter considera ordinem apostolicæ doctrinæ et prædicationis in eorum actis, primo cum Jesum illum virum a nazareth ad oculum demonstrant postea exhortantur et admonent ut credamus hunc ipsum Jesum esse Christum dei filium.

We should fearlessly proclaim him to be the Son of God *in the presence of men*, so that he might in the same way *acknowledge us to be his brothers in the presence of the Father.*[a] This is the covenant of our salvation, and the Holy Spirit is given to us as a sign and as the ark of this covenant.[b] [Christ] said, "*He who believes in me, 'Out of his body shall flow rivers of living water.'*"14 Christ *was saying this about the Holy Spirit, which those who believed in him were to receive.*[c] This is the word of the gospel, purifying hearts with faith, the word about which it is said, "*He who does not believe will be condemned.*"[d] This is the word of life, which John saw and touched,[e] and about which Peter said: "*You are the Christ, the Son of the living God, he who is coming into the world.*"[f] In another place he said, "*He commanded us to preach and testify that he was the one*"[g] about whom John the Baptist bore witness: "*I have seen and have borne witness that this is the Son of God.*"[h]

Paul said: "*I was crucified together with Christ, and the life I now live in the flesh, I live by faith in the Son of God, who loved me and gave himself for my sins.*"[i] Eternal life is promised only to those who believe that the crucified Jesus is the true Son of God. Indeed, God so loved and glorified his Son, the visible Jesus, that this single precept of faith, belief in Christ crucified, replaces the entirety of the law. Far greater advantage comes in observing [this precept] than in fulfilling the whole of ancient law. For [the law] never promised eternal life, as faith in Jesus Christ crucified does.[j]

Having forsaken this foundation of faith, our theologians and interpreters of scripture have never been able to understand what true justification is. Their blindness is so profound, that if the visible Christ were again to proclaim himself the Son of God, they would crucify him again, or, according to today's custom, set him on fire and reduce him to ashes. [If you wish] to get a solid understanding of their errors and to shed light on their mental darkness, consider carefully how [little] they display apostolic teaching and preaching in their own conduct. Especially since [the apostles] place Jesus, the man from Nazareth, right before our eyes, and encourage and advise us to believe that this same Jesus is the Christ, the Son of God.

---

[a] Luke 12:8-9, Matt. 10:32-33. [b] Exod. 25:22, 40:35-38. [c] John 7:38-39. [d] Mark 16:16. [e] 1 John 1:1.
[f] John 11:27. See also Matt. 16:16. [g] Acts 10:42. [h] John 1:34. [i] Gal. 2:20. [j] See Acts 13:39.

Item quod in eius nomine credentes remissionem peccatorum consequamur et iustificemur et hac fide iustificati verum pacem internum et spiritualem habemus, ut iam iam nos in cœlis esse sentiamus et ad hoc tendebat omnis Apostolorum cursus et prædicatio et Paulus ad hanc fidei in Jesum Christum obœdientiam destinatum dicit Apostolatum nec mirum si prædicare Jesum illum virum a nazareth esse verum dei filium erat hebræis [104] scandalum et gentibus stultitia cum etiam hodie Theologi nostri hoc stultissimum arbitrentur nec tam singulare dei misterium et beneficium agnoscere possint, quis enim nisi spiritu dei afflatus credere posset deum genuisse sibi filium hominem ex virgine passibilem et mortalem et supra omnem creaturam usque ad suam æqualitatem exaltasse per quem hominem omnem suam voluntatem et consilium adimpleret per eius suplicium et mortem mundum sibi reconcilians in quo solo sibi bene complacuit et in quo solo totus eius spiritus requievit, Quis inquam de homine tot et tanta misteria crederet et integra fide susciperet nisi pater ipse nos traheret et filium suum cordibus nostris insereret et universa scriptura nos planissime instrueret et fidem nostram penitus confirmaret hic est scopus et vita æterna, verum Theologi nostri qui scripturam per inanem philosophiam et subtilitates prave detorquent hanc dei benignitatem non agnoscentes et tam admirabile veræ pietatis misterium et relligionis nostræ fundamentum de filio dei crucifixo nec credere nec audire volentes statim cum Caipha exclamant Blasphemavit quia dixit filius dei sum, Jesus enim nulla de alio filio invisibili ratione habita seipsum visibiliter et palpabiliter demonstratum planissime dei filium toto orbe clamavit ut ex prima pauli prædicatione in actis manifestissime demonstratur. Sed Theologi nostri alium filium invisibilem et impassibilem nobis obtrudunt qui nihil facit ad propositum nostræ salutis [105] neque ad dei patris et misteriorum eius explicationem

[This is true justification:] that by *believing in his name*,[a] we might obtain *forgiveness of sins*[b] and be justified. And *justified by this faith*,[c] we obtain true internal and spiritual peace, so that we feel that we are almost in heaven. All the teaching and preaching of the apostles works towards this end. Paul says that *apostleship* is intended *to bring about the obedience of faith*[d] in Jesus Christ. No wonder that to preach Jesus the man of Nazareth as the true Son of God was *a stumbling block to Jews and folly to Gentiles*,[e] when even today our theologians deem it utter foolishness and are incapable of recognizing such a remarkable mystery and loving act of God.

Indeed, who, unless breathed upon by the Spirit of God, could believe that from a virgin God begot a human son, capable of suffering and subject to death, and that he raised [that son] above all creatures to an equality with himself? Or that he would fulfill his entire will and plan, *reconciling the world* to himself,[f] by means of the punishment and death of this man, [the Son] in whom he was alone *well pleased*,[g] and on whom alone his entire *Spirit rested*?[h] Who among us, I ask, could believe so many and such great mysteries and accept them in complete faith, unless the Father himself led us onward, implanting his Son in our hearts? All of scripture most plainly instructs us and thoroughly encourages our faith that this is the goal and our eternal life.

But our theologians, who perversely distort scripture with their empty philosophy and subtleties, and ignore God's benevolence, that wondrous mystery of true piety and the foundation of our religion – who wish neither to believe in nor to hear of the Son of God crucified – at once exclaim, like Caiaphas, "He has *blasphemed because* he has *said, 'I am the Son of God.*'"[i] For Jesus, having no idea of any other invisible Son, plainly proclaimed to all the world that he himself, who could be seen and touched, was the Son of God. This is clearly proven by Paul's first public preaching in Acts.[j] Our theologians, however, foist upon us another, invisible and non-suffering, Son, one who does nothing for our salvation nor helps us to understand God the Father and his mysteries.

---

[a] John 1:12. [b] Acts 2:38. [c] Rom. 3:26. [d] Rom. 1:5. [e] 1 Cor. 1:23. [f] Rom. 11:15. [g] Luke 3:22.
[h] Isa. 11:2. [i] Matt. 26:65 (though the wording is closer to John 10:36, where Jesus was responding to Jews who threatened to stone him). [j] Acts 9:20.

Err. 34b considera quæso tecum aliquantisper et in corde tuo recogita quid operetur illa unio filii invisibilis cum visibili? Christus enim Jesus ille visibilis tamquam verus et perfectus homo de spiritu sancto conceptus et de virgine natus a deo patre suo naturali omnem perfectionem potentiam et divinitatem accepit omnem dei patris sui voluntatem adimplevit, omne mandatum absolvit, omnia passus, omnia superavit, in illo est spes nostra, in illum fides, per illum salus et iustificatio, ille est vera lux, via, veritas, et vita, ille redemptor, ille <u>mediator dei et hominum</u>, in illo deus sibi bene complacuit, in illo totus dei spiritus requievit, per illum placata est ira dei patris, <u>per</u> illum <u>habemus accessum ad deum</u> et vitam æternam, illi data est omnis potestas in cœlo et in terra et omne iudicium in vivos et mortuos, sicut enim in carne venit in mundum humilis et abiectus salvare quod perierat sic in eadem carne gloriosus adveniet ingratos et incredulos iudicare.

Dic quæso in cuius fide et nomine sancti illi patriarchæ et prophetæ salutis suæ spem collocarunt? nisi in fide et nomine huius Christi visibilis qui futurus erat redemptor, in cuius nomine sancti illi apostoli tot signa prodigia et virtutes ædebant? nisi in fide et nomine huius christi crucifixi in cuius nomine et fide sancti illi martires sanguinem suum tam animose fuderunt totque suplicia constantissime pertulerunt? nisi in fide et confessione huius christi Jesu crucifixi qui prior animam suam pro ipsis posuerat **[106]** et suum pretiosissimum sanguinem pro eis tam libenter effuderat?

Quis obsecro pro illa secunda persona vel hypostasi sibi incognita mortem appetere voluisset? de qua nullam ex scripturis notitiam haberet, quis ab ea salutem sperasset? quæ redemptionem factura non erat quis ab ea gloriam et vitam æternam expectasset? quæ iuditium factura non erat, ubi quæso de hac unione unius filii invisibilis cum visibili vel unum iota in scripturis invenies, ubi de hac tua sophistica communicatione duorum?

Pray consider, for a moment, and reflect on this in your heart: what does the union of an invisible Son with the visible one achieve? For Jesus, the visible Christ, as a real and perfect man, conceived by the Holy Spirit and born of the Virgin, received from God, his natural father, all perfection, power, and divinity; brought to fulfillment all that his father willed; executed every mandate, suffered everything, and overcame all things. In him is our hope, in him our faith, through him our salvation and justification. He is *the true light*,[a] *the way, the truth, and the life.*[b] He is the redeemer and the *mediator between God and men.*[c] In him God was *well pleased.*[d] Upon him the entire *Spirit* of God *rested.*[e] By him the wrath of God the Father was appeased, and through him we have access to God and to eternal life. To him is granted *all power in heaven and on earth,*[f] and all *judgment over the living and the dead.*[g] And indeed, just as he came into the world in the flesh, humble and abject, to save those who had died, so too shall he come, full of glory, in that same flesh, to judge the ungrateful and the unbelieving.

Tell me, in whose faith and name did the holy patriarchs and prophets place their hope of salvation, if not in the faith and name of the visible Christ, who was, in time to come, to be their redeemer? In whose holy name did the apostles proclaim so many signs, miracles, and mighty works, if not in the faith and name of the crucified Christ? In whose name and faith did the holy martyrs courageously shed their blood, and steadfastly bear so many punishments, if not in the faith and confession of Jesus Christ crucified, who had earlier given his life for them and willingly spilled his own precious blood for them?

Who, I implore you, would want to seek death for the sake of that unknown second person or hypostasis, about which they could gain not the slightest inkling from scripture? Who could hope for salvation from that [person], which cannot bring about redemption? Who could have anticipated glory and eternal life on the basis of that [person] which was not going to deliver judgment? Where, I ask, in scripture will you find even a single iota about the union of one invisible Son with [another] visible one, or anything about your sophistical *communicatio* between two beings?

---

[a] John 1:9.   [b] John 14:6.   [c] 1 Tim. 2:5.   [d] Matt. 3:17.   [e] Isa. 11:2.   [f] Matt. 28:18.   [g] Acts 10:42

Unde hæc tam impia et blasphema unius et eiusdem filii dei visibilis et crucifixi divisio ac solutio? Nisi ex impurissimis illius Valentini hæresiarchæ lacunis cuius perversissimam opinionem sanctus ille dei vir Irenæus quinque libris erudite et copiose refutat præsertim libro iii ubi dicit et si unitos eos dicunt duos tamen Christos faciunt, alterum quidem passibilem alterum vero invisibilem et impassibilem et enim qui invisibilis et impassibilis est in passibilem et visibilem descendisse sententia quidem homicidialis dividens filium dei Jesum Christum crucifixum quod si quasi de duabus iuditium fiat numne longe melior invenietur qui passus est et pro persequentibus oravit, quam qui nihil horum fecit sed ab ipso Jesu in passione evolavit hæc Irenæus lib iii cap. 12. 18. 19. 20. et 21. ubi omnino videatur et hanc sententiam libenter repeto ut cognoscant Theologi nostri in quanto errore versentur et quam longe ab apostolica veritate recesserunt.

[107] Credamus igitur firmiter et intrepide fateamur Jesum illum crucifixum esse verum proprium et unigenitum altissimi dei filium verbum dei incarnatum visibile et passibile factum et in ligno suspensum ut Irenæus lib. 12. verbum dei homo factum est et verbum dei crucifixum est verus ergo dei filius vere passus mortuus et suscitatus est, non per idiomatum communicationem quæ ab istis sophisticis ad nihil aliud inventa est nisi ut unicum et individuum dei filium Jesum Christum cruci affixum dividant ac dissolvant.

Lege et percurre universam veteris et novi testamenti scripturam scrutare diligenter omnia prophetarum et Apostolorum Testimonia. Videbis luce clarius omnia ad Jesum illum visibilem et palpabilem referri, neque in alium dei filium aliamve personam

Where does such an impious and blasphemous division and sundering of one and the same visible and crucified Son of God come from, if not from the filthy wastepits of the heresiarch Valentinus? His utterly perverse opinions were fully and eruditely refuted by that saintly man of God, Irenaeus, in five books, and, especially in book 3, where he says, "Even if they say [the Sons are] united,"[a] they nevertheless make two Christs, "one certainly suffering, the other truly invisible and non-suffering. For the invisible and non-suffering one is [supposed] to have descended into the visible and suffering one."[b]

"This is indeed a homicidal idea, one that divides up the Son of God,"[c] "Jesus Christ crucified."[d] But "if anyone who supposes that there are two beings compares them, will not the [Christ] who suffered," and prayed for those who persecuted him, "be found to be far better than he who did none of these things, but rather took flight from Jesus's suffering?"[e] Thus says Irenaeus, in book 3, chapters 12, 18, 19, 20 and 21,[f] where this is all laid out. I gladly repeat these ideas here,[15] so that our theologians might recognize how wrong they are, and how far they have departed from apostolic truth.

Therefore, let us believe firmly and confess fearlessly that the crucified Jesus was the true and only begotten Son of God the Most High, the Word of God made incarnate, visible, and suffering, who was "*hung upon the cross*," as Irenaeus writes in Book [3, chapter] 12.[g] The Word of God was made man and the Word of God was crucified. Thus it was the true Son of God who actually suffered, died, and was restored to life – not by means of *communicatio idiomatum*, [a doctrine] which was invented by the sophists for no other purpose than to divide up and tear asunder the unique and indivisible Son of God, Jesus Christ, who was nailed to the cross.

Read carefully through the whole of scripture, both the Old and the New Testaments. Carefully scrutinize all the testimony of the prophets and the apostles. There you will see as clear as day that everything refers to the visible and palpable Jesus, and does not suit any other person or son of God.

---

[a] Irenaeus, *Adv. Hær.* 3.17.4 (PG 7a 931B).   [b] Condensed from Irenaeus, *Adv. Hær.* 3.16.6 (PG 7a 925B).
[c] Irenaeus, *Adv. Hær.* 3.16.8 (PG 7a 927A).   [d] Irenaeus, *Adv. Hær.* 3.12.2 (PG 7a 894A).
[e] Irenaeus, *Adv. Hær.* 3.18.5 (PG 7a 936A-B).   [f] Chapters 18-21 of Erasmus's edition of *Adversus Hæreses* correspond to chapters 16-19 in *Patrologia Græca*. See book 2, note 5.   [g] Irenaeus, *Adv. Hær.* 3.12.5 (PG 7a 898B), quoting Acts 10:39.

consentire et hæc est sincera fides, vera pietas, evangelica veritas, et relligio impolluta et vita æterna nempe credere et confiteri Jesum crucifixum esse, esse verum proprium et unicum dei filium de muliere factum caput ecclesiæ sanctæ dei, et qui hoc non credunt non ego sed dei spiritus pronunttiat eos non esse christianos nullumque habere cum Jesu christo fœdus aut commertium neque illius capitis membra esse quem ut verum caput non agnoscunt.

 Ego vero nunquam sperarem me esse filium dei adoptivum nisi naturalem haberem cognationem cum eo qui verus et naturalis dei filius est ex cuius filiatione nostra [108] filiatio pendet, nec unquam crederem me redemptum et deo conciliatum nisi hanc redemptionem et reconciliationem per sanguinem veri et unigeniti filii dei factum arbitrarer, oportuit enim filium dei pati mori et suscitari ut omne dei consilium impleretur et omnium misteriorum dei, perfecta consumatio fieret quia neque angelus neque ullus homo neque ulla creatura hoc sacratissimum expiationis misterium peragere potuisset neque divinæ iustitiæ satisfacere nisi ipsemet dei filius homo Jesus agnus immaculatus qui solus in conspectu patris mundus est et hostia acceptabilis et ideo scriptura clare pronuntiat quod unus sit deus pater a quo sunt omnia et unus dei filius per quem omnia homo christus Jesus dei et hominum mediator continue deum patrem pro nobis interpellans. Quamquam vero Jesus Christus dei filius sit ipsummet dei verbum corporatum visibile et passibile factum nunquam tamen verbum simpliciter et in sua prima forma incorporea et invisibili consideratum in scriptura filius appellatur nec voluit Joannes dicere, In principio erat verbum dei filius, et dei filius homo factus est sed ante nativitatem ex muliere semper verbum et non filium appellavit, filiatio enim nativitatem præsupponit et ad Christum solum pertinet seu ad verbum visibile et corporatum qui ex muliere filius factus est Gala 4. quod [109] si unum dei filium invisibilem et impassibilem per se aliquando consideremus nihil omnino illum nobis contulisse videbimus, immo nec ipsi patri satisfecisse, quomodo enim pater se in filio hominibus manifestasset?

This is genuine faith, true piety, the gospel truth, unpolluted religion, and eternal life: to believe and to confess that Jesus was crucified, that he is the own, true, and only Son of God, that he was born of a woman, and that he is the head of the holy church of God. Not I, but the Spirit of God declares that those who do not believe this are not Christians; that they have no covenant or fellowship with Jesus Christ; and that they are not members of [the body of] that head, whom they do not recognize as the true head.

Certainly I could never hope to be an adopted son of God, unless I possessed a natural physical relationship to the real and natural Son of God, on whose sonship our sonship depends. Nor could I ever believe myself redeemed and reconciled to God, unless I believed that this redemption and reconciliation was brought about by the blood of the true and only begotten Son of God. It was necessary for the Son of God to suffer and to die and be raised again, to fulfill God's entire plan, and to perfectly consummate all of God's mysteries. For no angel or man – nor any creature – could have accomplished this most holy mystery of expiation, nor satisfied divine justice, other than the Son of God himself, the man Jesus, the *spotless lamb*[a] who, alone in the eyes of the Father, was a pure and *acceptable sacrifice*.[b]

This is why scripture plainly states that there is *one God the Father, from whom all things are, and one* Son of God, *through whom all things are,*[c] *the man Jesus Christ, the mediator between God and men,*[d] who constantly appeals to God the Father on our behalf. Even though Jesus Christ, the Son of God, is truly *the Word* of God *made flesh,*[e] visible and capable of suffering, in scripture, the Word, simply considered, in its first, incorporeal and invisible form, is never called the Son. John did not mean to say, "In the beginning, the Word was the Son of God, and the Son of God was made man." Rather, prior to [its] being born out of a woman, John always calls it the Word and not the Son. For being a son presupposes being born and pertains solely to Christ, that is, to the Word made visible and corporeal, who is the *Son born of a woman* (Galatians 4).[f]

But if we consider the only Son of God to be basically invisible and non-suffering, we observe that he has conferred nothing at all on us, nor has he made any satisfaction to the Father. For how, in that case, could the Father have revealed himself to humanity in his Son?

---

[a] 1 Peter 1:19. [b] 1 Peter 2:5. [c] 1 Cor. 8:6. [d] 1 Tim. 2:5. [e] John 1:14. [f] Gal. 4:4.

quomodo visibilem suæ maiestatis imaginem præbuisset? quomodo se perceptibili specie cognoscendum dedisset? quomodo deus in carne manifestatus esset? quomodo novissime per filium suum nobis locutus esset? quomodo omnem suam voluntatem in terris per filium adimplevisset? quomodo per filium unigenitum facta esset redemptio? quomodo figuram Isaac a patre inmolari deus in filio suo vere consumasset? quomodo voluntas et veritas dei prædicata et verus dei cultus hominibus annuntiatus? quomodo tandem per filium omnia restituta et recapitulata fuissent? nisi omnia per verum et unicum dei filium visibilem et passibilem facta et adimpleta credamus.

Numne Johannes testificatur de verbo vitæ quod ipse vidit et palpavit numne vidit gloriam unigeniti a patre pleni gratia et veritate Numne unigenitus dei nobis nobiscum visibiliter habitavit. Numne tomas vidit et palpavit filium dei, dominum et deum suum et quod miri est si immortalis deus et pater verbum suum hominem esse voluit passibilem et mortalem ut per eum manifestaretur et omnia sua decreta atque misteria confundaret hic est filius ille dilectus in quo deus sibi bene complacuit a spiritu sancto in specie columbæ visibiliter [110] demonstratus in quo totus dei patris spiritus requievit homo Christus Jesus.

O ingentem dei bonitatem qui verbum suum hominem fecit ut in eo omne humanum genus beatificaret O inexplicabile divinæ Charitatis misterium et tamen boni Angeli huic sacrosancto exaltati hominis misterio non inviderunt sed potius deum ipsum glorificaverunt et hunc hominem ut verum et unicum dei filium coluerunt et adoraverunt hæc sunt quæ Theosophistæ nostri suis ampullis et sophismatibus turgidi, suis subtilitatibus et phaleratis dolis ambitiosi cognoscere noluerunt hunc divinissimum hominem non intelligentes, sed quandam quasi abiectam humanitatem appellantes et quemdam filium invisibilem quam secundam hypostasim vocant introducentes quam dicunt se illi humanitati univisse sustentando ipsam humanitatem quasi Christus ipse dei filius homo perfectissimus, et absolutissimus omni gratia virtute et divinitate a deo patre repletus et corroboratus alio sustentaculo indigeret quam patris,

How could he have physically presented a visible image of his majesty? How could he have made himself recognizable in a perceptible form? How could God have been manifested in the flesh? How could he, in latter times, have spoken to us through his Son? How could he have fulfilled his entire will on earth through his Son? How could redemption have been accomplished through his only begotten Son? How could God have truly accomplished in his own Son the paternal sacrifice prefigured by Isaac? How could the will and truth of God have been foretold and the true worship of God proclaimed to humankind? Finally, how could everything have been restored and recapitulated,[16] unless we believe that all things were fulfilled by means of the true and only Son of God, made visible and suffering?

Does not John bear witness *about the word of life*, which he himself *saw and touched*?[a] Did he not *behold the glory of the Father's only begotten [Son], filled with grace and truth*? Did not the only begotten [Son] of God visibly *dwell among us*?[b] Did not Thomas see and touch the Son of God, his *Lord and his God*?[c] And is it really so amazing that the immortal God and Father wished his Word to become a man, [who was] capable of suffering and death, so that through him [God] might be manifested and all his mysteries and decrees established together? This man Jesus Christ, is that *beloved Son* in whom God was *well pleased*, who was visibly identified by *the Holy Spirit in the form of a dove*,[d] and in whom the entire *spirit* of God the Father *reposed*.[e]

O immense goodness of God! He made his Word into a man, so that in him he might bless the entire human race. O inexplicable mystery of divine love! And yet the good angels did not become envious of this most holy mystery of the elevation of man, but rather glorified God, and worshipped and adored this man as the true and only Son of God. These are things which our theological sophists, with their bombast and turgid sophistry, their subtleties and cheap, gaudy tricks, have refused to recognize. Not comprehending this most divine of men, but calling him instead a kind of lowly human nature, they introduce an invisible Son, which they call the second hypostasis. This they claim united itself with a human nature in order to sustain that human nature – as if Christ himself, the Son of God, the most perfect man, completely filled and fortified with all grace, power, and divinity by God the Father, needed any other support than the Father.

---

[a] 1 John 1:1.   [b] John 1:14.   [c] John 20:27-28.   [d] Luke 3:22.   [e] Isa. 11:2.

Numne dixit pater in me est et ego in patre cur non dixit filius dei mecum est vel in me est nimirum quoniam ipsemet Jesus homo sanctissimus unicus est dei filius nec ullum alium dei filium sibi unitum vel coniunctum recognoscit ut garriunt isti sophistæ sed sese ipsum hominem visibilem et passibilem vere proprie simpliciter et immediate dei filium pronuntiavit [111] qui alium dei filium quærit vel considerat invisibilem et impassibilem illum sequatur. Mihi cum Paulo sufficit solus ille Jesus Christus crucifixus qui suo prætiosissimo sanguine immortali deo et patri me conciliavit qui unicus dei filius patri obediendo, patiendo, et moriendo divinæ iustitiæ copiosissime satisfecit et nos credentes dei filios et æterni regni cohæredes effecit. Nos enim livore eius sanati sumus, sanguine eius abluti, morte vivificati spiritu regeniti et omnes de plenitudine eius accepimus et sicut per verum hominem terrestrem et contumacem fuimus a deo patre maledicti, ita per alium hominem cœlestem et obedientem fuimus benedicti cui deus ipse pater omnipotentissimus velut unico filio dilectissimo et hæredi suo tantum gratiæ, potentiæ, virtutis, deitatis, honoris gloriæ et benedictionis contulit, quantum maxime conferre potuit ita ut omnia sua ei dederit eumque sibi in omnibus et per omnia adequaverit. Vide igitur quantum illi sanctissimo, et divinissimo homini dei filio Jesu Christo crucifixo secundum scripturas et evangelicam veritatem tribuere oporteat et hoc est quod deus pater Mosi prædixerat faciem meam non videbis sed posteriora mea videbis idest filium meum videbis et in filio visibili me cognosces, et ideo bene et conformiter respondit filius filippo patrem videre cupienti, philippe qui videt me videt et [112] patrem meum, item ego et pater unum sumus hoc est idem spiritus eadem potentia et voluntas nulla enim maior unitas omni respectu considerari potest quam inter deum patrem invisibilem et dominum Jesum Christum filium eius visibilem. Ipse enim est expressa et visibilis imago dei et patris sui invisibilis et licet deus pater per ea omnia quæ visibilia facta sunt cognosci potuit, longe magis tamen per verbum suum incarnatum et hominem factum Christum Jesum manifestatus est. Omnia enim per verbum dei patris facta sunt sed christus ipse velut filius ex ipso verbo factus est.

Did not [Christ] say, "*The Father is in me and I am in the Father*"?[a] Why did he not say, "The Son of God is with me," or "is in me?" No doubt the reason is that Jesus himself, the holiest of men, is the only Son of God. He did not recognize any other Son of God united or joined to himself, like the one the sophists prattle about, but proclaimed himself – the man who was truly visible and suffered – properly, simply, and without any intermediary, the Son of God.

Whoever seeks some other Son of God or believes him to be invisible and incapable of suffering, let him follow that [Son]. For me, as for Paul, all that is required is *Jesus Christ crucified*,[b] who, by his most *precious blood*,[c] reconciled me to the immortal God and Father. The only Son of God, by obeying the Father and by suffering and dying, completely satisfied divine justice and *made* us, as *believers, sons of God* and *co-heirs* of his *eternal kingdom*.[d] For we are *healed by his wounds*,[e] *washed by his blood*,[f] restored to life by his death, reborn in his spirit, and are all recipients of his abundance. And just as we were condemned because of a real, earthly, and disobedient man, so, too, we are blessed through another man, heavenly and obedient,[g] on whom, as his only, most beloved Son and heir, the omnipotent God the Father bestowed as much grace, *strength, power, divinity, honor, glory, and blessing*[h] as was in his power, thereby giving him everything that was his, and making him his equal *in all and through all*.[i] Therefore see how much [honor], according to scripture and the gospel truth, we ought to give to that most holy and divine man, Jesus Christ crucified, the Son of God.

This is what God the Father foretold to Moses: "*You shall not see my face, but you will see what comes after me.*"[j,17] That is to say, you will see my Son and, in my visible Son, you will recognize me. And accordingly the Son answered Philip well when he desired to see the Father, saying, "Philip, *he who sees me also sees* my Father."[k] He also said, "*I and the Father are one*,"[l] that is, "[we have] the same spirit, the same power and will." Indeed, we can imagine no greater unity in every respect than that between the invisible God the Father and his visible Son, the Lord Jesus Christ. [Christ] is the exact and visible image of God, his invisible Father. Although God the Father is recognizable in every visible thing, he was much more evident in Jesus Christ, his incarnate Word made man. For all things were made by the Word of God the Father, but Christ, as the Son, was made from the Word itself.

---

[a] John 14:11. [b] 1 Cor. 2:2. [c] 1 Peter 1:19. [d] John 1:12, Rom. 8:17, 2 Peter 1:11. [e] 1 Peter 2:24.
[f] Rev. 1:5. [g] See 1 Cor. 15:21-22. [h] Rev. 5:12. [i] Eph. 4:6. [j] Exod. 33:23. [k] John 12:45.
[l] John 10:30.

Nam ut toties repetere libuit et oportuit nihil aliud est Christus ille homo divinissimus dominus et deus noster nisi logos ille dei corporatus visibilis et passibilis factus dei filius unigenitus, in quo, per quem, et propter quem, omnia a deo patre facta et restituta sunt et hoc est nobilissimum et stupendissimum illud æterni consilii misterium quam paucissimis revelatum cui semper fuit contradictum.

Nunc quæso tecum reputa quanta lux ex hac tibi declaratione refulserit qui prius eras in tenebris nec unquam de deo et dei filio veram cognitionem acceperas sed in perplexo et confuso omnia credebas vide quomodo nunc omnia sunt tibi plana lucida et aperta et omnes ambages ac difficultates sublatæ, cognosce obsecro quomodo intelligendus sit unus deus invisibilis [113] qui est pater et unus dei filius visibilis Jesus Christus crucifixus sermo dei corporatus homo factus, servator, redemptor, conciliator, mediator, advocatus, rex, pontifex, iudex, dominus et deus noster, vide quam bene quadrem omnia quæ de uno deo patre et eius unigenito filio in scripturis dicuntur et præsertim in illo stupendo Joannis elogio, quod in principio idest ante omnia secula et omnem creationem erat verbum seu logos dei patris qui erat Christus ipse iam homo destinatus, aput ipsum deum patrem hoc est nondum mundo patefactus et qui erat deus ab ipso deo patre non idem ipsemet deus pater qui est super omnia secundum Ignatium ipsius Joannis discipulum ad Tarsenses sed verus deus de vero deo genitore per quem logon seu Christum dei patris omnia facta sunt et postea deffinito tempore idem logos in utero virginis homo factus est et sic in carne mundo patefactus visibilis palpabilis passibilis et mortalis cuius hominis seu verbi incarnati gloriam velut unigeniti dei patris Joannes ipse vidit dum cum eo habitaret tam ex signis et operibus quam ex illa transfiguratione resurrectione et in cœlum ascensione qui homo unigenitus dei patris logos eius corporatus fuit ab ipso patre omni benedictione gratia et veritate repletus

For as often as I must, and as long as you can stand it, [I will] continue to reiterate that Christ, the most divine man, our Lord and God, is nothing other than the *Logos* of God made flesh, visible and capable of suffering, the only begotten Son of God, in whom, *through whom, and because of whom* all things were made [a] and restored by God the Father. This is the greatest and most wonderful mystery of [God's] eternal plan, which has been revealed to very few, and which [revelation] has always been opposed.

Now reflect on how much light has shone forth for you from this book [*Declaratio*]. You were previously in darkness and had never acquired a correct understanding of God and the Son of God. Muddled and confused, you believed everything. Behold how everything is now plain, clear, and open to you, and how all the ambiguities and difficulties have been removed. Learn, I implore you, how to understand the one invisible God, who is the Father, and the one Son of God, the visible Jesus Christ crucified, *the Word* of God *made flesh* [b] and made man, [our] savior, redeemer, conciliator, mediator, advocate, king, high priest, and judge, our Lord and our God.

Observe how well I harmonize all is that is written in scripture about the one God the Father and his only begotten Son. [Note] in particular John's wonderful hymn of praise: *In the beginning* – that is, before all the ages and all creation – *was the Word* – or the *Logos* of God the Father, which was Christ himself, already destined to become a man. *[And the Word was] with God* the Father – that is, not yet revealed to the world – *and he was God* – from God the Father himself. [c]

"He is not the same God who is over all," according to John's disciple, Ignatius, in [his letter] to the Tarsians, [d] but he is "true God from true God," [e] the Father. *By means of* this *Logos* (or Christ) of God the Father, *all things were made.* [f] And subsequently, at the appointed time, this same *Logos* was made human in the Virgin's womb and was thus revealed to the world in the flesh: visible, palpable, capable of suffering, and mortal. John *beheld the glory* of this man, or incarnate Word, while *it dwelt* with him – *[glory] as of the only begotten [Son] of the Father*: the miracles and deeds he accomplished, as well as his transfiguration, resurrection, and ascension into heaven. This man, as t*he only begotten [Son] of* God *the Father*, was his *Word become flesh, filled* by the Father himself *with* all blessedness, *grace, and truth*. [g]

---

[a] Heb. 2:10.　[b] John 1:14.　[c] John 1:1.　[d] Pseudo-Ignatius, *Ad Tarsenses* 5 (PG 5 891B).
[e] From the Nicene Creed.　[f] John 1:3.　[g] John 1:14.

hæc omnia quæ Joannes ibi commemorat non ad filium aliquem incorporeum et invisibilem sed ad Christum illum visibilem et passibilem verum dei filium ab ipso Joanne visum et palpatum manifestissime referuntur neque alium dei filium nobis scriptura proponit vel commemorat præter quam illum met Jesum Christum hominem crucifixum qui fuit implementum et consummatio omnium consiliorum [114] et misteriorum dei patris.

Nunc te pie lector in spiritum paulisper collige et semota omni animi passione sincero corde diiudica, num hæc theologia de uno deo immortali et invisibili qui est pater ille conditor omnium et de unico eius filio visibili Jesu christo crucifixo per quem et propter quem omnia facta sunt videatur tibi planior sincerior et explicatior quam illa tenebrosa perplexa, confusa et intricata, de tribus in effectu deis æqualibus de personis hypostasibus, de duobus filiis visibili et invisibili de duabus naturis inæqualibus et distinctis simul unitis in uno agregato de communicatione idiomatum et suppositis connotativis et similibus nimiis quem* nihil prorsus habent commune cum evangelio Jesu Christi et de quibus ne unam quidem syllabam in universa tam antiqua quam nova scriptura invenies, infelix homo qui magis tenebras et calignem amas quam lucem dic quæso in quo sita est salutio tuæ fiduciæ si hominem illum sanctissimum et divinissimum Jesum redemptorem ita vilipendis, ut solam humanitatem voces ut solam humanitatem neges ab ipso deo genitum,** quam partem in eius sanguine et redemptione te habere confidis? quomodo speras illum pro te ante patrem supplicaturum? si illum verum dei patris filium non confiteris qui enim (inquit ille) non confitebitur me coram hominibus non confitebor et ego eum coram patre meo. Sed quam ille a nobis confessionem exigit? nisi [115] quod credamus et confiteamur illum esse filium dei, illum (inquit) qui pro nobis in ligno suspensus fuit primæ Io. 4. Nunquam enim aput gentiles et Judæos de re aliqua invisibili controversia fuit. Sed de Jesu illo homine visibili qui dicebatur Christus dei filius per generationem non per adoptionem cui propterea ab omnibus incredulis contradicebatur de quo tamen omnes prophetæ et Apostoli apertissime testificati sunt quod is vere filius dei esset dominus et deus noster benedictus et laudandus in sæcula.

---

* Should read *quæ*.   ** Should read *genitam*.

Everything John mentions here refers not to some incorporeal and invisible Son, but to the visible and suffering Christ, the true Son of God, who was unmistakably seen and touched by John himself. Scripture does not mention or present us with any Son of God other than Jesus Christ, the man who was crucified and who was the fulfillment and consummation of all the plans and mysteries of God the Father.

Now, pious reader, rally your spirit a little, and, setting aside every passion of the mind, judge with a sincere heart, whether this theology about one *immortal* and *invisible God*,[a] who is the Father and the author of all things, and his one visible Son, Jesus Christ crucified, *through whom and for whom all things* were made,[b] seems to you more intelligible, genuine, and straightforward than that shadowy, muddled, confusing, and complicated [theology] about three equal gods; about persons and hypostases; about two sons, [one] visible and [the other] invisible; about two unequal and distinct natures united together in one aggregate; about *communicatio idiomatum*, connotative *supposita*, and similar excrescences which have nothing whatsoever to do with the gospel of Jesus Christ, and about which you will find not one syllable in either the Old or the New Testament.

O unhappy one, you who love darkness and gloom more than light, please tell me, on what do you base your trust in salvation? If you so despise that most holy and divine man, Jesus our redeemer, that you call him merely "a human nature," and deny that this mere "human nature" was begotten by God himself, how can you be sure that you share in his blood and redemption? If you will not confess that he is the true Son of God the Father, how can you hope that he will pray for you before the Father? For he says, "*Whoever does not acknowledge me before men, I also will not acknowledge him before my Father.*"[c] But what confession does he require of us other than that we believe and *confess that he is the Son of God* (1 John 4),[d] he who was (as scripture says) *hung upon the cross*[e] for our sake? For the Gentiles and the Jews never argued about any invisible being, but about Jesus, the visible man who was called Christ: the Son of God by birth, not by adoption. Accordingly, all who do not believe [that Jesus is the Son of God] oppose what all the prophets and apostles most clearly testified: that he was truly the Son of God, our Lord and God, forever to be blessed and praised.

---

[a] 1 Tim. 1.17.   [b] Heb. 2:10.   [c] Matt. 10:32-33.   [d] 1 John 4:15.   [e] Acts 10:39.

Proinde non possum non vehementissime admirare quomodo antiqui illi theologi quos et moderni omnes secuti sunt ab hac planissima Apostolorum doctrina et apertissima evangelicæ lucis veritate de Jesu dei filio tam repente defecerint et ad illas imaginarias hypostases et deorum ac filiorum pluralitatem deflexerint. Novas et inauditas in scriptura voces confingendo per quas tota dei ecclesia conturbata est et in vacuissimas hæreses divisa puritas evangelii obscurata vera pietas et religio paulominus extincta. Quid veri? Quid sancti? quid boni? in tot voluminum miriadibus quos Theologi nostri iam a tot annis de relligione conflarunt inveniri potest? diviso et soluto (ut inquiunt Io. et Irenæus) Jesu Christi dei filio immo negato et destructo primo et potissimo evangelicæ veritatis fundamento quod est Jesus Christus crucifixus verus et unicus dei patris filius.

Milites Pilati dividentes vestimenta Christi quid aliud significarunt nisi istos hæreticos Valentiniatistas qui unicum dei filium patris Jesum christum crucifixum dividunt **[116]** ac dissolvunt. Sed invitis omnibus remanebit semper tunica inconsutilis quam nullus unquam dividere poterit sed tota aput Christi fideles integra remanebit, hi sunt qui Christum non dividunt. Sed unicum agnoscunt et adorant et quis non doleat hanc Christi domini sui divisionem? quis non suspiret lacrimetur et cum gemitu inenarrabili non exclamet, O altitudo dei quam admiranda sunt iuditia tua et inscrutabilia arcana consilii tui. Omnes homines errare permisisti et in suis inventionibus renitere ne quisquam sibi de veritate glorietur solus unigenitus tuus magister verax et infallibilis veritatem tuam docuit et prædicavit solus non erravit solus tenebras omnes discussit cum esset ipse vera lux, via veritas, et vita. Omnis homo mendax inventus est ut in solo Christo filio tuo veritatem gnosceremus. Pereant igitur omnes hominum inventiones et verbum tuum domine maneat in æternum.

What is more, I cannot but view with astonishment how quickly those theologians of old – whom all modern ones follow – abandoned the plainest teaching of the apostles and the clearest light of gospel truth regarding Jesus the Son of God, and turned to imaginary hypostases and a multiplicity of gods and sons, by fabricating new words unheard-of in scripture. Through these, the whole church of God has been shaken and divided by empty heresies, the purity of the gospel has been obscured, and true piety and religion nearly extinguished. What truth, holiness, or good can be found in the myriad volumes on religion which our theologians have concocted over the years? As John and Irenaeus say, they have divided and sundered Jesus Christ, the Son of God,[a] and have denied and destroyed the best and strongest foundation of gospel truth, which is Jesus Christ crucified, the true and only Son of God.

What does the dividing up of Christ's garments by Pilate's soldiers[b] prefigure, if not those heretical Valentinians who divide up and destroy the only Son of God the Father, Jesus Christ crucified? But whether they wish it or not, that *seamless garment*[c] will endure forever. No one will ever be able to tear it apart. Among Christ's faithful it will remain completely intact forever.

The [faithful] do not divide Christ but recognize and worship him as a single [being]. For who would not lament this division of their Lord Christ? Who would not sigh, weep, and cry out with an incredible groan: "O God most high, how wondrous are your judgments and inscrutable are your secret purposes. You have allowed all people to stray and to struggle, left to their own devices, *lest anyone should boast*[d] that he [possesses] the truth. Only your only begotten Son, the truthful and infallible master, taught and proclaimed your truth. He alone did not fall into error. He alone scattered all the shadows, because he himself was *the true light,*[e] *the way, the truth, and the life.*[f] *Every man* has been found *false,*[g] so that in Christ your Son alone we might recognize the truth. Let all the inventions of men therefore perish and *let your word, Lord, remain forever.*"[h]

---

[a] 1 John 4:3 (Vulgate). Irenaeus, *Adv. Hær.* 3.16.5 (PG 7a 924C-925A).   [b] Matt. 27:35, Mark 15:24, Luke 23:34, John 19:24.   [c] John 19:23.   [d] Eph. 2:9.   [e] John 1:9, 1 John 2:8.   [f] John 14:6.   [g] Rom. 3:4.
[h] Ps. 119:89.

Nunc audi Christiane fidelis confessionem meam quam ex tota mente et toto corde profiteor, ego pure sincere et firmiter credo atque confiteor hunc Jesum Christum hominem ex virgine natum passum mortuum et suscitatum cui omnes omnia debemus esse verum proprium et unigenitum dei filium dominum et deum nostrum qui nunc sedet gloriosus ad dexteram sui patris summi et invisibilis dei et qui ut verus homo dei filius rursus in carne gloriosus apparebit iudicaturus vivos et mortuos et quicumque hanc fidem aspernabitur iam iudicatus est et in peccato suo morietur, percurre scrutare et revolve quatuor evangelia universa Apostolorum acta et epistolas, non reperies vel unam lineam quæ de hac [117] fide non loquatur. Diligenter considera egregias illas ac disertas petri Marthæ Centurionis, Natanællii et Eunuchi de Christo Jesu confessiones quibus tamen nulla erat nec unquam fuit de alia re vel persona cogitatio quam de illo Jesu visibili crucifixo. Quid aliud cogitabat Paulus cum dixit fateor me nihil aliud scire præterquam Jesum Christum et hunc crucifixum et tum mirum est quod vir ille factus tam doctus et illuminatus vas electionis ad Christi prædicationem segregatum nihil unquam docuerit immo nec sciverit de illis personis seu hypostasibus de tribus deis æqualibus vel de uno deo triplici et trinomio de duabus naturis distinctis at unitis de duobus filiis de idiomatum communicatione et suppositis connotativis sed semper et ubique disserte et explicite prædicavit unum deum solum qui est pater a quo omnia, et unum filium dei solum qui est Jesus Christus crucifixus per quem omnia et per cuius sanguinem habemus redemptionem et remissionem peccatorum.

Quid igitur adhuc dubitamus, cum illis sanctis dei apostolis, et viris electis, nostram adiungere fidem et confessianem? fremat mundus, disputent philosophi, conspirent Theologi, persequantur impii, mactent lanientque tiranni, parentur carceres, vincula culei gladii, triremes, et incendia, nunquam tamen efficient quin istud sit verum et unicum Christianæ Relligionis fundamentum credere Jesum Christum illum visibilem crucifixum esse verum proprium et unicum unius dei patris filium ab ipso deo patre in utero virginis genitum

Now, faithful Christian, hear my confession, which I profess *with all* my *mind and all* my *heart*.[a] I simply, sincerely, and firmly believe and confess that this Jesus Christ, the man born of a virgin, who suffered, died, and rose again, the one to whom each of us owes everything, is the true and only begotten Son of God, *our Lord and our God*.[b] He is now *seated in glory at the right hand of* his Father, the almighty and invisible *God*.[c] As a real man and the Son of God, he will gloriously appear once more in the flesh, to *judge the living and the dead*.[d] Whoever rejects this faith *is already condemned*[e] and *will die in his sin*.[f]

Read through, examine, and reflect upon all four gospels, the Acts of the Apostles, and the epistles. You will not find even a single line that does not speak of this faith. Consider with care those illustrious and eloquent confessions [of faith in] Jesus Christ made by Peter, Martha, the centurion, Nathanael, and the eunuch.[g] They never so much as thought about any being or person other than the visible, crucified Jesus. Of what else was Paul thinking when he said, "*I confess that I know nothing other than Jesus Christ, and him crucified*"?[h] No wonder that this man, so wise and enlightened, the *chosen vessel*[i] set apart for the preaching of Christ, never taught or knew anything at all about persons and hypostases, three equal Gods – or, rather, one triple and three-named God – two natures distinct but united, two sons, *communicatio idiomatum*, and connotative *supposita*. He always and everywhere eloquently and plainly preached only *one God*, who is *the Father from whom all things are, and* only *one* Son of God, who is *Jesus Christ* crucified, *through whom all things are*,[j] and *through whose blood we gained redemption and the forgiveness of sins*.[k]

Why, then, should we any longer hesitate to unite our faith and confession with those chosen men and holy apostles of God? Let the world rage [against it], let philosophers dispute it, let theologians band together [against it], let the impious assail it, let tyrants tear it apart and destroy it, let them prepare prisons, chains, drowning sacks, swords, galleys, and flames, yet they shall never keep this from being the true and unique foundation of the Christian religion: the belief that the visible Jesus Christ crucified is the one and only Son of the one God the Father, begotten of the Father himself in the Virgin's womb.

---

[a] Matt. 22:37, referring to Deut. 6:5. [b] Rev. 4:11. [c] Matt. 25:31 (Erasmus); Mark 16:19, Luke 22:69, etc. [d] Acts 10:42. [e] John 3:18. [f] Ezek. 3:20. [g] Matt. 16:16 (Peter), John 11:27 (Martha), Mark 15:39 (centurion), John 1:49 (Nathanael), Acts 8:37 (eunuch). [h] 1 Cor. 2:2. [i] Acts 9:15. [j] 1 Cor. 8:6. [k] Eph. 1:7, Col. 1:14.

quod et in Apostolico simbolo expressissime [118] decantatur et hæc est vera fides et iusticia nostra hac fide iustificati pacem habemus erga deum patrem per dominum nostrum Jesum Christum eius filium bene dilectum et spiritus sanctus dei qui in nobis est, et cordis nostri parata conscientia testimonium reddit nobis efficatissimum quod sumus in vero et Christi veritatem habemus et quod ex deo nati sumus ut Joannes toties proclamat lex enim Christi non est sicut lex Mosis quæ erat scripta in tabulis lapideis nullam cordi præstans tranquillitatem vel securitatem, sed dicitur lex cordis et spiritus secundum Hieremiam et sic lex fidei cuius ratione eo ipso quod Christum cognoscimus et amplectimur firmiter in eum credentes, efficimur omnes filii dei patris per spiritum sanctificationis et regenerationis in filio suo Jesu Christo qui est caput nostrum et deus noster et hæc fides et spiritualis regeneratio donum dei est, quia non nisi patre trahente et revelante ad eius filii noticiam et amplexum perducimur et hæc lex non indiget ulla externa scriptione. Nam et si Apostoli nihil scripsissent si tum ex auditu tantum durasset nobis Christi cognitio semper mansisset hæc nova lux Jesu Christi interne Atramento descripta quam efficatia spiritus dei viventis in tabulis cordis imprimit.

Concludamus ergo hanc unam esse evangelicam veritatem et vitam æternam credere in unum deum patrem immortalem et invisibilem et in eum quem misit ille Jesum Christum filium suum crucifixum. Nemo enim ex corde dominum Jesum dicere potest nisi habeat spiritum dei. Unus ergo deus pater [119] omni* creator ut unus dei filius Jesus Christus crucifixus quibus sit laus honor et gloria in sempiterna sæcula. Amen.

---

* Should read *omnium*.

This, which is distinctly enunciated in the Apostles' Creed, is our true faith and righteousness. *Justified by this faith, we have peace with God* the Father *through our Lord Jesus Christ*, his well-beloved Son.[a] The Holy Spirit of God, who is within us, and our heart's own conscience provide us with the most effective testimony that we truly are in possession of Christ's truth and that we are *born of God*, as John so many times proclaims.[b]

For, unlike the law of Moses, which was written on tablets of stone and offers the heart no tranquility or security, the law of Christ is, as Jeremiah says, a law of the heart and spirit.[c] Thus it is a *law of faith*.[d] For since we come to recognize Christ and embrace him by firmly *believing in him*, we are all *made sons of God*[e] the Father by means of *the Spirit of sanctification*[f] and regeneration in his Son Jesus Christ, *who is our head*[g] and our God. This faith and spiritual regeneration is a gift of God, because, without the Father's revelation and guidance, we would not be led to the knowledge and the embrace of his Son. This law does not require any outward writing. For even if the apostles had not written anything, and knowledge of Christ had been preserved among us only by word of mouth, this new light of Jesus Christ would have endured forever, inwardly *inscribed* by the Spirit of the living God *on the tablets of our hearts*.[h]

Therefore we conclude [by saying] that this alone is the gospel truth and life eternal: to believe in one God the Father, *immortal and invisible*,[i] and in *him whom he sent*,[j] his Son, Jesus Christ crucified. For no one can speak of the Lord Jesus from the heart, unless he possesses the Spirit of God. There is, therefore, one God the Father, the creator of all things, and one Son of God, Christ crucified. Let them be given all praise, *honor, and glory, world without end. Amen.*[k]

---

[a] Rom. 5:1. [b] John 1:13, 1 John 3:9, 5:4. [c] Jer. 31:33. [d] Rom. 3:27. [e] John 1:12. [f] Rom. 1:4.
[g] Eph. 4:15. [h] Jer. 17:1. See also Jer. 31:33, Rom. 2:15. [i] 1 Tim. 1:17. [j] John 5:38.
[k] 1 Tim. 1:17, Rev. 5:13.

Apologia pro Michæle Serveto

A Defense of Michael Servetus

[18a] *Alphonsi Lyncurii Tarraconensis Apologia pro Michæle Serveto*

Egregiam tandem victoriam insignemque triumphum de prostrato adversario retulistis, en tandem iacet ille qui vobis adeo infestus et gravis in vestra dogmata et traditiones insultabat, tantus hostis, velut alter Hector Troianus a græcis tandem superatus abiit in cineres et favillas, erigite vobis trophæa ut tam præclari facinoris memoria nullo unquam tempore deleatur. Libros cudite et per orbem spargite ac dissipate, ut omnes ecclesiæ consulatum vestrum agnoscant, et de tam bene navata opera conservataque religione gratias agant. Vos nunc evangelicæ fidei et cristianæ rei publicæ contra omnia hæreticorum monstra fortissimos protectores assertores et vindices merito omnes intelligent atque laudabunt.

Sed iam operæ pretium videtur universam rei seriem exponere ut omnes insignem ~~justitiam~~ vestri progressus æquitatem intelligant. Non hic privati odii et simultatis atque invidiæ causas nominatim recensebo, quas omnibus satis notas esse existimo sed hominis detentionem et processum, quam brevissime et verissime potero enarrabo.

Michæl Servetus Villanovanus Tarraconensis medicæ artis peritissimus, Lucam illum medicum cuius plurima in evangelio laus est imitatus, cum plurimum ingenio valeret et de veritate relligionis mundum tumultuari nec non plurimorum scriptis et voluminibus infarciri satis ægre conspiceret animum suum ad sacras literas subinde transtulit in eisque omne suum studium et ingenium collocavit.

A Defense of Michael Servetus
by Alphonsus Lyncurius Tarraconensis

You have at last won a great victory and an impressive triumph over your prostrate adversary. Look, the man who was so dangerous to you, so critical of your dogmas, and who mocked your traditions, is finally dead! Such a mighty foe, like a second Hector of Troy at last defeated by the Greeks, has been turned into cinders and ashes. Erect a monument to yourselves, so that the memory of such a glorious crime may never be erased! Publish books [about it], and scatter and disperse them throughout the world, so that all churches may acknowledge your well-considered [actions] and thank you for your great zeal for the preservation of religion. Now everyone will justly recognize and praise you as courageous protectors, champions, and defenders of the gospel faith and the Christian republic against all the abominations of the heretics.

Nevertheless, at this point, it seems worthwhile to go over the entire sequence of events, so that everyone may appreciate the manifest justice of your legal proceedings. I will not here specifically review the causes of your personal hatred, rivalry, and jealousy, because I believe they are sufficiently well known to everyone. But I shall describe, as briefly and truthfully as possible, the arrest and trial of this man.

Michael Servetus of Villanueva in [the region of Hispania] Tarraconensis[1] was highly skilled in the art of medicine and followed in the footsteps of the physician Luke, whose chief glory is his gospel. Being a man of towering genius, and painfully aware that the world was in an uproar over the truth of religion and was full to bursting with the writings and books of many people, he thereupon turned his attention to sacred literature, and concentrated all of his efforts and genius there.

Cumque Lutheranos et Zwinglianos et Papistas de cæremoniis externis et ritibus atque primatu digladiari cognosceret interea vero circa veri et [**18b**] summi dei nec non domini Iesu Christi filii eius unigeniti cognitionem et substantiam atque misteria falso et impie convenire; aliquam diligentius rem scrutari cœpit ac de vero Deo et eius filio ex scripturarum fonte omnia maturius considerare.

Tandem ubi se aliquid (quod universo cristiano gregi profuturum esset) assecutum putavit Librum de erroribus trinitatis emisit in quo sententiam suam de Deo et dei filio libere explicavit docens unum tantum simplicissimum Deum neque trinum neque trinomium, neque divisum neque compositum scilicet æternum illum patrem et monarcham, rerum omnium authorem per verbum et spiritum suum omnia dispensantem, nec non et unicum ipsius Dei filium Iesum Cristum illum ex virgine Davidica natumneque alium filium Dei invisibilem ex scripturis ostendi, multa insuper alia tractans et affirmans quæ ~~modernis~~ recentibus scriptoribus præsertim Genevensibus (quos ille nominatim arguebat) quam maxime displicerent. Unde commoti illi atque irritati nec talem spiritum diutius ferre valentes, odiis, calumniis, insidiis persequi non destiterunt.

Cumque ille in gallicanis regionibus se plus nimio premi videret, nullumque sibi locum per æmulorum insidias relictum ubi securus degere posset tandem secum in animo statuit in Italiam ~~libere~~ transire ibique reliquum vitæ suæ tempus transigere, itaque collectis sarcinulis comparataque ex rebus et laboribus suis aliquanta pecunia itineri se infortunatus accinxit: et Genevam primum incognitus venit (neque enim de malo illorum erga se animo dubitabat) sed evangelicæ pietatis et mansuetudinis nonnulla spe confirmatus, et se non palam cognitum iri arbitratus ut per Sedunenses in italiam quam citissime emigraret iter suum illhac satis infeliciter instituerat Genevæ autem cum esset pænula et pileo tectus concionantem ministrum pedibus suis stans diligenter audivit. Verum a nonnullis cognitus [**19a**] et detectus eo ipso die comprehensus et carceri commendatus fuit. Res sic habet,

[Then] when he realized that the Lutherans, Zwinglians, and Papists, who were crossing swords over superficial details of ceremony and ritual and fighting for primacy of place, were at the same time falsely and impiously in agreement, not only about their conception of the true and highest God and his only begotten Son, the Lord Jesus Christ, but also about the [divine] substance and the mysteries, he began to examine the matter much more diligently. Drawing from the wellspring of scripture, he immediately began to reconsider everything regarding the true God and his Son.

Eventually, when he believed that he had discovered something that would be useful to the entire Christian flock, he issued his book, *On the Errors of the Trinity*, in which he candidly set forth his ideas about God and the Son of God.[2] He taught that there is only one uncompounded God, who is neither triple nor three-named, neither divided nor composite, who is undoubtedly the eternal Father and monarch, the author of everything, through whose Word and Spirit all things are arranged; and one Son of God, Jesus Christ, who was born of a virgin of the House of David. [He taught that] no other, invisible son of God was revealed in scripture.[3] He dealt with and asserted many other things as well, which were greatly displeasing to contemporary writers, particularly the Genevans, whom he attacked by name.[4] Whereupon [the Genevans], being upset and exasperated, and unable any longer to endure such a spirit, persecuted him incessantly, with hostility, slander, and treachery.

When [Servetus] saw that he was being hard-pressed in France, and that, because of the plots of his rivals, there was no place left where he could remain in safety, he finally decided to go to Italy to spend the remainder of his life there. Consequently, the unlucky man prepared himself for the journey by gathering together his few belongings and raising a little money from his labors and [the sale of the rest of] his possessions. He arrived in Geneva incognito because he had no doubt about [the Genevans'] bad feelings toward him. But, encouraged by the hope of evangelical piety and gentleness, and thinking that he would speedily make his way to Italy through the land of the Sedunians[5] without being openly recognized, he unfortunately decided to journey [through Geneva]. However, when he was in Geneva, attentively listening to a minister addressing public worship, although disguised in a cloak and cap and standing [in the back of the church], he was recognized and exposed by several people. On that same day he was arrested and imprisoned.[6] This is how it happened.

Accititius* quidam minister, aut ministri puer imo ut plerique aiunt ipsius ecclesiastæ coquus magistratum adiit, exponens adesse illhic hæresiarcham Servetum qui sanctissimam trinitatem pernegaret et cerberum tricipitem appellaret in ipsam Genevam et eius ministros perpetuo contumeliosum et pleraque alia de homine magistratui persuadens viatoris sibi copiam fieri postulans ut confestim detineretur ne ullo pacto elabi posset se cum illo carceribus offerens donec utrique ius fieret, sic enim illhic nescio quo more receptum est ut quicunque peregrinus et advena illhac transiens possit per quemvis alium de quovis facto etiam apud indos patrato postulari et reus fieri dummodo accusator se talioni subiiciens offerat se una cum accusato iudicium et censuram dicti magistratus se in carceribus subiturum donec uterque vel alteruter sibi sponsorem inveniat de iuri stando vel iudicato parendo.

Nunc audite tragœdiam probus minister vel coquus postulato reo confestim sponsorem adinvenit: pauper Servetus nullo ~~comperto~~ reperto fideiussore in carceres male detruditur illhinc non exiturus donec de pelle sua nundinatio peragatur, accusator personatus facto** liber et securus evasit. ~~Dii boni~~ Nunc qualis scenæ introitus dispicite (quæso vos pii et nullo affectu polluti) si accusator in capitali causa debuit fideiussoribus liberari? si talioni obstrictus iure dimitti potuit? reo carceribus mancipato? Quid si Michæl æquiores et rectos iudices nactus universalis concilii ~~iudicio~~ sententia absolvendus fuisset? et accusator talionis pœna feriendus? numquid et fideiussor ad capitalem pœnam vocatus esset? numquid sponsor ad flammas deductus? alienum facinus suo corpore luiturus?

---

* Should read *Ac citatius*.

** *Personatus facto*, a peculiar phrase, is likely a copyist's error for *personatus pacto*. See Horace, *Satires* 1.4.55.

A certain minister, or the servant of a minister, or, as many claim, the cook of the Church leader, [Calvin,][7] hastened to the magistrate, informing him of the presence of Servetus, the arch-heretic who denied the most holy Trinity, called it a three-headed Cerberus,[8] and was constantly contemptuous of Geneva and its ministers. He also persuaded the magistrate of many other things about the man, demanding that he be given legal power over the traveler, so that [Servetus] might be immediately detained and in no way allowed to escape. He offered to be kept in prison with [Servetus] until justice should be administered to each. For [in Geneva] – on what basis I do not know – any *stranger and sojourner*[a] passing through the city may be accused by anyone of any crime, even one committed in India, and made to stand trial.[9] Meanwhile the accuser, subjecting himself to the same penalty [to which the accused is liable], presents himself, along with the accused, to undergo in prison the judgment and sentence of the magistrate. [They remain in prison] until one or both of them can find a bondsman [to pledge that he will] stand trial or obey the legal judgment.[10]

Now hear the tragic tale. This worthy servant or cook, having pressed the charge, immediately found a bondsman, but poor Servetus, unable to find a guarantor, was wrongly tossed into prison, from which he would not emerge until the bargaining over his fate was concluded. The accuser, having played his part, was released free and clear. Now consider what this opening scene was like. I ask you – you who are pious and unsullied by influence – whether the accuser in a capital case should have been set free by bondsmen? Should the one who was bound under *lex talionis* [the law of retaliation] be dismissed, while the one he accused was thrown into prison? What if Michael had obtained fairer and more honest judges? Then if, by the judgment of the entire council, he had been absolved, his accuser should have suffered the punishment [to which the defendant had been liable]. In that event, would the bondsman also have been subject to capital punishment? And would the bondsman have been led into the flames to pay for the crime of another man with his own body?[11]

---

[a] Gen. 23:4, Ps. 39:12.

at qui naturæ ratio, æquitas et iuris censura huic ordini refragantur. Constat enim pro accusatore [**19b**] capitali, sponsorem seu fideiussorem recipiendum non esse sed ipsum una cum reo postulato personaliter detinendum donec de alterutrius crimine vel innocentia plene cognitum sit, videtis igitur quale fuerit initium Servetani processus quanta æquitatis et iustitiæ observatio.

Iam puto vos progressum reliquamque tragœdiæ partem vobiscum animo revolvere atque prope colligere. Quis vero tali initio non parem exitum divinasset. Solent enim fere omnia quodam naturæ vitio in deterius labi et (ut in proverbio est) quæ malo inchoata sint principio bonum exitum sortiri non possunt.

Videte nunc quid feceritis viri evangelici homunculum advenam et peregrinum professioni vestræ evangelicæ, et cristianæ caritati confisum tam fœde et ignominiose traduxistis, tam dire et immaniter exstinxistis. Ad vos ultro fidentemque sine tumultu, sine seditione, sine iniuria profectum accusastis, dolo tenuistis, carceribus intrusum peregistis et vivum tandem omni humanitate et misericordia prorsus exuti ardentibus flammis ~~coniectum~~ perussistis. O præclarum facinus nullis sæculis abolendum!

Hæccine est illa cristiana caritas? hæccine evangelica vestra professio, quam universo orbi persuadere tantopere studebatis? Docuit ne vos dominus et redemptor noster Iesus Cristus sic in hæreticorum causa procedere, qui hæreticum ab ecclesia pellendum, et loco ethnici habendum præmonuit, hæc ne a Paulo vase electionis didicistis? qui hæreticum hominem sæpe monendum et vitandum prædicavit, hunc ne morem vobis Ignatius, Ireneus, Augustinus, et cæteri patres orthodoxi per manus tradiderunt? qui veram dei ecclesiam pati non persequi solere dixerunt, et pro hæreticis pie orandum si forte per dei gratiam et benignitatem ad mentem et pœnitentiam reducantur.

But natural reason, equity, and the conduct of justice are [all] opposed to such a way of doing things. For it has been established that an accuser should not be allowed a guarantor, or bondsman, in a capital case, but that the accuser should be personally detained together with the defendant until such time as the guilt or innocence of each is entirely proven. Thus you can see what the legal procedure against Servetus was like from the outset, and to what degree [the rules of] fairness and justice were observed.

I believe that you are now ready to review and more nearly grasp the course of the trial and the rest of the tragedy. Given such a beginning, who could not foresee a corresponding outcome? Indeed, almost everything, through a kind of flaw in nature, tends to degenerate into a worse state, for, as the proverb says, "what begins badly is fated to end badly."[a]

Look at what you have done, you evangelicals! You have basely and disgracefully slandered and horribly and savagely killed this harmless man, this *stranger and sojourner*[b] who trusted in your evangelical profession and Christian charity. [Although] he trusted you, did not stir up any trouble or sedition,[12] and caused you no harm, you have accused him [of crime], detained him by treachery, tossed him into prison, prosecuted him, and finally, totally casting aside all humanity and mercy, burned him alive on a blazing pyre. What a noble crime, whose memory ought never to be obliterated!

Is this your Christian charity, your evangelical profession, about which you strove so hard to persuade the entire world? Is this the way our Lord and redeemer Jesus Christ taught us to treat heretics? [No, for] he counseled that heretics should [only] be expelled from the church and considered to be among the heathen.[c] Did you [then] learn these things from that *chosen vessel*,[d] Paul, who often preached that a heretical person should be admonished and shunned?[e] Is this the behavior exemplified for you by Ignatius, Irenaeus, Augustine, and other orthodox fathers? They were accustomed to say that the true church of God should endure, not persecute [heretics], and that heretics should be piously prayed for, so that, by the grace and kindness of God, they might perhaps return to their senses and repent.[f]

---

[a] Euripides, *Aeolus*, fr. 32: "From a bad beginning comes a bad end." [b] Gen. 23:4, Ps. 39:12.
[c] Matt. 18:17. [d] Acts 9:15. [e] Eph. 5:11, Titus 3:10. [f] Ignatius, *Epistola ad Ephesios* 9-10 (PG 5 651B-654A); Irenaeus, *Adv. Hær.* 3.25.7 (PG 7a 972A); Augustine, *Epistolæ* 100.1 (PL 33 366).

At saltem vos instruere debuit sapiens ille legisperitus Gamaliel ex principibus sinagogæ qui a sanguine apostolorum novam [20a] doctrinam promulgantium iussit temperari: et rem omnem deo committi quæ si mala esset, se ipsam dissolveret. Num vos scribis et Pharisæis si non mitiores saltem minime deteriores aut crudeliores esse decebat?

Sed quid egistis? Pauperculum virum ab omnibus destitutum, in manus vestras datum cum omni prius ludibrio et ignominia traductum flagranti incendio concremastis? Quid evangelio cum flammis? Existimastis forte illum in tanta sui animi angustia et ~~tribulatione~~ horrore et tanta mundi ignominia, opprobrio, sævitia et insultatione a clementissimo Deo fuisse derelictum? Absit, expendamus causam mortis. Unum solum Deum esse dicebat patrem illum domini Iesu Cristi a quo sunt omnia, atque hoc filius ipse fatetur et Paulus diserte testatur, vestrum trinitatis nomen irridebat, merito cum et nomen imaginarium et fœmineum sit, et vero deo contumeliosum qui nec sancta nec dea trinitas appellatur, nec triplex, nec trinomius, nec divisus, nec compositus est ut ex sacris literis discere potuistis. Unum solum unius altissimi dei filium agnoscebat Iesum Cristum ex virgine natum, ~~et~~ a Iudæis crucifixum humani generis redemptorem, atqui hoc est totius Cristianæ religionis fundamentum neque quidquam aliud prophetæ, Apostoli, et ecclesia sancta testantur.

Quid igitur? quid aliud dicere possumus? nisi illud ethnicum, omne in præcipiti vitium stetit. O si tantum iracundiæ æstum aliqua lenitatis temperie mitigare voluissetis, si calorem illum animis ebullientem temporis spacio refrigerari permisissetis, si tam ultrici libidini frena non laxassetis, quam alieni nunc ab ea occidendi hominis sævitia sive sententia videremini. Num pauperculus ille verum Deum negabat? quem unice tuebatur. Num dei filio seductorem Maumethem præferebat? qui solum Iesum Cristum crucifixum agnosceret in corde et ore semper haberet solum prædicaret, in eo solo spem et fiduciam omnem reponeret

You ought to have learned even from Gamaliel, one of the leaders of the synagogue, that wise expert in the law, who ordered [his men] to avoid shedding the blood of the apostles who were promulgating a new doctrine. He said that the whole matter should be placed in the hands of God, because [a doctrine] which was evil would destroy itself.[a] Ought you not to have been, if not more gentle, at least not markedly worse or more cruel than the scribes and the Pharisees?

But what did you do? This poor fellow, bereft of everything, was placed in your hands. Having first exposed him to every kind of ridicule and disgrace, you reduced him to ashes in a blazing fire. What has the Gospel to do with flames? Did you think that he, amidst such dread and anguish of spirit, confronted with the world's reproaches, taunts, rage, and attacks, had perhaps been abandoned by the most merciful God? Perish the thought!

Let us now look into the cause of his death. He said that there was *only one God, the father* of the *Lord Jesus Christ, from whom all things are*.[b] And this is what the Son himself declares and what Paul clearly attests. [Servetus] made fun of your word "Trinity." And rightfully so, since it is a made-up noun and feminine in gender. Truly, [the word] abuses God, who is called neither the Goddess nor the Blessed Lady Trinity, who is neither triple, nor three-named, neither divisible nor composite, as you could have learned from holy scripture. [Servetus] acknowledged only one Son of God the Most High, Jesus Christ, the redeemer of the human race, born of the Virgin, crucified by the Jews. This is the foundation of the whole Christian religion. The prophets, apostles, and the holy Church bear witness to nothing else.

What then? What else can we say, except [to mention] that pagan adage, "Every vice stands [on the edge] of a precipice"?[c] Would that you had chosen to temper such a great surge of wrath with some admixture of lenience. Would that you had allowed the passage of time to cool off that fever boiling in your minds. If you had not given rein to such a lust for vengeance, how far would you now be seen to be from that savagery or the idea that this man must be slain. Did that poor fellow deny the true God, whom alone he worshipped? Did he who acknowledged Jesus Christ crucified, and always had [Christ] in his heart and on his lips, who preached only [Christ], and in [Christ] alone placed all his hope and faith, prefer the seducer Muhammad to the Son of God?[13]

---

[a] Acts 5:34-39. [b] 1 Cor. 8:6. See, for example, *Err.* 15b-16a, 27a, 27b, 34b. [c] Juvenal, *Satires* 1.149.

quod si diversam opinionem circa [**20b**] nomen illud trinitatis et verbi interpretationem sive declarationem a comuni doctorum sententia, a vobis quoque recepta et approbata conceperat quam scriptura et rationibus se tueri posse et debere sperabat: erat ne tam repente et præcipiti iudicio damnandus et horrendo flammarum suplicio præsertim in evangelica et libera civitate, tam immaniter et ignominiose tradendus? Ubi patrum et procerum synodus convocata? qui de re tam ardua et seria mature dispicerent omni odio et humanis affectibus, seu ut vulgarius dicam, passionibus animi circumscriptis? Vos ipsi in unius animulæ interitum et accusatores et scribæ et iudices et executores fuistis: Dicite quæso, quem illi carceribus incluso patronum aut defensorem decrevistis? quam illi libertatem impune loquendi et rationes suas proferendi fecistis?

At dicetis disputavit nullis vinculis alligatus, libere loquutus est, dixit quæ voluit omnia gesta fideliter excepta, et aliis ecclesiis transmissa, reus mortis iudicatus est, bene habet tragœdia legitime peracta est. Quasi vero causam suam libere dixerit qui continue carceribus detentus nullius patroni aut confidentis sufragio adiutus sub iudicibus suspectis. Imo et capitali illum odio prosequentibus, et gesta (ut libuit) conscribentibus, nullo pro captivo gestorum conscriptioni assistente vel intercedente, nullius amici seu defensoris patrocinio fultus, quocum animi sui affectus et rationes miserandus exponeret.

Quid dicam? Breviter repeto, causam suam libere dixit? qui eosdem et capitales inimicos, et accusatores, et scribas, et iudices habuit et executores. Quis iam dubitet sub colore et prætextu divini zeli et publicæ vindictæ privatam ultionem non fuisse peractam? Quæ alia evangelica civitas vel ecclesia advenam et peregrinum virum quamvis hæresiarcham, nihil tamen in ea civitate moventem, tanta perfidia detinuisset, tam præcipiti iudicio damnasset, tam diro et anticristiano suplicio affecisset?

Even if he had conceived an idea about the word "Trinity" which diverged from the view generally held by the learned – which you also accept and approve – and an interpretation or revelation of the Word, which he hoped to be ready and able to defend using scripture and reason, should he therefore have been condemned by such sudden and precipitate judgment, and monstrously and disgracefully delivered to horrible punishment in the flames, especially in a free and evangelical city? When the council of the fathers and leading citizens was convoked, should they [not] have maturely deliberated over this difficult and serious matter, putting aside all human emotion (or, to put it in a more vulgar way, hurt feelings)? In the extinction of this one frail soul, you yourselves were the accusers, recorders, judges, and executioners. Pray tell me, what advocate or defender did you appoint for him when he was in prison? What freedom did you grant him to speak and make his arguments, without fear of punishment?

But you will say: "He was unshackled when he argued his case. He spoke freely. He said what he wished to say. All the proceedings were faithfully set down and sent on to the other [Swiss] churches. The guilty party was sentenced to death. It was done well. The tragedy was carried out legally." As if he, who was continuously held in prison, could have pleaded his case freely before untrustworthy judges who were bent on prosecuting him with the most deadly hatred and who wrote the record [of the trial] as it pleased them. There was no one to intercede on the prisoner's behalf or to help him compose a written defense. This unfortunate man was supported by no friendly defender or legal advocate, with whose aid he might have explained his state of mind and his arguments.[14]

What can I say, [except] to take a moment to ask again: Did he plead his cause freely, when the same people, his deadly enemies, were his accusers, recorders, judges, and executioners? Who could doubt that, under the show and pretext of religious zeal and public retribution, personal vengeance was carried out? What other evangelical city or church would, by means of such treachery, have detained a *stranger and sojourner*,[a] however heretical, who had stirred up nothing in that city, and condemned him with such hasty judgment, inflicting on him such a terrible and antichristian punishment?

---

[a] Gen. 23:4, Ps. 39:12.

Habuit quidem civitas vestra vidit et cognovit plurimos isthac transeuntes, in deum et veram religionem contumaces, impios, blasphemos et manifestos [21a] evangelii contemptores, imo et persecutores, quos tamen liberos securos et inofensos abire permisit: At vero hoc unum erat caput tantopere animis vestris infensum, oculis grave, auribus infestum: hoc unum caput erat tot laqueis et insidiis obsessum, tot telis expetitum, tot diris et imprecationibus devotum, en sic tandem præda in casses decidit, laqueos et insidias evitare non potuit: tandem suæ audaciæ et temeritatis pœnas dedit. Gaude Antoni, gaude et satiare en caput et dextram hominis qui in te moresque tuos stilum tam acriter strinxit, in tuos errores et vitia tam libere et licenter invectus, hoc Ithacus velit et magno mercentur Atridæ:

Quod si pacatiore animo iusticiæ leges consideremus, quanta mox iniustitia, quanta immanitas apparebit. Nemo enim sine dolo morte punitur. Quomodo autem doli is argui potest qui opinionem animo conceptam ut veram et evangelicam scripturis et rationibus tueri atque etiam mori pro ea paratus est? Neminem sane puto tam stupidi esse ingenii, tam hebeti consilio, tam comunis sensus expertem; qui in animum suum inducere possit, hominem velle ultro falsitatem sibi cognitam cum suo dispendio manifeste tueri: et pro ea non modo temporalem sed etiam æternam mortem oppetere. Quanquam enim permulti inveniuntur, qui pro temporariis commodis veritati cognitæ pro tempore refragentur, aut falsitati faveant simulantes. Nullus tamen unquam inventus est qui pro falsa opinione prudens sciensque mori voluerit: et animam suam ad æternum interitum gratis et sponte deducere præterea cum scrutatores cordium nullo modo esse possimus, quæ res soli deo præcipua est, de aliena conscientia iudicare temere non debemus, nec alienam fidem in deteriorem partem accipere, sed boni animi simplicitas et caritas suadent ut male opinantem vel sentientem, errore magis quam dolo peccare existimemus: et magis imprudentia labi quam se ipsum scienter prodere, et mortis æternæ vinculis obligare,

Indeed your city has seen and known many who have passed its way who were contemptuous of God and true religion, who were impious, blasphemers, and open disdainers of the gospel – even persecutors – whom you nevertheless allowed to pass through free, untroubled, and unhindered.[15] But this one person was so hateful to your souls, so odious in your eyes, and so dangerous to your ears, that he was beset with a great array of *traps and snares*,[a] ambushed with many weapons, and had a great many dire curses heaped upon him. Thus the prey finally fell into your nets, unable to evade those traps and snares. Finally he paid the penalty for his audacity and recklessness. Rejoice, [Mark] Antony, rejoice and be satisfied! Behold the head and the right hand of the man who wielded his pen so fiercely against your customs, who attacked your errors and flaws with such freedom and license![16] "This is what the Ithacan wishes, this is what the sons of Atreus would pay for so dearly!"[17]

But if we consider the laws of justice in a calmer state of mind, how much injustice, how much barbarity, soon appears! For no one who does not have evil intent is punished with death.[18] But how can anyone be convicted of having evil intent, who has an opinion that he considers true and evangelical, based on scripture and reason, and which he is prepared to defend and even to die for? I believe that there is no one of such dull intelligence, so feeble in understanding, or so lacking in common sense, that he would choose to defend what he knew to be false, when it was obviously not in his interest to do so. Would he seek not only his temporal but also his eternal death on behalf [of a falsehood]? For although many might, for a time, oppose a known truth or deceitfully approve a falsehood in order to gain worldly advantages, nevertheless, no one would knowingly and deliberately choose death, and freely and voluntarily offer up his soul to eternal destruction, for the sake of a false idea.

Furthermore, since only God has the power to look into a person's heart, we should not recklessly judge another person's conscience, nor disdain a faith different from our own. But the charity and candor of an honest mind urge us to consider that someone who holds wrong ideas or incorrect beliefs may not be guilty of deceit. For he may have fallen into error out of ignorance, rather than by knowingly betraying himself and shackling himself in chains of eternal death.

---

[a] Jer. 5:26.

fides enim et veritatis cognitio donum dei est: nec omnibus omni tempore [**21b**] datur. Spiritus ergo omnia iudicat, ipse autem a nullo sed a se ipso iudicatur. Quare iniquissimum est errantes spiritus, corporalibus pœnis velle constringere: et homines imprudenter labentes, atque falsa opinione deceptos, ultimo supplicio adiudicare, nunc addamus exempla. Si Martini Lutheri spiritus (cum deo placuit) in hoc excitatus fuit ut plerasque opiniones in religione Cristiana iam mille et trecentis ab hinc annis publico omnium patrum consensu comuniter Catholiceque receptas, præsertim (ut interim alias prope infinitas omittam) de transmutatione et adoratione panis simbolici, de purgaturio, invocatione divorum, cælibatu, libero arbitrio, et primatu Romanæ sedis, in dubium non modo revocaret, sed etiam editis voluminibus in totum convelleret, atque rescinderet, et falsas esse multis populis persuaderet, nec tamen quispiam nunc invenitur ex iis qui evangelium profitentur qui illum vel male egisse dicat, vel flammeis suppliciis dignum fuisse sentiat, qui ausus fuerit tot catholicas opiniones, tot sæculis confirmatas suo spiritu rescindere, et universam ecclesiam novis dogmatibus conturbare, et scismate manifesto antiquam aut saltem diutinam religionem proscindere, si uni inquam monacho germano, pacatis temporibus et florente Romana sede tantum licuit, cur Serveto Hispano viro bene docto et in sacris literis diligenter versato atque exercitato non licuit iam commotis temporibus et scismatibus superinductis et novis quotidie hominum opinionibus, interpretationibus, et decretis gliscentibus, unicam opinionem de hoc imaginario nomine trinitatis de quo ne syllaba quidem in scripturis invenitur, ab Ethnicis philosophis primum introductam, quam nec apostoli nec eorum discipuli unquam cogitarunt in dubium revocare? et scripturæ autoritate manifestisque rationibus erroneam, impiam, et absurdam ostendere?

For faith and the recognition of truth are gifts from God, and are not always given to everyone. Therefore, a spirit *judges all things; however, he is to be judged by no one else.*[a] For this reason, it is exceedingly unjust to attempt to constrain errant spirits with corporal punishments, and to condemn to the ultimate penalty those who imprudently fall into error and are deceived by false ideas.

Now let me add a few examples. God was pleased to so rouse the spirit of Martin Luther that, in his published works, [Luther] not only called into question, but completely shattered and demolished, a great many received opinions concerning the Christian church, which had been universally accepted by the general consensus of the church fathers for 1300 years. These included, among many other things, transmutation and adoration of the symbolic [eucharistic] bread, purgatory, invocation of the saints, celibacy, free will, and the primacy of the Roman See. [Luther] persuaded many people that these [doctrines] were false. Today, however, no one who professes the gospel claims that [Luther] acted badly or maintains that he should have been burned alive. [Luther] had the courage to demolish by the force of his intellect numerous universally-accepted ideas that had held sway for centuries. He upset the entire church with new teachings and [created] an open schism that tore the ancient or, at any rate, the long-established, religion asunder.

If all this was permitted to a German monk in a period of tranquility, when the See of Rome was flourishing, why, in a time of widespread tumult and schism, when new ideas arise daily and [new] interpretations and doctrines are spreading, was the Spaniard Servetus – a very learned man, carefully trained and well versed in sacred literature – not permitted this one belief about the imaginary word "Trinity"? [Why was he not allowed], based on plain reasoning and the authority of scripture, to call [the Trinity] into doubt and to prove that it was erroneous, impious, and absurd? For [the Trinity] was originally introduced by pagan philosophers. Not one syllable about it may be found in the scriptures. Nor did the apostles or their disciples ever give it a thought.

---

[a] 1 Cor. 2:15. This verse actually reads, "The spiritual person [*spiritualis*, the adjective being used as a noun, indicating a human being] judges all things..." Castellio, in his Latin New Testament, made it even clearer, expanding it to *spiritualis homo*.

Nullus spiritus contemnendus est, sed omnia probanda (ut inquit Paulus) et quod bonum fuerit amplectendum. Quotidie Deus novos spiritus excitat ad revelationem veritatis et iudiciorum suorum et [22a] usque in finem sæculi iugiter excitibit: ne quisquam hominum sibi blandiri queat se unum super omnes illustratum, sibi uni omnem veritatem patefactam, quinimo omnis homo mendax: et conclusit deus omnes sub mendacio et peccato, ut omnium misereatur et solus ipse verus et verax in sermonibus suis iustificetur, sed ut ad exempla redeam, an num Ulricus Zwinglius vir pius et doctus fervente et novo spiritu, Martini opinionem de eucharistiæ sacramento iam passim ab universa fere germania receptam aprobatam et doctissimorum hominum sufragiis confirmatam, nova scripturarum interprætatione dissolvit, probabilioremque demonstrare conatus est, licet Martinus verborum proprietati magis hæreret, Ulricus autem scripturæ tropum et figuram agnosceret, quæ controversia tanto hinc, inde studio, tot aculeis inter ipsas evangelicæ professionis eclesias agitata est, et usque in hodiernum diem tot contentiosis et famosis libellis agitatur, ut nisi deus optimus manum admoveat, non sit spes tantam contentionem usque in diem iudicii consopitam iri: Adeo pertinax est quisque sui nominis et studii defensor. Verum ~~illi~~ Lutherus ~~scilicet~~ et Zwinglius summos principes fautores et corporis sui protectores habuerunt, ut sine ullo persecutionis et supliciorum metu possent quicquid vellent libere promulgare atque ita efectum est ut orbem suis voluminibus et doctrina compleverint, studiisque divisis multas ecclesias excitarint quæ licet se invicem scriptis et parum modestis arguant, ~~hæreseos~~ lacessant, hæreseosque insimulent, nullum tamen illarum membrum exustum est, aut flammarum anticristiano suplicio iudicatum.

No spirit should be condemned, but we ought to *test all things*, as Paul says, and *embrace what is good*.[a] Every day God arouses new spirits to a revelation of his truth and his judgments, and he will continually arouse them until the end of the world. Let no one delude himself that he alone is enlightened above all others and that all truth has been revealed to him alone. For *everyone is false. God has confined everyone in* sin and falsehood *so that he might show mercy to everyone*, and that *he*, being alone *true* and truthful, might be *justified in his words*.[b]

To return to my examples: Did not that pious and learned man Ulrich Zwingli, having the fervent and revolutionary spirit of Martin [Luther], refute, by means of a new interpretation of scripture, an idea about the sacrament of the Eucharist which was then generally accepted, approved, and sanctioned throughout Germany by the assent of the learned, and endeavor to provide a more plausible [understanding of the Lord's Supper]? While Martin adhered more closely to the literal meaning of words, Ulrich discerned the tropes and figures of speech in scripture.[19]

Among the churches of the evangelical profession, this controversy has been so eagerly pursued on every side, with so much mutual criticism, and continues to rage in so many contentious and renowned books even to the present day – each party being so dogged a defender of its reputation and position – that, unless Almighty God[20] were to put his hand down, so great a controversy could not be expected to abate until the day of judgment. However, both Luther and Zwingli had great princes as patrons and protectors of their physical safety. This allowed them to freely promulgate whatever ideas they wished without fear of persecution or punishment. Thus, although they filled the world with their books and doctrines, stirred up a multitude of churches with their opposing theological views, and debated in their writings (and quite immodest ones at that), attacking each other and exchanging charges of heresy, none of their limbs was scorched, and none of their adherents has been sentenced to the antichristian punishment [of death] by fire.

---

[a] 1 Thess. 5:19,21. [b] Rom. 3:4, 11:32.

At vero pauper Servetus advena et peregrinus omni amicorum et procerum sufragio destitutus, non habens ubi caput reclinare posset, sed ubique insidiis et persecutione vexatus, vix unum libellum de errore triadis potuit publicare, in quo demus [**22b**] et ipsum alicubi excidisse, nec omni prorsus errore vacasse (quod sane omni homini peculiare est) bono tamen zelo et divinæ veritatis studio ferebatur, in qua promovenda quamvis id quod maxime contendebat vivens assequi non potuerit, plura tamen dixit ex scripturæ sententia, plurima revelavit adnotatione dignissima, quæ hactenus passim occulta aut certe neglecta videbantur. Denique bonam ille operam in hoc saltem navasse dicetur et a posteris laudabitur quod tepidos et dormientes spiritus ad unius veri et summi Dei nec non et filii eius unigeniti cognitionem diligentius perquirendam excitavit.

Nempe recentes Theologi, qui se evangelicos profitentur et veræ doctrinæ assertores prædicant, in religionis cauda duntaxat omne studium posuerunt, circa inferiora elementa strenue et diligenter elaborarunt, opiniones diu receptas de primatu Romani pontificis, quem verum Anti-cristum esse testantur, de missa, purgatorio, sacramentis, confessione, pœnitentia, satisfactione, ciborum delectu, divorum invocatione, imaginibus, votis monasticis, cælibatu, libero arbitrio, et prædestinatione, de quibus nec dum inter ipsos convenit et aliis ecclesiæ Romanæ cærimoniis fortiter oppugnantes verum, ut dixi, circa caudam duntaxat laborarunt, solam papismi causam subvertere cupientes, cæterum caput ipsum penitus negligentes circa veri dei et filii eius unigeniti cognitionem, nihil omnino studii, operæ, et diligentiæ posuerunt, sed cum ipsis papistis simpliciter transierunt falsum et erroneum illorum vadum secuti: Sophisticas et imaginarias illas de trinitate chimæras unanimiter aprobantes, nec in tali philosophia papam et suos pro Anticristo habuerunt: sed adhuc spiritu sancto aflatos concesserunt.

On the other hand, poor Servetus, *a stranger and a sojourner*,[a] without the backing of friends and princes, *having nowhere to lay his head*,[b] and everywhere beset by plots and persecution, was with difficulty able to publish just one little book on the errors of the triad.[21] In this, we grant, he occasionally went too far and was not entirely free from error, [a failing] which, of course, he shares with every human being. Nonetheless, he was carried away by his good intentions and his passion for God's truth. But although during his lifetime he could not achieve what he most greatly strove for, nevertheless much that he said was based on the meaning of scripture, and he revealed a great many things most worthy of note, which previously had lain scattered and hidden, or at any rate had been overlooked. In short, it can be said that at least he did his best and that he will receive the praise of posterity. For he roused lukewarm and drowsy spirits to more diligently seek knowledge of the one, true, and highest God, and also of his only begotten Son.

Of course, current theologians who proclaim that they are evangelical and defenders of true doctrine merely concentrate their efforts on the tail of religion. They labor strenuously and diligently on the lesser elements, those long-received beliefs promulgated by the Roman Pope (whom they maintain is really the Antichrist) about the mass, purgatory, the sacraments, confession, penance, atonement, dietary rules, invocation of the saints, images, monastic vows, celibacy, free will, and predestination. Although they still have not come to complete agreement among themselves, they fight bravely against these and other ceremonies of the Roman Church. But, as I have said, while they have concentrated all their efforts on the tail, eager only to undermine the cause of popery, they have meanwhile totally neglected the head of religion, expending no effort, zeal, or careful study on achieving an understanding of the true God and his only begotten Son. Rather, following the papists, they have merely taken the same false and erroneous path, pursuing sophistical and imaginary chimeras of the Trinity and giving them their unanimous approval. In this kind of philosophy they did not consider the Pope and his followers to be the Antichrist, but allowed that, at least in this regard, [the papists] were inspired by the Holy Spirit.

---

[a] Gen. 23:4, Ps. 39:12. [b] Matt. 8:20.

Cum vero de articulis caudæ rogarentur, cur omnes receptas et catholicas [23a] opiniones tam strenue oppugnarent et convellerent, respondebant quicquid a papis et eorum scholasticis asseclis traditum aut receptum esset, nihil habere veritatis, sed omnia falsa, corrupta et depravata, nihilque a Romana ecclesia (quam Anticristi sedem et Satanæ synagogam appellant) boni, sancti, veri, aut puri prodire posse, cum nullam sancti spiritus scintillam prorsus haberet, sed satanico spiritu in omnibus et per omnia manifestissime regeretur.

Mox ubi ad caput ventum est, et Deus spiritum Daniellis excitavit qui seniorum errores et pecata corrigeret, qui veternum e mentibus excuteret, docens eos in cognitione veri Dei et filii euis Iesu Cristi negligenter versatos, cum papistis graviter hallucinatos, longeque de veritatis semita fuisse digressos. Bone deus qui rumores, qui tumultus, quæ incendia, confestim hæresiarcham exclamarunt: in necem coniurarunt: insidias et laqueos tetenderunt: miris modis pauperculum persequentes tandem in eorum manus delapsum vivum et clamantem Iesum dei filium flammis ardentibus consumpserunt, asserentes papistas in hoc articulo bene sensisse, et veritatem docuisse; seque cum illis in hac re probe convenire, en quam repentina vocis mutatio Anticristi ecclesia de sancta trinitate optime sentit: nec non et de hæreticis comburendis. Quemadmodum igitur in trinitatis articulo unanimes convenerunt, sic etiam in flammarum supplicio hæreticis adhibendo concordes fuerunt, nisi quod evangelici aliquanto mitiores qui non hæreticum (ut papistæ) prius laqueo præfocant quam ignem admoveant, sed vivum flammis extinguunt Perilli et Phalaridis ~~sevitiam~~ exemplum non modo æquantes sed longe etiam superantes,

Thus, when asked why they vigorously opposed and overthrew all the received, catholic opinions about the articles in the tail [of religion], they answered that whatever was handed down or accepted by the papists and their scholastic hangers-on contained nothing of the truth, but was entirely false, corrupt, and depraved. [They said] that nothing good, sacred, true or pure could emerge from the Roman Church – which they called seat of the Antichrist and the *synagogue of Satan*[a,22] – since it possessed not a single scintilla of the Holy Spirit, but was plainly ruled in and through all things by the spirit of Satan.

Soon, however, when the head [of religion] became the subject, God roused the spirit of our Daniel [that is, Servetus], who corrected the errors and sins of the elders and shook the torpor from their minds, teaching that they were careless in their understanding of the true God and his Son Jesus Christ and that they, like the papists, were hallucinating wildly and wandering far from the path of truth. Good God, what shouting [was heard]! What an uproar! What a conflagration! They immediately cried out that he was an arch-heretic and conspired to murder him. They spread out *traps and snares*[b] and persecuted the poor fellow in an amazing fashion. Finally, he fell alive into their clutches. As he called out to Jesus the Son of God, they reduced him to ashes in a blazing pyre, thereby proclaiming that, in this article [of faith], the papists possessed an excellent understanding and a true doctrine [of the Trinity]. In this regard, [the evangelicals and the papists] were in complete agreement.

See how quickly [the evangelicals] changed their tune! The church of the Antichrist [was now felt] to be quite correct in its thinking about both the holy Trinity and the burning of heretics. Therefore, just as they were of one mind on the article of the Trinity, so too did they concur in using fire to punish heretics. Perhaps the evangelicals were somewhat "gentler" in that they did not, like the papists, first strangle the heretic with a noose before they administered the fire, but burned him alive, in a manner not only equaling [the cruelty of] Perillus and Phalaris,[23] but even far surpassing them.

---

[a] Rev. 2:9, 3:9.   [b] Jer. 5:26.

hæc est illorum Cristiana pietas, evangelica caritas, et religiosa professio, domini Iesu Cristi humilitatem, patientiam, benignitatem, longanimitatem et misericordiam scilicet imitantes, satis potuit infallibilis veritas et [23b] magister optimus admonere et exclamare: discite a me quia mitis sum et humilis corde, discite quid est, misericordiam volo, non sacrificium, sinite zizania crescere usque in diem messis ne forte et triticum eruatis; si quis vos et ecclesiam audire noluerit, sit vobis tanquam ethnicus et publicanus; hæreticum hominem post admonitiones sæpe factas evitate, tantum absit ut quemquam occidatis filius hominis non venit perdere quemquam sed salvare, et deus optimus non vult mortem peccatoris, sed magis ut convertatur et vivat, diligite inimicos vestros, orate pro persequentibus vos eisque bene facite, mihi vindictam et ego retribuam, si quis dixerit diligo deum, et fratrem suum oderit, mendax est: qui enim fratrem suum quem vidit non diligit, deum quem non vidit quomodo diligere potest? Charitas ex deo est, et omnis qui diligit ex deo est, qui vero non diligit, is deum non novit hæ sunt Cristi voces, hæc spiritus sancti oracula, quæ cordibus vestris evangelicis infixa esse debuerant, non impiorum dogma et ritum in proximi perditionem amplecti non cum anticristianis ad fidelium suplicia convenire.

Sed iam video cavillos vestros quibus supra scriptas ~~flammas~~ sententias prave detorqueatis. At nihil proficitis, piis enim et charitate præditis spiritibus imponere non potestis. Frustraque illis persuadere contenditis, an ne proximi vestri in Iesum Cristum dei filium baptizati et evangelicam fidem ex animo profitentis et corpus et animam, quantum in vobis fuit, perdere studuistis? pro cuius vita et salute Cristus mori voluit, si errore lapsum sciebatis corpus exstinguere non debuistis, si dolo peccantem (quod est ab omni verisimilitudine maxime alienum) longe minus pro causa fidei perdere debebatis, corpus et animam interimentes,

So this is their Christian piety, evangelical charity, and religious profession! Of course, for one who imitates the humility, patience, kindness, forbearance, and mercy of the Lord Jesus Christ, who is the infallible truth and the best of teachers, it is enough to warn and exclaim: "*Learn from me, for I am gentle and humble of heart.*"ᵃ "Learn *what this means* [when God says]: *'I desire mercy, not sacrifice.'*"ᵇ "*Let the tares grow until the day of harvest, lest you root up the wheat as well.*"ᶜ "*If he refuses to listen to you and the church, let him be to you like a gentile and a tax collector.*"ᵈ After you have given a heretical person frequent warnings, avoid him, but refrain from killing anyone.

"*The Son of man* did not *come to destroy* anyone but *to save* [*the lost*]."ᵉ "Almighty *God does not desire the death of the* sinner, *but rather that he be converted and live.*"ᶠ "*Love your enemies, pray for those that persecute you,* and *do good* to them."ᵍ "'*Vengeance is mine, and I will repay,*' [*says the Lord.*]"ʰ "*If anyone says 'I love God,' and hates his brother, he is a liar. He who does not love his brother whom he has seen, how can he love God whom he has not seen?*"ⁱ "*Love is of God, and all who love are of God; truly, he who does not love does not know God.*"ʲ These are the words of Christ, these are the utterances of the Holy Spirit, words which ought to be *engraved on your* evangelical *hearts*.ᵏ Instead, you embrace the dogmas and rituals of the impious in order to destroy your neighbors, joining with the antichristians in punishing the faithful.

I now see the mocking way in which you perversely twist the foregoing statements. But *it profits you nothing*.ˡ For you cannot impose your views on pious, loving souls. You attempt in vain to persuade them that you did not try your best to *destroy both the body and the soul*ᵐ of your neighbor, [a man] who was baptized in Jesus Christ the Son of God, who professed a heartfelt evangelical faith, and for whose life and salvation Christ chose to die. If you knew that he had fallen into error, you [still] should not have destroyed his body. It is one thing if you knew that he was sinning intentionally (which is quite unlikely), but, by no means, should you have destroyed him on account of [his] faith, [trying to] kill his body and his soul.

ᵃ Matt. 11:29.   ᵇ Matt. 12:7, quoting Hosea 6:6.   ᶜ Matt. 13:29-30.   ᵈ Matt. 18:17.
ᵉ Mark 1:24, Luke 4:34 (not to destroy); Matt. 18:11, Luke 19:10 (save the lost).   ᶠ Ezek. 18:23.
ᵍ Matt. 5:44, Luke 6:27-28, 35.   ʰ Rom. 12:19, based on Deut. 32:35.   ⁱ 1 John 4:20.   ʲ 1 John 4:7-8.
ᵏ 2 Cor. 3:3.   ˡ 1 Cor. 13:3.   ᵐ Matt. 10:28.

quia clementissimus deus benignus, patiens, et longanimis est et multæ misericordiæ nec vult mortem peccatoris, sed ut ad pœnitentiam revocetur: An scitis fidem esse donum dei? et duodecim esse horas diei, et primo quoque temporis momento posse errantem corrigi, peccantem converti, cæcum illustrari, infidelem [24a] reduci, hæreticum ~~reuniri~~ revocari, publicanum iustificari, et latronem glorificari, hæc sunt omnipotentis dei admiranda opera et iudicia cuius viæ omnes misericordia plenæ, et manus ad sublevandum minime abbreviata, quam vos tamen vestro præcipiti iudicio et ultrici consilio, ausuque temerario et præcurrere et præscindere voluistis, truculentorum et immanium iudicum exempla sequuti, qui reum aliqua privata ratione sibi ipsis invisum, morti adiudicatum quanta possunt ~~claritate~~ celeritate ad supplicium præcipitant: ne forte regis gratia superveniens, reum ab eorum manibus liberet et saluti vitæque restituat. Sed certe cristianum erat, evangelicum erat, et religiosæ professioni consentaneum, hominem peregrinum in manus vestras traditum humaniter admonere, scripturis evincere, ad unitatem in charitate reducere, perseverantem vel propellere vel durius agendo, ~~carcerius~~ honesta custodia asservare: et pro illo deum orare si forte ad sanam mentem et pœnitentiam reduci posset quod sane magis sperandum fuit si et veritas et charitas a parte vestra stetissent, sic animæ Domino lucrifiunt: sic veræ religionis cultus augetur, et ecclesiæ sanctæ unitas conservatur. Hæc ex scripturis et interni spiritus testimonio adeo plana et aperta sunt ut nisi pertinaci cavillatione et invicta malitia dissimulari non possint et quicquid editis libellis magis verborum pompa ~~et elegantia~~ quadam, quam veritatis simplicitate refertis persuadere conati sitis, et tantum facinus excusare, nihil tamen proficitis quinimo piorum animos amplius ofendistis et tyrannorum opinionem de cremandis hæreticis magis impie confirmastis,

For the most loving God *is kind, patient, long-suffering, and full of mercy.*[a] He does not desire the death of a *sinner* but wishes to *summon* him *to repentance.*[b] Do you not know that *faith is the gift of God,*[c] that *there are twelve hours of daylight,*[d] and that in the first minute of that time one who is in error can be corrected, a *sinner converted,*[e] one who is blind made to see,[f] an infidel restored, a heretic regained, a *tax collector justified,*[g] and a thief glorified?[h] These are the *marvelous works and judgments* of Almighty God.[i] *All his ways are filled with mercy,*[j] and *his hand* is very quick *to raise up.*[k]

Nevertheless you, with your precipitate justice and vengeful policy, preferred to rush forward with reckless abandon to tear [Servetus] apart. You followed the example of cruel and inhuman judges, who hasten to punish an accused person, whom they, for personal reasons, detest and deem worthy of death, lest a royal pardon arrive and free the accused from their clutches, restoring him to life and safety. But certainly it would have been Christian, evangelical, and in keeping with your religious profession, to kindly admonish such a stranger who had been placed in your custody, to convince him with scripture, to lovingly lead him back into unity, and, if he persisted [in his ways], to cast him out [of the city]. Or if you wished to apply harsher methods you might have detained him in prison under proper conditions, and prayed to God for him, hoping that he might be recalled to sound thinking and repentance. This latter outcome was certainly more to be anticipated if truth and love, on your part, had prevailed. This is how souls are gained for the Lord. Thus is reverence for true religion furthered and the unity of the holy church preserved. This is so plain and obvious, both from scripture and the witness of the spirit within us, that it cannot be concealed except by persistent quibbling and unconquerable malice.

You accomplish nothing by publishing those little books, crammed more with pomposity of speech than simplicity of truth, to try to persuade [us] to excuse the crime. Rather, you have amply succeeded in offending the souls of the pious, and have impiously lent your support to the policies of tyrants regarding the burning of heretics.

---

[a] 1 Cor. 13:4, Ps. 86:5, Ps. 103:8.   [b] Matt. 9:13.   [c] Eph. 2:8.   [d] John 11:9.   [e] James 5:20.
[f] See, for example, Matt. 11:5.   [g] Luke 18:13-14.   [h] See Luke 23:43.   [i] Ps. 105:5.
[j] Ps. 25:10, James 3:17.   [k] See Mark 1:31, 9:27.

verum quianam aliter fecissetis? qui nunquam verum deum nec verum dei filium cognovistis quos imaginarias quasdam relationes semper existimastis, nonne bene prædixit Cristus quod pii persecutionem paterentur et affligerentur ab iis qui nec patrem nec ipsum cognoscerent. Quis dei spiritus vos unquam ad tam immane facinus perpulisset? Quando unquam persuadebitis vel [24b] posteris vel ecclesiæ in evangelio renascenti vos Cristiane evangelice et religiose fecisse cum legent vel audient vos tam atroci vindicta, impiorum armis succinctos, privatam causam re ipsa satagentes, hominem peregrinum pietati vestræ confisum, ad vos sponte profectum, solum et indefensum, omni sufragio destitutum, vestro id est capitalium inimicorum arbitrio ventilatum, lancinatum, cum immortali odio ignominia et ludibrio traductum, tam crudeliter et immaniter exstinxisse: corpus et animam (quantum in vobis fuit) occidere properantes.

Audete negare, si potestis, vos ei non fuisse gravissimos inimicos et eius scriptis nominatim non ofensos? eius sanguinem non totis animis expetivisse? omne consilium et operam in tollendo adversario et gravissimis suppliciis afficiendo, non adhibuisse, mortem eius et oprobrium ridentibus oculis non aspexisse, ad suplicium eunti illusoriis verbis non insultasse?

Quid mœres? quid gemis? quid suspiras? Si opinio tua vera est, cur non lætus et gaudens abis? Tales erant perfidorum in dei filium voces; si filius Dei es, descende de cruce, et credemus tibi, O cristianam pietatem, o evangelicam charitatem, o præclarum facinus pro tutela et quiete ecclesiæ excogitatum. Quis tam ferreus et Neronianus hæc audiens non horrescat? Quis tam Busiricus et adamantinus hæc siccis oculis legat?

At deerat adhuc spectaculo nænia confestim editus est libellus omnem progressum et iudicium probans, fuit nimirum illa oratio funebris quæ exstincti cineres commendaret.

Indeed, how could you have done otherwise – you who have never known the true God or the true Son of God and who have always set store by imaginary "relations"?[24] Did not Christ accurately predict that the pious would suffer persecution and be tormented by those who did not know either the Father or himself?[a] Could the spirit of God ever have compelled you to [commit] such an inhuman crime? How will you ever persuade posterity, or the church which is being reborn in the gospel, that you have acted as evangelical and religious Christians, when they read or hear that you, with such savage vengeance, armed with the weapons of the impious, and, in truth, preoccupied with a private grudge, so cruelly and inhumanly destroyed the body and soul of a stranger, who trusting in your piety, alone and defenseless, completely without rights, came to you of his own free will? In other words, he was subjected to capital punishment by the will of his mortal enemies. He was torn apart, mocked, and vilified with undying hatred, as you hastened to murder him as quickly as possible.

Dare to deny [these charges], if you can. Were you and he not the worst of enemies? Were you not personally offended by his writings? Did you not vigorously demand his blood? Did you not focus all your plans and actions on doing away with your adversary and causing him to suffer the most painful of punishments? Did you not look upon his death and humiliation with smiling eyes? Did you not insult him with mocking words as he went forth to meet his punishment?

Why are you so mournful? Why do you moan and sigh? If your [legal] position was correct, why did you not emerge from this [event] happy and joyful? These words were spoken by the faithless to the Son of God: "*If you are the Son of God, come down from the cross and we will believe in you.*"[b] O Christian piety! O evangelical love! What a splendid crime devised for the protection and peace of the church! Who, upon hearing these things, is so cruel and Neronian as not to cringe in horror?[25] Who is so inflexible and Busirus-like as to read this with dry eyes?[26]

But this spectacle as yet lacked a funeral dirge. A little book was immediately issued approving the proceedings in the trial and the judgment that was rendered.[27] That doubtless was the funeral oration which was meant to grace the ashes of the deceased.

---

[a] John 15:20-21, 16:2-3.   [b] Matt. 27:40,42.

Accendite flammas, o tyranni: hæreticos a vobis iudicatos, scindite, laniate, torrete, cineres dispergite, pacem imperiis et sedibus vestris stabilite: Quid dubitatis? quid hæretis? quid cessatis? Perdite, mactate, devorate, humano divinoque iure fas est evangelicos ecclesiastes et Theologos luculentissimos laudatores habetis.

Sic, sic deo maximo rite litatur: sic evangelium recte propagatur, sic ecclesiæ pax et unio concordiaque conservatur, hostes [25a] scilicet hæreticos ferro flammisque tollendo, mortuus non luctatur. Nunc tandem cognoscent hæretici evangelio gladios et flammas non deesse, nunc tandem sapit ecclesia quæ hæreticos didicit de viventium terra delere, et zizania de medio tritici eradicare, nimium mitis cristus, stultus Gamaliel, fatui paulus, Ignatius, et Augustinus, qui hæreticos dimitti et zizania succrescere voluerunt, vos Gamaliele, paulo, Ignatio et Augustino immo Christo ipso multo prudentiores et doctiores, maiori spiritu et iudicio præditi, qui ecclesiæ vestræ tam bene consulere didicistis. Vos igitur pacis et quietis evangelicæ restitutores omnes ecclesiæ unanimes imitentur: vos collaudent, celebrent et erectis trophæis ad sidera tollant. Dixi.

Kindle your flames, O tyrants! Rend asunder those judged by you to be heretics, tear their flesh, roast them, scatter their ashes, that you may establish your empires and thrones in peace! Why are you in doubt? Why hesitate? What is holding you up? Slay, slaughter, and gobble them up! It is your human and divine right. The leaders of the evangelical church and its most brilliant theologians are even now singing your praises.

So this, then, is the most proper way to worship Almighty God. So this is the right way to propagate the gospel. So this is the way to preserve peace and concord in the church. The enemy, that is, the heretics, are to be extirpated with steel and fire. A dead man does not fight. Now at last let the heretics know that *fire and sword*[a] are part of the gospel message. The church finally understands and has learned to exterminate any such heretics from *the land of the living*,[b] to uproot the tares from the midst of the wheat.[c] Christ was far too gentle. Gamaliel was a dolt. And Paul, Ignatius, and Augustine were fools. They all wanted heretics to be let go and the tares to continue growing. But you, who have provided such excellent counsel to your church, are far more skillful and learned than Gamaliel, Paul, Ignatius, and Augustine – even than Christ himself – and are more greatly endowed with spiritual gifts and judgment. Therefore it is you, the restorers of evangelical peace and quiet, whom every church should single-mindedly imitate. Let them praise and celebrate [what you have done] and set up victory monuments rising up to the stars. That is all I have to say.

---

[a] Isa. 66:16. [b] Isa. 53:8. [c] See Matt. 13:29-30.

Theses de filio Dei et Trinitate

Theses about the Son of God and the Trinity

Theses de filio Dei et Trinitate

[16a] 1. Pater et filius duæ hypostases, sive res realiter distinctæ, hoc est duo æterni spiritus distincti, et consequenter, duo dei, duo domini, duo lumina, alterum ex altero genitum et productum, uniti tamen et omnino coniuncti in omni divina perfectione, et in una divinitate. Tertull. contra Praxeam. Lact. li. 4 ca. 6. Ignatius ad Magnesios.

2. Tres sunt de filio dei sententiæ, prima est Irenei, Verbum esse Dei æternum filium, eundemque factum hominem in tempore.

3. Secunda Valentini, duos esse filios unitos simul, alterum dei filium invisibilem, et impassibilem: alterum visibilem et passibilem.

4. Tertia Serveti, verbum ante incarnationem non fuisse filium.

5. Calvini atque aliorum, patrem et filium esse vere duas personas substantiales, et tamen esse unum tantum eundemque deum.

Affirmare deum esse simplicissimam unamque substantiam, aut spiritum simplicissimum immutabilem: et esse tres, repugnat. Nam quod objicitur vere tres hypostases, et unam substantiam, apud omnes eruditos nihil valet, cum unum idemque significent, nimirum substantialem rem, et non qualem.* Vide Laur. Vallam in Eleg. ubi de persona contra Boethium.

---

* Should read *qualitatem*.

Theses about the Son of God and the Trinity

1. The Father and the Son are two hypostases, or really distinct beings, that is, two distinct eternal spirits, and consequently two Gods, two Lords, two lights, one born and produced from the other, but united and completely joined together in every divine perfection and in one divinity. Tertullian, *Against Praxeas*.[a] Lactantius, book 4, chapter 6.[b] Ignatius, [letter] to the Magnesians.[c]

2. There are three ways of thinking about the Son of God. The first is that of Irenaeus: the Word is the eternal Son of God, and it was made man in time.[d]

3. The second is that of Valentinus: there are two sons united together, one the invisible and non-suffering Son of God, the other visible and capable of suffering.[e]

4. The third is that of Servetus: the Word prior to the incarnation was not the Son.[f]

5. That of Calvin and others: the Father and the Son are truly two persons in substance. Nevertheless, they are one and the same God.[1]

To affirm that God is an absolutely simple and unitary substance, or an absolutely simple and unchanging spirit, is incompatible with there being three [persons]. For to propose that there are three hypostases and one substance holds no weight among the learned, since these [terms, *hypostasis* and *substance*,] denote one and the same thing: that is, a substantial being and not a quality.[2] See Lorenzo Valla, *De Elegantiis*, where he treats of persons, arguing against Boethius.[g]

---

[a] Tertullian, *Adversus Praxean* 9 (PL 2 164A-C). [b] Lactantius, *Divinarum Institutionem* 4.6 (PL 6 461A-463A), quoting Hermes Trismegistus. [c] Ignatius, *Ad Magnesios* 6-7 (PG 5 763B-766A).
[d] Irenaeus, *Adv. Hær.* 3.16.7 (PG 7a 926C). This passage is quoted at length in *Decl.* 22.
[e] Irenaeus, *Adv. Hær.* 3.17.4 (PG 7a 931B). Quoted in *Decl.* 25. [f] *Err.* 93b.
[g] Lorenzo Valla, *De Elegantiis Latinæ Linguæ* 6.34. The same passage is cited in "Religionis Christianæ" 1 and *Decl.* 78.

Si tres hypostases sunt unus solus deus, sequitur, unum in tres substantias divisum, aut ex tribus conflatum, aut trinomium, ut Ireneus ait: aut unum deum genericum, imaginarium, prædicabilem, trium substantiarum, aut personarum substantialium, ut genus de formis, et forma ultima de individuis, absurdum. Si unus et idem deus simplex et individuus, homo factus est, necessario sequitur, patrem et spiritum s. incarnatos esse aut deum simplicem et indivisibilem esse in partes divisum, ita ut una pars facta sit F. altera S. S. tertia remanserit pater. O absurditatem.

Si pater filius et S. S. tres sunt hypostases, tresve spiritus, et unaquæque est deus, ergo tres sunt Dii: est enim Deus appellatio supremæ autoritatis, et potestatis. Unde et Moses Deus Pharaonis, et Cyrus Israelis neque Paulus negat esse multos Deos in cœlo et in terra, sed unum tantum esse summum, omnis deitatis caput, idest patrem omnium atque autorem. [**16b**] Ut igitur pater et filius duo domini dicuntur, sic ut duo dei, duo reges, duo lumina. Nam pro subiectorum numero et prædicatorum numerus est confitendus: in quo tamen non confundatur unitas substantiæ, quæ tota refertur in patrem, tanquam in fontem.

Trinitas nomen est quiditativum abstractum a numero ternario, nomen quo neque Apostoli, neque eorum successores, Ignatius, Policarpus, Ireneus, Origenes, Cyprianus, Lactantius, sed Græci nimirum subtiles invenerunt, ut et illa, hypostasis, persona, natura, proprietas, unitas, essentia, substantia, suppositum, subiectum, individuum, connotativum, humanitas, communicatio, et id genus alia.

Unus deus, unus dominus etc.

Nobis unus est deus, qui est pater omnium, etc. Multi in cœlo et in terra dii et domini etc. Angeli in cœlo, in terra reges etc.

Unus deus, et unus mediator etc.

Hæc est vita æterna, etc.

If the three hypostases are one God only, then what follows is absurd: that the one is divided into three substances, or is formed out of three, or is three-named, as Irenaeus says;³ or that the one God is a concept, like a genus, predicable of three substances or substantial persons, in the way that a genus [is predicable] of species, and the ultimate species⁴ [is composed] of individuals. If one and the same God, simple and undivided, was made man, it necessarily follows that the Father and the Holy Spirit became incarnate; or that the simple and indivisible God is divisible into parts, so that one part is the Son, another the Holy Spirit, while the third remains the Father. How absurd!

If the Father, the Son, and the Holy Spirit are three hypostases – or, if you prefer, three spirits – and each one is God, then there are three Gods. In fact, "God" is a name [indicating] supreme authority and power. Hence Moses was a god to Pharaoh and Cyrus to Israel.ᵃ Nor does Paul deny that there are *many gods in heaven and on earth*,ᵇ but only one [of these] is the supreme [God] and the head of all deity, that is, the Father and author of all things. Therefore, since the Father and [the Son] are called two Lords, [they must be] two Gods, two kings, two lights. For it must be conceded that the number of predicates corresponds to the number of subjects, in which the unity of substance, which refers entirely to the Father as the source, cannot be a mixture.

"Trinity" is an quidditative noun derived from the number three, a term which was not used by the apostles or their successors – Ignatius, Polycarp, Irenaeus, Origen, Cyprian, or Lactantius – but which was clearly invented by the subtle Greeks, who also coined hypostasis, person, nature, property, unity, essence, substance, *suppositum*, subject, individual, connotative, humanity, *communicatio*, and other such [terms].

One God, one Lord, etc.ᶜ

For us there is *one God* who is *the Father of all*, etc.ᵈ [*There may be*] many *gods and lords in heaven and on earth*,ᵉ etc. *Angels in heaven and kings on earth*, etc.ᶠ

One God, and one mediator, etc.ᵍ

This is eternal life, etc.ʰ

ᵃ Exod. 7:1, Isa. 45:3. See *Decl.* 61, 69; *Err.* 11b, 13b.   ᵇ 1 Cor. 8:5.   ᶜ 1 Cor. 8:6.   ᵈ Eph. 4:6.
ᵉ 1 Cor. 8:5.   ᶠ Isa. 24:21.   ᵍ 1 Tim. 2:5.   ʰ John 17:3.

Si hæc trinitas, unus est Deus in substantia, sequitur unum eundemque deum se genuisse, sibi imperasse, et paruisse: se ipsum in mundum mississe, etc. id genus omnia. Sequeretur etiam substantiae simplicitatem considerantibus, omnes tres incarnatos esse.

Si filius dei est similis et æqualis patri Deo, et exp[ressa] imago substantiæ eius, et imago invisibilis dei, ergo non est ille deus cui similis dicitur. Ubi enim aliquid simile dicitur, et imago, ibi pluralitas et distinctio.

Cum oratio nostra ad patrem fieri debeat, per filium: si ad ipsam trinitatem fiat, totus hic ordo pervertetur, et iam nulla oratio fit per filium ad patrem.

Patris, filii et S. S. unitas, est voluntatis, amoris, consensus, omnis perfectionis, non substantialis, et identitatis. Tert. in Praxeam.

Clarifica me pater ea gloria et claritate quam habui apud te, priusquam hic mundus fieret. Magna fuit Christi gloria cum vidit se a deo productum et genitum deo æqualem, virtute et potestate: et per se omnia creanda, regenda et conservanda.

Nullum esse dei filium præter Jesum Christum visibilem, et passibilem vide quid responderit cæco illuminato. Et Angelus virgini, vocabitur f. d.

Generatio ex simili. Deus est spiritus: ergo filius dei ante carnem, erat spiritus. Ignatius. Lactantius.

[17a] .... et primus
.... productus, et primus
.... et primus in gloriam apud
.... [per] verbum facit deus, primo mundi et omnium
.... et nondum hominem, creationem
.... expiationem hominis perditi per verbum
est natum, et passum: Tertio, totius hominis istan[tem ulti]onem, et iudicium, per verbum hominem gloriosum.

If this Trinity is one God in substance, it follows that one and the same God gave birth to himself, commanded and obeyed himself, sent himself into the world, and everything else of that sort. It will likewise follow, taking into account the simplicity of the substance, that all three were incarnated.

If the Son of God is similar and equal to God the Father, and the express image of his substance, and the [visible] image of the invisible God, then he is not the God to whom he is said to be similar. When something is called similar, and an image, you have a distinction and a plurality.

Since our prayer to the Father must be through the Son, if we pray to the Trinity, the whole arrangement is subverted, and hence no prayer comes to the Father through the Son.

The unity of the Father, the Son, and the Holy Spirit is one of will, love, harmony, and every perfection, not one of substance and identity. Tertullian in *Against Praxeas*.[5]

Glorify me, Father, with that glory and splendor which I had with you before the world was made.[a] Great was the glory of Christ when he beheld himself brought forth by God and born equal to God in might and power. And through him all things were to be created, ruled, and preserved.

There is no Son of God other than the visible and suffering Jesus Christ. See how he answered the blind man who had regained his sight.[b] *And the angel said to* the virgin, "*he shall be called the Son of God.*"[c]

Something that is generated comes from a similar [thing]. *God is spirit.*[d] Therefore the Son of God, before he was flesh, was spirit. Ignatius.[e] Lactantius.[f]

....and first
....was brought forth, and first
......................................and was first in glory among
.......[through] the Word, God makes first of all ... of the world and all
....and not yet man, creation
........................the atonement of lost man through the Word
[which] was born and suffered. Thirdly, [the threatened retribution] and judgment of all mankind, [made] glorious by the Word.

---

[a] John 17:5 (Erasmus, Vulgate). [b] John 9:35-37. [c] Luke 1:35. [d] John 4:24. [e] Pseudo-Ignatius, *Ad Tarsenses* 6 (PL 5 891C-894B). [f] Lactantius, *Divinarum Institutionem* 4.8 (PL 6 465B-466A).

Christus cum esset in forma dei, etc., idest cum esset Deus de deo, ipsique æqualis, non voluit sua illa autoritate et potestate uti, regna et imperia invadendo, nec diabolum sua possessione per vim spoliando, quam in hoc mundo usurpabat, nec suos hostes ulcisci, quod potuisset: in summa noluit sua illa divina in omnes potestate per vim, et rapinam abuti, sed in hac vita quasi servus omnibus subiectus esse, omnia extrema ab extremis hominibus patiendo, atque a deo ipsam crucis ignominiosissimam mortem.

Deus manifestatus est in carne. Deus nimirum verbum, quod erat in principio apud deum, et erat deus.

Ubicumque in divinis literis invenitur unum esse Deum, nec extra eum alium ullum esse Deum: illum esse primum et ultimum etc. intelligitur pater ille, pater Jesu Christi, qui solus est Deus a se, et cuius potestate, Christus est Deus, et S. S. est deus etc. Quia cum ita loquitur, non facit ut filium suum Deum de deo, excludat, sed falsos illos deastros* et ab hominibus factos. Vide Ignatium ad Antiochenses.

Ego et pater unum sumus, voluntate, potestate, consensu, amore, ut illa, ut unum sint, sicut et nos unum sumus. Spiritus aqua et sanguis unum. Qui plantat, et qui rigat unum.

Si deus ex sua substantia filium genuit, aut facta est mutatio et deminutio in deo: aut ipsemet se genuit, non alterum: aut si hoc non est, nec est filius de dei substantia, sed ex nihilo creatura. Solutio, alia est generatio terrena, alia divina terrena fit cum alteratione, quoniam a composito generante fit: divina a simplicissimo.

---

* The uncommon word *deaster* was used by Castellio in his Latin New Testament (1551) in place of *idolum* to mean a false or pagan god (for example, at 1 Cor. 8:4).

Although Christ was in the form of God, etc., that is, although he was God from God and *equal to* him, he did not wish to possess that which was his own by authority and power,[a] seizing kingdoms and empires. Nor did he wish to strip the devil of his possessions by using power which he had usurped in this world. Nor did he wish to punish his enemies, which he could have done. In brief, in everything he refused to abuse his divine power by means of force and *usurpation*, but in his mortal life, like the lowliest of *servants*, he was submissive, suffering every extremity at the hands of the vilest of men, and, from God, a most disgraceful *death upon the cross*.[b]

God was manifest in the flesh.[c] God – evidently *the Word, which was in the beginning with God, and was God.*[d]

Everywhere one looks in sacred scripture, there is one God, and *apart from* him, *there is no other God.*[e] He is *the first and the last*, etc.[f] The Father is understood to be the father of Jesus Christ. He *alone is God*[g] in himself, and by his power Christ is God, and the Holy Spirit is God, etc. For when [scripture] says this, it does not exclude [God's] son from being "God of God," but rather excludes those false, inferior gods, and those fabricated by men. See Ignatius's [letter] to the Antiochenes.[h]

I and the Father are one,[i] in will, in power, in harmony, in love, as [scripture says], *that they may be one as we are one.*[j] *The spirit, the water, and the blood are one.*[k] *The one who plants and the one who waters are one.*[l]

If God begot the Son from his own substance, a diminution and change has taken place in God. Otherwise he has begotten himself, not another. Or else the Son is not of the same substance as God, but is a creation from nothingness. The solution: earthly generation is one thing, divine generation another. Earthly generation involves alteration, since the generating is being done by a composite, while divine generation arises from absolute simplicity.

---

[a] Phil. 2:6. [b] Phil. 2:6-8. [c] 1 Tim. 3:16. [d] John 1:1. [e] Deut. 4:35, Isa. 45:5. [f] Rev. 22:13.
[g] Ps. 86:10. [h] Pseudo-Ignatius, *Ad Antiochenos*, 1 (PG 5 899A). [i] John 10:30. [j] John 17:22.
[k] 1 John 5:7-8. The Johannine Comma. See *Declaratio*, book 5, note 1. [l] 1 Cor. 3:8.

[17b]..
sed [comm]unicat[io]..................................
ut lumen de ....
Nicæna sinodus..
Deus per filium suum omnia............................
testificatus est per spiritum s. omnia.................
confirmavit et ....
Spiritus s. officium est ea sanctificare ....
aliquid munus uti vult................................
quo unxit me ad evangelizandum ....
accipite s. s. quibus renasceritis....................
idcirco per excellentiam dicitur s. s. et .... sunt
spiritus administratorii etc..........................

THESES ABOUT THE SON OF GOD AND THE TRINITY

....
but *communicatio* ....
as light of [light]. ....
the Council of Nicaea. ....
God, through his Son, [made] all things[a] ....
bore witness through the Holy Spirit, all things ....
affirmed and. ....
the role of the Holy Spirit is to sanctify them. ....
some service when he wishes. ....
who *has anointed me to evangelize*[b] ....
receive the Holy Spirit by which you will *be born again*[c] ..
therefore, through merit, is called [by] the Holy Spirit and .... are
ministering spirits, etc.[d] ....

---

[a] Heb. 1:2. [b] Isa. 61:1. [c] Acts 8:17, John 3:5. [d] Heb. 1:14.

De vera Dei et filii eius cognitione sermo

A Discourse on the True Knowledge of God and his Son

[99] *Michælis Serveti Tarraconensis de vera Dei et filii eius cognitione sermo antequam Genevæ combureretur*

Qui tres substantiales personas seu hypostases in Divinis statuunt, tres aequales per naturam Deos nobis insinuant. Tres enim res substantiales distinctas et differentes nobis proponunt, et unamquamque illarum rerum (seu ut vocant) Hypostasium, Deum esse volunt. Inde necessario tres Deos aequales et distinctos faciunt. Cum enim personae seu Hypostases illae re et numero differentes singulatim de Deo praedicentur: Necessario sequitur tot esse praedicata quot subjecta, et juxta numerum personarum deorum quoque numerum multiplicari. Et licet unum tantum Deum nobis verbis praedicent, in effectu tamen et re ipsa, tres nobis Deos in intellectu repraesentant. Nullus est enim intellectus tam acutus et sincerus, qui, non videat tria sibi colenda proponi. Quomodo autem illa tria, quorum unumquodque Deus est, unum Deum numero esse intelligat, nemo unquam dicere potuit, vel docere. Relinquitur ergo et in spiritu et in intellectu insolubilis illa perplexitas et confusio inexplicabilis, quod tria sunt unum, et unum sunt tria. Quamvis enim, ad unum Deum totus intellectus intendat, et dirigatur, unumque sibi Deum in spiritu colendum proponat, et se ad unitatem tota acie colligat, confestim tamen tria distincta objecta se offerunt, et ante mentis oculos obversantur, quorum unumquodque Deum esse cognoscit, et sic tres in effectu Deos aequales et distinctos sibi repraesentari, videns inter unum et tria confusus succumbit, et hic est exitus illius Graecanicae Triadis seu triplicitatis.

*A Discourse by Michael Servetus of Tarraconensis
on the True Knowledge of God and his Son
[delivered just] before he was burned [at the stake] in Geneva*

Those who think that there are three substantial persons or hypostases in the Godhead, are suggesting that there are three Gods equal in nature. For they tell us that there are three different and distinct substantial beings, and wish each of those beings – or hypostases, as they call them – to be [called] a God. Hence, they are necessarily creating three equal and distinct Gods. For since those persons or hypostases, which differ in being and number, are each separately predicated of God, it necessarily follows that there are as many subjects as there are predicates, and that the number of Gods is multiplied to correspond to the number of persons. And although with their words they proclaim to us [that there is] only one God, in fact and in actuality they present three gods to our understanding. For it does not take a very sound and penetrating intelligence to see that they are proposing three beings to be worshipped. However, no one has ever been able to say or explain how these three, each of whom is a God, count as one God. Thus both the spirit and the understanding are left [to deal with] the impenetrable perplexity and irresoluble confusion of "three are one" and "one is three." For although the entire mind may incline and be directed toward one God, and may propose one God to be worshipped in spirit, and may with all its cleverness infer a unity, nevertheless three distinct objects are immediately presented to the mind's eye, each of which it recognizes as a God. Beholding, as it were, three equal and distinct Gods, and caught between the one and the three, [the mind] collapses into confusion. This is the end result of the Greekish Triad or triplication.

Quodsi revoluto velo ad SacroSanctae Script. verbum velut ad lydium lapidem rem omnem exploremus, et iuxta ipsius Dei eloquia, veram de Deo cognitionem exquiramus, cessabit dubio procul omnis confusio et perplexitas: et nil in se repugnans intellectus noster admittere compelletur.

Primum itaque sciendum est, Deum nomen esse appellativum, omnis potentiae Dominii, et superioritatis et proprie illi convenit, [**100**] qui super omnes est, qui est omnium princeps, Rex regum et Dominus dominantium, a quo omnia sunt et dependent, qui est solus Pater omnium ac Creator.

Minus autem proprie sumptum, etiam creaturis convenire potest ut quicunque habet potestatem et superioritatem, Divinitus sibi concessam super aliquem, hic Deus illius dici possit. Velut Moses dictus est Exo: 7.1.* Deus Pharaonis. Et Cyrus Esa. 45.3. Deus Israelis. Et si liceat exempli tantum gratia profana sacris adiungere, Augustus Caesar, Deus Virgilii et Lentulus Deus Ciceronis, quia fuit Author restitutionis suae.

Et hac ratione scriptura appellat Deos, quos summus et Aeternus Deus aliqua gratia, virtute et privilegio supra alios decoravit et sublimavit. Unde Psalmista Ps. 82.6. Ego dixi dii estis et filii excelsi omnes. Ex Exod. 22.28. Dominus domus ad Deos applicabitur et ad Deos utriusque causa perveniet. Ii autem non natura dii sunt, sed per gratiam, et donum summi Dei. Ideoque nunquam eo deitatis nomine appellantur quod soli supremo Deo convenit. Nam tales dii et Domini apud Hebraeos, quibus haec nomina divinitatis proprie distinguuntur Elohim, vel Adonai nuncupantur, neque unquam proprio et singulari, nomine quod est Iehova, designantur, licet dominum.

[Hic aliquid deest in autographo, ex quo haec desumsi.]

Et ideo Paulus ubique initio suarum epistolarum sic praefatur Gratia et pax a Deo Patre nostro et Domino nostro Iesu Christo.

---

* The use of verse numbers in the Bible citations in this document (and the Protestant numbering of the psalms) suggests that the text has been edited, either by the seventeenth-century editor, Stanislas Lubieniecki, or by some earlier transciber. A good many of these Bible citations have verse numbers that are different from those found in modern Bibles. Rather than pointing out all the differences, we have omitted verse numbers from the English translation. Chapter and verse as per the Lubieniecki version can be found in the Latin text. The footnotes to the English text give full citations using modern verse numbers.

But if we draw back the veil and test the whole matter by using the words of Holy Scripture as a touchstone, and if we seek a true knowledge of God according to God's own utterances, all confusion and perplexity will definitely come to an end. Then our minds will not be forced to accept anything self-contradictory.

First, it should be known that "God" is an appellative noun, indicating all power, dominion, and superiority. It properly applies to him *who is over all*,[a] chief of all, *king of kings, Lord of Lords*,[b] *from whom are all things*[c] and on whom all things depend, who alone is the Father and creator of all things.

In a less proper sense, however, [the name "God"] can also be applied to creatures. Anyone to whom God has granted power and superiority over another can be called that other's God, just as Moses in Exodus 7 is called *a god to Pharaoh*[d] and Cyrus, in Isaiah 45, *the god of Israel*.[e] And if one is permitted to add profane examples to sacred ones, Augustus Caesar [is called] the God of Virgil[f] and Lentulus, the God of Cicero – since [Lentulus] brought about the restoration [of Cicero's rights].[g]

In this way scripture calls gods those whom the Most High and Eternal God has distinguished and exalted above others with grace, power, and privilege. Whence the Psalmist, in Psalm 82, says: *I say, "You are gods, and all of you are sons of the Most High."*[h] From Exodus 22: *The master of the house will be brought before the gods, and the case of both parties will be placed before the gods*.[i] These, however, are gods not by nature, but through the grace and gift of the highest God. Thus they are never called by the divine name which belongs to the only supreme God. For, among the Hebrews, such gods and lords, to whom these divine names properly belong, are called *Elohim* and *Adonai*. They are not, however, ever designated by the proper and singular name, *Jehovah*, that is, the Lord.

[…][j] Thus Paul always begins his epistles with the preface: *Grace and Peace from God our Father, and our Lord Jesus Christ*.[k]

---

[a] Eph. 4:6. [b] 1 Tim. 6:15, Rev. 17:14, 19:16. [c] 1 Cor. 8:6. [d] Exod. 7:1. [e] Isa. 45:3. [f] Virgil, *Eclogue* 1.6-8.
[g] Publius Cornelius Lentulus (Spinther) (fl. 63-48 BCE), when a consul of Rome (57 BCE), had Cicero recalled from exile. Cicero, *Pro P. Sestio Oratio* 144; *Oratio post reditum* 4.8. [h] Ps. 82:6. [i] Exod. 22:8-9 (Vulgate).
[j] Lubieniecki noted, "Here something is missing from the manuscript from which this is taken."
[k] Rom. 1:7, 1 Cor. 1:3, 2 Cor. 1:2, Gal. 1:3, Eph. 1:2, Phil. 1:2, 2 Thess. 1:2, Philem. 1:3. This was a common formula at the beginning of epistles.

Caeterum tres aequales deos per naturam, constituere summa blasphemia est et impietas execrabilis. Oportet enim ad unum omnia referri, nempe ad eum, qui omnium author est, et omnia pro sua voluntate creavit. Ille enim solus per naturam a seipso Deus est, Caeteri vero quicunque a se ipsis dii non sunt, rationem deitatis ab illo uno Deo Patre accipiunt et agnoscunt, et dii de Deo dicuntur. Potest enim summus ille et Princeps Deus creaturas sanctificare et divinitate replere. Tres autem deos per naturam aequales nullo modo constituere possumus alioqui et tres rerum conditores, seu Pantocratores et tres Patres necessario constituere [**101**] oporteret. Soli enim Patri, qui a se ipso Deus est, et qui omnia condidit, Dei nomen simpliciter convenit et is solus simpliciter et absolute Deus appellatur.

Iam ergo ex praedictis facile deduci potest, quomodo Dominus noster Iesus Christus verus Dei filius etiam Deus dicatur. Nam suae deitatis ratio a Deo Patre suscipitur, et verus Deus de vero Deo nuncupatur, Deus quidem Omnium creaturarum, non autem Deus Patris, qui ei cuncta subiecit. Quin imo Pater ipse qui solus per naturam a seipso Deus ut etiam ipse filii Dominus et Deus est, dicente filio Ioh. 14.28. Vado ad Patrem, qui maior me est. Ioan. 20.17. Vado ad Patrem meum et Patrem vestrum, ad Deum meum, et ad Deum vestrum. Matth. 27.46. Deus meus quare dereliquisti me. 2. Apoc. 3.13. Scribam super illum nomen Dei mei, et nomen civitatis Dei mei. Nec convenit hic eorum interpretatio qui dicunt haec filium loquutum, ut hominem, non ut Deum. Quibus respondetur, quod ratio deitatis, quae est in filio, etiam ut homini convenit, est enim filius homo deificatus, seu divinitate repletus, ideo non tollitur Patris superioritas in ipsum filium. Quanquam enim filius factus est nobis a Patre Dominus et Deus et caput nostrum: Attamen Pater et Dominus et Deus et caput ipsius filii est. I. Cor. 11.3. Et filius patri subiectus est. I. Cor. 15.28. Et paternae domus oeconomus atque administrator. Hebr. 3.8. Itaque filius ut Deus noster et caput nostrum deitatem ac superioritatem Patris in se ipsum recognovit.

Besides, to set up three Gods equal in nature is the height of blasphemy and an execrable [act of] impiety. For all things ought to be referred back to the One, namely, to him who is the author of all things and who created all things through his own will. For by nature he alone, in and of himself, is God. All the rest, who are not Gods in and of themselves, receive, and acknowledge [that they receive], their mode of deity from the one God the Father, and are called gods because of [him]. For the highest and chief God is able to sanctify [his] creatures and fill them with divinity. However, we can in no way set up three Gods equal in nature. Otherwise, it would be necessary to set up three creators of things, or *Pantocrators*,[1] and three Fathers. For the name "God" plainly suits the Father alone, who is, in and of himself, God, and the author of all that is. He alone is simply and absolutely called God.

From what has been said, it can now easily be seen how our Lord Jesus Christ, the true Son of God, is also called God. For he receives the nature of his deity from God the Father. He is called "true God of true God,"[a] the God, indeed, of all creatures. He is not, however, the God of the Father, who made *all things subject to him*.[b] On the contrary, only the Father is, by nature and in and of himself, God. [The Father] is also the Lord and God of the Son, as the Son says in John 14: *"I go to the Father, who is greater than I"*;[c] *"I go to my Father and your Father, to my God and your God"* (John 20);[d] *"My God, why have you forsaken me?"* (Matthew 27);[e] *"I will write on him the name of my God, and the name of the city of my God"* (Revelation 3).[f] Nor is it a useful interpretation to say that the Son was here speaking as a man, not as God. My answer to [those who would say this] is that the nature of deity that is in the Son is also appropriate to [him] as a man (for the Son is a deified man or [a man] filled with divinity). Therefore, the superiority of the Father is not withheld from the Son. For although the Son was made Lord over us by the Father, and our God and head, nonetheless, the Father is the Lord, God, and head of the Son himself (1 Corinthians 11).[g] And *the Son is subject to* the Father. (1 Corinthians 15).[h] He is steward and administrator of his Father's house (Hebrews 3).[i] Therefore the Son, as our God and our head, acknowledged the Father's deity and superiority to himself.

---

[a] From the Nicene Creed. [b] 1 Cor. 15:28. [c] John 14:28. [d] John 20:17. [e] Matt. 27:46. [f] Rev. 3:12. [g] 1 Cor. 11:3. [h] 1 Cor. 15:28. [i] Heb. 3:6 (Erasmus).

Inde Propheta hanc duplicem deitatis rationem Patris et filii diserte explicans dixit, ad filium Psa. 45.3, 7, 8. speciosus forma prae filiis hominum diffusa est gratia in labiis tuis propterea quod Sedes tua, Deus, in seculum seculi, virga directionis, virga regni tui dilexisti iustitiam et odisti iniquitatem, propterea quod unxit, Te Deus, Deus tuus oleo laetitiae prae consortibus tuis.

Ecce quomodo David in spiritu vocat filium Deum, et Patrem Deum filii. Nam sedes tua Deus, et unxit te Deus vocativi casus sunt, et ad filium referuntur. Dum postea subiungit Deus tuus de Deo [102] Patre loquitur, qui filium unxit et sanctificavit. Similiter sapientia, quae Dei filium repraesentat, sic exclamat Eccles. 24.16. Et radicavi in populo honorificato et in partes Dei mei hereditas illius.

Proinde iam luce clarius liquere puto unicuique scripturis ahhaerere volenti, filium esse Deum a Patre, et tanquam Deum a patre omnibus constitutum, deitatem ac superioritatem Patris in se recognoscere, licet apud Graecos et Latinos haec divinorum nominum distinctio non inveniatur et omnes uno communi Dei nomine appellentur. Unus igitur per naturam Deus a seipso, aeternus, summus, supremus, immortalis, invisibilis, incomprehensibilis, lucem habitans inaccessam, qui omnia condidit, omnia gubernat, a quo omnia sunt, et dependent. Hic est ille Deus Deorum, Rex Regum et dominus dominantium, Iova Pater, quem solum scriptura simpliciter et absolute, Deum et Patrem appellat. Patrem quidem omnium universalem, proprie vero et singulariter Domini Dei nostri Iesu Christi, quod et diserte explicat Paulus dicens. I. Cor. 8.5. Nam et si sunt qui dicantur Dii, sive in caelo, sive in terra (quemadmodum sunt Dii multi, et Domini multi) 6. Nobis tamen est Unus Deus ille Pater, ex quo omnia et nos in ipso et unus Dominus Iesus Christus per quem omnia et nos per ipsum.

And so the Prophet, eloquently expressing the twofold nature of deity, that of the Father and of the Son, in Psalm 45 said to the Son: *You are more beautiful in form than the sons of men; grace is poured upon your lips; for your throne, God, is for ever and ever, and the royal scepter is the scepter of justice, you love righteousness and hate wickedness, and therefore your God has anointed you God with the oil of gladness above your fellows.*[a]

Behold how David, being full of the Spirit, calls the Son God and calls the Father the God of the Son. For [the word "God" in the expressions] "*your throne, God*," and "*anointed you, God*" is in the vocative case and refers to the Son. When he says "*your God*," he is speaking of God the Father, who anointed and sanctified the Son. Similarly Wisdom, which represents the Son of God, in Ecclesiasticus 24 exclaims: *I took root in an honored people and in the portion of my God, their inheritance.*[b]

Hence, I believe it is as clear as day, to anyone who wishes to adhere to [the words of] scripture, that the Son is [made] God by the Father. And, established by the Father as the God of all, he acknowledges the deity and superiority of the Father, although this distinction of divine names is not found among the Greeks and the Latins, and all are called by the single common name, God [*theos/deus*]. [There is,] therefore, by nature, one God in and of himself, eternal, most high, supreme, *immortal, invisible*, incomprehensible, *dwelling in light inaccessible*, who established everything and governs everything, *from whom all things are* and on whom they depend.[c] This is the *God of gods, King of kings, and Lord of lords*,[d] Jehovah the Father,[2] the only one whom scripture simply and absolutely calls God and Father. He is indeed the universal Father of all, who is properly and particularly [the God] of our Lord and God, Jesus Christ, as Paul clearly explains in 1 Corinthians 8, when he says: *For although there may be those who are called Gods, whether in heaven or on earth, just as there are many gods and many lords, yet for us there is one God, the Father, from whom are all things, in whom we exist, and one Lord Jesus Christ, through whom are all things, and through whom we exist.*[e]

---

[a] Ps. 45:2,6,7. [b] Ecclesiasticus (Sirach) 24:12. [c] 1 Tim. 1:17, 6:16; 1 Cor. 8:6.
[d] Deut. 10:17, 1 Tim. 6:15, Rev. 17:14, 19:16. [e] 1 Cor. 8:5-6.

Unde palam hoc sit nomine deitatis etiam creaturas decorari, per gratiam tamen et concessionem Unius supremi Dei, qui est Deus Deorum, Princeps et Pater omnium supra omnia per omnia et in omnibus. Eph. 4.6. in quem veluti unicum, summum, et naturalem a seipso Deum, caeteri omnes referuntur eique subiiciuntur et obediunt, et haec Deorum inferiorum pluralitas, nullam affert confusionem neque divinae unitati praeiudicat, Cum omnis creatura laudet Deum creatorem et illum solum velut summum et supremum Deum respiciat et suspiret, Solum colat et adoret, de quo universa scriptura testatur, quod non sit alius Deus praeter illum. Deut. 6.4. Audi Israel dominus Deus tuus Deus unus est. Et Deut. 10.17. Iehovah Deus magnus potens et terribilis, qui non [103] accipit personam neque respicit munus. Et Psa. 50.1. Deus Deorum locutus est. Et Paulus ad Gal. 4.8. imo tum quidem quum ignoraveritis Deum, serviebatis iis qui non natura sunt Dii. 9. At nunc quum agnoscatis Deum quomodo convertimini retrorsum ad impotentia et egena. I. ad Timoth. 6.15. Quem temporibus suis ostendet ille beatus et solus princeps, Rex regum et Dominus Dominorum 16. Qui solus habet immortalitatem, lucem habitans inaccessam, quem vidit nemo hominum, neque videre potest. I. Thess. 1.9. ut serviretis Deo vero et vivo. 10. Et expectaretis filium eius e caelis quem suscitavit a mortuis Iesum. I. Tim. 1.17. Regi aeterno, immortali invisibili, soli sapienti Deo honor sit, et gloria in secula seculorum Amen. I. Tim. 2.5. Unus Deus unus etiam mediator Dei et hominum Homo Christus Iesus. 6. Qui seipsum dedit in redemptionis precium pro quibusvis. I. Timo. 6.13. Praecipio tibi coram Deo qui vivificat omnia, et Iesu Christo qui testatam fecit coram Pontio Pilato bonam professionem. Tit. 2.11. Illuxit enim gratia Dei illa salutifera omnibus hominibus, erudiens nos ut abnegata impietate et mundanis cupiditatibus, moderate, et pie et juste vivamus in praesenti seculo. 13. Expectantes beatam illam spem et illustrem adventum gloriae magni illius Dei, ac servatoris nostri Iesu Christi, 14. Qui dedit semet ipsum pro nobis ut redimeret nos ab omni iniquitate. etc.

Hence it is clear that even creatures are honored with the name of deity. This is, however, by the grace and permission of the one supreme God, who is God of Gods, pre-eminent, and *Father of all, above all, through all, and in all* (Ephesians 4).[a] Since he is the unique, Most High, and natural God, in and of himself, all the others are derived from him, are subject to him, and obey him.

This multiplicity of inferior Gods presents no confusion and does not prejudice the divine unity, since every creature praises God the creator, respects and longs for him as the most high and supreme God, and worships and adores him alone, about whom all of scripture bears witness that *there is no other God beside* him.[b] *Hear, O Israel, the Lord your God is one God* (Deuteronomy 6).[c] *Jehovah, the great, the mighty, and the terrible God, who does not distinguish between persons, and does not care for a bribe* (Deuteronomy 10).[d] *The God of Gods has spoken* (Psalm 50).[e]

And Paul [said] in Galatians 4: *Formerly, when you did not know God, you served them that by nature were not Gods. But now, when you know God, how can you turn back to poor, weak [elemental spirits]?*[f] 1 Timothy 6: *Which at the proper time he shall reveal, the blessed and only Sovereign, the King of kings, and Lord of lords, who alone has immortality, dwells in light inaccessible, whom no human has seen, or can see.*[g] 1 Thessalonians 1: *To serve a living and true God and to await his Son from heaven, Jesus, whom he raised from the dead.*[h] 1 Timothy 1: *To the eternal King, immortal, invisible, to the only wise God, let there be honor and glory for ever and ever. Amen.*[i] 1 Timothy 2: *One God and one mediator between God and mankind, the man Jesus Christ, who gave himself as a ransom for all.*[j] 1 Timothy 6: *I charge you, in the presence of God who gives life to all things and Jesus Christ who, in his testimony before Pontius Pilate, made the good confession.*[k] Titus 2: *For the grace of God has appeared for the salvation of all men, training us to renounce impiety and worldly desires, and to live soberly, piously, and justly in this world, awaiting the blessed hope and the illustrious arrival of the glory of the great God, and our Savior Jesus Christ, who gave himself for our sake, to redeem us from all iniquity,*[l] etc.

---

[a] Eph. 4:6. [b] Deut. 32:39. [c] Deut. 6:4. [d] Deut. 10:17. [e] Ps. 50:1. [f] Gal. 4:8-9. [g] 1 Tim. 6:15-16.
[h] 1 Thess. 1:9-10. [i] 1 Tim. 1:17 (Erasmus). [j] 1 Tim. 2:5-6. [k] 1 Tim. 6:13. [l] Titus 2:11-14.

Vide igitur quomodo scripturae inter Deum et Dei filium semper distinguere soleant: et, si diligenter inspicias, videbis scripturam semper: tribus vel quatuor locis exceptis, simpliciter et absolute appellare Patrem Deum et Iesum eius Christum ac filium. Differt tamen filii divinitas ab aliis diis. Quare Deus Pater alios deificavit et santificavit ad mensuram, veluti filios adoptivos et ideo Moses et Cyrus particulares dii fuerunt Pharaonis et Israelis, Christum vero, ut proprium filium, benedictum Deus sine mensura sanctificavit et totum spiritu suo S. atque omni divinitate replevit, de cuius plenitudine, nos omnes accepimus.

Nec praedictis adversatur, quod filius deitate, potentia et gloria Patri [104] adaequatus sit, quoniam omnis deitas, gloria et aequalitas filii a Deo Patre est, et tanquam donum Patris a filio recognoscitur, dum inquit, Matth. 28. Donata mihi est omnis potestas in caelo et in terra. Et Petrus Act. 2.16. Quod Dominum et Christum facit Deus hunc Iesum quem vos crucifixistis: Et Paulus, Phil. 2.10. Quapropter Deus summo extulit illum honore, et dedit illi nomen super omne nomen, ut in nomine Iesu omne nomen curvetur caelestium, terrestrium et inferorum, Heb. 1.8. Et adorent eum omnes Angeli Dei. Eph. 1.22, 23. Qui suscitavit Christum ex mortuis, et sedere fecit ad dextram suam in caelestibus super omnem principatum et pietatem et virtutem et dominationem, et omne nomen quod nominatur non solum in hoc seculo sed etiam in futuro. Et omnia subiecit, pedibus eius, et ipsum dedit caput super omnia ipsi Ecclesiae, quae est corpus ipsius, plenitudo eius, qui omnia in omnibus adimplet. Hebr. 1.13.* Cui unquam Angelorum dixit, filius meus es tu, ego hodie genui te. 8. Thronus tuus in seculum seculi, Virga directionis virga regni tui. 13. Sede a dextris meis donec posuero inimicos tuos scabellum pedum tuorum. Et Ioh. Apoc. 5.12. Dignus est agnus ille mactatus qui accipiat virtutem, et divitias et sapientiam et fortitudinem et honorem et gloriam, et benedictionem.

---

* Should read *Hebr. 1.5.*

See, therefore, how the scriptures are always accustomed to distinguish between God and the Son of God. If you look carefully you will see that scripture, except for three or four passages,[a] always simply and absolutely calls the Father "God," and calls Jesus his Christ and Son. However, the divinity of the Son differs from that of other gods. God the Father deified and sanctified others, to a certain extent, as adoptive sons.[b] Thus Moses and Cyrus were, in a partial way, gods to Pharaoh and Israel. However, *God sanctified Christ without measure*,[c] as his own blessed Son, and filled him completely with his Holy Spirit and with all divinity.[d] We have all partaken of this fullness.[e]

To say that the Son is equal to the Father in divinity, power, and glory does not contradict the aforesaid, since all of the Son's deity, glory, and equality is from God the Father, and is acknowledged by the Son as a gift from the Father. In Matthew 28 he says, *"All power in heaven and on earth has been given to me."*[f] And in Acts 2 Peter [says], *"God has made him Lord and Christ, this Jesus, whom you crucified."*[g] And in Philippians 2 Paul [says], *Therefore God has highly exalted him and given him a name above every name, that at the name of Jesus every knee should bow, in heaven, on earth, and under the earth.*[h] Hebrews 1: *"Let all God's angels worship him."*[i] Ephesians 1: *He who raised Christ from the dead, and made him sit at his right hand in heaven, above all rule, piety, power, and dominion, and every name that is named, not only in this age but also in that which is to come; and he has put all things under his feet, and has made him head over all things for the church, which is his body, filled with him who fulfills everything in all things.*[j] Hebrews 1: *To what angel did he ever say, "You are my Son, today I have begotten you"?*[k] *"Your throne is for ever and ever, the righteous scepter is the scepter of your kingdom."*[l] *"Sit at my right hand until I make your enemies your footstool."*[m] And in Revelation 5: *"Worthy is the lamb who was sacrificed, to receive power and wealth and wisdom and might and honor and glory and blessing."*[n]

---

[a] Isa. 9:6; John 1:1-3, 20:28; Rom. 9:5. [b] Eph. 1:5. [c] John 3:34. [d] See Col. 2:9.
[e] John 1:16. [f] Matt. 28:18. [g] Acts 2:36. [h] Phil. 2:9-10. [i] Heb. 1:6. [j] Eph. 1:20-23.
[k] Heb. 1:5 [l] Heb. 1:8, quoting Ps. 45:6. [m] Heb. 1:13. [n] Rev. 5:12.

Et ideo Paulus hanc filii deitatem et cum altissimo Deo Patre aequalitatem non respectu ipsius Patris, sed respectu creaturarum intelligendam esse declarat. I. Cor. 15.27. Nam omnia subiecit sub pedes eius; quum autem dicat quod omnia subiecta sunt, palam est quod hoc dicatur extra eum qui subiecit ei omnia. 28. cum autem subiecta fuerint ei omnia tunc et ipse filius subiicietur ei, qui subiecit ei omnia ut Deus sit omnia in omnibus.

Quamvis autem filius dono Patris se virtute et gloria, et potentia aequalem Patri factum agnosceret, noluit tamen illo aequalitatis dono abuti et illud in tyrannidem et rapinam convertere ut Paulus ait. Ad Phil. 8.* Ipse se summisit factus obediens usque ad mortem, mortem autem crucis. 9. Quapropter Deus ipsum in summam extulit sublimitatem, ac omnia coelestia terrestria ac inferna eidem subiecit. Deum ac Dominum ab omnibus creaturis adorandum proposuit, breviter, tantum virtutis, potentiae, gratiae, benedictionis, [105] gloriae et Deitatis in filium suum dilectissimum contulit omnipotens Pater, quantum maxime conferre potuit, et in aequalitate sua et trono suo collocavit tantumque honoris filio, quantum sibi ipsi exhiberi voluit. Proinde, qui filium non agnoscit, Patrem quoque negat. Nullum enim datum est hominibus (Act. 4.12.) nomen sub caelo, in quo salutem sperare oporteat praeterquam in nomine filii Dei, Domini Nostri Iesu Christi, qui est Verus Dominus et Deus noster, ut Thomas Ioh. 20.28. Paulus et Ioannes verissime confessi sunt. Cui propterea cum Deo Patre, Maximo et clementissimo Deo, sit Laus honor et gloria in Sempiterna Secula Amen.

---

* Should read *Phil. 2*.

And thus in 1 Corinthians 15 Paul declares that the deity of the Son, and his equality with the most high God the Father, is to be understood not with respect to his Father, but with respect to creatures: *For he has put all things in subjection under his feet. But when it says, "All things are put in subjection under him," it is plain that he is excepted who subjected all things to him. When, however, all things are subjected to him, then the Son himself will also be subjected to him who subjected all things to him, that God may be all in all.*[a]

However, although the Son realized that by gift of the Father he was made equal to the Father in power, glory, and might, he refused to abuse the gift of equality or to convert it into tyranny and theft. As Paul says in Philippians 2: *He humbled himself and became obedient unto death, even death on a cross. Therefore God has highly exalted him, and made all things, in heaven, on earth, and under the earth, subject to him.*[b] He established him to be worshipped by all creatures as God and Lord.

In short, the omnipotent Father bestowed on his most beloved Son as much power, strength, grace, blessing, glory, and deity as he could possibly bestow.[c] And [the Father] established [his Son] in equality with himself and on his throne, because he wished as much honor to be paid to the Son as to himself. Thus *he who does not* acknowledge *the Son*, denies *the Father* as well.[d] *For there is no other name given to men under heaven, by which we ought to hope for salvation* (Acts 4),[e] than the name of the Son of God, our Lord Jesus Christ, who is our true Lord and God, as Thomas (in John 20),[f] Paul, and John have most truthfully confessed. To whom, therefore, with God the Father, the all-powerful and most merciful God, let there be praise, *honor*, and *glory, world without end. Amen.*[g]

---

[a] 1 Cor. 15:27-28. [b] Phil. 2:8-10. [c] See Rev. 5:12. [d] John 5:23. [e] Acts 4:12. [f] John 20:28.
[g] 1 Tim. 1:17, Rev. 5:13.

Letter to the Italian Congregation in Geneva

Carissimi in Cristo Iesu fratelli, perche occorse hieri in publica congregatione parlar et disputar de l'unità de Dio contra la mia voglia, perche non voleva intrare quello articolo tanto profondo et alto che à gran pena et cum difficoltà si puo con parole explicare, maxime in tanto numero de auditori et essendo io stato come vi pare de molto diversa et contraria opinione de voi, fosti tutti di me grandemente scandalizati riputandomi heretico et malitioso. Niente di manco non fu risciolti li luoghi et argomenti della scrittura per me addutti. Ma la cosa restò che si dovesse scrivere sopra di questo et non piu contendere presentialmente cum parole.

Acciò adunque cognosciate che in me non è malitia né passione, ma un spirito lieto et sincero, et che per niente voglio essere ostinato, essendo raggionevolmente instrutto. Vi dico et protesto dovanti il Signor Dio che risolvendomi voi li luoghi et argomenti che me inclinano in questa openione piu che alla vostra, et la gratia di Dio mi faccia capace di puotervi ben intendere, vi prometto accettarla di tutto il cuore et spirito mio, et alli altri fratelli communicarla et deffenderla.

Adunque vi per l'honore di Dio pigliate le parole mie in buona parte et charità, perche havete veduto l'animo mio sincero verso di voi, che nel primo articolo son stato d'accordo con voi, doppo che son stato ben inteso, et non ho simulato, anchora in questo dell'unità di Dio sono andato sincero et senza malitia, perche puoteva in una parola acquetarvi simulando cum voi, et dicendo cum malitia ch'io era della openion vostra et credeva come voi. Ma perche non voglio ni intendo ingannar me stesso et simular cum Dio, fui contento dire liberamente l'oppenione nella quale el spirito mio piu inclinava, aggiungendo in parte le cause ragioni et authorità che me facceano in cotal oppenione inclinare.

Et doppo vedendo que tutti voi eravate di questo molto et molto contra di me exagerati, et che per ogni modo volevate l'oppinione vostra prevalere, Io dissi queste parole a buon fine, che se volevate ch'io credesse ch'el padre et figliolo sono un medemo dio, ch'io lo direbbe et crederia nel modo però che la scrittura dice: *Ego et pater unum sumus*. Et perche ne il mio dire fu inteso, ni anco l'animo mio, tutti furono di questo gravemente offesi et scandalizati, stimando ch'io mi beffasse di sua maestà. Cosa horrenda e dal spirito mio mai pensata.

Dearest brothers in Jesus Christ:

When, contrary to my wishes, I was required to speak publicly to the congregation and to argue for the unity of God – I did not then wish to examine such a profound and lofty article [of faith], one that could only be put into words with great effort and difficulty, especially before such a large audience – you were all greatly scandalized, and considered me heretical and false, because, as it seems to you, my opinions are so different and opposed to yours. Anything that I failed to make clear can be obtained from the passages and arguments of scripture which I cited. But the nature of the subject is such that I need to supply a written statement and no longer to rely on oral argument.

You know there is no ill-will or anger in me, but rather a joyful and sincere spirit. I by no means wish to be obstinate, if I am given reasonable instruction. I say to you – and before the Lord God I insist – that it is your duty to reinterpret for me those passages and arguments that have inclined me to my opinion rather than to yours. May the grace of God enable me to understand you. And I promise to accept [anything you have well explained] with all my heart and spirit, and to communicate and defend it to other brethren.

Therefore, for the honor of God, accept what I have to say charitably and in good part, because you have seen how sincere I am with you. In the beginning I was in agreement with you. Since that time I have been very straightforward and have not dissimulated. On the question of the unity of God, I am again being frank and sincere. For I could placate you with just one word, if I were to lie to you, falsely claiming that I agree with you and believe as you do. But because I neither wished nor intended to deceive myself or to be false to God, I chose to freely discuss the belief which I favored, providing some of the arguments and authorities that made me prefer it.

Seeing, however, that all of you were becoming more and more incensed with me on this subject, and that you were utterly determined that your own view should prevail, I generously proposed that, if you wished me to believe that the Father and the Son are the same God, I would say it and believe it, but only in the way that scripture states: "I and the Father are one."[a] And since what I said was meant to convey what I truly thought, you were all deeply offended and scandalized, thinking that I was mocking [God's] majesty – a horrible thing, which I never contemplated doing.

---

[a] John 10:30.

Si che per dire brevemente et chiarire come io questa unità intendo et capisco, dico in questo modo, che essendo il padre et figliolo due cose substantiale, o vero come si dice due hypostasi realmente et veramente distinte, intanto, che l'una non è l'altra, et ogniun de loro è vero Dio, l'uno Dio genitore, l'altro Dio genito, l'uno Dio mittente, l'altro Dio misso, l'uno Dio corporeo, l'altro Dio corporato, l'uno della scrittura regolarmente chiamato Dio, l'altro Signore, non posso altramente col mio intelletto capire se non do dei, l'uno existente da l'altro.

Per che intendo che Dio et Domino sono nomi appellativi signifficando potestà et superiorità. Et così intendo il figliolo esser Dio da Dio padre, lume de lume, et vero Dio de vero Dio. O veramente il padre Dio da sé et figliuolo Dio dal padre, et però la scrittura al solo padre un Dio referisse et questo pigliando cotal nome de Dio in concreto applicandolo specifice ad esse hypostasi o vero persone distinte ut singulis.

Ma pigliandolo in abstracto et in commune a tutte le hypostasi in sieme, dico il Padre et figliuolo esser una medema divinità et una divina essentia. Item dico il Padre et il figliolo esser dui potenti et sapienti, et tamen una potentia et sapientia, et così intendo la scrittura dove dice: *Ego et pater unum sumus*, et dove dice: *Paulus et Apollo unum sunt*. L'uno et l'altro era apostolo di Dio et veramente due apostoli et tamen un medemo apostolato. Et in questo modo l'intelletto mio facilmente capisse questa unità de molte hypostasi. Et in fino adesso non la posso capire altramente, maxime che in concreto et individuo uno sia tre et tre uno. Per che mi par che questo ripugni ad ogni intelletto.

Per il che vi priego, carissimi fratelli, *in visceribus caritatis* et per l'honor et la gloria di Dio, che deposta ogni amaritudine verso di me, volliate con la scrittura dichiarare et explicare questa unità di tre hypostasi distinte in tal modo che el mio intelletto e d'altri fratelli la possino ben capire et risolversi mediante la gratia di Dio a laude et gloria di sua maestà et pregar Dio per noi, et perche il tempo è breve et gia doveria essere in Padova all'officio et vocatione mia.

To describe briefly and clearly how I conceive of and understand this unity, I will put it thus: the Father and the Son are two substantial beings, or, as they say, two truly distinct hypostases. While one is not the other, each of them is the true God. One is God the begetter, the other is God the begotten. One is God who sent, the other is God who was sent. One is God made flesh, the other is the God who made him flesh. One is usually called "God" in the scriptures, the other is called "Lord." I cannot grasp how they could be anything other than two gods, one of whom derives his existence from the other.

I mean by this that "God" and "Lord" are appellative nouns signifying power and superiority. And thus I mean that the Son is God from God the Father, light of light, true God of true God.[a] In other words, the Father is truly God in and of himself, and the Son is God from the Father. For, according to scripture, "the one God" refers to the Father alone. Understanding it this way, and looking at it in concrete terms, the name "God" applies particularly and individually to [each of] the hypostases, or truly distinct persons.

Taking all the hypostases together, in the abstract and in the commonly understood way, I say that the Father and the Son are the same divinity and are one divine essence. Likewise, I say that the Father and the Son are two powers and wisdoms, and yet a single power. Thus do I understand scripture when it says: "I and the Father are one,"[b] and when it says, "Paul and Apollos are one."[c] Each man was an apostle of God. Truly there were two apostles. And yet there was one common apostolate. In this way, my intellect easily comprehends the unity of the many hypostases. And even now I cannot understand it differently, for otherwise, in concrete and individual terms, one would then be three and three would be one. In my view, that [idea] is repugnant to every intellect.

Thus I pray you, dearest brethren, "with charity of heart"[d] and for the honor and glory of God, that you, with all bitterness against me put aside, turn to the scriptures to clarify and explain this unity of three distinct hypostases in such a way that my intellect and that of other brethren can understand it well. Because time is short and I really need to return to Padua to pursue my professional duties, you will have to resolve the matter yourselves, with the help of God's grace, for the praise and the glory of his majesty. Pray to God for us.

---

[a] From the Nicene Creed. [b] John 10:30. [c] 1 Cor. 3:8. Paul says that he and Apollos have one purpose.
[d] 1 John 3:17. Sometimes translated "in the bowels of compassion."

Io promettovi avanti Dio et di buona fede mandarvi di Padova tutti li luoghi, argomenti et raggioni et authorità de dottori che mi pariranno esser ripugnanti alla vostra oppenione, acciò possiate ben considerar l'articolo et con la gratia de Dio ad ogni spirito satisfare, acciò siamo un medemo corpo et spirito in Giesu Cristo nostro Signore a cui sia honor et gloria in secola. Amen.

Per il tutto vostro
Mattheo Gribaldo
manu propria.

I promise before God, and in good faith, to send you from Padua all the passages, arguments, reasons, and patristic authorities which appear odious in your eyes. Once you have carefully considered this article [of faith about the unity of God], then, with God's grace [I hope that] you may be able to satisfy every spirit. Then once more we would be one, the same in body and spirit, in Jesus Christ our Lord, to whom be honor and glory forever. Amen.

       For all of you
       Matteo Gribaldi
        in my own hand.

Religionis Christianæ

προγυμνάσματα

Preliminary Exercises

on the Christian Religion

[1] *Religionis Christianæ* προγυμνάσματα

Unus Deus, unus Dominus, unus spiritus sanctus, una fides, et unum baptisma. Unus est deus æternus, ille pater a quo omnia, et ut unus Iesus Christus per quem omnia, sed in omnibus non est scientia.

Hæc est vita æterna cognoscere æternum patrem solum deum verum, et filium quem ipse misit Iesum Christum filium suum.

Verus et summus deus, cum sit spiritus simplicissimus perpetuo invisibilis et immutabilis, personam non habet. Persona enim qualitatem mutabilem proprie significat. Ideoque recte et apposite dixit Laurentius Valla, personam non magis convenit deo quam bruto.

Trinitatis nomen factitium est, et quidditativum ex ternario numero humana inventione deductum, Græci τριάδα vocant. Proinde impium et blasphemum est, verum et summum deum spiritum simplicissimum, deum Trinitatem vel deum τριάδα appellare. Eadem ratione factitia non minus, immo magis etiam deum unitatem dicere licebit, cum unitas trinitatis vocabulo correspondeat, et trinitas ad numerum personarum, et unitas ad essentiam secundum Theologos referatur.

Æternus pater domini nostri Iesu Christi, est verus ille et summus deus, fons et caput omnis essentiæ et divinitatis, cuius infinita et incomprehensibilis essentia, omnia capit, omnia implet, omnia sustentat. Itaque impium et blasphemum est, æternum patrem primum verum et summum deum, a quo uno cœtera omnia creata et increata dependent, alterius dei vel essentiæ personam naturam seu proprietatem dicere vel existimare.

Preliminary Exercises on the Christian Religion

One God, one Lord, one Holy *Spirit, one faith,* and *one baptism.*[a] *There is one* eternal *God, the Father, from whom are all things, and one Jesus Christ, through whom are all things.*[b] But not everybody understands this.

This is eternal life: to recognize the eternal Father, *the only true God, and* the Son, *whom* he *sent, Jesus Christ*, his son.[c]

The true and highest God does not possess personhood, since he is a completely uncompounded spirit, forever invisible and unchanging. For "person" properly indicates a changeable quality. Thus, Lorenzo Valla spoke correctly and appositely [when he said], "Personhood no more suits God than it does a brute beast."[d]

"Trinity" is an artificial term and is quidditative, being derived by human invention from the number three. The Greeks call it the "Triad." Accordingly it is impious and blasphemous[e] to call the true and highest God, who is a completely uncompounded spirit, God the Trinity or God the Triad. On the basis of this same artificial reasoning, it would be at least as correct to call God a unity, since "unity" is the same kind of term as "trinity": trinity reflects the number of persons, while unity, according to the theologians, refers to essence.

The eternal Father of our Lord Jesus Christ is the true and highest God, the source and origin of all being and divinity, whose infinite and incomprehensible essence holds everything, fills everything, and sustains everything. Therefore, it is impious and blasphemous to say or to suppose that the eternal Father, the principal, true, and highest God, the one on whom all other created and uncreated things depend, is a person, nature, or property of another God or essence.

---

[a] Eph. 4:4-6. [b] 1 Cor. 8:6. [c] John 17:3.
[d] Lorenzo Valla, *De Elegantiis Latinæ Linguæ* 6.34. The same passage is cited in "Theses" 16a and *Decl.* 78.
[e] The phrase "impium et blasphemum" also follows immediately after the Valla citation in *Decl.* 78.

Cum pater æternus summus deus omnia secundum beneplacitum suæ voluntatis per filium et spiritum sanctum fecisse, vivificasse legatur, nusquam tamen legitur, deum aliquem per ipsum patrem velut personam seu proprietatem suam quicquam fecisse, dispensasse, vel disposuisse. Ideo scriptura de æterno deo patre semper loquens et sentiens, dicit deum sibi filium genuisse, per filium omnia condidisse, filium in munndum misisse, per filium novissime locutum, per filium sibi mundum reconciliasse, et filium in gloriam ad dexteram suam recepisse, nusquam tamen dixit, deum patrem filium generavisse, in mundum misisse, a mortuis suscitasse et glorificasse.

Unigenitus veri et summi dei filius Dominus noster Iesus Christus, non venit in mundum, ut alicuius alterius dei præterquam patris sui voluntatem faceret et consumaret. Neque deum alium discipulis suis adorandum proposuit, mundove prædicavit quam ipsum æternum patrem, qui illum genuit, misit, glorificavit. Impium igitur est alium sibi deum proponere quam deum Iesu Christi ab universa scriptura nobis tantopere commendatum.

[2] Vera et sancta dei Ecclesia Catholica et apostolica, semper æternum patrem deum nostri Iesu Christi, in cunctis suis precibus et desideriis tamquam verum deum oravit et adoravit per Iesum Christum unigenitum filium, ab ipsoque patre fonte omnis divinitatis omne bonum omnemque gratiam per filium recognovit tanquam a solo deo et patre luminum, a quo bonum donum et omne datum optimum sua infinita benignitate procedit. Nec unquam alium deum quam patrem ipsum æternum in suis deprecationibus invocavit.

Si trinitas illa ex numero personarum seu proprietatum, ut aiunt, collecta deus esset, iam dei quatuor necessario nobis emergerent, Deus pater, Deus filius, Deus Spiritus Sanctus, et Deus illa Trinitas ex omnibus simul iunctus et eductus illorum enim quilibet vere deus est, nec tamen ipsorum quisquam deus trinitas est, quare et deum patrem, et deum filium, et deum spiritum sanctum, et deum Trinitatem prædicta ratione fateri.

While the eternal Father, the highest God, is said to have made and brought all things to life through the Son and the Holy Spirit, *according to the good pleasure of his will*,[a] nowhere is it written that some other God, [acting] through the Father, as his person or as [one of] his properties, made, arranged, or ordained anything. Thus scripture, speaking about and having in mind the eternal God the Father, always says that God begot a son for himself, established everything through the Son,[b] *sent the Son into the world*,[c] *spoke through the Son in the latter days*,[d] *reconciled the world to himself* through the Son,[e] and received the Son in *glory at* his *right hand*.[f] However, [scripture] never says that God the Father [as a person of the Trinity] begot the Son, sent him into the world, *raised him from the dead, and glorified him*.[g]

The only begotten son of the true and highest God, our Lord Jesus Christ, did not come into the world in order to perform and fulfill the will of some other God than his father. He did not tell his disciples to worship another God, nor did he proclaim to the world any God other than the eternal Father, who begot him, sent him, and glorified him. It is therefore impious to set up another God than the God of Jesus Christ, the God who is so expressly commended to us by all of scripture.

God's true and holy, catholic and apostolic church,[h] in all its prayers and petitions, has always prayed to and worshipped the eternal God, the Father of our [Lord] Jesus Christ, as the true God, through Jesus Christ his only begotten son. It has ever recognized that every good thing and every grace that comes through the Son is from the Father, the source of all divinity, the sole God and *the father of lights. Every* good *gift and every excellent thing* proceeds from his boundless loving kindness.[i] And [the church] has never invoked any God other than the eternal Father in its prayers.

If, as [theologians] claim, the Trinity, assembled from a number of persons or properties, is God, then four Gods necessarily emerge: God the Father, God the Son, God the Holy Spirit, and God the Trinity, all of them joined together and brought forth at once. For whichever of [the persons of the Trinity] truly is God, none of them is God the Trinity. By this reasoning, it must be admitted that there is a God the Father, a God the Son, a God the Holy Spirit, and a God the Trinity.

---

[a] Eph. 1:5 (Erasmus). [b] 1 Cor. 8:6, Heb. 1:2, 2:10. [c] John 10:36. [d] Heb. 1:2. [e] 2 Cor. 5:19.
[f] Matt. 25:31 (Erasmus), Mark 16:19. [g] 1 Peter 1:21. [h] From the Nicene Creed. [i] James 1:17.

Si pater filius et spiritus sanctus unius dei Trinitatis personæ seu proprietates habentur, ut vulgo existimant, utique totus ille deus filium non genuit, neque misit in mundum, sed una tantum ipsius proprietas aliam proprietatem genuit, misit, glorificavit, unique proprietati alia proprietas paruit et supplecavit, ridiculæ nimirum Theologicæ fundamenta.

Nos verum et summum deum patrem illum æternum omnium rerum authorem cum universa scriptura credimus et confitemur, nempe qui filium genuit, opificem in creando habuit, in mundum misit et glorificavit. Cæterum illum deum factitium, confusum, quem humana subtilitas in locum veri et summi dei substituit, nullo pacto agnoscimus nec profitemur.

Si pater, filius, et spiritus sanctus, unus et idem numero deus ut vulgo dicunt, recte vereque diceretur, utique necessarium esset, patrem quoque et spiritum sanctum simul cum filio in utero Virginis fuisse corporatos, quando quidem unus et idem numero deus, natura et substantia simplicissimus atque individuus, partim visibilis et corporatus, partim invisibilis et incorporatus censeri non potest.

Pater, filius, et spiritus sanctus, cum tres sunt spiritus sive tres substantiæ spirituales, non autem qualitates, unus et idem numero dici non possunt, esset enim repugnantia in adiecto, manifestaque in essentiali veritate contradictio. Quare scriptura rectissime ipsos unum esse naturaliter dixit unitate scilicet coniunctionis et unanimitatis, non singularitatis et identitatis, quod et Tertullianus adversus Praxeam hæreticum Sabellianum verissime sensit et explicavit. Et Ioannes filium dei verbum, deum apud deum, et ecclesia de deo fuisse, manifestissime testantur.*

Nullum omnino deum verum summum et simplicissimum nobis scriptura proponit, quam primum illum omnium rerum authorem, qui solus a seipso, et sine principio deus est αὐτόθεος ab origene recte nuncupatur,

---

* Should read *testatur*.

If, as is generally supposed, the Father, the Son, and the Holy Spirit are to be considered persons or properties of one God the Trinity, then that entire God certainly did not beget the Son, nor did it send him forth into the world. Rather, one of its properties alone begot, sent forth, and glorified another property. And this other property obeyed and supplicated the [first]. [This is] undoubtedly the basis for a ridiculous theology.

We, [however], together with all of scripture, believe in and confess the true and highest God, the eternal Father, the author of all things. Everyone agrees that he begot the Son, employed him as his craftsman in the work of creation, sent him forth into the world, and glorified him. But in no way do we recognize or profess that other artificial and commingled god, which human subtlety has substituted for the true and highest God.

If it is correct and accurate to say that the Father, the Son, and the Holy Spirit are one and the same God in number, as is commonly claimed, then it would certainly have been necessary for the Father and the Holy Spirit, as well as the Son, to have been made flesh in the Virgin's womb. For it cannot be supposed that God, one and the same in number, uncompounded and undivided in nature and substance, is partly visible and corporeal and partly invisible and incorporeal.

The Father, the Son, and the Holy Spirit, since they are three spirits or three spiritual substances – and not three qualities – cannot be called one and the same in number. For that would be a contradiction in terms and would be clearly at variance with basic truth. Accordingly scripture most correctly says that these three are one in nature.[a] This unity is, of course, a unity of unanimity and mutual love, not one [that indicates that they are] one and the same. This also Tertullian, [writing] against Praxeas, the Sabellian heretic, correctly understood and explained.[b] And John most plainly affirms that the Son of God is the Word, God with God,[c] and that the church is from God.[d]

Scripture does not present to us any true, highest, and most simple God, other than the principal author of all things, the only God, who is by himself and without a beginning.[e] Origen rightly calls him *autotheos*, God in himself.[f, 1]

---

[a] 1 John 5:7.   [b] Tertullian, *Adversus Praxean* 22 (PL 2 183C-D). See "Theses" note 5.   [c] John 1:1.
[d] 1 John 4:6.   [e] Isa. 37:16, Ps. 90:2.   [f] Origen, *Commentaria in Evangelium Joannis* 2.2 (PG 14 110A-B).

nempe æternum illum patrem, qui et filium et spiritum sanctum non necessitate, ut vulgo putant, sed benefica voluntate seu suæ imperceptibilis essentiæ communicatione produxit, [3] per ipsum filium spiritum unigenitum omnia creans, et per ipsum spiritum paracletum omnia vivificans atque confirmans, quibus sit laus et sempiterna gloria.

Dominus noster Iesus Christus, redemptor noster verus, et unigenitus altissimi filius, cum discipulos suos de veri et summi dei cultu diligenter institueret, illisque modum et formam recte orandi et adorandi præscriberet, solum patrem ut verum et summum deum tota mente ac spiritu orandum colendumque proposuit et commendavit. Quod si alium deum aliamve divinam essentiam præter æternum patrem filius ipse novisset, cuius dei vel essentiæ pater una tantum persona natura seu proprietas esset, utique divinam illam essentiam ut verum et summum deum, integro et perfecto cultu orandum atque adorandum omnibus proposuisset. Dei enim et filii eius omnia perfecta sunt opera.

Paulus ille vas electionis, et organum veritatis, cui omnia divina misteria celitus revelata fuerunt, deum illum Trinitatem penitus ignoravit, quinimmo unum solum verum et summum deum nobis colendum perpetua atque diserta confessione testatus est, nempe æternum illum patrem, a quo uno omnia, et unum dominum Iesum per quem omnia. Porro unum deum, unum dominum, unum spiritum, unam fidem, unum Baptisma, pro fundamento veræ relligionis semper edocuit et prædicavit. Quod si ille deum Trinitatem cognovisset, procul dubio ipsum pro sui apostolatus munere gentibus annunciasset.

Cum igitur æternus ille pater domini nostri Iesu Christi caput et principium omnis essentiæ, fons et origo omnis divinitatis, perpetua unigeniti filii sui et apostolorum suorum confessione solus verus et summus deus universo orbi fuerit annunciatus, qui filium suum ut mundum redimeret ad nos in carne transmisit, æterno patri, summo deo et simplicissimo spiritui Trinitatis nomen factitium et complexum et in genere discordans nulla penitus ratione conveniat, eandem ipsam Trinitatem pro vero et summo deo velle agnoscere et adorare summæ est dementiæ et impietatis.

He is, of course, the eternal Father, who brought forth the Son and the Holy Spirit, not out of necessity as is commonly supposed, but by his own good will or by the sharing of his imperceptible essence. Through the only begotten Son-spirit, he created all that is, and through the Paraclete-spirit he vivified and strengthened all things. To these [three] *let there be* praise and *glory for ever and ever*.[a]

Our Lord Jesus Christ, our true redeemer and the only begotten Son of the Most High, when he carefully instructed his disciples on the worship of the true and highest God, and directed them in the correct manner and form of prayer and worship, indicated and designated the Father alone,[b] as the true and highest God, to be prayed to and worshipped *with all our mind and soul*.[c] If the Son had known of some other god or divine essence besides the eternal Father, of which the Father was just one person, nature, or property, assuredly he would have presented this [other] divine essence as the true and highest God, to be prayed to and venerated in pure and perfect worship. For all the *works* of God and his Son *are perfect*.[d]

Paul, that *chosen vessel*[e] and instrument of truth, to whom all divine mysteries were revealed from heaven, was completely unaware of the god Trinity. Rather, he testified, in a timeless and eloquent confession [of faith], that only one true and highest God should be worshipped by us. Of course [he meant] the eternal Father, *from whom* alone *are all things, and one* Lord *Jesus, through whom are all things*.[f] Again, he always taught and proclaimed *one God, one Lord, one spirit, one faith, and one baptism*[g] as the basis of true religion. But if he had known about the god Trinity, in his capacity as *apostle to the Gentiles*,[h] he unquestionably would have preached about it.

Since, therefore, the eternal Father of our Lord Jesus Christ, the head and chief of all being, the everlasting source and origin of all divinity, was proclaimed to all the world by the confession of his only-begotten Son and the apostles as the only true and highest God, who sent his son to us in the flesh in order to redeem the world – and since, as well, the artificial and complex name "Trinity" is different in kind and totally unsuited to that completely uncompounded spirit, the highest God, the eternal Father – to wish to recognize and venerate this same Trinity as the true and highest God is the height of madness and impiety.

---

[a] Rev. 5:13, 1 Tim. 1:17. [b] For example, in the Lord's Prayer, Matt. 6:9. [c] Mark 12:30. [d] Deut. 32:4. [e] Acts 9:15. [f] 1 Cor. 8:6. [g] Eph. 4:4-6. [h] Rom. 11:13, Gal. 2:8.

Quod si patrem et filium eundem numero deum cum communi grege dicimus, innumera profecto absurda et repugnantia necessario consequentur nempe eundemmet deum semetipsum genuisse, sibi ipsi mandasse et paruisse, seipsum in mundum misisse, sibi ipsi dixisse filius meus es tu, de seipso testimonium præbuisse, seipsum in gloriam recepisse, et ad deteram suam collocasse, et patrem ac spiritum sanctum simul cum filio incarnatos fuisse, quæ plane consequentiæ omnino ridiculæ falsæ et impiæ sunt ab universa scriptura penitus alienæ.

Quicumque igitur sacrosanctæ scripturæ interpretes tres substantias, sive tres spiritus æternos, re et numero distinctos eundem numero deum Trinitatis nomine nuncupatum sibi constituerunt, imaginarias hominum traditiones magis quam veritatem et simplicitatem ipsius scripturæ secuti, miris sine dubio modis hallucinati sunt, et in errores innumeros impegerunt.

Nec mirum magnopere est, antiquos illos Doctores deum hunc Trinitatem, nimium subtiliter excogitasse, a scripturæ veritate penitus aberrantes. Iam enim Christiana relligio humanæ auctoritati et inventioni nimium tribuere ceperat, et a simplicitate doctrinæ apostolorum longe deflectere, quemadmodum enim in cœna Domini et quottidiana dominici corporis oblatione omnes [4] evidenter errasse vos ipsi egregie docuistis.

Quod si antiqui omnes ex illo sancto Iesu Christi mysterio commemorationis nihil integrum aut parum retinuerunt, quid mirum si ex omnibus aliqui et sane pauci etiam, et veri et summi dei cognitione primitus aberrarunt, alium deum imaginarium et confusum loco veri et simplicissimi atque purissimi dei temere surrogantes, quem postea errorem improvidi successores velut Epimetheus Pandoram totis ulnis amplexi sunt. Porro abusivus ille Eucharistiæ ritus usque ad nostra tempora conservatus, non omnino scripturæ fundamento destitutus videbatur, quem tamen saniori adhibita interpretatione, et maturiori iuditio confirmati penitus emendastis.

To agree with the common herd, that the Father and the Son are the same God in number, inevitably leads to countless absurdities and contradictions, because then God will have begotten himself, commanded and obeyed himself, sent himself forth into the world, said to himself, "*You are my son,*"[a] borne witness to himself, raised himself up to glory, and placed himself at this own right hand. And the Father and the Holy Spirit will both have been made incarnate along with the Son. All these are consequences which are obviously entirely ridiculous, false, and impious, as well as totally alien to all of scripture.

Therefore, the interpreters of holy scripture who have set up for themselves three substances or three eternal spirits, distinct in being and number, have followed the imaginary traditions of man rather than the truth and simplicity of scripture, so that God, reflecting that number, is called by the name "Trinity." They have without a doubt been wildly hallucinating and have stumbled into countless errors.

Nor is it any great wonder that the ancient doctors [of the church], having strayed far from the truth of scripture, have contrived this god Trinity with such extreme subtlety. For even then, the Christian religion had begun to depend too much on human authority and invention, and had already departed greatly from the simplicity of apostolic teaching. [Because of this] you yourselves have admirably taught that everyone had clearly gone astray in regard to the Lord's supper and the regular offering of the Lord's body.

But if all the ancients retained nothing sound, or very little, of the sacred mystery of the commemoration of Jesus Christ, what wonder is it then if some of them, even just a few, strayed at the outset from an understanding of the true and highest God and substituted another imaginary and composite deity in place of that true and simplest and most pure God. Their unwary successors afterwards embraced these errors with open arms, just as Epimetheus embraced Pandora.[2] Distorted as it has been, the rite of the Eucharist, maintained into our own times, has never seemed entirely devoid of a basis in scripture. You, however, have thoroughly corrected this ritual, relying on a sounder interpretation and a more mature judgment.

---

[a] Mark 1:11.

At vero hic deus Trinitas, a paucis primum inventus et a multis postea susceptus universæ scripturæ contrarius, vos etiam acerrimos protectores invenit, qui etsi pro eius fundamento ne syllabam quidem ex universa scriptura producere valeatis, hunc tamen tam impium et manifestum errorem una cum papistis mordicus et usque ad sanguinem propugnatis, non alia certe ratione, nisi quod hunc ipsi errorem primi non animadvertistis, sed cum cætero grege parum cogitantes et imprudenti iuditio devorastis quem nunc revomere salvo honore vestro et vestri nominis æstimatione, vos non amplius posse, vobis certe nimis impie persuadetis.

Verum quicquid sibi universus mundus persuadeat, quicquid maligni ipsius calliditas moliatur, stabit perpetuo fidelis et incorrupta veritas, ab ipso dei filio et eius apostolis firmiter complantata, unum esse verum et summum deum, nempe æternum illum patrem, a quo omnia: et unum unius dei filium Iesum Christum, per quem omnia, quibus cum sancto spiritu sit sempiterna gloria. Amen.

But [although it is] contrary to all scripture, you have become the fiercest protectors of this god Trinity, which was at first invented by a few and [only] afterwards accepted by many. Even if you are unable to produce a syllable in all of scripture upon which to base it, nonetheless you, together with the Papists, tenaciously hold onto this impious and manifest error and are willing to fight to the death for it. The only reason you do this is that you failed to notice the error at the outset. Along with the rest of the herd, you have devoured it with little thought and poor judgment. You have quite impiously persuaded yourselves that you cannot now disgorge it without losing your honor and your good name.

Nevertheless, whatever the whole world finds persuasive, or whatever the devil himself, in his artfulness, devises, this is ever the faithful and uncorrupted truth, firmly planted by the Son of God and his apostles: *there is one* true and highest *God*, namely, *the* eternal *Father, from whom are all things, and one Jesus Christ*, Son of the one God, *through whom are all things*.[a] To them, with the Holy Spirit, *let there be glory, for ever and ever. Amen.*[b]

---

[a] 1 Cor. 8:6. [b] Rev. 5:13, 1 Tim. 1:17.

Chronology and Notes

	Historical Events	Reformation Events
1498	Vasco da Gama in India	
1499	Holy Roman Emperor grants Swiss independence	
1502	Last voyage of Columbus	
1503		
1505	Construction of St. Peter's Basilica begins Poland becomes a democracy of nobles	
1506	Sigismund I, king of Poland	
1507	Leonardo da Vinci, *Mona Lisa*	
1509	Henry VIII, king of England	
1511		Erasmus, *Praise of Folly*
1512	Michaelangelo, Sistine Chapel ceiling	Fifth Lateran Council begins
1515	Francis I, king of France	
1516	Thomas More, *Utopia*	Erasmus New Testament in Greek and Latin
1517	Ottomans conquer Egypt	Luther, Ninety-Five Theses
1519	Charles V, Holy Roman Emperor Voyage of Magellan	
1520		
1521	Cortez conquers Mexico	Diet of Worms; Luther: "Here I stand"
1522	Ottomans conquer Rhodes	Complutensian Polyglot Bible
1524	Peasants' Revolt in Germany Latin edition of Josephus published in Basel	Reformation established in Strasbourg and Mümpelgard (Montbéliard)
1525	French defeated at Pavia; Duchy of Milan becomes Imperial possession	Parlement of Paris prohibits Lutheranism
1526	George, Count of Mümpelgard Ottomans capture Budapest	Tyndale, New Testament in English Erasmus edition of Irenaeus

CHRONOLOGY

Servetus and Calvin	Gribaldi and his Circle	
	Birth of Vergerio	1498
		1499
		1502
	Birth of Curione	1503
	Birth of Gribaldi (approx.)	1505
		1506
		1507
Birth of Calvin		1509
Birth of Servetus		1511
		1512
	Birth of Alciati (approx.)	1515
	Birth of Biandrata	1516
		1517
		1519
	Birth of Gentile (approx.)	1520
		1521
		1522
		1524
Servetus begins service with Quintana (approx.)	Birth of Lelio Sozzini Birth of Gonesius (approx.)	1525
		1526

	Historical Events	Reformation Events
1527	Sack of Rome by Imperial army	
1528		
1529	Ottoman siege of Vienna	Diet of Speyer condemns Lutheranism; some German princes protest Marburg Colloquy: Protestant unity on everything but Eucharist
1530	Coronation of Charles V	Diet of Augsburg: Augsburg Confession
1531		Death of Zwingli; Bullinger succeeds him in Zurich
1532	Machiavelli, *The Prince* Rabelais, *Gargantua and Pantagruel*, book 1	
1533	Pizarro conquers Peru	Thomas Cranmer, archbishop of Canterbury
1534	First voyage of Jacques Cartier	Luther, Bible in German Henry VIII head of Church of England Placards affair in Paris leads to persecution of Protestants
1535		Fall of anabaptist kingdom of Münster Thomas More executed
1536	French occupy Savoy Bern conquers Gex Anne Boleyn executed	Death of Erasmus Tyndale burned at the stake Dissolution of the monasteries in England
1537		

CHRONOLOGY

Servetus and Calvin	Gribaldi and his Circle	
Valladolid Assembly		1527
Servetus studies in Toulouse		1528
Servetus returns to Quintana		1529
Servetus attends coronation of Charles V in Bologna Servetus in Basel		1530
Servetus in Strasbourg *De Trinitatis Erroribus*		1531
Dialogorum de Trinitate Servetus pursued by Inquisition		1532
Calvin implicated in Nicolas Cop's reform speech; goes into hiding Servetus in Paris		1533
Servetus makes appointment to debate Calvin; fails to show up Calvin flees France Servetus works as editor in Lyons		1534
Calvin in Basel Servetus edits Ptolemy geography	Gribaldi marries Georgine Carraxe, heiress of Farges (approx.) Gribaldi teaches in Toulouse	1535
Calvin issues first version of *Institutes* Calvin called to Geneva	Bern court upholds Gribaldis' claim to Farges	1536
Caroli challenges Calvin on Trinity Servetus studies medicine in Paris	Gribaldi teaches in Cahors	1537

	Historical Events	Reformation Events
1538	Battle of Preveza: Ottomans defeat Imperial fleet	
1539		Great Bible in English
1540		Pope Paul III approves Jesuit order
1541	Transylvania becomes autonomous (paying tribute to Ottoman Empire)	
1542		Roman Inquisition established
1543	Death of Copernicus; *De Revolutionibus Orbium Cœlestium* published; Vesalius, *De Humana Corporis Fabrica*	
1545		Council of Trent begins
1546	Schmalkaldic War	Death of Luther; Anabaptist gatherings in Vicenza begin
1547	Edward VI, king of England; Württemberg surrenders to Imperial army	Roman Inquisition penetrates Venice
1548		Diet of Augsburg: Augsburg Interim imposed on German states such as Württemberg and Strasbourg
1549		Consensus Tigurinus between Calvin and Bullinger on Eucharist; Book of Common Prayer

Servetus and Calvin	Gribaldi and his Circle	
Calvin exiled from Geneva Servetus tried in Paris for practicing astrology Servetus moves to Charlieu		1538
	Birth of Fausto Sozzini	1539
	Gribaldi teaches in Valence	1540
Calvin returns to Geneva Servetus in Lyons; begins editing Pagnini Bible		1541
Servetus practices medicine in Vienne	Curione flees Italy Gribaldi is known to be Protestant	1542
	Gribaldi teaches in Grenoble	1543
Servetus finishes editing Pagnini Bible		1545
"Libertine" opposition to Calvin Servetus corresponds with Calvin, sends him draft of *Christianismi Restitutio*		1546
Jacques Gruet executed for trying to subvert church order in Geneva	Curione settles in Basel	1547
	Gribaldi teaches in Padua Death of Francesco Spiera	1548
	Vergerio flees Italy	1549

	Historical Events	Reformation Events
1550	Christoph, duke of Württemberg	Anabaptist convention in Venice
1551		Castellio, Bible in Latin Estienne prints Bible with verse numbers Manelfi confesses to the Inquisition
1552	Elector of Saxony drives Imperial forces from Germany	Treaty of Passau: religious freedom to Protestant princes
1553	Mary, queen of England	Radziwiłł, chancellor of Lithuania, begins to protect Protestant preachers
1554		First Reformed Church synod in Poland John Knox to Geneva
1555		Peace of Augsburg: rulers in Holy Roman Empire can determine faith in their own territories Inquisitor becomes pope Oxford martyrs: Latimer and Ridley
1556	Philip II, king of Spain	Cranmer burned at the stake Laski to Poland to take charge of Reformed church
1557		Francis Dávid elected supervisor of Transylvanian Protestant churches Colloquy of Worms: dialogue between Catholics and Protestants

Servetus and Calvin	Gribaldi and his Circle	
	Pietro Perna leaves *De Trinitatis Erroribus* with Gribaldi in Padua	1550
Jerome Bolsec disagrees with Calvin on predestination and is banished	Gonesius to Padua	1551
Calvin learns about impending publication of *Restitutio*		1552
Restitutio printed Calvin informs Inquisition; Servetus arrested in Vienne; escapes from prison Servetus arrested, tried, and executed in Geneva	Gribaldi in Geneva during trial of Servetus; entertains Lelio Sozzini; begins lecturing on Servetus	1553
Calvin publishes *Defensio* Castellio (with Sozzini and others) issues *De Hæreticis* Castellio writes *Contra libellum Calvini*	Gribaldi writes *Apologia*; speaks at Italian Church in Geneva; writes letter to Italian Church Curione publishes *De Amplitudine*	1554
Calvin publishes commentary on the Harmony of the Gospels Calvin executes political opponents and destroys the power of the Libertines	Gribaldi teaches in Tübingen Gribaldi and Sozzini sign confessions for Bullinger Gribaldi meets with Calvin and Geneva ministers	1555
	Vergerio travels to Poland Biandrata arrives in Geneva Gonesius at synods in Poland	1556
	Gribaldi stabbed in Bern; hearing at Tübingen; flight from Tübingen; trial in Bern; banishment Vergerio in Krakow Curione investigated in Basel	1557

	Historical Events	Reformation Events
1558	Elizabeth I, queen of England	Protestantism re-established in England
1559	Treaty of Câteau-Cambrésis ends war between France and Spain; Piedmont and Savoy returned to Duke of Savoy	Knox returns to Scotland First Reformed Church synod in France
1560	Catherine de Medici, regent of France	Scottish Reformation
1561		Edict of Orleans: halts persecution of Huguenots
1562		Wars of Religion begin in France
1563	Duke of Guise assassinated *Foxe's Book of Martyrs*	Thirty-nine Articles Council of Trent ends
1564	Great plague in Europe Gex returned to Savoy Birth of Shakespeare, Galileo	Death of Martin Borrhaus
1565	Siege of Malta	Minor Reformed Church (antitrinitarian) established in Poland
1566	Death of Suleiman the Magnificent	Francis Dávid openly unitarian
1568	Death of Christoph of Württemberg	Edict of Torda: religious toleration in Transylvania
1569	Union of Poland and Lithuania	
1571	Battle of Lepanto: European coalition fleet defeats Ottomans	
1572		St. Bartholomew's Day massacre

Servetus and Calvin	Gribaldi and his Circle	
Calvin meets with Italian Church	Gribaldi returns to Farges Alciati and Biandrata flee; Biandrata to Poland with Sozzini Trial of Gentile at Geneva Perna establishes his own press	1558
Calvin issues final version of *Institutes*	Gribaldi returns to teach in Grenoble Murder of Zaleski; discovery of *Declaratio* in Tübingen	1559
	Gribaldi dismissed from Grenoble	1560
	Sozzini writes *Brevis Explicatio* (approx.)	1561
	Gentile and Alciati to Poland Death of Lelio Sozzini	1562
	Biandrata to Transylvania	1563
Death of Calvin	Death of Gribaldi Death of Orazio Curione	1564
Death of Farel	Death of Vergerio	1565
	Valentino Gentile executed Death of Agostino Curione	1566
	Biandrata and Dávid, *De falsa et vera*	1568
	Death of Curione	1569
		1571
		1572

Notes

Introduction

In addition to the specific citations below, information in the introduction is from the following sources:

On Servetus:

Roland H. Bainton, *Hunted Heretic* (1953; revised edition, Providence: Blackstone Editions, 2005).

Actes du procès de Michel Servet, in *Calv. Op.*, 8:721-872.

On Gribaldi:

Francesco Ruffini, "Matteo Gribaldi Mofa," in *Studi sui Riformatori Italiani* (Turin: Edizione Ramella, 1955), 45-126.

On Gribaldi and his successors:

Frederic C. Church, *The Italian Reformers, 1534-1564* (New York: Columbia University Press, 1932).

Earl Morse Wilbur, *A History of Unitarianism*, vol. 1, *Socinianism and Its Antecedents* (Cambridge, MA: Harvard University Press, 1945).

George Huntston Williams, *The Radical Reformation*, 3rd ed. (Kirksville, MO: Truman State University Press, 2000).

On the discovery of the Declaratio manuscript and the investigation at Tübingen:

Stanislas Kot, "L'Influence de Servet sur le mouvement antitrinitarien en Pologne et Transylvanie," in Bruno Becker, ed., *Autour de Michel Servet et de Sébastien Castellion* (Haarlem: H. D. Tjeenk Willink & Zoon N.V., 1953).

[1] *Historia Mortis Serveti* (1554) in Johann Lorenz Mosheim, *Anderweitiger Versuch einer vollständigen und unpartheyischen Ketzergeschichte* (Helmstadt, 1748) 448-451, translated into English by Alexander Gordon as "An Account of the Death of Servetus," in Bainton, *Hunted Heretic*, 149-154. At La Madeleine there were no morning services; see Philip E. Hughes, ed. and trans., *The Register of the Company of Pastors of Geneva in the Time of Calvin* (Grand Rapids: Eerdmans, 1966), 40.

[2] Procès de Servet, in *Calv. Op.*, 8:770, 8:782.

3 Philip E. Hughes, *Register of the Company of Pastors of Geneva in the Time of Calvin* (Grand Rapids: Eerdmans, 1966), 54.

4 *Apologia* 18b. For the location of *La Rose d'Or* and the church, see Clifford M. Reed, ed., *A Martyr Soul Remembered: Commemorating the 450th Anniversary of the Death of Michael Servetus* (Prague: International Council of Unitarians and Universalists, 2004), 115, 118.

5 Marcel Bataillon, "Honneur et inquisition: Michel Servet poursuivi par l'Inquisition espagnole," *Bulletin Hispanique* (Jan.-Mar. 1925), 5-17.

6 There is controversy about both Servetus's birthdate and birthplace. See Bainton, *Hunted Heretic*, 2 (birthdate) and 171-172, note 2 (birthplace).

7 On the Valladolid Assembly, see Marcel Bataillon, *Erasme et l'Espagne* (1937; Geneva: Droz, 1998) and Lu Ann Homza, "Erasmus as Hero, or Heretic? Spanish Humanism and the Valladolid Assembly of 1527," *Renaissance Quarterly* (Spring 1997), 78-118.

8 Roland H. Bainton, "The Present State of Servetus Studies," *Journal of Modern History* (Mar. 1932), 89, quoting a variant text of *Christianismi Restitutio* from the Edinburgh ms. See also Alexander Gordon, "Servetus and America," *Christian Life* (Oct. 24, 1925), 360.

9 Oecolampadius to Bucer, July 18, 1531, in *Calv. Op.*, 8:866.

10 Girolamo Aleandro, April 17, 1532, in Hugo Laemmer, ed., *Monumenta Vaticana Historiam Ecclesiasticam sæculi XVI* (Freiburg im Breisgau, 1861), 110.

11 See, for example, *Err.* 64b (Trinity); 93b-94a (person); 22b-24a (unity); 95b-96b (hypostasis, substance, etc.); 12b-13a (God).

12 *Err.* 9b-10a, 58a-59a (Christ is God); 2a-5b (Christ is a man); 79b (Christ has no prior existence); 59a, 93a (Word transformed); 80a (God's operation in other worlds); 112b-113a (blended nature); 106b (image).

13 *Err.* 85a-b (no internal distinctions); 19a-b (difference in nature); 13a-b (not Arian); 23a-b (harmony of will); 76a-77a (no need for *communicatio idiomatum*, Father does not suffer). Interestingly, the argument for the unity of God and Christ by means of agreement in spirit was also made by Calvin, when he was himself accused of Arianism. See *Calv. Op.*, 7:313.

14 *Err.* 90a (face of God); 62a (procession of the Spirit); 9a (adoption); 67a (filled with God).

15 *Rest.* 168-173.

16 Servetus's contribution to medical science was known by a few physicians and scholars shortly before the end of the seventeenth century, but it was not generally acknowledged until the eighteenth century. See John F. Fulton, *Michael Servetus, Humanist and Martyr* (New York: Herbert Reichner, 1953), 42-43.

17 Calvin to Farel, Feb. 13, 1546, in *Calv. Op.*, 12:283.

18 Théodore de Bèze [Beza], *L'Histoire de la vie et mort de feu M. Jean Calvin* (Geneva, 1657), 16.

19 John Calvin, *Defensio orthodoxæ fidei de sacra trinitate contra prodigiosos errores Michælis Serveti Hispani* (1554; in *Calv. Op.*, 8:453-644), 8:481, 494. See also Procès de Servet, in *Calv. Op.*, 8:748-749 (point 37).

20. Myconius to Bullinger, in *Calv. Op.*, 10.2:103.
21. Karl Barth, *The Theology of John Calvin* (Grand Rapids: Eerdmans, 1995), 309-383.
22. *Apologia* 18b.
23. *Historia Mortis Serveti*; Procès de Servet, in *Calv. Op.*, 8:735-741.
24. "Requête de Servet à la Seigneurie," in Procès de Servet, in *Calv. Op.*, 8:797.
25. Guillaume Farel to Ambrose Blaurer, Dec. 10, 1553, in *Calv. Op.*, 14:694.
26. *Historia Mortis Serveti*.
27. Madeleine E. Stanton, "Bibliography of Servetus," in Fulton, *Michael Servetus*, 84-86.
28. Kot, "L'Influence de Servet," 93.
29. Roland H. Bainton, *Servet, el hereje perseguido*, trans. Ángel Alcalá, (Madrid: Taurus, 1973), 223. Bainton, *Hunted Heretic*, 228-229.
30. Ángel Alcalá, introduction to *Miguel Servet: Obras Completas*, vol. 2, *Primeros escritos teológicos* (Zaragoza: Larumbe, 2004), 2.1:lxxii. (Volume 2 of *Obras Completas* is in two parts, the Spanish in vol. 2.1 and the Latin in 2.2.)
31. Alcalá, introduction to *Obras Completas*, 2.1:lxxiii; Bainton, *Servet, el hereje perseguido*, 223; Kot, "L'Influence de Servet," 94.
32. See, for example, *Decl.* 12, where a Bible reference from *Erroribus* ends up attached to the wrong quotation in *Declaratio*. For a full discussion see book 1, note 13.
33. *Passibilis* (capable of suffering), is used 47 times in *Declaratio*; *visibilis* (visible), 174 times; *crucifixus* (crucified), 64 times; *redemptio* (redemption), 36 times; *mysterium* (mystery), 33 times; *unigenitus* (only-begotten), 32 times; *sanguis* (blood), 26 times; *peccatum* (sin), 25 times.
34. *Err.* 42b-43a; *Rest.* 35-36.
35. *Decl.* 54-55, 77.
36. *Decl.* 21-26.
37. For example, the quotation of the "Testimonium Flavianum," from Josephus (*Decl.* 14).
38. In book 1 of *Erroribus*, Servetus cited Augustine, Basil, pseudo-Clement, Cyprian, Gregory Nazianzus, Hilary, Ignatius, pseudo-Ignatius, Irenaeus, John of Damascus, Justin Martyr, Lactantius, Maxentius, Origen, Tertullian, and Theophylact. In book 1 of *Restitutio*, dropping only Lactantius, Servetus added Ambrose, Athanasius, pseudo-Athanasius, pseudo-Augustine, Cyril of Alexandria, Epiphanius, Isidore of Seville, Jerome, Liberatus, Polycarp, and Socrates Scholasticus.
39. *Err.* 27a.
40. *Decl.* 21.
41. Compare, for example, the different renderings of Isaiah 7:14 ("Behold a virgin shall conceive and bear a son, and shall call his name Immanuel"):
    Declaratio Ecce virgo concipiet in utero et pariet filium et vocabunt nomen eius Emanuel
    Vulgate Ecce virgo concipiet, et pariet filium. Et vocabitur nomen eius Emmanuel
    Restitutio Ecce virgo prægnans, et pariens filium et vocabis tu mater nomen eius Immanuel
    Pagnini Ecce virgo prægnans et pariens filium et vocabis (tu mater) nomen eius el-Himmanu

42 The word *neoteric* originally referred to a once-new style of Hellenistic poetry, the proponents of which included Callimachus and Theocritus.

43 *Decl.* 93.

44 *Decl.* 18, 29, 90-91.

45 Carlo Ginzburg, ed., *I Costituti di Don Pietro Manelfi* (Florence: Sansoni, 1970), 34-35. See also John Martin, *Venice's Hidden Enemies: Italian Heretics in a Renaissance City* (Baltimore: Johns Hopkins University Press, 2004), 99-112.

46 *Decl.* 103.

47 *Decl.* 18. For a full discussion see book 2, note 3.

48 Vergerio to Bullinger, Apr. 29, 1559, quoted in Kot, "L'Influence de Servet," 92.

49 For a review of some of the early literature, see Uwe Plath, "Nocheinmal 'Lyncurius'. Einige Gedanken zu Gribaldi, Curione, Calvin und Servet," *Bibliothèque d'Humanisme et Renaissance* (1969), 583-586.

50 The Roman province of Hispania Tarraconensis at one time covered about two-thirds of the Iberian peninsula. Under Emperor Diocletian, Hispania Tarraconensis was divided into four parts, leaving only the Ebro river valley and the territory between the Ebro and the Pyrenees in Tarraconensis proper. This region corresponds to the later kingdoms of Aragon and Navarre.

51 Some, based upon the meager information provided by "Alphonsus," have speculated that the author of *Apologia* might be an otherwise unknown Spaniard; see Robert Wallace, *Antitrinitarian Biography* (London, 1850), 2:168-169; Alcalá, introduction to *Obras Completas*, 2.1:lxx. There is no reason, however, to believe that this material is any less fictitious than the pseudonym itself.

52 He called Valla "a man preeminent in all disciplines, especially in sacred literature." *Decl.* 78.

53 Delio Cantimori, *Eretici Italiani del Cinquecento* (Florence, Sansoni, 1939), 175-176.

54 Apollonius of Rhodes, *Argonautica*, 1.153-155; Plutarch, *Moralia* 1083D.

55 Erasmus, *Moriæ encomium*, § 53.

56 Kot, "L'Influence de Servet," 91-92; David Pingree, "The Apologia of Alphonsus Lyncurius," in John A. Tedeschi, *Italian Reformation Studies in Honor of Laelius Socinus* (Florence: Felice Le Monnier, 1965), 200-201; Cantimori, *Eretici Italiani*, 175-176; Uwe Plath, *Calvin und Basel in den Jahren 1552-1556* (Theologischer Verlag Zürich, 1974), 156-163.

57 Williams, *Radical Reformation*, 957.

58 Pingree, "Apologia," 200-201; Williams, *Radical Reformation*, 957.

59 Arguments based upon handwriting can be found in Pingree, "Apologia," 199-200; Plath, "Nocheinmal," 583-595; Carlos Gilly, *Spanien und der Basler Buchdruck bis 1600* (Basel: Verlag Helbing & Lichtenhahn, 1985), 299-303.

60 Wallace, *Antitrinitarian Biography*, 2:38.

61 "Historia Dialogorum Coelii Secundi Curionis de Amplitudine beati Regni Dei," *Amœnitates Literariæ* 12 (1730), 593, 597-598.

62 Delio Cantimori and Elisabeth Feist, *Per la Storia degli Eretici Italiani del Secolo XVI in Europa* (Rome: Reale Accademia d'Italia, 1937), 64.

63 The passage in question is Lorenzo Valla, *De Elegantiis Latinæ Linguæ* 6.34. See *Decl.* 78; "Theses" 16a; "Religionis Christianæ" 1.

64 "Theses" 16a; Cantimori and Feist, *Per la Storia*, 64 (*Brevis Explicatio*).

65 Cantimori and Feist, *Per la Storia*, 10.

66 Antonio Rotondò, "Nota Critica" in *Lelio Sozzini Opere* (Florence: Leo S. Olschki, 1986), 305-306; Plath, "Nocheinmal," 608-609.

67 Gilly, *Spanien*, 307-318.

68 For example, Beza to Bullinger, Jan. 1, 1556, in *Calv. Op.*, 16:2; Leandro Perini, "Ancora sul libraio-tipografo Pietro Perna e su alcume figure di eretici italiani in rapporto con lui negli anni 1549-1555," *Nuova Rivista Storica* 51 (1967), 398-399.

69 Perini, "Ancora," 399.

70 Alain Dufour, "Deux lettres inédites de Pierre Viret," *Revue de théologie et de philosophie*, 3rd series 11 (1961), 226; Williams, *Radical Reformation*, 950.

71 Martin, *Venice's Hidden Enemies*, 51-56, 73; Basil Amerbach to Boniface Amerbach, June 24, 1555, quoted in Church, *Italian Reformers*, 221.

72 Matteo Gribaldi, *Historia de quodam, quem hostes Evangelii in Italia cœgerunt abiicere agnitam veritatem* (1549), translated into English by Edward Aglionby as *A Notable and Marvailous Epistle* (1550). See M. A. Overell, "The Exploitation of Francesco Spiera," *Sixteenth Century Journal* (Autumn 1995), 626-628; Martin, *Venice's Hidden Enemies*, 125-128.

73 Gribaldi, *Historia de quodam*, quoted in Ruffini, *Studi sui Riformatori*, 58.

74 Antonio Santosuosso, "Religion *Moreveneto* and the Trial of Pier Paolo Vergerio," in Joseph C. McLelland, ed., *Peter Martyr Vermigli and Italian Reform* (Waterloo, ON: Wilfrid Laurier University Press, 1980), 50; Gribaldi to Calvin, Nov. 13, 1549, in *Calv. Op.*, 13:448.

75 Oporinus to Francesco Ciceri, July 25, 1551, quoted in Perini, "Nota e documenti," 152; Guglielmo Grataroli to Ulrich Iselin, 1560, quoted in Perini, "Nota e documenti," 162.

76 Sebastian Castellio, *Contra libellum Calvini* (1554), 22, quoted in Friedrich Trechsel, *Die Protestantischen Antitrinitarier vor Faustus Socin*, vol. 2, *Lelio Sozini und die Antitrinitarier Seiner Zeit* (Heidelberg, 1844), 55.

77 *Decl.* 63-67.

78 *Decl.* 67, based on *Err.* 13a-b.

79 Williams, *Radical Reformation*, 952.

80 *Decl.* 89, based on *Err.* 23b-24a.

81 Jerome Friedman, *Michael Servetus: A Case Study in Total Heresy* (Geneva: Droz, 1978), 65.

82 *Decl.* 33-34, 90.

83 *Decl.* 17-18, 49-53, 67, 107-108.

84   Calvin to Zurkinden, July 4, 1558, in *Calv. Op.*, 16:463-464. See also Calvin to Count George of Mümpelgard, May 2, 1557, in *Calv. Op.*, 16:463-464.

85   Castellio, *Contra libellum Calvini*, 22-23, quoted in Trechsel, *Antitrinitarier*, 2:55-56.

86   Vergerio to Bullinger, Oct. 3, 1553, in *Calv. Op.*, 14:633; Philip Gallicius to Bullinger, Oct. 19, 1553, in *Calv. Op.*, 14:649.

87   Basil Amerbach to Boniface Amerbach, Oct. 23, 1553, in *Matthæi Gribaldi et Basilii Amerbachii ad Bonifacium Basilii patrem Amerbachium epistolæ* (Basel, 1922), 4.

88   Grataroli to Iselin, in Perini, "Nota e documenti," 162.

89   Basil Amerbach to Boniface Amerbach, Oct. 19 and Dec. 5, 1553, in *Amerbachium epistolæ*, 1, 8.

90   Plath, *Calvin und Basel*, 150-152.

91   Gribaldi's letter to the Italian congregation is included in this volume, 229-235.

92   Vergerio to Bullinger, Sept. 6, 1554, quoted in Wilbur, *History of Unitarianism*, 1:216.

93   Church, *Italian Reformers*, 164-165.

94   Ginzburg, *Pietro Manelfi*.

95   Ruffini, *Studi sui Riformatori*, 71-72.

96   "Gribaldi Confessio: Exemplar Turicense," in *Calv. Op.*, 15:856-857.

97   Vergerio to Bullinger, Aug. 22, 1555 in Trechsel, *Antitrinitarier*, 2:288; Vergerio to Bullinger, Sept. 14, 1555, in *Calv. Op.*, 15:767; Bullinger to Beza, Dec. 3, 1555, in Trechsel, *Antitrinitarier*, 2:287; Beza to Bullinger, Jan. 1, 1556, in *Calv. Op.*, 16:1-3.

98   Calvin to Melchior Wolmar, 1555, in *Calv. Op.*, 15:644.

99   Beza, *Vie et mort de Calvin*, 70.

100 Hughes, *Register of the Company of Pastors*, 311.

101 Beza, *Vie et mort de Calvin*, 70-71.

102 Calvin to Count George of Mümpelgard, May 6, 1557, in *Calv. Op.*, 16:463-465.

103 This phraseology was used by Eusebius of Caesarea (c.260-c.340), whose theology was intermediate between that of Arius and what would become the orthodox position in the fifth century, long after the Council of Nicaea (325).

104 "Gribaldi Confessio: Fides di Gribaldi," in *Calv. Op.*, 15:856.

105 Kot, "L'Influence de Servet," 82.

106 Beza to Bullinger, Jan. 1, 1556, in *Calv. Op.*, 16:2.

107 Vergerio to Amerbach, March 7, 1556, quoted in Church, *Italian Reformers*, 234.

108 Curione to Johann Sturm, June 25, 1550, quoted in Church, *Italian Reformers*, 156.

109 Church, *Italian Reformers*, 267.

110 Vergerio to Duke Christoph of Württemberg, June 17, 1557, in Eduard von Kausler and Theodor Schott, *Briefwechsel zwischen Christoph, Herzog von Württemberg und Petrus Paulus Vergerius* (Tübingen, 1875), 141.

111 Calvin to Count George of Mümpelgard, May 6, 1557; Geneva Council to Count George of Mümpelgard, May 1557, in *Calv. Op.*, 20:451.

112 Boniface Amerbach, note appended to "Religionis Christianæ," in Cantimori and Feist, *Per la Storia*, 81.

113 Gribaldi to Curione, May 21, 1557, in Trechsel, *Antitrinitarier*, 2:295.

114 The Athanasian Creed was not actually formulated by the fourth-century Greek-speaking church father, Athanasius of Alexandria, but was likely composed a century later by a writer of Latin in Gaul. It is not a brief, general creed, like the Apostles' Creed or the Nicene Creed, but rather a detailed and precise exposition of the orthodox doctrine of the Trinity.

115 University of Tübingen Law Faculty archives, quoted in Cantimori and Feist, *Per la Storia*, 86.

116 Christoph of Württemberg to the senate of the University of Basel, Aug. 12, 1557, in Cantimori and Feist, *Per la Storia*, 90.

117 Cantimori and Feist, *Per la Storia*, 86-87, 90-91.

118 Cantimori and Feist, *Per la Storia*, 91.

119 Cantimori and Feist, *Per la Storia*, 91; Vergerio to Bullinger, Aug. 4, 1557, in Trechsel, *Antitrinitarier*, 2:296.

120 The other members of the commission were Wolfgang Wissenburg and Simon Sulzer. Sulzer had leanings towards Lutheranism, which had already lost him his pastorate in Bern.

121 Cantimori and Feist, *Per la Storia*, 91-92; Basel archives, in Church, *Italian Reformers*, 288-289; Curione's statement to the Basel commission, Sept. 7, 1557, in Perini, "Nota e documenti," 163.

122 Gribaldi to Tübingen University, Aug. 8, 1557, cited in Wilbur, *History of Unitarianism*, 1:220.

123 Zurkinden to Calvin, June 13, 1558, in *Calv. Op.*, 17:207.

124 Council of Bern to the Duke of Württemberg, Aug. 20, 1557, quoted in Church, *Italian Reformers*, 238.

125 Haller to Bullinger, Sept. 14, 1557, in *Calv. Op.*, 16:623.

126 Haller to Bullinger, Sept. 14, 1557, in *Calv. Op.*, 16:624.

127 Zurkinden to Calvin, Feb. 10, 1554, in *Calv. Op.*, 15:19-22; Zurkinden to Calvin, June 13, 1558, in *Calv. Op.*, 17:207.

128 Haller to Bullinger, Sept. 14, 1557, in *Calv. Op.*, 16:624; Gribaldi to Haller, undated, in Trechsel, *Antitrinitarier*, 2:299.

129 Johannes Haller, Wolfgang Musculus, Johannes Weber, and Moritz Bischoff.

130 Haller to Bullinger, Sept. 17, 1557, in *Calv. Op.*, 16:635.

131 "Gribaldi Professio Fidei," in *Calv. Op.*, 16:636-637.

132 Haller to Bullinger, Sept. 20, 1557, in *Calv. Op.*, 16:636; Zurkinden to Calvin, June 13, 1558, in *Calv. Op.*, 17:207.

133 Gribaldi, *Historia de quodam*.

134 Gribaldi to Haller et al., Apr. 24, 1558, in Trechsel, *Antitrinitarier*, 2:301-302; Zurkinden to Calvin, June 13, 1558, in *Calv. Op.*, 17:207-208.

[135] Gribaldi to the Tübingen faculty, May 6, 1558, in Cantimori and Feist, *Per la Storia,* 88.

[136] *Apologia* 21a.

[137] Gribaldi to the Tübingen faculty, May 6, 1558, in Cantimori and Feist, *Per la Storia,* 87-89.

[138] Vergerio to Duke of Württemberg, Aug. 11, 1558, in Kausler and Schott, *Briefwechsel,* 183.

[139] Jacques Berriat-Saint-Prix, *Histoire de l'ancienne université de Grenoble,* 2nd ed., (Paris, 1839), 25-30.

[140] Claudius Courtoys to Calvin, Dec. 17, 1563, in *Calv. Op.,* 20:215.

[141] Beza, letter, Aug. 5, 1567, *Epistolæ Theologicæ,* 338, quoted in Wilbur, *History of Unitarianism,* 1:222.

[142] Jules Bonnet, *La Famille de Curione* (Basel, 1878), 47-51.

[143] *Apologia* 18b.

[144] Plath, "Nocheinmal," 597, 599.

[145] *Apologia* 18b.

[146] *Apologia* 24b. See *Apologia,* note 27.

[147] Georg Tanner to Boniface Amerbach, Feb. 1554, cited in Church, *Italian Reformers,* 206; Gribaldi to Amerbach, Feb. 13, 1554, in *Amerbachium epistolæ,* 10-11.

[148] Plath, "Nocheinmal," 588, 606.

[149] Plath, "Nocheinmal," 608-609.

[150] *Decl.* 3-4.

[151] Stanislas Lubieniecki, *Historia Reformationis Polonicæ* (Freistadt, 1685), 98; Stanislas Lubieniecki, *History of the Polish Reformation and Nine Related Documents,* trans. George Huntston Williams (Minneapolis: Fortress, 1995), 160.

[152] Johann Lorenz Mosheim, *Anderweitiger Versuch einer vollständigen und unpartheyischen Ketzergeschichte* (Helmstadt, 1748), 451.

[153] Testimony of Francesco Scudieri to the Inquisition at Padua, June 27, 1560, in Perini, "Ancora," 399. Gilly argues that this booklet was *Declaratio.* Gilly, *Spanien,* 316. *Declaratio,* however, as we have seen, was not completed until after Gribaldi went to Tübingen.

[154] Beza to Bullinger, Jan. 1556, in *Calv. Op.,* 16:2.

[155] Cantimori and Feist, *Per la Storia,* 81-85; Plath, "Nocheinmal," 592. If Plath is wrong, then the follow-up document, if it was ever sent, has yet to be found.

[156] Calvin to Duke Christoph of Württemberg, May 6, 1557, in *Calv. Op.,* 16:465.

[157] Record of Celio Curione's testimony to the Commission of Inquiry in Basel, Oct. 2, 1557, in Cantimori and Feist, *Per la Storia,* 91-92; Duke Christoph of Württemberg to the Basel Council, Aug. 22, 1557, in Cantimori and Feist, *Per la Storia,* 91.

[158] Vergerio to Bullinger, Aug. 4, 1557, in Trechsel, *Antitrinitarier,* 2:296.

[159] Vergerio to Duke of Württemberg, Jan. 11, 1563, in Kausler and Schott, *Briefwechsel,* 372.

[160] Cantimori and Feist, *Per la Storia,* 86.

[161] Haller to Bullinger, Sept. 14, 1557, in *Calv. Op.*, 16:623-4.

[162] For example: *Decl.* 80 (supreme Father); 68 (apparent reference to Jove); 73 (Son subordinate to the Father); 75 (laughing at the Trinity); 76 (sophistical delirium). References to *communicatio idiomatum* and to the ante-Nicene fathers in *Declaratio* are many.

[163] Haller to Bullinger, Sept. 14, 1557, in *Calv. Op.*, 16:624.

[164] *Decl.* 17.

[165] Kot, "L'Influence de Servet," 82.

[166] Duke Christoph of Württemberg to his councilors, Mar. 26, 1559, in Kausler and Schott, *Briefwechsel*, 200-201.

[167] Kot, "L'Influence de Servet," 83-85.

[168] Lubieniecki, *Polish Reformation*, 443-444, note 183 (Jan Drohojowski); 547-548, note 552 (Stanislas Lutomirski); Kot, "L'Influence de Servet," 82.

[169] Bainton, *Hunted Heretic*, 34-35.

[170] Vergerio to Bullinger, Apr. 29, 1559, in Kot, "L'Influence de Servet," 92.

[171] Vergerio to the Duke of Württemberg, Jan. 11, 1563, in Kausler and Schott, *Briefwechsel*, 372; Kot, "L'Influence de Servet," 91.

[172] Kot, "L'Influence de Servet," 91-92.

[173] Lubieniecki, *Polish Reformation*, 160.

[174] Christopher Sandius, *Bibliotheca Anti-trinitariorum* (Freistadt, 1684), 41.

[175] Lubieniecki, *Polish Reformation*, 174; Wilbur, *History of Unitarianism*, 1:287-288.

[176] Calvin to Alciati, Oct. 11, 1554, in *Calv. Op.*, 15:265; Calvin, *Brevis Explicatio Impietatum*, in *Calv. Op.*, 9:389.

[177] "Calvinus de Blandrata," in *Calv. Op.*, 19:40.

[178] Wallace, *Antitrinitarian Biography*, 2:112-117; Pierre Bayle, *Dictionnaire historique et critique* (Paris, 1820) 1:389-393.

[179] Biandrata to Calvin, undated, in *Calv. Op.*, 17:169-171.

[180] "Calvinus de Blandrata," in *Calv. Op.*, 19:39-41.

[181] Nevertheless, Zurkinden believed that, however bad Gribaldi and Biandrata might appear to be, they both wished to be "brothers in Jesus Christ." Zurkinden to Calvin, June 13, 1558, in *Calv. Op.*, 17:207-208.

[182] Peter Martyr Vermigli to Calvin, July 11, 1558, in *Calv. Op.*, 17:250. See also Lubieniecki, *Polish Reformation*, 184.

[183] Lubieniecki, *Polish Reformation*, 176-188; James Miller, "The Origins of Polish Arianism," *Sixteenth Century Journal* (Summer 1985), 236-239.

[184] Kot, "L'Influence de Servet," 94-103.

[185] Salvatore Spiriti, *Memorie degli Scrittore Cosentini* (Naples, 1750), 64-66.

[186] Its third paragraph reads: "We condemn and detest the error of those who say that the Father, considered simply in terms of his essence – and since he is (as they say) the only true God – begot his son. This amounts to saying that the divine majesty, glory, essence, and, in sum, true divinity, pertains to the Father alone, and that Jesus Christ and the

Holy Spirit are gods who proceed from him. In this way, the unity of the divine essence is divided or separated." The confession, in Italian and Latin, is printed in *Calv. Op.,* 9:385-388. There is an English translation in Gaston Bonet-Maury, *Early Sources of English Unitarian Christianity* (London, 1884), 247-248.

[187] Beza, *Vie et mort de Calvin,* 126-129; Benedicto Aretio [Aretius], *Valentini Gentilis iusto capitis supplicio Bernæ affecti brevis historia* (Geneva, 1567), 8, 10, translated into English by Robert South as *A Short History of Valentinus Gentilis the Tritheist* (London, 1696), 19-20, 25.

[188] Aretio, *Short History of Valentinus Gentilis,* 40-47, 121-122; Calvin, *Impietas Valentini Gentilis,* in *Calv. Op.,* 9:373-384, 389-90.

[189] *Decl.* 85, 89; "Theses" 16b, 17a; "Protheses" in *Impietas Valentini Gentilis,* in *Calv. Op.,* 9:377-379.

Notes on Sources, Transcription, and Translation

1. Stuttgart Hauptstaatsarchiv, A 63 Bü 25.
2. *Miguel Servet: Obras Completas,* ed. Ángel Alcalá, vol. 2.2 (Zaragoza: Larumbe, 2004), 535-625.
3. Öffentliche Bibliotek, Universität Basel, Ms. Ki. Ar. 26a, fol. 16a-17b ("Theses"), 18a-25b (*Apologia*); A IX 74:2a ("Religionis Christianæ").
4. *Calv. Op.,* 15:52-63 (*Apologia*); Delio Cantimori and Elisabeth Feist, *Per la Storia degli Eretici Italiani del Secolo XVI in Europa* (Rome: Reale Accademia d'Italia, 1937), 57-60, 81-85 ("Theses" and "Religionis Christianæ").
5. *Calv. Op.,* 15:246-248.
6. Friedrich Trechsel, *Die Protestantischen Antitrinitarier vor Faustus Socin,* vol. 2, *Lelio Sozini und die Antitrinitarier Seiner Zeit* (Heidelberg, 1844), 460-461.
7. Stanislas Lubieniecki, *Historia Reformationis Polonicæ* (Freistadt, 1685), 99-105.
8. Lubieniecki, *Historia Reformationis Polonicæ,* 100.
9. Richard Wright, *An Apology for Dr. Michael Servetus* (Wisbech, 1806); Stanislas Lubieniecki, *History of the Polish Reformation and Nine Related Documents,* trans. George Huntston Williams (Minneapolis: Fortress, 1995).
10. David Pingree, "The Apologia of Alphonsus Lyncurius," in John A. Tedeschi, *Italian Reformation Studies in Honor of Laelius Socinus* (Florence: Felice Le Monnier, 1965), 202-214.

Declarationis Jesu Christi filii Dei

Preface

1. *Geneva Allobrogum* or *Colonia Allobrogum* were Roman names for Geneva. The Allobroges, mentioned by Julius Caesar (*Gallic War* 1.6) were a Gallic tribe that founded Geneva, then settled in the area between the Rhône and Geneva. Horace spoke of them as treacherous (*Epodes* 16.6). Juvenal called a certain orator, Rufus, an Allobrogian Cicero (*Ciceronem allobroga*), or a backwoods orator, for speaking in a barbaric way

(*Satires* 7.214). The reference to the Allobroges by the learned writer of this preface may have been intended as a slighting reference to Geneva and Calvin.

2   Servetus famously called the Trinity a three-headed Cerberus (*Rest.* 119). This was one of the accusations made against him when he was arrested in Geneva. It was included in the sentence pronounced against him. *Calv. Op.*, 8:728.7, 738.7, 828.

3   Servetus certainly studied the works of these three church fathers, especially early in his life. But, early and late, he studied many others as well, some of whom he approved and others with whom he greatly differed. Although Servetus did favor the early church fathers for the reason mentioned by "Alphonsus," it cannot be said that he devoted his life to their study, for his ideas are based upon a much larger set of sources. Gribaldi relied more heavily on Irenaeus and Ignatius than Servetus did. "Alphonsus" includes Tertullian in this short list because the passages copied into *Declaratio* from *Erroribus* include many of Servetus's Tertullian citations.

4   The claim that "hypostasis" is a medical, rather than a theological, term is made by Gribaldi (*Decl.* 78) but not by Servetus. In both *Erroribus* and *Restitutio*, Servetus used the word "hypostasis" as if it were a legitimate theological term. However, in his medical work, *On Syrups*, he used "hypostasis" to mean solid matter in urine.

5   The reformers, including Calvin, criticized Roman Catholics for imagining that communion bread was actually God. See Calvin, *The Supper of Our Lord*, 43; *Institutes* 4.17.13.

Book 1

1   Tertullian of Carthage (fl. c.200-c.210) was the earliest major Latin Christian writer. Because he wrote, "What has Athens to do with Jerusalem, or the academy with the church?" his theology was thought to be untainted by Greek philosophy. He insisted upon the full humanity of Christ, who was both the man Jesus and the divine Word. Although his Trinitarianism, formulated to counter gnosticism and modalism, was relatively orthodox by later standards, it included proto-Arian subordination of the Son to the Father. As he believed in strict asceticism and the authority of continuing revelation, he was classified as a Montanist heretic and, despite his importance as a pioneer Christian apologist and theologian, was never canonized.

2   Apollos of Alexandria was an early Christian teacher who promoted a form of Christianity under Jewish law, which was inconsistent with Paul's mission to the Gentiles. He preceded Paul in Ephesus, where Paul's associates, Priscilla and Aquila, tried to correct him (Acts 18:26). Following Paul in Corinth, he stirred up faction and contention over both ritual and belief (1 Cor. 1:11-18). In Acts 18 the importance of these differences is minimized.

3   In this text, "the Prophet" indicates David.

4   Clement's *Recognitions* is part of a body of literature which purports be a first-hand account of the travels and preaching of the apostle Peter, but which was probably composed in the fourth century.

5   The Latin demonstrative pronouns *hic* [this] and *ille* [that], in the masculine singular form, are often used to mean not merely "this" or "that," but "this man" or "that man." Following Servetus (*Err.* 3b), Gribaldi argues that the use of these pronouns to refer to Christ shows that he is a man.

6   According to the orthodox formula adopted by the Council of Chalcedon in 451, Christ has two natures: a divine nature and a human nature.

7   *Communicatio idiomatum* is a Christian doctrine referring to the sharing of attributes, or the communication of properties, between the human and divine natures of Christ. By *communicatio idiomatum* one might say that God suffered on the cross or that Jesus created the world. This teaching evolved from ideas about the relationship between the natures of God and Christ proposed by some of the earliest church fathers. The phrase itself was introduced into the vocabulary of the scholastics in the 1250s.

8   Following Servetus (*Err.* 4a-b), Gribaldi is contrasting two words, both often translated into English as "man": *homo*, meaning a human being, and *vir*, meaning an adult male person. Since the word *homo*, in orthodox Christian doctrine, has a specialized theological meaning when applied to Christ, the Bible texts which refer to Christ as *homo* would not necessarily demonstrate to all readers that Christ was a human being in the commonly accepted sense of the word. Texts which refer to Christ (or to Old Testament figures understood to be types of Christ) as *vir* carry fewer theological overtones.

9   The grammatical term "demonstrative pronoun" is related to the Latin verb *demonstro*, meaning "point out." Servetus had made this point more clearly (*Err.* 4b): "Carefully consider the nature of the demonstrative pronoun, and you will recognize that [pointing out] is the original meaning of the word [demonstrative]."

10 In this text, "the Apostle" indicates Paul.

11 According to the nominalist school of scholastic philosophy, a connotative entity is a derivative or secondary one, which must always be applied to an absolute entity. An absolute entity is an irreducible entity that can be named, but not defined.

12 According to scholastic philosophy, a *suppositum* is a self-subsistent substance, something that can be considered a subject. A rational suppositum (*suppositum naturæ rationalis*) is a person.

13 In *Erroribus* (*Err.* 5a), this quotation from Psalms was preceded by a quotation from 2 Peter 1. In adapting this material, Gribaldi mistakenly attached the citation to the wrong quotation.

14 Hebrews 2:5-8 quotes (and reinterprets) Psalm 8:4-6. The psalm speaks of "the son of man" as being "a little lower than the angels." In Hebrews, "the son of man" is taken to mean Christ, and the psalm is quoted as if it said, "You have made him *for a little while* lower than the angels."

15 "Truth itself" was an epithet of the second person: Christ or the Logos. See John 14:6: "I am the way, and the truth, and the life."

16 Josephus (37-c.100), author of *The Jewish War* and *Antiquities of the Jews*, was a Jewish historian. After he became a Roman citizen and client of the ruling Flavian dynasty, he was known as Flavius Josephus.

17 This celebrated passage, known as the "Testimonium Flavianum," is thought by many to have been revised by Christians in order to bring it in line with their theological beliefs. The text used here is nearly identical to the Testimonium passage in the Latin edition of Josephus printed in Basel by Johann Froben (Frobenius) in 1524.

Book 2

1. All of these names are associated with the belief that Joseph was the father of Jesus. Carpocrates, a second-century gnostic, believed that Jesus, though not divinely begotten, was able to transcend the material world because of his purity. The Ebionites were a second-century Jewish-Christian sect who believed that Jesus was the Messiah but not divine. (The name Ebionites means "the poor"; it does not derive from a person named Ebion.) Cerinthus was an early second-century Ebionite. Photinus, a fourth-century bishop deposed for heresy, may have held views similar to those of the Ebionites.

2. In 1550 a group of Italian Anabaptists meeting in Venice voted to adopt a profession of faith saying that Joseph was the father of Jesus. See Introduction, xxvii.

3. The Greek "inferential word" in Luke 1:35, *dio* [wherefore], can be translated into any of several Latin words meaning "wherefore" or "therefore," including *ideo, ideoque, idcirco, propterea*, and *quapropter*. The precise meaning of the word, and its translation into Latin, was a point of contention because Servetus used it as part of an argument about the nature of Christ. Saying, "Ponder the word *quapropter*," he argued that only the man, and not the Word, can be called the Son of God (*Err.* 6a).

    Calvin, in the section on Luke 1:35 in his *Harmony of Matthew, Mark, and Luke* (1555), translated *dio* in three different ways: as *quapropter, propterea*, and *ideo*. His comment makes it clear that he had Servetus in mind: "Heretics, who imagine that [Christ] became the Son of God because he was begotten as a man, point to the causal word, *ideo*, as the cause of him being called the Son of God."

    Gribaldi was almost certainly familiar with this work. He felt it necessary to marshall three inferential words – *quapropter, idcirco*, and *ideoque* – in order to respond adequately to Calvin's argument. Thus, this seemingly unnecessary accumulation of adverbs makes more sense when it is viewed as part of a conversation started by Servetus in 1531, answered by Calvin in 1555, and rebutted by Gribaldi around 1557.

4. Irenaeus (c.140-after 190), born in Asia Minor, became bishop of Lyons around 178. He lived before the terminology of Trinitarianism existed and before some of the doctrines that make up Trinitarian theology had been fully developed. He stressed the unity of God while asserting that the human Christ and the Holy Spirit were both fully God. Many who were later considered heretics – including Sabellians, Arians, Patripassians, and even Socinians – could find support for their views in Irenaeus, although more orthodox thinkers may, with at least equal justice, claim him to be on a line of evolution from Paul to the Cappadocian Fathers or Augustine.

5. Gribaldi's citations of Irenaeus are from the edition prepared by Erasmus, printed in Basel by Froben in 1526. The chapter numbers in this edition are somewhat different from those in *Patrologia Græca*.

6. Irenaeus's great work (c.180), commonly known as *Adversus Hæreses* (sometimes called *Adversus* or *Contra Valentinum*), was written to combat the Valentinians, gnostics who held that the Son of God descended on the man born of the Virgin.

7. Recapitulation is a doctrine, developed by Irenaeus, based upon the Greek word *anacephalaiosis* found in Ephesians 1:10. For Irenaeus, recapitulation has the sense not of simple repetition or summarizing, but of repetition in a way that corrects and renews. The word is used ten times in book 3 of *Adversus Hæreses*.

8   Tertullian did not endorse this sentiment, but attributed it to his opponents, the followers of the Patripassian preacher, Praxeas.

9   Ignatius (c.50-c.110), bishop of Antioch, is known through the letters he wrote to various Christian communities while en route to martyrdom in Rome. He urged Christians to avoid disunity by suppressing heresy and submitting to the authority of bishops. The specific heresies mentioned in the letters are gnosticism and docetism (the idea that Christ was not really human but only appeared to be).

10 The conjunction of *lippi* [half-blind men] and *tonsores* [barbers] derives ultimately from Horace, *Satires* 1.7.3.

Book 3

1   See book 2, note 1.

2   According to Irenaeus, John was living in Ephesus, on the west coast of Asia Minor, when he wrote his Gospel in order to refute the error of Cerinthus; see *Adversus Hæreses* 3.1.1 (PG 7a 845A-B) and 3.11.1 (PG 7a 879C-880A). Jerome, in the prologue to *Commentariorum in Evangelium Matthæi* (PL 26 18B-19B), said that John wrote against "Cerinthus, Ebion, and others who denied that Christ came in the flesh," because he was asked by most of the bishops and by many churches in Asia Minor to write about the divinity of Christ. In the introduction to his commentary on the gospel of John (1553), Calvin mentioned Jerome and the theory that John wrote to oppose Ebion and Cerinthus.

3   Eusebius, *Historia Ecclesiastica* (PG 20 551B-C), citing Clement of Alexandria, said that John composed his gospel "last of all." The sense of the church fathers is that, while the other evangelists were interested in recording events and uninterested in laying out doctrine, John, at a later date and in response to faulty doctrine, was inspired by Christ to set down information about the Godhead. See John Chrysostom, *Homiliarum in Matthæum* 1.3 (PG 57 1). Most modern scholars agree that John was the last of the gospels to be written.

4   This is a controversial passage not accepted by most modern scholars. It appears to be an interpolation based upon a second-century formula for baptism, inserted because of the mention of that rite. The verse was known and quoted by Irenaeus, *Adversus Hæreses* 3.12.8 (PG 7a 901D).

5   By "our Ebionites" Gribaldi means the Italian Anabaptists. See book 2, notes 1 and 2.

6   Gribaldi is comparing his opponents to the Valentinians. See book 2, note 6.

7   The definite article *ille* is not, in fact, commonly used with *filius Dei* in the Latin Bible. This argument, which Gribaldi took from Servetus (*Err.* 9a), is based on the Greek. Servetus inserted the word *ille* to convey the force of the Greek definite article in passages such as John 1:34 and Acts 9:20.

8   The Bonosians were adoptionists who lived in Spain and southern Gaul in the fifth though seventh centuries. They were named after Bonosus (fl. late fourth century), bishop of Sardica (modern Sofia, Bulgaria), who was condemned for claiming that Mary gave birth to other children after Jesus. Bonosus himself, however, was not an adoptionist.

Book 4

1. Modern scholars are divided as to how the original Greek of this verse should be punctuated. It could mean "… comes Christ, who is God over all, blessed forever." It could also mean "… comes Christ. God, who is over all, be blessed forever." The former reading, first adopted by Irenaeus, was generally accepted during the Reformation.

2. The double translation of the Hebrew word *Elohim* – "gods" (*dii*) and "angels" (*angeli*) – reflects the fact that these two translations into Latin are found in the various Latin Psalters current in the early sixteenth century. Gribaldi would have been aware that Servetus had discussed the word *Elohim* (*Err.* 14b), quoting this same verse from Hebrews.

3. The idea that Cyrus was made the God of Israel comes from Servetus (*Err.* 13b). Isaiah 45:3 in the Vulgate reads *Ego dominus qui voco nomen tuum Deus Israel*. Servetus interpreted this to mean that the Lord is calling Cyrus – understood by Servetus as a type of Christ – "the God of Israel." More likely, however, the passage should be read, "I, the Lord, the God of Israel, who call you by your name."

4. Christian theology distinguishes two kinds of grace (*gratia*): *grata* and *gratuita*. The first is given to elevate human beings and the second, given only to Christ, is the free gift of divine union with the human nature. See, for example, Aquinas, *Summa Theologiæ* 3.2.10.

5. Following the teaching of Arius (c.250-336), a presbyter of Alexandria, the Arians believed that Christ was subordinate to and not of the same substance with the Father. To them Christ was only of similar substance and created after the very beginning. The Arian rallying cry was, "There was a time when he was not!" Arians nevertheless believed that Christ existed before the beginning of creation and that he was the creator. They considered the Holy Spirit subordinate to the Son. In 325 Arius was declared anathema by the Council of Nicaea. The controversy lasted throughout the fourth century, being put to rest by the Council of Constantinople in 381.

6. When Gribaldi says here, "Speaking of the Son of God in Hebrews 1, the Apostle says *Elohim*," he is making reference to an argument made by Servetus (*Err.* 14a-b), which is discussed at greater length later on (*Decl.* 70-71). See note 8 below.

7. The Vulgate and other early printed versions of Psalm 90:4 in Latin have *hesterna* [yesterday] instead of *externa* [outward]. *Externa* is a variant found in a few Latin manuscripts and it is used by some medieval and Renaissance writers (e.g. Riccoldo of Monte Croce and Pietro Alighieri). It may have resulted from a copying error in the Latin Psalms. We do not know why Gribaldi used this unusual version of Psalm 90. It appears twice (here and *Decl.* 86), so it is unlikely to be a copying error in the manuscript of *Declaratio*.

8. Hebrews 1:8 reads, "Of the Son he says, 'Your throne, O God, is forever and ever.'" The quoted passage is from Psalm 45:6. Psalm 45 is a royal wedding psalm; verses 1-9 are addressed to the king, and verses 10-16 are addressed to the queen. In the sixteenth century, this psalm was thought to be about Solomon, who was regarded as a type of Christ. Therefore, when the king in the psalm is addressed as "O God" (*Elohim*), this was taken as a reference to the divinity of Christ.

   Today, the meaning of Psalm 45:6 seems more problematic. Does this verse, in fact, address a human king as "God"? Some believe that the psalm should be read, "Your divine throne…" or "God has enthroned you." It is also possible that the psalm incorporates elements from other ancient Near Eastern cultures, in which kings were regarded as divine.

9   Subsistence (*subsistentia*) is that which underlies existence. This word is similar in meaning and appearance to the word "substance" (*substantia*). In spite of subtle differences of meaning, the two words are often used interchangeably.

    The Greek word *hypostasis*, translated straightforwardly into Latin, would be *substantia*. Theological confusion arose because the Latin church translated *hypostasis* as *persona*, and affirmed that there were three *hypostases*, or persons, but only one substance in God. This compelled them, for consistency's sake, to translate *hypostasis* not as *substantia*, but as *subsistentia*. Accordingly, in orthodox theology, in Christ, two substances (natures) are united in one subsistence (hypostasis or person); while in the Trinitarian Godhead, three subsistences (one of them being the unified Christ) are united in one divine substance or essence. See Calvin, *Institutes* 1.13.6.

    Servetus followed the common practice of using *hypostasis* and *subsistentia* interchangeably (see, for example, *Rest.* 51) – the practice which Gribaldi is criticizing here.

10 The parallel passage from *Erroribus* mentions Turks, Scythians, and barbarians. Scythians were thought, in ancient times, to be among the more barbaric of barbarians. They are discussed by Herodotus in book 4 of *Histories*.

11 An example of the kind of teaching referred to here is the passage Calvin added to the 1559 edition of the *Institutes*: "The whole fifth book of Augustine *On the Trinity* is concerned with explaining this matter. Indeed, it is far safer to stop with that relation which Augustine sets forth than by too subtly penetrating into the sublime mystery to wander through many evanescent speculations." *Institutes* 1.13.19.

12 Lorenzo Valla (1407-1457) was an Italian humanist philologist, educator, and theologian. He is most celebrated today for having exposed as a forgery the Donation of Constantine, a document which purportedly gave the western part of the Roman Empire to the Roman Catholic Church. Having questioned the authenticity of this and other church documents, ridiculed the Latin of the Vulgate, criticized scholastic philosophy, and accused St. Augustine of heresy, Valla was often in trouble with the authorities in Rome. His *Annotations on the Latin Text of the New Testament* (1442-57) inspired Erasmus's *Annotations on the New Testament* (1516). His works on Latin style, including *De Elegantiis Latinæ Linguæ* (1441-48), rejected medieval Latin, and set a new standard modeled on the best writers of ancient Rome.

13 Anicius Manlius Severinus Boethius (c.480-524), a Roman politician who served under the Ostrogoth ruler of Italy, Theodoric, was suspected of political disloyalty and eventually executed. While imprisoned he wrote his most celebrated work, *The Consolation of Philosophy*. His works include translations and commentaries on Porphyry and Aristotle and several theological treatises, including *The Trinity is One God, and Not Three Gods*.

14 In *Liber de Persona et Duabus Naturis contra Eutychen et Nestorium* 3 (PL 64 1343C-1345B), Boethius defined person as "an individual substance of a rational nature." After allowing his logic to lead him to the conclusion that there are three substances in the Trinity, he admitted that this usage of words is forbidden by the church. In *De Elegantiis Latinæ Linguæ* 6.34, Lorenzo Valla criticized Boethius for equating person with substance and for having three substances in God; however, his primary concern was not with theology, but with the misuse of language.

15 This word is found in Isidore of Seville, *Etymologiarum* 8.5.68 (PL 82 304C). Some codices read *Tritoitæ*, others read *Tritheistæ*.

Book 5

1. This passage is known as the "Johannine Comma." It had long been thought to be a genuine Bible text, one of the most important in the defense against Arianism. Erasmus thought it spurious because he did not find it in Greek manuscripts of the New Testament. Unknown to the Greek church fathers, who would have cited it had they known of it, the Comma is now generally conceded to be a fourth-century North African interpolation and is omitted in most modern Bibles.

2. In the Greek text of John 1:1, the word *theos* [God] precedes *ho logos* [the Word]. But *theos* is anarthrous (without an article), while *logos* has an article (*ho*). Thus, according to the rules of Greek grammar, the anarthrous word *theos* is a predicate noun. This is rendered in the Latin of the Vulgate (and Erasmus) as *Deus erat Verbum*, preserving the word order of the Greek but omitting the article. Gribaldi reads *Deus erat Verbum* in the Greek manner (as "the Word was God") and cautions against misinterpreting the Latin (as "God was the Word").

   In the English expression "the Word was God," the word order unambiguously conveys to us that "the Word" is the subject and "God" is the predicate. Word order did not serve this function in classical Latin or Greek. By the sixteenth century, however, Latin was becoming less inflected, and word order was becoming more significant. Thus, the obvious way of reading *Deus erat Verbum* would indeed have been "God was the Word." In order to convey the correct meaning, Gribaldi suggests revising the Latin text to *verbum illud erat deus* – thus reversing the order of the words, and adding the demonstrative pronoun *illud* to correspond to the Greek article.

3. Quotations from the Old Testament are common in the New Testament, but Acts 13:33 is one of the few passages which attempts an explicit identification of the source of the quoted material. The problem is that there is no single agreed-upon method for numbering the psalms, even today. Some manuscripts of Acts give the source as the first psalm, some say the second psalm, and some merely say "the psalms." The Vulgate says Psalm 2. Erasmus opted for Psalm 1 and Gribaldi follows him.

4. In scripture the Greek word *apator* [without a father] is used only in Heb. 7:3. There, it says that Melchizedek, identified as a type of Christ in Heb. 6:20, is *apator* and also *ametor* [without a mother]. These words could imply that a person's parentage was unknown or illegitimate. They could also imply divinity, since a self-existent and unbegotten God has no parents.

5. See book 2, note 2.

6. *Corpus organizatum* or *organicum* (translated here as "physical body") is a scholastic term, used by Peter Lombard, Aquinas, and Scotus, meaning something with a physical or organic structure.

7. See book 2, note 1.

8. When talking about Mary in Luke 1:42, *fructu ventris* is rendered "fruit of her womb." In the psalm it is translated "fruit of his body." Neither seems to fully support the interpretation in Irenaeus, particularly as it is understood here: "fruit of his belly."

9. See book 2, note 6.

10. The argument and the quotation are from Calvin, *Commentary on Philippians* 2:6 (1548):

I admit, of course, that [in this passage] Paul does not mention the divine essence of Christ. It does not follow, however, that the passage does not effectively counter the impiety of the Arians, who imagined that Christ was a created God, inferior to the Father, and who denied that he was of the same substance. For how can there be equality with God without theft, except within the unique essence of God? ... Not even all the devils that there are could tear this passage away from me.

11 The Vulgate renders the Greek word *plouton,* meaning either riches or god of the underworld, as *divinitas* [divinity]. Erasmus uses the similar word *divitias* [riches]. Here, interestingly, we have both.

12 Theophylact of Bulgaria, archbishop of Achrida (c.1050-after 1107). This is a reference to his *Commentary on Philippians* 2:6 (PG 124 1163B-C) and 2:9 (PG 124 1166B), where he says that by "the form of God" Paul meant "nature" (*ousia*) and that the human nature of Christ could be called God.

13 In the first half of the sixteenth century, "evangelical" meant what we now call Protestant. It was then the term most commonly used to identify Lutherans, Calvinists, and others who wished to reform the Church. The word "Protestant" originally identified those reforming German princes who found themselves outvoted at the Council of Speyer in 1529. It did not develop a non-political meaning until much later. The word "evangelical," meaning those who wished to champion the Gospel, better described how the early reformers thought of themselves.

14 There is nothing in the known versions of the Old Testament which matches the scriptural source that is here quoted by Jesus.

15 A very similar passage, including many of the same quotations from Irenaeus, is found a few pages earlier (*Decl.* 100).

16 See book 2, note 7.

17 The idea that God's back (or back parts) refers to the Messiah is found in Tertullian, *Adversus Marcionem* 4.22 (PL 2 415C-D): "At the end he says, 'And then you shall see my back.' He wished to reveal, not the loins, or the calves of the legs, but the glory of later days."

Apologia pro Michæle Serveto

1 The Roman province of Hispania Tarraconensis included the territory which was later known as the Kingdom of Aragon, Servetus's native land. See Introduction, note 50.

2 For a discussion of the inaccuracies in this short outline of Servetus's life and works, see Introduction, xlviii-xlix. Gribaldi was unaware of *Restitutio* and thought of *Erroribus* as the culmination of Servetus's theological writing.

3 This is a good summary of Gribaldi's theology, but a rather inaccurate depiction of what Servetus believed.

4 Servetus did not, of course, attack Calvin or any of the Genevan leaders in *Erroribus*. He did attack Calvin much later, in letters which were published as an appendix to *Restitutio*.

5 The Sedunians are mentioned in Julius Caesar, *Gallic War* 3.1. Their territory corresponds to the present Canton of Valais, in southeastern Switzerland, at the other end of Lake Leman from Geneva.

6   The material in this section is much more accurate than the information on Servetus's earlier life. It is consistent with what Servetus said in his testimony at the trial. See *Calv. Op.*, 8:770.

7   The nominal accuser was Nicholas de la Fontaine, Calvin's secretary.

8   Servetus did not think that the Trinity was a Cerberus – certainly not as he conceived the Trinity. Rather he claimed that those who accepted orthodox Trinitarian theology worshipped a three-headed Cerberus. Based upon this misunderstanding of his views, Servetus stood charged with blasphemy.

9   The Genevan magistrates, in fact, had no jurisdiction over what Servetus did, or may have done, to promote heresy elsewhere.

10 With respect to the imprisonment and bail of accusers, and the use of proxies who could be imprisoned in place of eminent persons, the proceedings were in accordance with articles 12-15 of the *Caroline Code*, promulgated under the Holy Roman Emperor Charles V in 1532.

11 Under the *Caroline Code*, the accuser, or his bondsman, is not actually liable to undergo the same punishment that the accused might suffer if convicted. The accuser is imprisoned, or freed on bail, only to assure that, if the charges prove to be baseless, he will pay the court costs and any damages to the defendant assigned by the court and be available to face charges of slander or calumny. According to the ancient *Code of Justinian* (9.2.17), however, the accuser would be in peril of execution in a capital case. Since Servetus was condemned to death under provisions of that code (perhaps 1.5.8 and 1.6.2), Gribaldi maintained that it would have been more fair and consistent for the Genevans to have followed its stern provisions with regard to accusations. Of course, no one in the sixteenth century would have held that the severe and outmoded *Code of Justinian* ought to be applied in its entirety. The danger, however, was that provisions of the code might be selectively applied, as in this case, to suit the purposes of the prosecution.

12 The Genevans would have jurisdiction over seditious acts committed in their city. Albert Rilliet, in "Relation du procès criminel intenté à Genève, en 1553, contre Michel Servet," *Mémoires et documents publié par la Société de l'Histoire et d'Archéologie de Genève* (1844), contended that Servetus was really punished for sedition. There is, however, no clear evidence to prove that Servetus was, or ever intended to be, a danger to the government of Geneva. See Roland Bainton, "Servetus and the Genevan Libertines," *Church History* (June, 1936).

13 In the Geneva trial, Servetus was accused, among many other things, of writing approvingly of the Quran and Islam. *Calv. Op.*, 8:765.

14 Servetus was unjustly denied counsel. Because of this, and his own desperate situation, he made intemperate remarks to the court which were found to be both offensive and suggestive of guilt. Crucially, he had no one to advise him about either the content or the applicability of the *Code of Justinian* and to argue this before the court.

15 This is an appeal to precedent. In the time leading up to Servetus's arrest there were a number of other foreigners detained for blasphemy, notably Jerome Bolsec, who was exiled from Geneva in 1551.

16 This classical reference to the slaughter of a personal enemy, upon the pretext that it was for the good of the state, is quite pointedly aimed at Calvin. Marcus Tullius Cicero had attacked Mark Antony, whom he thought to be acting in a high-handed fashion,

in a series of celebrated speeches, the *Philippics*. As a condition of joining the Second Triumvirate with Lepidus and Octavian, Antony had Cicero declared an enemy of the state. After Cicero was apprehended and put to death, Antony had his head and hands cut off and publicly displayed in the Forum.

17 Virgil, *Aeneid* 2.104. When captured by the Trojans, Sinon, a supposed fugitive from the Greek army at Troy, says that he has been persecuted by Ulysses and the sons of Atreus, Agamemnon and Menelaus. Sinon tells the Trojans that if they kill him, they will be doing just what their enemies, the Greek commanders, most desire. Similarly, according to Gribaldi, the Council of Geneva was manipulated into killing Servetus in order to gratify Calvin's desire.

18 This is a legal principle for determining whether a homicide is a murder, and thus subject to capital punishment: the commission of an act does not make a perpetrator culpable unless his mind is guilty [*actus non facit reum nisi mens sit rea*]. If one believes, as many did in the sixteenth century, that to promote heresy is to kill souls, then, in order to prove a heretic a murderer of souls, it would be necessary to demonstrate malice aforethought.

19 Luther, though he rejected the Roman Catholic dogma of transubstantiation (that the bread and wine were physically transformed by consecration into the body and blood of Christ), taught consubstantiation (that two realities existed in the elements: physical food and the spiritual presence of Christ). Zwingli, on the other hand, thought of communion as a simple commemorative partaking of bread and wine.

20 *Deus optimus* appears to be short for *Deus optimus maximus* [God the best and the greatest], an epithet of the Roman god, Jupiter, which was later adopted by some Christians, including Erasmus and some Polish Socinians, as a description of God the Father.

21 In fact, Servetus published three books on the Trinity: not only *De Trinitatis Erroribus* and *Christianismi Restitutio*, but also *Dialogorum de Trinitate* (Dialogues on the Trinity, 1532).

22 Martin Luther called the Roman Catholic Church the synagogue of Satan (Luther, *Opera Latina* 7:530, quoting Rev. 2:9, 3:9). He referred to the Church as the seat of the Antichrist in a letter to Jean Lange (Johannes Angelus) in 1529.

23 Phalaris (fl. 560 BCE), tyrant of Sicily, was famous for his cruelty. Perillus of Athens invented a bronze bull in which Phalaris roasted his victims. Both Phalaris and Perillus ended their lives inside the bull.

24 "Relations" here is a term drawn from debates within scholastic philosophy. William of Ockham thought that the "relations" or "formal distinctions" used by Duns Scotus to distinguish between the various persons of the Trinity were inventions of the human mind. Thus they could be described as imaginary. See *Err.* 41a.

25 According to Tacitus, the Roman emperor Nero (37-68 CE) made Christians the scapegoats for the great fire in Rome and had many crucified, burned at the stake, or torn apart by dogs.

26 In Greek mythology, Busirus sacrificed to his gods all those who visited his city. "Was it for this I vanquished Busirus, who defiled his temples with the blood of strangers [*peregrino cruore*]?" Ovid, *Metamorphoses* 9.182-183.

27 This is a reference to Calvin's *Defensio Orthodoxæ Fidei*, issued in January 1554.

Theses de filio Dei et Trinitate

1 This may refer to the idea, later called *extra Calvinisticum* [the "Calvinistic extra"], that the human nature of Christ is finite and in one place, while the nature of the Word is infinite and ubiquitous. See *Institutes* 4.17.30.

2 The Greek word *hypostasis* is often translated as *substantia* [substance] in Latin. See *Declaratio*, book 4, note 9.

3 The word *trinomio* [three-named] is not found in Irenaeus, but is mentioned in pseudo-Ignatius, *Ad Philippenses* 2 (PG 5 922B-C). It is also employed by Gribaldi in *Apologia* 18b and *Decl.* 117.

4 According to scholastic literature commenting on Aristotle's *Categories*, an "ultimate species" is one that cannot be subdivided into other species.

5 Contrary to what Gribaldi claims here, Tertullian did assert that the Father, Son, and Holy Spirit are one in substance. He was, however, adamant that these three persons are not identical. Tertullian's purpose in *Adversus Praxean* was to argue against those who "would have the Two [Father and Son] be One." He denied that the Word is coeternal with God, explaining that the Greek term *Logos* refers, not to the Word, or second person of the Trinity, but to God's reason or consciousness (*Adv. Prax.* 5, PL 2 159C-160B). According to Tertullian, the oneness of the Father and the Son consists of "unity, likeness, affinity, and love," in the Father's love for the Son, and in the Son's obedience to the Father's will (*Adv. Prax.* 22, PL 2 183C-D). In general, *Adversus Praxean* presents a view of the relation between the Father and the Son that is so close to being Arian that it is easy to see why it appealed to antitrinitarians like Gribaldi.

De vera Dei et filii eius cognitione sermo

1 The Greek word *pantocrator* means all-powerful one, ruler of all, and almighty (Latin, *omnipotens*). It is used of God the Father in 2 Cor. 6:18 and in the Apostles' Creed. In the Greek Orthodox Church, *Pantocrator* is a title often applied to Christ.

2 In Latin this is *Iova Pater*, which looks suggestively like Father Jove, a possible classical reference. In *Declaratio*, however, where *Iova* is also used, the context indicates that Jehovah, or Yahweh, is intended.

Religionis Christianæ προγυμνάσματα

1 Calvin asserted that the Son was *autotheos* in response to the teachings of Valentino Gentile, a friend and follower of Gribaldi. See *Institutes* 1.13.25.

2 The story of Pandora was first recorded by Hesiod in the eighth century BCE. The Titan Prometheus ("forethought") incurs the wrath of the gods by revealing to humankind the arts and sciences of civilization, including the use of fire. In retaliation, Zeus sends forth Pandora ("all-giving") bearing a jar containing all the evil gifts of the gods. Knowing that Prometheus will be too cautious to accept such a gift, Zeus sends Pandora instead to Prometheus's impulsive brother, Epimetheus ("afterthought"). In Hesiod's version of the myth, Zeus says, "I will give men an evil thing in which they may all be glad while they embrace their own destruction." The story is thus emblematic of the human propensity for making unwise choices.

www.ingramcontent.com/pod-product-compliance
Lightning Source LLC
Chambersburg PA
CBHW050614300426
44112CB00012B/1505